# From This Moment On

# SHANIA TWAIN

# From This Moment On

**ATRIA** PAPERBACK

New York   London   Toronto   Sydney   New Delhi

**ATRIA** PAPERBACK
A Division of Simon & Schuster, Inc.
1230 Avenue of the Americas
New York, NY 10020

First Atria Paperback edition May 2012

**ATRIA** PAPERBACK and colophon are trademarks of Simon & Schuster, Inc.

For information about special discounts for bulk purchases, please contact Simon & Schuster Special Sales at 1-866-506-1949 or business@simonandschuster.com.

The Simon & Schuster Speakers Bureau can bring authors to your live event. For more information or to book an event contact the Simon & Schuster Speakers Bureau at 1-866-248-3049 or visit our website at www.simonspeakers.com.

Designed by Joy O'Meara

Manufactured in the United States of America

10  9  8  7  6  5  4  3  2  1

The Library of Congress has cataloged the hardcover edition as follows:

Twain, Shania.
From this moment on / Shania Twain. — 1st Atria Books hardcover ed.
p.   cm.
1. Twain, Shania.   2. Country musicians—Canada—Biography.   I. Title.
ML420.T953A3 2011
782.421642092—dc22
[B]
                                          2011005554

ISBN 978-1-4516-2074-0
ISBN 978-1-4516-2075-7 (pbk)
ISBN 978-1-4516-2076-4 (ebook)

*For my son, Eja*

# Contents

## Why Look Back?

Like most people, I have secrets. I have sibling secrets, friendship secrets, parent secrets, lover secrets, and other secrets, but that still leaves much to tell of my life that is not "secret." On the other hand, secrets I've promised to keep are safe with me; I believe I can tell my life story without breaking these vows, and also without compromising my integrity. Long after this book has been read, secrets that have been entrusted to me will eventually die with me.

We all have our share of secrets and dirty laundry, but for me personally, I feel that the sooner I learn to relax and laugh about them, the sooner I can enjoy the relief that comes with that liberation and release. I see writing this book as a process of washing my laundry and hanging it out in the sun and fresh air to dry. A sort of emotional cleansing.

I read a quote by a woman who said she'd never write a book as a vow to take her secrets with her to her grave, but I found her thinking to be rather dramatic; after all, how many secrets can one person have? Is she implying that her whole life is a secret? How could anyone already living a full, adult life not have something worth writing about that would be of interest and possibly meaningful to someone else? Surely, if you've lived a life worthy of inspiring even one other person, you could do that and still maintain a healthy, personal, private boundary. In the end, maybe it's simply more a question of whether you *want* to write a book or not.

Expressing the joy and pain in my life through writing has forced me to read the good and the bad with my eyes wide open, letting the pages become a mirror reflecting a self-portrait in bold black and white. It's been both challenging and incredibly liberating. I spent quite a bit of time discussing the pages of my life with many friends and family during the process of writing this book, in a more open way than ever before. In an atmosphere similar to sitting around a campfire, we found ourselves reminiscing, exchanging stories, and sharing from the heart as we reflected together. For my sister Carrie and I especially, it's been a particularly bonding experience gathering around our memories. The campfire spirit of laughing and singing from deep down, sharing freely and honestly, feeling safe to join in around our circle of comfort and trust.

With this book, I hope readers also feel the community spirit of the campfire and the urge to participate from the heart. To laugh and cry along with the pages, feeling that we are all around the same campfire.

I read this once about fire, and it rings so true to me: "Fire can give wings of courage, compassion, and devotion. Fire is obstinate and heady and absolutely not subtle. It is seen as the force burning inside us, giving us an iron willpower to go for our goals, bestowing upon us the passion to do it with all of ourselves, resulting in the honor and freedom to do it without backstabbing and with an open face."

My life has had its ups and downs, but there is always more than one side to a person's story. The flip side of those challenges—the joys and positive swings, the pleasures that came like the good along with the bad—are a promise of inevitable contrast, necessary to maintaining the delicate component of balance.

I believe deeply that everything is relative. We need the bad to appreciate the good, and vice versa. We need something unexpected to happen in order for us to realize that everything else was expected. It's in our relation to those things that we are able to decide how we feel and the level of intensity of those feelings. Such is relativity. There's no getting off life's roller coaster once it's rolling, so you might as well try to understand it as best you can so you might flow with the curves and actually enjoy the ride. In my life, there have been sharp turns and unexpected falls; what I thought were my "life's most embarrassing moments," or things that I thought would kill me once, I can, in some cases, now reflect upon with a grin. I now find it therapeutic to share some of the experiences, and find it rewarding when they hold value in the life of someone else as well.

Albert Einstein wrote in his *Autobiographical Notes,* "I do, in fact, believe that it is a good thing to show those who are striving alongside of us how our own striving and searching appears in retrospect." I read this passage after I'd finished writing this book, and it perfectly expresses my own feelings about sharing my life story.

The process of writing it all down forced me to revisit a lot of times and places from my past, as well as relive a tidal wave of emotions. Memories can be like nightmares. Some people fight them, but others might feel that the only way out of the nightmare is to freeze and remain frozen. I remind myself regularly of how grateful I am for the self-survival exercise of brushing and combing through my thoughts and memories. The endless fingering through thousands of what, at times, seemed to be hair roots for lice eggs clinging to each strand for dear life, trying to hang on long enough so they get the chance to hatch and infest my head like creepy, crawly nightmares. Once they hatch, everything has to be stripped down and either thrown away or washed over and over again. I've heard that putting all your laundry outside overnight in the middle of winter works to kill the cycle of reproduction of these unwelcome nightmares, but what about thoughts and emotions? What do you do with them when they start keeping you up at night and nesting in the roots of your very sanity? Sticking them outside for the night in the middle of winter would only turn you into an ice cube, a frozen block so cold you might never be warm again. This is what happens sometimes to hearts so broken and minds so haunted they don't know what to do. They can't find the strength to labor over washing and rinsing and washing and rinsing again, till all the nightmares are cleaned out.

Sometimes during such episodes of what feels almost like border-line insanity, it may seem easier to just stay comfortably numb with drugs and alcohol. Many suffering souls take this route, but I don't recommend it. Personally, I find it safer to face the pain and allow yourself to feel it. It hurts like hell once you start to thaw, but the alternative—freezing to death spiritually and emotionally—is worse. Thawing a broken heart, spirit, or mind is painful no matter how you became numb in the first place, but a wise friend's advice worked very well for me. She told me that when the storm picks up, I should lean into the wind instead of turning away from it if I wanted to keep my balance. Running with the wind at my back would only give it the advantage to knock me over. She was right. Better to brace yourself and face it head-on.

There have been moments in my life when I wasn't so confi-dent tomorrow would ever come, so once I began writing this book, it started crossing my mind more regularly that perhaps I'd better hurry up and document my life story in case I run out of time. Hurry to ensure that my story would not be put together with half-truths someday, misconstrued through articles and various other media ex-ploitation. I'm also writing this in order for my son, Eja, to have an honest and complete account of my life should I not get the chance to tell him about it myself—just as my mother never got the chance to tell me more about herself. She died in a car accident at the age of forty-two, three years younger than I am now. It's an empty, helpless feeling to have so many questions for my mother and know that they will never be answered. The finality of mortality and the fact that you can never go back and get your questions answered directly has often frustrated me and left me feeling helpless, with a longing impossible to satisfy. I don't want my son to have to draw conclusions about me based on bits and pieces of memory or other people's recollections, but instead from my own heart and mind. This has been a key reason behind why I decided to document my life story.

I thought that maybe I could tell a sweeter version of my experi-ences, so the reader could get the gist of what my life has been, while

I avoided telling about the punches and focused more on how I rolled with them instead. Although I did manage to roll with the punches some of the time, other times they hit me square in the head. I struggled for a while about how to get started with writing this book without telling the whole story, but no matter at what angle I attempted this, I concluded that there is no way of telling a story with integrity if you don't have the conviction to tell it without ducking and hiding the whole way. It was important for me to clearly explain the context and still be satisfied that I'd written an honest autobiography. Without braving through the painful explanation of the most difficult moments, the story is half empty, half true, and could even end up being misleading as a result. The complete picture is worth telling if your intent is to share the truth about yourself, how it's shaped who you've become, how you once thought, and how you think now after what you've learned and what it is you've learned.

When I told a friend of mine who's lived a very interesting life so far that I was writing my autobiography, he said to me that although he has much to write himself, his fear of overwhelming his sensitive friends and family, who are inevitably associated with his story, led him to give up on documenting his fantastic journey for as long as it was practical, as so many people he knows are still alive. I think the likelihood of him outliving almost everyone he knows, although possible, isn't very promising. Even if he does, will he have the capacity to write his story then? That leaves millions of people who may never benefit from his remarkable story. For me, personally, there is a great deal of meaning in writing about my life in the event anyone ever finds my experiences useful as a guide in some way, or as inspiration to endure their own struggles. That maybe someone will find it helpful in a fellowship-like communication of one human being sharing with another. I believe sharing my life story serves more purpose than keeping it to myself, and I recommend writing your life story even if you don't plan on sharing it publicly, and noting in your will that by a specific year, for example, your story should be given to specified people for private use only. Autobiographies are not only for the purpose of public reading. In my case, as a public personality, I decided to use the platform of fame to hopefully inspire those looking for comfort, so that they can know they are not alone in the things we might have in common. No matter who we are, human suffering does not discriminate.

I have been quite closed about my private life until now for a couple of reasons. Not only was I embarrassed to reveal certain details to even my closest friends, it bothered me to look back on some of the more painful things, and I preferred to leave them as forgotten. Other aspects of my life I simply took for granted as not holding much value or being relevant or important enough to bother sharing.

The most obvious question is, "Why look back?" As I already explained, I wrote this book for the sake of thoroughly and accurately documenting my life and so that it might be of some help to others; but it has also been a positive force in keeping me moving forward during some personal lows, helping to prevent me from getting bogged down in self-pity, shame, depression, disappointment, and fear. In dealing with these emotions rather than avoiding them and coming to terms with them so I could move on to the future without missing the present, this book is that precious piece that bridges the past to the future. I had a certain level of discomfort while writing about my past but feel more at peace with it now that I've revisited it and given it a chance at a new understanding. Now that I have a midlife level of maturity and experience, it's as though the past is allowed to be a part of who I am now and not just of who I was, as if it was something I didn't want to be associated with anymore. But I knew deep down that those experiences were imprinted on me in the grooves of my memory, in the very formation of my character, and as permanent stamps on my emotions. I still thought I was "okay" with keeping painful things in their rightful place of "things that have already happened and can now be forgotten" and that I was perfectly fine being passive, confident that I was currently unaffected by what was now behind me, with no need to ever "go there" again.

I have to say, it's been satisfying bringing myself up-to-date with myself, if you will, through writing this book. I can see now that I was missing out on some wonderful feelings and emotions from the memories of my youth as a result of closing the book too tightly behind myself—leaving the chapters to collect dust on a shelf so high above arm's reach that it would take too much effort to reopen them down the road. Much to my relief, in some instances I can say there were things I thought would be a lot scarier than they actually were when revisiting them, and it surprised me how things seemed so much smaller in retrospect. It's like the giant tree at the end of your grandparents' driveway, which you thought only Jack from *Jack and the Beanstalk* could ever be brave enough to climb. But when you go back as an adult, that towering tree might now be dwarfed in comparison to the magnified lens you once saw it through as a tiny child.

Before I started writing, this pretty much summed up my attitude toward the past: "That was then; tomorrow's another day." I did that because some of my past was painful, and this outlook helped me stay afloat. Now I see that in closing off part of my past, I also missed what was happening to me in the present. I was always in a rush toward tomorrow. Sometimes addressing things openly at the time they happen prevents "getting stuck" later on.

I was unhappy. My life had been a fight for security, a place in the world, the chance to pursue my goals. From a very young age, I grew up with the mind-set of a survivor, like a boxer in the middle of the ring, constantly spinning and turning, ready to punch anyone coming at me. Life was not going to knock me down! I had to make it. So I didn't let anyone close enough to find a weakness that could undermine me. I lived in this survivor mode into my adult years and through the ascent of my music career. Long after I'd achieved success and security, I still kept my dukes up, as if no one told me that the fight was over or that I was at least between rounds. It was exhausting living in this defensive state, and other than being tired of it, I also slowly began to feel more confident that life wasn't necessarily trying to beat me up all the time.

The bell still sounds for my defensive survival mode now and

then, but I practice not responding to it. I now find it more worthwhile trying to accept that my days will unfold as they will. That's not
to say I've become complacent. I've just redirected that strength to
pursuing the fun stuff.

I also no longer sweat the discomfort of sharing the past, the
present, or the voyage along the way. And I don't see any point in
keeping my story to myself, as explaining about life with my parents,
for example, might inspire and give strength to many suffering men
and women out there who can relate to and benefit from my parents'
challenges, and from the courage they displayed during some of the
more difficult times. It would be a shame for their life's experiences
to have died along with them. Better to remember even their pain as
a source of inspiration than to forget them in vain. My parents were
conscientious people with good intentions. If they were alive today
to reflect on the years when my brothers and sisters and I were growing up, they might not feel that they'd lived up to their good intentions. There were plenty of times when the Twain family didn't have
enough to eat, lacked warm clothes in the frigid Northern Ontario
winters, and lived in a cramped, rented apartment or house with no
heat. The perpetual undertow of financial instability took its toll in
other ways, as it usually does, compromising my parents' love for each
other at times and no doubt feeding my mother's recurrent bouts of
depression.

Because of the unpredictable periods of instability in my childhood home, I didn't feel that I could really rely on my parents to be
consistent caregivers or protectors of me. I didn't know what to count
on from one day to the next—calm or chaos—and this made me anxious and insecure. It was hard to know what to expect, so it was easier to just be ready for anything, all the time. But I understand and
forgive my parents completely for this because I know they did their
best. All mothers and fathers have shortcomings, and although there
were circumstances during my childhood that to some may seem extreme, if one could say my parents failed at times, I would say they
did so honestly. They were often caught up in circumstances beyond

their control. If my parents were here today, I'd tell them what a great job they did under the conditions. I would want them to feel good about how they raised me. I would thank them for showing me love and teaching me to never lose hope, to always remember that things could be worse and to be thankful for everything good in my life. Most important, they taught me to never forget to laugh. I thank them for always encouraging me to look on the bright side; it's a gift that has carried me through many challenges. They may not always have been the best examples, or practiced what they preached, but it was clear they wanted better for us. That in itself was exemplary.

Ultimately, I am responsible for how I live my life now, and what I make out of it. In fact, I am actually grateful for what I've gone through and wouldn't change a thing—although I admit I wouldn't want to live it over again, either. Once was enough.

# From This Moment On

# 1

## So *That's* What Happened to Me

Eileen Morrison waits to meet her newest grandchild, her only daughter Sharon's second baby. It's a hot summer day, and Sharon is in labor. She's a bird-framed twenty-year-old with long, skinny legs, a pale face as bony as her knees, and a sharp nose. Agile and double-jointed, especially in the hips, Sharon has spent years doing gymnastics. She is a chatty, energetic young woman who enjoys telling of her amazing flexibility, like how she can cross her legs around the back of her neck or stand with them slightly straddled, bend all the way back, and with no hands pick up a rag placed on the floor between her feet. With her *teeth*. Sharon is warm, kind, and quick to laugh, in a loveable, widemouthed, high-pitched cackle.

Sharon's delivery is long and complicated, with not enough relief for her pain. No epidural. The obstetrician's voice betrays little hope as he informs her that the baby is breech, no longer moving, and is still in the birth canal. When she is finally delivered, there is no sound, no movement, no life.

While Sharon lies on the delivery table, the doctor quietly hands her a cigarette and lights it. That's right: a cigarette, in the delivery room. The young woman understands that she has to be prepared for the worst. She's delivered a blue baby, stillborn.

Except, miraculously, the baby girl is alive! Even more remarkable, she will have suffered no ill effects from the temporary lack of oxygen during the stressful delivery. (Not to mention the smoky delivery room!)

While I was growing up, my mother used to frequently tell me the story of my turbulent, dramatic entrance into the world—the worst of her four deliveries, she always said. Looking back, sometimes I can't help but think to myself, *So that's what happened to me.* Ha! It explains a lot.

In this smoky Canadian delivery room on August 28, 1965, I was born. The same year the Rolling Stones had their first number one hit, "(I Can't Get No) Satisfaction," Malcolm X was assassinated, and the movie musical *The Sound of Music* was released. My birth wasn't as noteworthy as the more history-making moments taking place that year, but for my mother, a miracle had happened. We both survived that difficult birth.

I was named Eilleen Regina Edwards: Eilleen, after my mother's Irish-born grandmother, Eileen Morrison; and Regina, after my biological father's mother, whom we called Grandma Edwards. My grandmother Eileen was born in County Kildare, Ireland, to English parents named Lottie Reeves, from Wales, and Frank Pierce, from England. While my grandmother was still a small child, the Pierces migrated to Piney, Manitoba, to begin farming. I haven't personally investigated the Edwards family genealogy myself, but my understanding of what my mother explained is that they had a mixed background of French-Canadian and Native Indian. And since the name Edwards originated in England, it's possible they may have been British at some point in their family background. The exact percentages of which blood on whose side is a bit of a mystery, as is the case for many Canadians. The first European explorer to reach Canada, the Italian navigator Giovanni Caboto (better known from school textbooks as John Cabot), is believed to have landed in Newfoundland in 1497. Over the coming centuries, explorers from many nations around Europe followed, and the melting pot between Europeans and Native Canadians began, which is pretty much what I am a product of. I wouldn't feel as though I were exaggerating in saying I'm quite the Heinz 57, considering the cross of so many nationalities over the centuries.

My mother, Sharon May Morrison, had a difficult life. When she was sixteen, she lost all of her teeth in an accident at school while crouched behind home plate playing catcher (or back catcher, as we call it in Canada) during a softball game. A batter swung mightily at a pitch and connected. As he took off toward first base, he flung the heavy bat behind him—smack dab into Sharon's face, knocking her out cold. Most of her teeth were shattered from the blow. Reconstructive techniques weren't as sophisticated as they are today, and so the only solution to giving her anything to smile about (or smile with, for that matter) was to pull out even the few remaining undamaged teeth and fit her for dentures. One can only imagine her horror as a teenage girl, regaining consciousness and discovering that her teeth were gone and her smile would never be the same again. I'm sure she must have felt robbed of her youth, to some extent. False teeth are for grannies, not adolescent girls, who are so self-conscious about their appearance as it is, and for whom life should be full of reasons to smile.

At eighteen, Sharon fell in love and got engaged. She was expecting her first child with her fiancé, Gilbert, but he was killed in a car accident shortly before my older sister, Jill, was born. The following year, 1964, my mother met and married my biological father, Clarence Edwards. I was their first child, followed two years later by my little sister, Carrie-Ann. My mother and Clarence divorced when I was still a toddler. From the one faded photograph my mother kept from their wedding day, I formed a vague impression of my father. He was a fairly short man, with an olive complexion and dark hair. I could tell from the photograph that both Carrie and I inherited his eyes, hazel green and almond shaped, as, clearly, we didn't have the small, round, chocolate eyes of our mother. I was curious about him: to see the color of his eyes up close, to hear what his voice sounded like, to know his personality, but I didn't know him or develop an attachment, and I didn't miss someone I didn't know.

Growing up, I knew he existed, that he apparently never had any other children, didn't remarry but had a longtime girlfriend with children of her own, that he worked as a train engineer, lived in Chapleau, and had five or six siblings. I did often wonder what he thought of me and if he cared. I believed he probably did, as my mother told me it was more my father Jerry's wish for Clarence not to be a part of our lives to avoid confusion in the family. Jerry was the one toiling with the day-to-day challenges of raising kids that weren't his own, and he expressed his feelings clearly in regard to choosing one or the other—that I couldn't have both fathers in my life. I accepted that as being fair enough.

The divorce between my mother and Clarence left her a single parent with three little girls. She turned to her mother for support, and we moved into my grandmother Eileen's tiny farmhouse just outside of Timmins, in a small district called Hoyle. I don't remember my grandmother working outside the home, but I do recall my mother having the odd waitressing and cashier job for short periods of time. But otherwise she was at home with us girls. Being a single mother in the 1960s was not a desirable position to be in, as it wasn't common for young women to further their education and become professionals, able to earn enough to provide for a family. Ideally, most girls finished high school, got married to a good provider, and started having children. This was the norm, and my mother was clearly well outside that norm.

My mother had little family in Ontario: only one brother in Timmins with five children of his own. The rest of her relatives still lived out west, where our great-grandparents had originally settled after emigrating from Ireland.

By the time my mother started having children of her own, my grandmother had long been a widow to my grandfather George Morrison. He had become terminally ill with a severe case of gangrene to his legs when my mother was still quite young. She was raised alone with my grandmother because her older brother was fifteen years her senior and was gone from the house when my mother was still a small child.

Grandma Eileen was pretty: fair skinned, with exotic blue eyes and pronounced cheekbones. She was tall and slender but had a heavier frame than my mother, who took after her thin, brown-eyed father. My grandmother genuinely possessed both inner and outer beauty and had a warm way about her that made me feel safe and nurtured. She was the one who filled the house with a calm concern for everyone.

I remember my grandma making us Cream of Wheat cereal, which she'd boil to lumpless perfection and serve up with brown sugar and fresh whole milk delivered each morning by the milkman. Grandma was good at keeping the house in order, like making sure our sheets and pillowcases stayed fresh, and there was always something baking in the oven, like bread, pie, or butter tarts. She used to leave her pies to cool on the windowsill, just like I'd see the women do in TV commercials for Crisco shortening. Her blueberry and apple pies were especially delicious. Blueberry pie was my favorite of the two. The berries were ready for picking only during a short period, from mid-July to early August, which made them even more special, since we weren't able to get them any other time of the year. A fresh, warm slice was my much-deserved reward for my long mornings of picking the tiny berries and then suffering the runs from eating more from my pail than I actually took home. Oh, how I miss those blueberry pies!

To help pass the time waiting for the pies to cool, I'd play out in the fields with my sisters, running through the tall, golden grass, and I felt like a child that might have lived on the set of 1960s TV programs like *Green Acres* or *Bonanza*. I was happy and liked life. The fields were not owned by my grandmother, but they butted right up to the little farmhouse we lived in, as if they belonged to us. Summer seemed long in a good way at the farmhouse in Hoyle.

Are these warm, fuzzy memories from my first five years what I *want* to remember? Or was it really that nice when my grandma Eileen was with us? I'm not sure, but I believe that it probably was that good, since I've heard only nice things about her from anyone who ever knew her. More than the details, I especially remember feeling cared for and content when my grandma Eileen was there.

My sister Jill, two years older than me, was the first to start school. I can remember watching her enviously, my nose pressed up against the living room picture window, as she'd walk down to the end of the driveway to catch the school bus. I was excited for her but felt left out; I wanted to go, too. Even then, at the age of three or so, I craved independence and felt the urge to head out somewhere new. As far back as I can remember, I was restless and eager to "go," even if I didn't know where I was going. I didn't know what happened once my big sister disappeared on that huge, yellow bus; I just knew that I didn't want to be *not* going.

It took my mother a few heartbreaks and several children before she found the man with whom she would live out the wedding vow "Till death do us part." When I was around four years old, my mother met and married a man named Jerry Twain.

Jerry, an Ojibway Indian, was born and raised in the northern region of Ontario; his mother came from the Mattagami Indian Reserve and his father from the Bear Island Reserve in Temagami. Jerry had a bright, charming personality with a playful character and plenty of jokes and pranks up his sleeve. He had a particularly identifiable laugh that very visibly jerked his Adam's apple up and down. He often cupped his hand over his mouth when he laughed hard from the gut, snorting and gasping for air through his fingers. He loved a good laugh. Jerry was generous and friendly, with a sharp mind and a witty sense of humor. A good friend of my mother's named Audrey Twain had introduced her to Jerry, her younger brother.

My new stepdad was not much taller than my mother; around five foot ten—maybe five eleven if you include his thick brush of black hair. Jerry had a sort of unidentifiable, almost universal ethnic look about him, and I remember that he'd often joke about how when he'd met some people from Asia one time, they thought he was one of their own and started speaking to him in their native language—until they heard him reply in his local accent, with some *th*'s pronounced as *t* and pinched, long-held, almost sung vowels. He always got a kick imagining himself being mistaken for a Mexican, for example, or maybe someone from the Middle East. I recall seeing Saddam Hussein on the news for the first time years ago and thinking, *Whoa, that guy looks so much like my dad!* Although Jerry's most prominent features were his dark skin, deep brown eyes, and black hair, one of his grandfathers, Luke, was of Scottish heritage, with blond, wavy hair and light blue eyes. Interestingly, I was told that my grandpa Luke had been raised on an Indian reservation from infancy. The dash of Caucasian physical traits showed up in Jerry's light sprinkle of freckles on his face and especially in the texture of his kinky hair; he didn't have the straight, shiny locks usually associated with Native North Americans. Other than his waves and the few freckles, though, he looked very obviously ethnic. The question was of which origin. Carrie and I both agree that he resembled George Jefferson from the comedy series *The Jeffersons*. Not only did his looks remind us of our dad, but they also shared the same quirky humor.

We all moved to a moderately small split-level rental house on Norman Street, in Timmins, similar in size to my grandma Eileen's farmhouse, only with a more open concept, with a combined kitchen and living area. However, the living room was a couple of steps below the kitchen, which added several feet to the ceiling and made the home seem more spacious than it actually was. The Norman house sat on a residential street, just outside of the town center, and our house was one of the many small houses spaced about twenty feet apart that lined the street on either side. Most houses in Timmins are two-by-four timber-framed construction and average about a thousand square feet, with three bedrooms, one bathroom, and a basement. Compact homes are more the norm for practical reasons, as they're more efficient for insulating and heating during the cold winters. Timmins was historically a gold mining town. It has a wide river running along its banks called the Mattagami, where the loggers used to send tons of raw cut logs down the current to the mills. Logging is still a part of the area's industry, but the felled trees are now hauled by transport trucks to the lumberyards. Mining and forestry are the primary industries in the region, and Timmins's population has grown from 29,000 in the sixties to around 43,000 today.

Our grandmother moved with us to the Norman house. Jerry didn't resent having his new mother-in-law under the same roof as his new family. Far from it. He loved my grandma Eileen for her kind, nurturing, honest nature (to say nothing of her scrumptious pies). "She is a saint," he used to say.

I have some vivid memories from the Norman house, like my first dishwashing lesson. My grandmother propped me up on a stool and let me make a sudsy, wet mess at the kitchen sink, basically. The first fighting I remember between my mom and Jerry also occurred in the Norman house. I don't recall my grandmother ever being home when they fought, and I never heard her comment about it. It's hard to imagine, though, that she was not aware of the violence, as she and my mother were so close and there would have been the obvious physical signs of bruising and soreness. My father had only good things to say about my grandma Eileen and I only ever saw her be kind to him, regardless of what she knew, thought, or may have felt about his relationship with her daughter. Although she never expressed it in front of us children, I can only assume it would have disturbed her deeply to know it was an abusive relationship.

One fight between my parents that happened in the Norman house stands out as especially vivid. I don't remember the exact cause, but these episodes tended to follow a familiar pattern. My father had a fairly jealous streak, so it could have been related to that. Or it's likely that my mother might have been nagging him about not having enough grocery money, something we were beginning to experience more frequently. That was the source of most of their conflicts. Jerry wasn't lazy—he always worked—but I'm not even sure if he had his full high school education, so he was limited to working for minimum wage, although he changed jobs frequently in search of a fatter paycheck. But bills still never seemed to get paid on time. We moved a lot, often because we couldn't pay the back rent on one place, so we'd start over at another address until we fell too far behind there. It was a perpetual cycle, moving in order to run away from bills my parents couldn't pay.

My mother pressured my father hard when he couldn't provide. Now, it was stressful enough on him to know that he couldn't make ends meet for his family of five, let alone having my mother nag him about it to no end. But to be fair, she had nowhere else to vent her anxiety and frustration. It was humiliating to have to go to friends or family for help; that was a last resort reserved for moments of absolute desperation.

In a small house where emotions are running high, few secrets are hidden from little ears. Typically, my mother would nag, and my father would ignore her at first. As the tension mounted, so did the volume of their voices, then the verbal insults, until one of them would nudge or slap the other. From there it wouldn't take long for things to escalate into full-scale physical fighting. We kids understood that money was often tight, and the root of many of my parents' arguments was the stress of trying to survive financially.

My sisters and I usually cowered behind a closed door or in a side room where we couldn't see what was happening, only hear when violence broke out. But, unfortunately, I recall this particular fight in our new home with plain, visual detail.

My mother was a featherweight and so easy to push around. Jerry had her on the bathroom floor by the toilet, and, grabbing her hair, he slammed her head against the side of the basin, knocking her out cold. I could see Jerry repeatedly plunge my mother's head into the toilet bowl, then pull it out again. I remember wondering, *Why is he trying to drown her when she's already dead?* I wanted to scream, "Stop, you already killed her!" I wanted to stop him, but I was too afraid. My mother was limp and lifeless. I cried for her and felt completely humiliated to see her so helpless, drenched with the water from the toilet and a wet piece of toilet paper dangling from her chin.

The enormity of that helplessness transferred to me, and I felt as limp as she was. I'd never seen anything like it before or ever felt such confusion or panic. Dressed in only our pajamas, my sisters and I watched from as far away as we could get: on the tiny porch on the outside of the entrance door, in the freezing snow that came up over our bare feet. We were freaking cold and freaking out, shivering from fear, with tears streaming, lungs screaming, red-faced, and scared shitless. I can clearly remember screeching at the top of my lungs as if someone were killing me personally. Absolute, bloody murder was ripping out of my throat. The life was gone out of my mother, and I felt as if my brain were about to burst from screeching so hard and so loud. I was in hysterics, crawling out of my skin with fear, feeling as helpless as my poor mother lay at the base of the toilet, seemingly drowned.

The disturbing scene continued to play out in front of me like a movie, framed by the open door of the bathroom. It was surreal, as if I were not really there, only looking in from somewhere else.

Suddenly, several big men in dark uniforms and heavy boots walked past us on the porch and into the house. Their hard soles clopping across the floor, the static-y voices on their radios snapped me back to reality. Someone, probably a neighbor, had called the police. They escorted my dad outside and into a squad car that had pulled up in the driveway. Much to my shock, my mother was not only still alive but coherent enough to convince the officers that she was "okay." She was staggering and breathless but could speak. As I reflect on the memory, I recall how her hair clung to her head in random clumps, hanging down her face and neck, and the top half of her pajamas was soaked through to her skin.

Everyone was acting like it was going to be all right, almost not making enough of what just happened. My mother made as little of it all as possible, putting on a brave face, acting unshaken by her obvious state of distress. She would have said something like, "Everything is fine, officers, I'll be all right. Thank you for coming. Have a good night."

The end of the drama was quite swift once the police arrived.

After breaking things up, they nodded and filed out the door, but what if my mother needed medical attention? Surely she should have at least been examined. No one was sent to check on her—or us, for that matter. We were traumatized, and the only person there to help us cope with the aftermath of the horrific events of that night was my beaten, broken mother. Today, forty years later, with the far greater awareness of spousal abuse and the victim's tendency to downplay the violence, make excuses for the abuser—even blame herself for the offender's actions—the situation would be investigated further and handled more thoroughly. Back then I was relieved that the police at least ended the fighting just by showing up. And with that, everything returned to normal. Until the next time.

As confusing and painful as it was to witness these battles between my parents, I was comforted knowing that I was not alone, that my sisters were there, too. We were all going through it together. And even though I was only four years old when family violence entered my life, it also occurred to me that my parents were caught up in it, and it wasn't their fault. What I mean is, sure, I hated the violence while it was happening, but I didn't hate *them*. I felt sorry for them. They were aware of how their behavior was affecting us—I could sense them eyeing us with worry even as they screamed at each other—but by the time things had degenerated into physical abuse, the two of them were just too far gone emotionally to be able to put out the fire they'd both had a hand in starting.

The guilt and shame they clearly felt after each incident, I sensed, weighed a ton; knowing us kids were watching must have been awful. I felt sorry for their shame and didn't have the heart to hold it against them even at that very young age. Each time, I just wanted it to be over, behind us and forgotten. Once a fight ended, I only wished for life to go back to normal, as quickly as possible, like nothing ever happened.

I mean the good part of normal, when they weren't fighting with each other, my parents displayed love and affection toward each other. My dad often winked at my mom deliberately when he knew we were looking, so we'd blush and get all coy. He enjoyed annoying her with surprise pinches to her backside. He'd come up behind her with his finger to his lips, hushing us to be included in getting the rise out of her. He openly complimented my mom in general, especially her legs, saying that they were beautiful and that she should wear skirts more often to show them off. My mother was openly flattered by my father's adoration of her, and I sensed a genuine love between them. Although I wanted to protect my mom against my dad when they fought, I didn't actually resent my dad for the fighting or blame him more. I felt they were both victims of the economic struggle, the key reason for the violent outbreaks, and that they both should have known better and were both responsible for letting their arguments get out of control. I did feel more sorry for my mother, though, because she was the physically weaker of the two, and therefore more vulnerable, but I didn't feel she was any less responsible for instigating the commotion.

When my turn finally came to start school, the urge to follow my big sister suddenly dimmed once I realized I was to go spend my day with a lot of strangers. I'm not sure what I was expecting, but Jill seemed to enjoy school, and I was curious about what she was enjoying. I have always had an inquisitive nature, ready to explore and discover, but I was uncertain about sharing new experiences with people I didn't know. I preferred to be alone rather than with strangers, and was quite content being solitary as a child. In fact, I am still very much like that now. Not lone*ly*, but alone with my thoughts, emotions, and reflections.

That first day of school, I felt insecure and utterly panicked as my mother walked me into the first classroom I'd ever seen and handed me over to the kindergarten teacher. "Eilleen," the woman instructed, "why don't you go sit down on the carpet with the other children." She would say something like "Go on now!" while gesturing for my mother to leave, before I could say anything about it. As my mother turned to walk away, the most furious hurricane of emotions swept over me. My face became hot, and my eyes welled up with tears that blurred her figure until all I could see was a dark, tall blob leaving the room. Just like that, she was gone.

I hated this! I was miserable and gutted that my mother could leave me with this lady I didn't even know and kids I didn't want to know. But what I *did* know was not to run after my mother and beg her to stay. I felt I needed to be brave and act like a big girl. I remember feeling that I was supposed to stay, my mother had to go, and that I wasn't allowed to make a fuss about it. I felt the anxiety of separation from her and the intense struggle not to show it.

The day got better as it went on. "Music time!" the teacher announced. We were allowed to rummage through the music box and pull out whatever instrument we wanted to play. There were sticks with ridges that you could rub together to make clicky sounds, a variety of shakers, tambourines, bells, and other noisy, percussive instruments. Now, *this* was getting fun! I enjoyed my first music session and couldn't wait till the next one. Unfortunately, music time lasted only a few minutes each day; then it was time to spread out our blankets on the floor and take a nap. This frustrated me to no end, as it seemed that just as we got started playing music, it was already time to stop. I wanted to play with the instruments the whole day. It's obvious to me now that my strong desire to create music—a true passion—was developing even then. This was my first experience of having my hands on musical instruments, and it was all I wanted to do.

By the time I graduated from high school, I had attended seventeen different schools. In fact, I didn't even make it through kindergarten without our family moving not once but twice. It was difficult being the new kid so often, but I can see how I benefited from learning how to adjust to change.

I was seven when my parents had their first child together, Mark. My brother wasn't even out of diapers yet before they adopted a second son. Audrey Twain, Jerry's older sister, died shortly after giving birth to a boy named Darryl. There was no question about what to do under the tragic circumstances; both my mother and my father did not hesitate to take their nephew into our home. With that, the "Twain Gang," as my mom used to call us—five children from two mothers and four fathers—was now complete.

A real blend of this and that, the Twain Gang was off chugging through life, a crazy, happy, sad, dysfunctional, destructive, loving, violent roller-coaster ride, to a head-on collision.

# 2

# Timmins, 1971

In the summer of 1971, around the time of my sixth birthday, we left the Norman Street address for a small rental home on Bannerman Street on the east side of Timmins. In September I began the first grade at Mattagami Public School, where the principal's name was Mrs. Partridge. I thought that maybe she was related to the singing family on TV's *The Partridge Family*. The world was still very small to me at the age of six, so it made perfect sense—although I did question why "my" Mrs. Partridge lived in Timmins, Ontario, while the Mrs. Partridge played by Shirley Jones lived in a fictional small town in Northern California. It was hard at such a young age to consider that people with the same last name were not necessarily related. I thought the only Twains that existed in the world, for example, were us, and that anyone with the name Twain must be our relatives. The only other use of the word *partridge* I'd heard of at six years old was what I knew as a wild, medium-sized pheasant, hunted by locals in the fall. I was having trouble connecting all these long-distance dots. Although the United States was our next-door neighbor, to me it seemed worlds away, a country you read about in stories and saw on TV and in movies. I had trouble determining the difference between what was real and only real on TV.

On the school playground, a bold white line divided the boys' area from the girls' area; although our classes were coed, we were separated during recess. I'm not sure what the purpose of separating the sexes really was, but I assumed it was intended to keep the boys from kissing the girls when the teacher wasn't looking. Mrs. Partridge would gaze down from her second-floor office window, which afforded her a bird's-eye view of the entire playground, and anyone who dared to cross the line could expect to be hauled upstairs to her office for punishment. Don't ask me what type of punishment, because I was never brave enough to find out. Mrs. Partridge scared me, even though I never had any particular reason to feel that way. The braver kids used to call her "the old bird," but as a child I tended to avoid trouble and although it was only harmless naughtiness, I wouldn't have been caught dead mocking Mrs. Partridge.

Once a week, we had show-and-tell first thing in the morning. Anyone willing to participate could get up in front of the class and share whatever hobby or interest he or she wanted. It might be something such as a stamp or coin collection, vacation photos, or a grandfather's war helmet, but preferably something unique to that person. Although I was outgoing in many ways, I shriveled up whenever I was put on the spot or made the center of attention.

So I surprised even myself when I volunteered to sing a song for show-and-tell. I'd fallen in love with singing from the age of three. There was always music playing at home, although there was no one musical in my immediate family to influence me to become a singer. I just naturally sang along with whatever music was on. My earliest recollection of consciously singing was sitting in the field that stretched out behind my grandma's Hoyle farmhouse. I used to sing "Baa Baa Black Sheep" and "Twinkle, Twinkle, Little Star" repeatedly to myself. Actually, at first I just hummed the melodies, rolling the notes around in my mouth and enjoying the buzzing sensation of my tongue against my teeth until it tickled so much from the vibration that I had to stop, desperate to scratch the itchiness. And I was intrigued by the feeling of the resonance, how it seemed to fill the whole cavity of my head.

It's common for vocal instructors to teach singers specific exercises and techniques that help develop voice resonance in order to improve sound projection, pitch control, and tone quality. A well-known vocal warm-up exercise, for example, entails creating a buzzing sensation in the lips and tongue while humming "*Umumumumum.*" Hmmmm, that sounds familiar! The tickle on the tongue and lips is the indication that the exercise is being done properly, that the vocalist is successfully resonating the sound. What I now know is an actual vocal technique was instinctively sound play for me at three years old. I'd discovered an internal instrument and was learning how to play it. I was finding my voice.

From that moment on, I sang all the time: to the car stereo (either the radio or the eight-track tape), whatever was playing around the house, with restaurant jukeboxes. Everywhere there was music playing, I was singing along. It was how I spent most of my recreational time, much in the same way that other kids my age caught butterflies in jars or collected lucky pennies in a tin. I listened to music and learned songs. I was in love with all the music genres I'd been exposed to as a small child. Rock, pop, folk, and country. I couldn't have been more than four years old when "He Ain't Heavy, He's My Brother," a big harmony-laden hit by the Hollies, came on the radio. I was struck by the profound message in the lyrics, agreeing with the sentiment, championing the words, thinking, *Ya, everyone deserves a helping hand, understanding!* The song's meaning provoked an awareness in me of sensitivity toward humanity. I respected the singer for feeling so generous and tolerant toward others less fortunate and weaker than himself. I was impressed that he was so willing to help carry someone else's heavy load. *What a nice guy,* I thought. I also interpreted that he might be implying that no matter where people are from or where they're going, they are worthy of compassion, and this, to me, spoke out against what, of course, I know now as prejudice.

My mother and Jerry were not together yet, and still in the safe home of my grandmother, I had not yet experienced hunger, nor had I any sense of what it was like to be deprived of any basic necessities. Neither had I been introduced to the realities of a mixed-race family environment yet, especially not one of a social minority. In fact, I hadn't even considered that skin could be identified by color. I believe I saw the last of my innocence when I was three. This was the last period in my life I remember living without fear, panic, and insecurity for the welfare of myself and those close to me. At this tender age, my voice was still fun to use, and I didn't understand anything about the role of fathers because up to Jerry coming into our lives, I had no recollection of a father present, just my mother and my grandmother. I didn't know anything about whether my mother was happy or not, nor did I worry myself about the future.

Music continued to grow as a passion for me both as a singer and as an enthusiastic listener. On a purely sonic note, I was drawn by the sounds of the Supremes' records. Every song was as exciting as the last in a long string of hits. Specific songs that stand out in my memory from that time were the Beach Boys' "Good Vibrations," the Turtles' "Happy Together," "Crimson and Clover" by Tommy James and the Shondells, and one I couldn't get out of my head: "Seasons in the Sun" by Terry Jacks. I was so sad for the singer, as in the song he was dying, and I especially felt his pain when he sang "Good-bye, Papa, it's hard to die, when all the birds are singing in the sky." Music moved me, and I was emotionally affected by the sounds and the storytelling. I remember people remarking, "Oh, listen to that tiny girl sing!" as I sang along with everything with deep emotion and sincerity. Not everyone was appreciative, though; sometimes I heard, "Eilleen, you're getting on our nerves. Now stop singing!" I never did, though.

Not unexpectedly, my mother was my biggest fan. Now, my mother couldn't sing to save her life, but she could tell that I had an ear for music. My singing made her emotional and often teary eyed. One time, when I was about five, the two of us were in the car together, and this new brother-sister duo called the Carpenters came on the radio. I was in awe of the smooth, silky depth of Karen Carpenter's voice, layered with her own harmonies stacked with her brother's voice, which created that luscious, distinct vocal blend they had together. The brother-sister sound poured out of the tinny car radio speakers like pure honey. Wow! No speakers could make the Carpenters sound bad. Hearing Karen sing always gave me chills.

One of my favorites to sing along with was "Rainy Days and Mondays." I liked to double Karen's voice, but on a different note, pretending to be her backup singer. I couldn't resist singing along to the beauty of her voice, but I wanted to hear her, not sing over her notes. I tried to follow Karen's lead part by following the melody line like a shadow. The blend felt so satisfying to me. My mother, however, was taken aback.

"Eilleen!" she exclaimed. "What are you doing?"

"This part's more interesting," I explained. I loved to harmonize, and couldn't get enough of listening to pristine and sometimes complex vocal arrangements executed ingeniously by artists such as the Beach Boys, the Mamas and the Papas, Bread, and the Bee Gees, to name a few. Later, in my teens, I would study other groups known for their multipart harmonies: the Eagles, Fleetwood Mac, the Doobie Brothers, Earth, Wind & Fire, ABBA. And more Bee Gees—it's hard to top the three brothers' combination of talent and the similar voice quality that comes from sharing DNA.

Although my preference was to always take the harmony part, my mother encouraged me to sing lead. "You're my little singer, not my little *backup* singer," was her reasoning. The urge I felt to go straight to the harmony parts so often, I believe, was probably a true reflection of my personality. An aspect of my nature that preferred being in the company of others to enjoy my singing. I appreciated the concept of group singing, the team spirit and group effort, especially once I learned to play guitar at eight years old.

I became more influenced by singer-songwriter-type artists who accompanied themselves on acoustic guitar. This allowed for a more intimate group sound that I would say has made the biggest impression on my acoustic-style songwriting. When I plunk out songs on the piano, as I don't actually play piano but use it as a songwriting tool, my melodies and feel are very different from when I use the guitar. Guitarist-songwriters such as Dolly Parton, Willie Nelson, Gordon Lightfoot, and Jim Croce impacted my writing, but I think the group artists did even more. Bands such as the Poppy Family and Crosby, Stills and Nash drove me crazy with creative inspiration, like the sky was the limit, and I loved their songwriting and the three individual voices they put together to create a cluster of sound. I just couldn't believe it, I was so amazed.

This was really where my heart was, singing words and melodies that sit with ease in my throat. I strive for this again now. I got away from the more organic way of using my voice when I began singing live, commercial rock in my late teens and am only getting back to the folkish, acoustic artist style of singing I enjoy singing the most. I will always be a great fan of the voice that expresses itself with no inhibition of imperfection. The concern to vocalize emotion without flaw, I believe, only obstructs the flow of honesty and integrity in the expression. I have a great appreciation for classical music, which in my experience, through the bit of exposure I've had on and off over the years through vocal lessons and having dated a classical orchestra conductor, has made me realize that there is little room for improvisation or personal adaptation. I admire the complexity in the compositions of classical music and also the incredible discipline it requires to execute a high standard of performance, but my favorite piece of music written by a classical musician is the film score from *The Mission*. I don't believe it's considered "classical," but rather a soundtrack for a Hollywood movie. Nevertheless, it's a symphony of masterfully combined sounds that appeals to me in the same vein as classical music. The creative and unique approach Ennio Morricone took with *The Mission* soundtrack was what I consider "contemporary classical," but I don't believe it is actually called that, technically.

Although my taste in music was broad from the beginning, my own personal style continued to develop more in the vein of an acoustic singer-songwriter. The song I chose to sing to my first-grade class was called "Take Me Home, Country Roads." The response wasn't at all what I'd expected. Some of the kids started snickering and giggling. I was so embarrassed that I came *this* close to stopping mid-song and bolting out of the room in tears. But it seemed too late to give up, so I finished, much to my relief, although I distinctly remember feeling that I never wanted to sing in front of my peers again! However, the children's cruelty didn't end there. On the playground that afternoon, some of them ridiculed me, calling me a show-off. I couldn't understand it. My family always enjoyed it when I sang and never gave me the impression that I was "showing off." In fact, they *wanted* me to sing for them.

My traumatic public debut at show-and-tell was pretty disheartening, to tell you the truth, but I loved music too much to let it discourage me from singing. The same year during first grade, I joined the school choir, figuring that singing as part of a group probably couldn't be too bad. Plus, there'd be a lot of harmonizing; I liked that. Without my mother's pushing me, though, I might not have tried out. She accompanied me to school for the evening audition in front of the music teacher who directed the choir. First, I had to sing solo, then with the full ensemble. I didn't know anything about singing in a choir. I didn't understand how to *not* improvise the notes. It was awkward being told exactly what part to sing and being expected to remain strictly in unison with the several other voices on my same part: melody. Despite my obvious lack of experience, the director was visibly impressed by my voice and accepted me, even though I was one year below the minimum-age cutoff. That made some kids jealous and their parents annoyed. Once again, I heard calls of "show-off!" and accusations that I craved attention. The last thing I wanted was to stand out from the group of singers. I wanted to blend in like everyone else. I also wanted to explain that I sang simply because I enjoyed it, just like they might have played soccer or taken riding lessons. By this point, I felt targeted and bullied for being good at something. Being the "little singer" wasn't so fun. Not a good start to a career that would dominate the next few decades of my life.

• • •

I'm looking at a photo of me, my dad, Carrie, and our dog Peppi posing on the front steps of the house on Bannerman. It's my little sister's first day of kindergarten. The one-bedroom home, a tiny, wood-framed box shape with wood plank siding, sat behind the landlord's larger house. Perhaps our little house was originally the garage or storage shed of the main house. It was small enough for me to assume that it had possibly been a secondary building of that sort, converted into a rental dwelling. Regardless of what its original use may have been, this small, wood-framed square house was now the Twain home to a family of six. In the two years that we lived there, it served as the stage for plenty of Twain Gang drama, including poverty, violence, and the arrival of my baby brother Mark, my mother's fourth child.

This little house shook when there was a physical ruckus going on inside. There wasn't much space, so during a struggle, there was lots of banging into things and no room to avoid tumbling into furniture and corners. My parents once had an argument during a birthday celebration for my dad. My mom had surprised him by baking a spice cake. I loved her spice cake! It had an apple-cinnamon flavor with vanilla icing. But this day, they began fighting, and it soon became a physical struggle. At the sound of their yelling, I poked my head around the corner and saw this peculiar brownish stuff on my mother's head and face and I immediately thought of a scary movie I'd seen once, where a knife thrower, as part of a circus stunt, threw knives at a spinning wheel that had a woman strapped to it. He hit the woman right in the neck, cutting her throat open. It was an old movie with cheap visual effects, and in that scene, a brownish, mince-type stuffing came out of her wound. Although it wasn't very convincing as real bodily insides coming out, the texture I now saw caked on my mother reminded me of it. I panicked. *Her brains are coming out! She's going to die! He's killed her!* I was convinced that my mother was dead. But what I saw wasn't the minced insides; six-year-old me had jumped to conclusions. It was the birthday cake she'd baked for him, which he'd thrown in her face. I felt conflicting emotions: relief that my mom was okay, but sadness, too. How could he be so mean and humiliate her like that after she'd done something so nice for him and gone to the trouble of baking him this delicious cake?

But the Bannerman Street house saw far worse fights than that. During my mother's pregnancy on Bannerman, far into her last term, as I remember her tummy being well pronounced already, they got into an angry spat, and Jerry tossed her around the room like a rag doll, banged her head against the wall, and then kicked her while she was on the floor and curled up, trying to protect her stomach. I didn't know anything about pregnancy, but it was instinctively obvious to me that if you beat the shit out of a woman with a baby in her belly, you could hurt—or kill—the baby. Thankfully, both of them lived.

Between the beatings from my dad, living in a cramped house with four kids, one of them an infant, and money being tight as usual, my mother was increasingly edgy. Adding to the stress, Grandma Eileen was in the hospital dying. I don't remember why my grandmother no longer lived with us by the time I was six. I do remember my mother being very stressed after coming home from hospital visits to my grandmother, very emotional about how helpless she felt not being able to stay with her through the night, and deeply distressed that the nurses couldn't give my grandmother water when she was so parched and desperate to drink. Apparently with her heart condition, angina, and the treatment she was under, a very limited liquid intake was necessary, as my mother explained. It hurt her so much to see her own mother suffering.

My grandmother died while we were still living on Bannerman, the same time period my mother delivered the first boy in the family. My grandmother specifically asked my mother that if the baby was a boy, to name him Mark, and she did.

One of my sister Carrie's most vivid memories from the Bannerman house was her routine of waiting for my dad to get home from work. He always saved his lunch dessert for Carrie; she had a real sweet tooth and sat on the front step each afternoon, waiting for him to return so she could rush his lunch box. She'll never forget the time she clipped open the aluminum hinged box to find a plastic bag filled with water and two goldfish swimming about. She named her new pets Goldie and Silvy. They sat on display at the top of the fridge of our tiny kitchen in a round glass bowl. In her memory, it was the sweetest gift he ever gave her. We both remember our father as a kind, thoughtful man, and because the contrast between his two sides was complicated for us small children to comprehend, we tended to hold on to the sunny side rather than the darker side.

The Bannerman house certainly saw its share of personal hardships, and it showed in my mother's behavior. She would spend hours putting together our Halloween costumes, like the ones shown in the photo included in this book, with me as a fairy princess with a tinfoil wand and crown, Carrie in her clown suit, and Jill in a "squaw outfit," as my dad called it. She pulled herself into the spirit of life for us kids, and I realize now how much courage that must have taken for her to keep us happy and feeling as if we had some normalcy in our lives. Yet on the other hand, there could be a hurricane of domestic instability, sometimes all in the same day. But she was only so strong, and she inevitably took it out on us sometimes. One time I had the stomach flu and woke up in the middle of the night feeling nauseous. I called for her as I stumbled out of bed and staggered across the kitchen on my way to the washroom. I didn't make it, vomiting all over the floor. It was the first time in my seven-year life I'd ever thrown up. I didn't understand what was happening to me, and I was scared. With my mother now at my side, I vomited again, this time on myself as well as on her.

I was crying and weak and wanted only to be held while I tried to catch my breath. To my shock, my mom grabbed me by the shoulders and shook me hard. "I can't believe what a mess you made!" she scolded furiously. "Now I have to clean all this up. It's the middle of the night, for Christ's sake!" Aside from the odd slap across the head or tight grip on my arm when I got on her nerves, either by talking too much or not paying attention, I'd never felt my mother being so angry with me before.

Looking back on it now, and being a mother myself, I understand her lack of patience that night. She had three other kids to wake up for in a few hours, and now, in the middle of the night, I'd given her a big mess to clean. I wish I'd had the maturity then to comfort her and tell her I understood. But being seven years old, I didn't understand. How could I? The idea that adults can live challenging lives full of struggles and suffering is beyond a child's comprehension. All I knew was that her behavior upset me, making me feel worse than I already did.

How can four children and two adults sleep in a tiny one-bedroom house? The only bedroom was on the second floor, and that was where my parents slept, while my two sisters and I slept in single bunk beds wedged into the corner of the stairwell at the base of the steps leading down from their room. Our baby brother's crib was tucked under the stairs, across from our bunk beds.

Jill's "seniority" earned her the luxury of sleeping alone in the top bunk; Carrie and I shared the bottom bed. Not only was it pretty cramped, especially as we grew—this arrangement continued until I was twelve—but my little sister was a bed wetter until about the age of ten. Boy, did I used to get pissed (sorry, Carrie!) at her when I'd feel something warm and wet soaking my pajamas in the middle of the night. Sometimes I was able to avoid it by jamming myself up against the wall or shifting to the foot of the bed; I'd throw a coat over myself and leave her in the puddle of pee with a grunt and try to get back to the business of sleeping. But other times there was no dry spot to take refuge in, and so I'd have to go through the whole process of waking up Carrie-Ann, changing her pajamas, placing a towel over the wet spot, and putting on fresh bedding. Much to my astonishment, and my annoyance, if I didn't shake her awake, she'd just carry on sleeping peacefully as if nothing had happened!

• • •

We girls had unusual amounts of independence and responsibility for children our ages. With Carrie in tow, Jill and I used to walk over an hour to the public swimming pool in the neighboring town of Schumacher. It was a long distance for six- and eight-year-old kids, let alone for a tiny four-year-old. In 2010 Carrie and I went back to Timmins and took that exact walk again, from our old front door on Bannerman to where the pool used to be, just to step back through the distance of time. What took us over an hour nearly forty years ago was still a forty-five-minute walk for us as adults. We were impressed at how our little legs were able to take us so far from home as well as all the way back again. Sometimes when we look back at the scale of things from when we were little, we often find them so much smaller and shorter than we remembered them. Not in this case! But more than the distance, we marveled at how we ever managed, at such young ages, to make our way back and forth without supervision, especially when you consider that there were no sidewalks along the busy highway with traffic whizzing past. It was dangerous. My sisters and I didn't think twice about it at the time, but in retrospect—and being a mom myself—it does strike me as rather eyebrow raising, as nowadays most parents don't even let their kids walk down to the corner alone before they reach their teens.

Jill, being the oldest, naturally shouldered most of the responsibility. She was incredibly mature and conscientious, always taking good care of Carrie and me. My parents often gave her the task of paying utility bills while the three of us were on our way to the pool, or to Hollinger Park, or to the local bowling alley—bowling being one of our favorite activities. My dad worked long hours at the local mine at this point, and my mother had a part-time job at a department store called Marshalls. We took care of ourselves a lot and did many of the errands while they worked.

Even at age seven, I was painfully aware that our family was dysfunctional compared to most. Other families seemed to behave more like the families I saw on TV: sibling squabbles over taking too much time in the bathroom, parents disagreeing over whether to have the in-laws over during the holidays, how to tell the kids the dog ran away, things like that. The television series I used to watch in the late sixties and early seventies included *Bonanza, The Flintstones, The Addams Family, Gilligan's Island,* and one of my favorites, *The Brady Bunch*. These families—even the animated Flintstones of Bedrock—always worked out their problems reasonably, learning important life lessons and morals in the process.

In contrast, something was seriously wrong in our home, so whenever I encountered another dysfunctional family, the signs were all too familiar to me, and I'd feel compassion for them, silently recognizing what we had in common. I could relate to the likely struggles in their home life. I was sensitive to others who showed signs of neglect or abuse such as poor hygiene, bad teeth, regular absenteeism from school, overly introverted or extroverted behavior, parents you never saw, even when they were invited to participate in school functions, and unexplained injuries. I believe suffering children recognize one another. I personally never talked openly to anyone, even other kids I felt sorry for or related to, about my own inner struggle with my childhood. Many kids don't because children naturally care for their parents and families and feel protective of them, not wanting to expose any dysfunction in the family for fear of the family breaking up or someone getting in trouble. Exposing a parent or someone a child loves can make him or her feel guilty or disloyal, which is how I would have felt. Kids might hide painful feelings also because they are embarrassed by their situation, feeling they might be criticized, and are afraid of being exposed and humiliated. My personal experience was that if I were ever to have shared a violent scene between my parents with a teacher or a friend who then told her parents, I knew my father could be arrested, and I was afraid of being alone with my mother not being able to provide for us. I felt that if anyone knew about certain situations in our home, everything would fall apart. Fear and guilt were primarily what kept me quiet.

I remember one friend the same age as me named Charlotte, a girl with long, golden braids. She lived on the other side of the alley behind our house. Her mother was a meek, dusty-gray-haired woman who gave me the impression that she had neither the energy nor the time to wash her grungy kitchen floor. One Saturday morning, I went to play at Charlotte's house. Just as I arrived, her mother was rushing out the door to go to work. Instead of playing, Charlotte and I were assigned the chore of scrubbing the floor while her mother was gone. Our seven-year-old method was to fill up a pail with hot water and a half quart too much of Javex bleach (that's the brand name for Clorox in Canada) and flood the surface with it until it was about a half inch deep from corner to corner. Next we swished the mop around for a while, squeezing the dirty water into the bucket. Last but not least: let it air dry.

Proud of our little housekeeping duty, we were ready for some play. Charlotte's father was still in his bathrobe, watching TV in the bedroom. He called us in and invited us to jump on the bed, which we were eager to do. As we jumped up and down, giggling, his bathrobe opened to reveal an ugly, dangling organ surrounded by a ghastly bush of hair. The man made no effort whatsoever to cover himself; he just lay there coolly, clearly aware that he was intentionally exposing himself to a couple of little girls, one of whom happened to be his own daughter.

I had never seen anything like this sausage-like thing before, and it scared me. Picturing the scene *still* gives me shivers. I ran out of the house and kept running until I was standing in our kitchen, gasping for breath. No one asked me where I'd been, nor did I volunteer the information. It never would have occurred to me to tell my parents about the frightening experience; to be honest, I didn't want to burden them, as things were stressful enough in our household. *Mom and Dad have enough to worry about without having to worry about me,* was my thinking.

I was, however, concerned for Charlotte and felt guilty for leaving her there with her father, and his gross, disgusting thing, without telling anyone. I knew there was definitely something wrong with that scenario, but I didn't have the courage or maturity to know what to do except feel uncomfortable and confused. I believed there was nothing I could do for her, and I believe that she had her problems, I had mine. That sense of helplessness is how I would describe how I felt during many crises growing up, with me consciously detaching myself from the suffering, even though I felt every bit of it. I did my best to distance myself from it mentally, a mind-over-matter-type approach. All I felt I "could" do was to move forward, look ahead and not behind. As a parent, I know that if my child told me about a similar experience at a friend's house, I'd march right over there and bonk the guy on the head, then report his ass to child protective services. I'd like to think that had my mother known, she would have been just as alarmed—although instead of bonking the child offender on the head, she probably would have bonked *me,* to try to scare the wits out of me so I never went back there again. That would have been her way of protecting me, and I suppose it would have worked, although I was sufficiently freaked out without her help. *No way* was I ever going back to Charlotte's house.

When my grandmother died in 1972, my mother was devastated and thrown into intense grief, crying all the time and at the drop of a hat. I can't imagine how lost and alone she must have felt with three little girls and a new baby, trapped in a violent, roller-coaster marriage with barely enough money to get by. Now she had lost the one person who had always been there for her. Everyone loved my grandma Eileen, including my dad, who always spoke of her with immense respect, but no one more so than my mother. And certainly no one was as dependent on her as my mother was; just the mere mention of my grandmother would bring her to tears.

Not long after my grandmother died and my new baby brother began to crawl, we moved to a basement with more living space. Although it was roomier—at least my sisters and I now had our own bedroom—I didn't like it so much. Our bedroom carpet was so thick with skank that I didn't want it touching my bare feet. I decided we needed to pull up the carpet and throw it out. I'm not sure what my parents thought of the idea, but they didn't try to stop me, in any case. When I began peeling back the dirty thing, what I saw made me want to throw up on the spot: what seemed like zillions of disgusting, squirming white *things,* like moving rice, bending and squiggling on the bare floor where the carpet had been. I'd never heard of maggots before, but I knew that they were insects, and I knew that insects shouldn't be living under the carpet. Rather than complain, I slapped the filthy carpet back down and simply pretended that our revolting little guests weren't there. The way I figured it, better for them to be living *under* the floor covering and out of sight. The carpet remained.

We rented the apartment from an elderly couple that lived upstairs. They were always sweet to me whenever I'd pass them on my way to the corner store or to the neighborhood church to light candles for my grandmother and our little dog Peppi, who'd also died not long after her. I missed them both so much and found comfort lighting a candle for each of them along with saying a prayer that I wished they hadn't gone, and that I hoped to see them again someday. I believed the candles would help light their way to the Heavenly Father, to God Himself. And feeling that my candle was very important, I visualized the flame literally helping them see their way through what I imagined was somewhere dark.

One afternoon on my way back from the church, the old man from the upstairs apartment called to me from his chair on the front porch. "Come here!" he said with a friendly wave of his hand.

Although I was shy, I didn't want to be rude, so I slowly entered through the white picket gate and climbed up to the porch. "Would you like some candy?" he asked. I nodded yes. I was a bit nervous about being alone with him and accepting candy, but I didn't see the harm. After all, he wasn't a complete stranger.

"Why don't you come inside while I look for the candy?" he suggested. Ordinarily, his wife joined him on the porch, literally every day. I noticed that she didn't appear to be around.

"Where is your wife?" I asked innocently.

"In the hospital," he replied softly. I felt sorry for him, thinking that maybe his wife would die like my own grandmother had so recently. As I was going through these sad thoughts, he found what he was looking for. Placing the candy on the table, he told me to come sit on his lap. I did, and he let me take one piece. Being in that house, eating candy while sitting on his knee, was the most unnatural, uncomfortable position I'd ever been in. I just wanted to turn into liquid and drip through the floorboards down to our basement apartment below.

Suddenly I felt his rough hand on my leg. Then, slowly but in one fluid motion, he slipped it underneath my T-shirt and onto my tummy, before settling on my chest. I hadn't started developing yet and was too young to relate my chest to sex in any way, but I knew this wasn't right and froze. How was I going to get out of this grip I found so repulsive? Break away from the dirty feeling of being held up against this man who was making me so anxious? I didn't know if I should resist; I mean, he wasn't hurting me, and I'd accepted his offer of candy. My hesitation stemmed from not being able to determine where the boundary was between responding to my instinct for suspicion and fear, and my urge to be a good little girl, showing respect and kindness by obeying my poor, elderly neighbor, whose wife was sick and could die. Suddenly, an idea:

"I'd better go see if my mother needs me for something," I piped up, trying to act like it was an innocent thought, not an excuse he would see through. It took a lot of courage to stand up and walk out of that house, as I knew I was defying an adult's authority. Once I headed for the door, I just kept going and didn't look back, hoping with all my might that he wasn't going to try to stop me. *That was close,* I thought. Close to *what,* exactly, I didn't know at the time; I just knew that something so wrong was happening and that I was vulnerable and somewhere I wasn't supposed to be. Somewhere dangerous, and I'm just glad I had the presence of mind to figure out a way to get out of there.

Once again, I didn't report this incident to my parents or to anyone else. I actually blamed myself for getting into the situation in the first place, probably because I felt that's how my mother would have reacted if I'd told her. In retrospect, it strikes me as ironic that my mother was my excuse to escape but not my refuge; also the fact that I lied to the old man, hoping he'd be alarmed by the prospect of my mother expecting me, when the reality was that she had no idea where I was and wouldn't have worried about me unless I wasn't home after dark. I was on a very loose leash—too loose, I feel now. I can think of several occasions when I was very lucky that something more traumatic or dangerous didn't happen to me while I was farther away from the nest than I should have been at my age.

It goes without saying that parents are responsible for their children's well-being. We can't leave things to chance, or expect our kids to "know better" (not without our teaching them, that's for sure), or assume that they'll always report potentially dangerous scrapes to us. Children want to please their parents, and, right or wrong, they may withhold information for fear of disappointing their mom and dad or making them angry. I'm not advocating holding our kids' hands everywhere they go, but there needs to be regular communication and not so much distance that they feel neglected. You know, children may act annoyed at being checked on and monitored, but as long as you can say honestly that you aren't smothering them, such parental attentiveness actually makes them feel loved and secure.

Certainly my mother and my father went through periods where they were aloof and even negligent. Yet I can't say that I didn't feel loved. I just accepted the fact that they weren't always capable of being there for me to the extent that I wished they would be. They didn't choose to be that way. Circumstances—mainly poverty—prevented them from being the ideal parents that, in their hearts, they probably had hoped to be. I honestly don't believe that I'm making excuses for them, although I can see how some may think that I'm rationalizing their behavior. Life isn't like a TV series. There is no perfect parent. I do realize, however, growing up the way we did, we probably saw our parents' shortcomings earlier than perhaps other kids do. I feel that we were certainly exposed to too much, too young.

But then, even with my son, although I have the best intentions, I'm sure I'm not always the mother he expects me to be. I have to say that the understanding I've reached about my own mother and my father has allowed me to be more forgiving toward myself when I fall short of my own expectations as a mother. No parent can be perfect in every situation or all the time (and this applies to our other roles in life as well, be it spouse, relative, or friend), no matter how much he or she may want to be or try. Ultimately, I've realized that my responsibility is to *do* my best, whether I succeed or not. My parents deserve the same degree of understanding and compassion that I afford myself and those around me. Anyone who gives a good, honest effort wins my respect every time, and in that regard, my mother and my father deserve my thanks.

# 3

## Tomboy

Moving day *again*, just months later. I'm not unhappy about it, though. To be leaving our maggot-infested bedroom in the basement apartment belonging to the dirty old man? I'm packed and ready to go! Especially since we're relocating to a city called Sudbury, located about four hours south of Timmins. I've never lived in a city before, so I am excited about the prospect of a place with real skyscrapers. This will be the year I get into my first physical fight and win my first gold award of excellence in track-and-field, as well as discover the excruciating pain of breast development. I won't realize it until later, however, that Sudbury is a *small* city compared to Toronto or New York, for example, and that I wouldn't find real skyscrapers there.

The apartment house on King Street in Sudbury was an upgrade for us compared to our last two houses in Timmins. By that I mean it was clean, new, and spacious enough for me to not be embarrassed if a friend came over.

King Street was where we welcomed the fifth child to the family, when my parents adopted Darryl, my father's nephew. Audrey, my dad's sister and the one who first introduced my parents, took an overdose of pills and unfortunately succeeded at taking her own life. Darryl was just a baby, still in one-piece sleeper pajamas (you know, the kind with the enclosed feet), and wasn't walking yet when my parents took him in. I remember enjoying having another baby around and thought he was *soooo* cute. I nicknamed him "Bay," and it stuck as a cutesy, short form for baby. The five of us kids' bedrooms were in the basement of the apartment house, with the boys sharing a room, Jill tucked into a makeshift bedroom that was really the furnace room with extra space for a bed, and Carrie and I continuing to share a room, sleeping in a single bed.

We didn't live in the Sudbury house for more than one school year, but it seemed like a lot happened during that time. One of the most painful memories of that period, at least as far as I was concerned, was the excruciating swelling of my breasts, signaling the start of puberty, even though I was only going on nine years old. One of the first days at my new elementary school, I accidentally bumped one of my new little bumps on the corner of my desk. It generated such a sharp, piercing pain, my eyes welled up with tears.

I somehow suppressed the urge to cry, though, because I was much too tough a tomboy to whine about a little discomfort. I mean, I used to challenge friends to thigh-punching contests to see who could withstand the hardest blow, while at night I ran around with the boys pulling pranks, like sneaking into parking lots and letting the air out of people's tires. I was the only girl and much more concerned with fitting in with the boys than making friends with girls. One day, when my mother asked what I thought I wanted to be when I grew up, I announced that I wanted to be a man.

I didn't mean *literally*. But as I edged toward adolescence, I imagined myself growing up to be a solid, strong, athletic woman, not a soft, fussy, screechy one. So this new shape that my body was about to take on may have presented serious pain, and my eyes watered, but I was going to ignore it and hold it back.

One thing I learned quickly about playing tough, though: there's always someone tougher. One day another tomboy, two years older than me, and bigger, taller, and stronger, challenged me to a fight after school. I was scared and went through the whole day with knots in my stomach. This girl was a real bully—the genuine article—and there was no way out of it. At the sound of the dismissal bell, I tried to avoid her by dashing out the school doors and hightailing it for home, but she eventually caught up to me. The "fight" took no more than ten seconds: she shoved me to the ground, then sat on me, squeezing all the air out of my lungs. I couldn't breathe, and I panicked. The girl was just too heavy to budge. I guess she sensed my desperate struggle for air and realized it was time to get off me. Or maybe she was just bored, since I didn't present much of a challenge. In any event, it was over, and I was relieved to be alive.

Being a nine-year-old tomboy, I didn't fuss much about my appearance like some of the other girls did. "Didn't fuss much" might be putting it mildly: I used to skip brushing my teeth, not really understanding the point of maintaining a Colgate smile. Oddly enough, I ended up becoming friends with my former nemesis, the toughest tomboy in town. She invited me over to her apartment for a sleepover, and I remember her mother handing me a toothbrush before bedtime, since I hadn't brought my own. I found it odd that they actually had a bedtime brushing routine, for as with so many other things, my parents were far more lax about our caretaking.

Truthfully, I learned more about personal hygiene from school and friends than I learned at home, because my parents didn't fuss in that way. I learned to be very self-sufficient with personal care. If I ran out of clean socks, for example, I had to hand wash a pair myself. I often went to school with oily hair, and it was only after a classmate insensitively told me how dirty my hair was—wrinkling up her nose like she didn't want to get too close—that I realized I'd better start shampooing more regularly.

I frequently longed for the more traditional family environment: Mom prepares breakfast in the morning, then sends the kids off to school with a hand-packed lunch, maybe even making some home-baked cookies ready as a snack for when they come home from school, then shoos them off to play till dinnertime, reminding them to stay nearby where she can keep her eye on them. No sooner does Dad appear in the doorway than Mom serves up a delicious dinner. The whole family sitting around the table, discussing their day while they eat. For dessert, a tall glass of milk accompanied by homemade pie or cake. Then time for a bath and brushing teeth, followed by a bedtime story, a kiss on the forehead, a tuck of the sheets, lights out, and the words "Sweet dreams" called out softly from the bedroom doorway. This was the dream childhood to me. The dream care and comfort of family life. This was what it seemed other families had, and I longed for it.

In our house, Jill read Carrie-Ann and me our bedtime stories. My dad did often tuck us in, though probably more to stop our chatter. "That's enough, girls, time to go to sleep," then it was lights out as he left the room. We tended to talk back and forth for as long as we could till my dad would poke his head back in and say, "I mean it, now, you three, not another word." He treated us all equally, I thought, though Mark was his only biological child out of the five of us, but he went out of his way to make sure we felt like his own. We girls were in charge of taking care of ourselves and shepherded the boys through their daily routines as well, which is probably why I wasn't always as clean as I should have been. We kids tended to our own cuts and scrapes, which I considered sort of like badges of honor. I was proud of my war wounds, being a tomboy, especially the ones I earned without showing that it hurt. I was damned if I was going to be caught crying over a cut. This stiff-upper-lip attitude, however, did make me miss out on attention I probably needed at times, the kind of fussing that lets you know someone cares. Instead I felt singing was really the only thing that got my parents' attention.

The King Street basement bedroom was quite dark and stuffy, tucked down in a far corner and isolated enough from the rest of the house that you could barely hear the sound coming from my room. I sang out loud to mid-1970s records such as Brownsville Station's "Smokin' in the Boy's Room," Jim Stafford's "Spiders & Snakes," and "Rock the Boat" by Hues Corporation. My hand-me-down red-and-white plastic K-tel record player spun for hours as I played the few vinyl records I had over and over again, as loud as the toylike turntable would go.

Our apartment house was in a fairly crowded residential area called the Flour Mill, which was within walking distance of the Sudbury city center. The neighbors behind our building were a French-Canadian family with two kids, a boy and a girl both around my age. The mom was a good caretaker to her family, I thought. I could tell she was a great cook just from the delicious aromas of homemade food that drifted over to our apartment from their little house. The fresh, comforting scent of laundry detergent blew out of their dryer vent and gave me the impression that she kept her family clean and their home tidy. There were freshly washed clothes hanging on her line every day. This family lived in a very small space that seemed as if it had been converted from a one-story garage. The entrance was flush with the ground level and had a low, flat roof. They couldn't have been much better off than we were, if at all, but they seemed to function better somehow. In the evening, you could hear their quiet conversations broken occasionally by boisterous laughter as they sat around a table playing cards together. I envied the fact that the neighbor kids' laundry was done while they were at school, so they didn't have to worry whether or not they'd have something clean to wear to school the next day or if they could expect dinner on the table each night. I was jealous of their reliable, consistent life. What I could see from this family was that you could be poor without being dysfunctional. That regardless of how modest your means, kids should still be clean and fed. I felt sorry for myself. I was humiliated that someone else's mother had to be the one to show me how to floss my teeth, to point out that I wasn't brushing properly or regularly enough.

Over the next few years, I noticed my mother withdrawing from her family and friends, going in and out of what I can now see was depression. Sometimes she was up and around, participating in family life; other times she was in bed for long periods of the day, leaving us kids to fend for ourselves. It was hard to predict when she would be in a state of attentive motherhood or in bed with the covers over her head, but I came home late from playing one afternoon after school to find her waiting for me like any worried mother would be when her child is late getting home. Except that she met me at the door with an extension cord in hand and proceeded to whip me with it, scolding, "Where the hell have you been?! I was worried sick about you. Never do that again!" I don't recall ever doing that again; the welts I developed from that beating instilled enough fear in me that I was very mindful of the time from that day on.

My mother didn't often lose her temper with me, but when she did, it was impactful. I can't say my mother was violent by nature, but the way she expressed herself when she was angry was excessive, like whipping me with an extension cord, for example, or giving me a sharp slap across the face. Like I said, it didn't happen often, but if I were to dare talk back, *smack!*

My dad, on the other hand, wasn't as temperamental. His discipline of us kids was more deliberate and controlled, unlike his arguments with my mother. At bedtime he'd give us three girls warnings to be quiet and go to sleep. If we pushed it too far, he'd line us up and give us the belt on the bum: three for Jill, two for me, and one for Carrie. Other offenses called for more severe consequences, but I never remember getting the belt just for getting on his nerves or even for talking back. That usually got a kick in the ass, but at least not a slap in the face, which to me is the more degrading of the two. For the most part, I considered my dad to be a fair disciplinarian with me. I could tell that he didn't feel good about it: in fact, he used to explain why he had to discipline me, and I accepted it as something a responsible father felt he had to do, like he had no choice but was doing what good parents do, which is to keep their kids in line. But then there was that other side to my dad, where he almost seemed to become a different person: violent and out of control, especially toward my mother.

I don't think you need a psychology degree to attribute my mother's depression at least partly to years of physical abuse, and not just from Jerry. When I was ten years old or so, she confided that she had a history of being beaten by men. My mother explained that one time, my grandmother Eileen was at home and heard a moaning in the alley behind her house. When she went out to investigate, she found an unrecognizable, battered woman, her face swollen and bloody, lying on the ground wincing in pain, in and out of consciousness. She got her to the hospital, and only once the young woman was cleaned up did my grandmother realize that it was her own daughter. I was horrified by this story. She went on to tell me that her marriage to my biological father had also been violent. Clarence was the jealous type, is how my mother put it, and when he lost his temper he became physically explosive. Although I didn't personally know my father, the fact that he would do this to my mother really affected me. In fact, it made me afraid of him. Carrie and I talk now about how we forgive him and hold nothing against him, no matter what the truth was. I personally wish him peace, as I now have peace and understanding that those early years were turbulent for reasons I don't feel entitled to judge.

My mother's face told the story of an abused woman. She'd obviously been bruised so many times that her skin coloring was now permanently uneven, with thumbprint-sized patches of bluish-purple and tiny red broken blood vessels, speckled in blotches here and there. There were several periods when for months at a time, my mother would hardly leave the house, even to walk up to the corner store. She would send us kids for the essentials: Export "A" cigarettes, instant coffee, a can of Carnation evaporated milk, and if there was enough change left over, a Hershey Cherry Blossom. My mother's favorite, it was a small egg–sized chocolate shell with a maraschino cherry in the center. A sweet syrup would pour out when you broke through the chocolate. The Cherry Blossom was my dad's frequent makeup offering to my mom after a fight, as well as the no-fail pleaser on Valentine's Day and Mother's Day.

My mother often didn't feel good about the way she looked and didn't want other people to see her. Christmastime got her out more, though, and with a bit of sprucing up, she'd gather up her courage, and we'd go to my uncle Don's for a visit or hop around to some of my dad's relatives in town. When I had performances, she got herself together to come with me. She never missed those, yet it was hard to get her to meet my teachers or other parents. I feel she was too insecure about herself to feel comfortable in normal family environments such as schools or neighborhood events. She did like the odd night out at bingo, though. Any outing where she had to meet people, she'd ask me to apply foundation to her face to cover the blotchy patches, and I'd style her hair with a curling iron and Final Net spray. As I dabbed on the foundation, it seemed as though it should have still been as painful as the day she was beaten, as her skin appeared bruised in places. Certainly the memories of how she got them would have been.

When my mother spoke of Clarence, my biological father, she never sounded bitter or hateful, even when describing the violence between them. "We just rubbed each other the wrong way," she'd say with a shrug. Although my mother spoke of Clarence as someone who hurt her, she never did so with malice or anger. Any resentment she may have felt toward him never transferred to me, and she explained that they fell in love but just weren't meant for each other. She never blamed him or disrespected him in her tone. She only sounded sad and disappointed that things turned out the way they did. Given my age, I don't know that she should have been so graphic with me in describing the violence, but then, if she had waited until I'd reached a more appropriate age, perhaps the past would have died with her in the car accident. Her explanations of my biological father's violent behavior, although disturbing, helped answer why he wasn't part of our lives.

It did leave me confused, though, as to why she would fall in love and marry back into a violent relationship. As an adult, however, I'm more sympathetic regarding why my mother remained in this abusive cycle. Psychologists explain many reasons why this happens, and in my mother's case, I believe at least a few of them clearly applied, like the reality of economic struggle, the responsibility of children, low self-esteem, and not enough family or social support; the fact that I believe she entered her relationships out of love, and even abuse, doesn't make those feelings just disappear. What I got out of my own observations of my mother is that leaving is easier said than done. Make no mistake: trying to break free from an abusive relationship, especially with the responsibility of children in tow, takes extreme courage.

# 4

## Roast Beef Families

Jerry may have had his problems, on the one hand, but he was also a man of high principles on the other. As I describe the scary side of my dad through these pages, it's important to me that the reader keep in mind the context of the situation: he was just twenty years old when he married my mom—who was two years his senior—so young to have taken on the responsibility of raising three little girls with the type of dedication and sincerity that he did. I find that very admirable and tremendously brave, as he didn't have any children of his own when they married, so he had no parenting experience. How many young men would have done what he did: claiming us as his very own and, later, adopting his nephew Darryl? Jerry adamantly banned the words *stepfather*, *stepbrother*, and *half sister* from our household. He insisted that the Twain Gang of five children was united. I was all for simplifying the reconstructed family language terms, accepting it as something that made me feel as if I belonged all the way and not just partway. It mattered to me that once my dad took me on as his own daughter, I was treated like his daughter. It was a commitment that felt more real because he insisted the terms we used to identify our roles in the family be all or nothing. No half this or half that. It would have insulted my dad if I'd ever referred to him as my stepfather, for example, or to my brothers as my half brothers. Because I was so young when he assumed the father role in my life, I hadn't established that role with my biological father, and there was no confusion for me. Perhaps had I been older, it would have been more complicated, and, of course, in some circumstances, *step* terms are appropriate.

My dad always struggled to find steady work that paid enough to support all of us. When I was ten, he landed a job at the Sudbury Bureau of Indian Affairs. It didn't pay well, or certainly not enough to support our family, but as a Native Canadian with minimal education, he was proud to work there. I remember my dad coming home from his job quite emotionally drained. One of his responsibilities required that he visit various Ontario Indian reservations, assess the conditions in which the people were living, and comment on any of the grants for community improvements such as road repairs, community safety services, and various other things that might be necessary for the quality of life on the reservation.

He'd say things to us like, "You know, kids, we don't have much, but we're so lucky. I visited a reserve this week to review a request for a basketball net to be installed in the school gym along with a supply of balls. I randomly stopped in at a private home on my way out and saw that the house had no floor, only dirt, and there was a toddler crawling around with a shitty diaper so weighed down from not being changed for so long, it was dragging along the ground. The mother was drunk, sprawled out on the couch, slurring at me with her tongue against her toothless gums. I was so depressed by this, how can I support the recommendations to install sporting equipment for kids on this reservation, when there were issues in the community like this not being dealt with?" He'd say this with his head in his hands. He felt that the money was going in all the wrong places and that his job was futile.

Although our family saw some rough times, some of the stories my dad would tell about what he saw during his time with Indian Affairs showed us that we were actually doing pretty well in comparison. My father would tell me about how some Native communities in Canada had alarmingly high rates of suicide, rape, incest, child abuse and neglect, alcohol and drug abuse, and other social problems—all at a higher rate than most non-Native populations in Canada. Still, living outside the reservation in the white world, when we were kicked out on the street because my dad couldn't afford the rent, I remember vividly asking my parents, "Why don't we just go live on a reserve so we don't have to worry about where we're going to live all the time?" Although my father was bringing home these depressing stories about life on some reservations, from my perception of things, though the relatives on our family reserve in Temagami lived modest lives, they didn't seem to suffer from the extreme scenarios my father witnessed through his work in Indian Affairs. In fact, they seemed to be doing better than we were, for the most part.

I had fond memories of summer stays on the Temagami Reserve as a kid, and I assumed that life on all reservations would be as fun as it was there, with plenty of food to go around, roofs over every-one's heads, always lots of music and dancing, and the kids running around with much more freedom than in town. Dad's relatives had no prejudice toward us girls and treated us like their own. We felt welcome there, but my father just didn't want to live on a reserva-tion, and that was it. Even as a child I could see the irony of the social and domestic struggles of our own family and my father's job with Indian Affairs, as he tried to improve the quality of life for other Native families. My father was disheartened with the statistics he saw firsthand in certain Native communities, and by the fact that his job didn't do anything to help the neediest of his own people, espe-cially since he could only report the social problems he witnessed; he couldn't follow up on them, as he didn't work for the Social Services Department. I believe my father felt ultimately that in order to break the cycle of poverty, you had to be able to help yourself, because in his opinion, if you were Indian, the government certainly wouldn't. I wonder if he felt that moving onto a reserve and allowing the govern-ment to support us was like giving in to the very system he resented for the Native people: taking the handout in exchange for remaining under the thumb. I can see how he may have felt, that being poor but integrated was better than being comfortable but segregated.

He was also caught up in a cycle of his own that he was trying to break. His parents were heavy drinkers, yet my father veered away from that path, and I saw him drink only occasionally. He also broke the cycle by not relying on welfare. He was the only one of his immediate family to successfully remain independent of welfare. He took pride in that, and it was important to him to be able to set a good example.

To qualify for the position my father had at Indian Affairs, he'd taken some college courses in night school while working a day job. I admire him so much for bettering himself in order to give us a better life. There's more irony here: a Native man (a minority) trying to give his adopted white (majority) children a better future and doing everything he could to avoid handouts from the government. My mother also believed in him and encouraged him to strive to reach his potential—although nagging was probably more like what she did. But her heart was in the right place, and my dad appreciated her support. My mother stood behind him, and Jerry always worked hard at everything he did.

Probably because he now had a government job with an impressive-sounding title, my dad managed to swing a mortgage so that we could buy our very first house, on a cul-de-sac in the neighboring working-class community of Hanmer. It was in an area people referred to as "the Sticks," I suppose because the houses were built up against the bush line of the Sudbury outskirts. This wasn't really forest, but more like low-growing bush—sort of brush, hence the term *sticks*? For the first time in my young life, we enjoyed a semblance of stability, staying there into my high school years. I finished grade school at Redwood Acres, went on to Pinecrest Junior High, and then transferred to Capreol High School, all in the Hanmer area.

I liked our house on Proulx Court, with its light green siding and faux brick panels at the base. Though it was just a simple bungalow, it was bigger than any of the other places we'd lived. (Carrie and I still had to share the same single bottom bunk bed, however.) How great was it to have more space? Sometimes, when my parents were out and I was bored, I would move the bedroom furniture all over the house, just for something to do. A friend would be over, and the two of us would pull beds apart and drag them into the living room, then switch sets of belongings from one bedroom to the other. Looking back now, I find it strange that my mom and my dad were so cool about it, as it's kind of odd for a ten-year-old to orchestrate a home renovation, so to speak, with little reaction from the parents. I think it was my way of superficially changing things in an environment I had so little control to actually change.

We had our own backyard for the first time, and I spent many hours there playing with grass. Not just picking it; I loved to take tall-stemmed grass with long, wide blades draping down in a swoop that I'd split with my fingernail to create the effect of hairlike strands. Each grass had its own name and character, like a Barbie doll. Then I'd put on little plays, giving each of them different accents and personalities, like the mean one, the mother, and so on. I loved acting out roles through them and found making up stories to be a great escape that whisked me to another place. I was very private about this make-believe play, as I felt embarrassed to share it with anyone else my own age. Although my little sister, Carrie, understood, and she joined in sometimes, I remember telling her quite seriously to never tell anyone that I played with grass.

The stories were always complete fantasy and never about reality or drawn from my own life. This was an escape. I enjoyed pretending that my grass people were from far away, like England or somewhere exotic like Egypt, for example. I've often thought that maybe I should have become an actress, since I enjoyed being in someone else's skin so much, but I think it's more that I enjoyed being *out* of my own skin. I can't say that I would have been any good at *real* acting, but it sure would have suited my need to be someone else for a while, molding the characters and stories as I desired.

This also held true for my songwriting, which started the same year I began playing with grass. I was ten when I wrote my first songs, and the backyard was a great place to hide and write. When I escaped into my creative world of "putting" stories to music, like when I played with my grass dolls, I lost myself in a world of fiction.

Usually after some solitary time in the backyard, I'd hear my mother calling out for me. I wouldn't answer. What a terrible thing to do to your own mother, but I didn't want to be disturbed. I wanted to preserve this state of escape for as long as I could and pretend I wasn't there. I needed someplace with a secret door that I could enter and close behind me so no one could follow. My backyard spot was actually inside a patch of brush that sat in the center of the one-acre lot behind the house. I trimmed a path through the branches and made a cavity on the inside as my hiding place. I could make small twig fires in there without being seen. This branchy cave was a place where I could forget about the piles of laundry I would spend the coming Saturday hand washing and hanging on the line, or if it was raining, the hours from midafternoon to eleven at night in the Laundromat. Instead it was necessary for my mental health to be able to experience, even if just in my imagination, an existence without worries of what we would eat this week without money for groceries.

My mother loved to hear my new song ideas, and I'd play them for her occasionally, after much coaxing. I kept my songwriting to myself during my childhood as much as I could, since I didn't see the point in sharing it. It was my personal thing, like a diary I kept with no intention of ever sharing it with anyone. It pleased my mother when I included her in my music, though I often needed time alone with music. To really ensure privacy with my thoughts and creativity beyond the backyard hideout, I'd put my guitar in its case, some matches in my pocket, and walk up the road about twenty minutes, then go off into the bush to have my fire. No one would find me there. I was safe to sing and talk to grass to my heart's content.

Our house had a basement with a dirt floor. We kept chickens down there for a while, as my dad figured it would save money to raise our own and have free eggs. We had a few hens and a banty rooster. At the same time, we planted potatoes in the backyard along with a few

other root vegetables. We also started scavenging nearby fields for potatoes left over from the fall harvest. You could pick them for free, so
why not? If you dug and kicked the dirt enough, you could go home
with a decent yield. My dad was being innovative with these hobby-
farming, potato-scavenging ideas, and I thought they were clever ways
of helping to keep us fed through periods when money was scarce.

That said, I *hated* picking potatoes. Not so much because of the
physical work of bending and digging on your knees, but because
every once in a while I'd thrust my hands into the loosened, tilled soil
and pull up a muck-like slime of putrid, rotted potato. The stench
is almost impossible to wash off your hands once it gets in the pores
and up into the fingernails. Even worse was pulling up a potato and
discovering that it doubled as a condo for potato worms. Ever see
one? They are large, fat, white, and *so* disgusting. I used to gag at the
mere sight of them, and coming face-to-face with one of these gooey
creatures dangling from my potential dinner was enough to make
me swear off spuds for life. But potatoes were a staple in our house,
especially during picking season. I was turned off of potatoes for a
while, but beggars can't be choosers, so down the hatch they went—
even if sometimes I had to choke them down.

As for the chickens, I was my dad's head-chopping assistant. I
didn't like the idea of this and was a little nervous about the whole
thing, but he talked me through each step, and off we went with
being off with their heads. My father warned me that once the head
fell away and he let the chicken go, it would run around for a minute or so before finally falling over dead. That idea freaked me out.
But I had to suppress my girlish squeamishness and be the tomboy
I wanted to prove to my father I could be. I felt he was relying on
me to help him, as Carrie and the boys were too young, and I'm not
sure that Jill would have been up for doing it. Although I was on the
verge of adolescence, I felt obligated to fulfill my role as his son-
slash-daughter for a while longer.

My job was to hold the chicken's head in my hand, pressing
its beak firmly against the brick that served as the chopping block.

While my dad held its body still with one hand cupped over it, he brought down the axe on the bird's neck with his other hand. The instant the blade made contact, I let go and ran as fast and as far away as I could, as I was sure that the decapitated chicken would chase me. You know the expression "run around like a chicken with its head cut off"? That's exactly what it did: running frantically, senselessly, and directionless. There was little blood, though, and it was all over very quickly. Phew! Boy, was I glad when the raising-chickens phase came to an end.

My dad had a playful sense of humor. One night, after everyone had gone to bed, we heard my mother give out a high-pitched shriek. I was alarmed, thinking maybe they were fighting again, but when I went to their bedroom door, she was laughing. My mom had gone to bed and turned out the lights. My dad waited until she was settled in, then he quietly joined her in the dark, with his feet up on his pillow beside her and a lit cigarette between his toes. All she could see next to her was the orange tip of the cigarette in the black and leaned over to kiss him on the face. That's when she let out the screech. I thought that was a clever one.

Reflecting back as I write my life story, nothing feels better and cozier than my bare feet on my clean kitchen floor, and with dinner already on at five in the afternoon. The air is filled with the aroma of onions, garlic, thyme, rosemary, and slowly stewing potatoes (I love potatoes now), the sun is shining, my son is playing happily with a school friend, I snuck in a ten-minute nap this afternoon, my first spring roses on my deck are up, the birds are singing, and I feel all warm and fuzzy. Content. This is what's really happening to me today: order, comfort, not just on TV or in my imagination, but in my real life in my own home. I savor these days and remind myself not to take them for granted, as I realize it's not every day that you have the chance to enjoy the simple things.

I've already run around straightening every curtain, vase, carpet, and chair, opened all the right windows, lit a fragrant candle, poured myself a glass of fresh-squeezed orange juice, and sat down in my chair, which is perfectly positioned at just the right angle to take in the most of the view over Lake Geneva and the Swiss Alps, to write. Nature is my favorite painting. I like nesting and enjoying a perfect home setting. With everything in place, I can relax and enjoy the picture-perfect moment. Freeze-frame it for as long as it will last. Then my son runs in with a bloody knee and smudges his muddy fingers on the sliding glass doors; the dogs trot along behind him, wet, and proceed to shake themselves dry all over the floor. Yup, these are the components that complete the scene of a truly perfect day. The peace may be broken in my quiet setting, but by something that makes me smile, like the warm, humorous scenes of one of my favorite Norman Rockwell paintings, *No Swimming,* depicting everyday, real-life perfection where something goes wrong but still makes you smile.

When I was a kid, I longed to have moments alone to myself, just so I could dream about how ideal life could be. I always imagined other homes having dinner on the stove, and I fantasized about the great food they would be getting ready to eat. Their lawns the perfect green and manicured, car just washed and polished, and parked very straight in the driveway, a couple of kids playing basketball at the net mounted up above the garage door, their golden retriever sprawled out in the sun, and me watching, dreaming, wishing things could be as ideal for us as they were on the other side of the street. I wanted us to be like them. I called them "roast beef families" because their dinners often smelled of roast beef. To me, if you could eat roast beef so often, then you must have been rich. By contrast, the Twains were pretty much a "ground beef family," off the reduced-price rack, and that's when we were lucky. For the most part, it was soups, stews, or other dishes where the meat could be spread out over several meals. Often, though, we didn't have enough for even that.

All my senses would sharpen as I'd sit and observe this roast beef family basking in its perfectly pleasant life. We had one such family across the street from us on Proulx Court, which was a horseshoe-shaped "court" with a string of bungalows on either side. Roast beef families frequently barbecued on summer weekends, and the smell of their steak sizzling would almost kill me. I was dying with envy knowing they could eat so deliciously all the time. It didn't seem fair, and I felt sorry for myself and perpetually hungry when I smelled something I couldn't have.

In our house, when the cupboards were otherwise empty, we ate what we called goulash, which in reality consisted of boiled milk poured over broken pieces of dry white bread and topped with brown sugar. Very hard to feel satisfied no matter how much goulash you fill up your belly with when you have a neighbor who is sitting down to his juicy, barbecued steak for Saturday lunch and his roast beef dinner that evening. Now it's strikingly ironic to me how, as a vegetarian, I no longer yearn to eat any sort of animal, yet my childhood envy was to eat the rich man's food: meat.

For us, goulash became a staple; there were times when we would eat it for every meal for days. Funny enough, I really liked it and still do, but it was hard to swallow when my taste buds were begging for something more savory and succulent. I recently rediscovered goulash in the Middle East, to my surprise. I went to Dubai for a recreational weekend trip in 2009, and one of the desserts offered in a very nice restaurant I was eating at was goulash! Although it's also made with bread, sugar, and milk, the sugar is different and not like our Canadian brown sugar, which I think makes it taste best. This Middle Eastern version was good, though, and it brought me back to the days when this was my meal two to three times a day. Ironically, I was eating this poor man's dish at a luxury five-star hotel in the desert, worlds away. *Whoa*, I thought, *it really is a small world after all*.

I spent a lot of my youth jealous of what other people ate. When our cupboards were empty, my school lunch was likely to contain a "poor man's sandwich," as my dad used to call it, given that it included only two ingredients—mustard or mayonnaise spread on two slices of white bread. A poor man's lunch box for a poor man's lunch was an empty plastic bread bag. That was a bit embarrassing, as most kids had a proper container for carrying their lunch, or at least a brown paper lunch bag. On days when we had no bread left, I lied about why I had no lunch and told the teachers and my classmates that I forgot it at home or that I wasn't hungry—anything to deflect attention or prying questions.

Leave it to my dad to make lemonade out of lemons, or in this case, a poor man's sandwich. Its origin goes back to one morning when I went to make myself lunch for school, only to discover that we had nothing to put between the bread. "Of course there's something to make sandwiches with!" he piped up cheerily. He opened a jar of mustard, grabbed a butter knife, and gave me a demonstration. "Voilà!" he exclaimed, wearing a wide grin. Then he took a giant bite of this meager sandwich, as if to say, "You see? Problem solved. Nothing to worry about. All is good in the world." I was grateful for his solution and so relieved that I wouldn't have to go to school empty-handed once again. My father lived by the optimistic outlook "Where there's a will, there's a way." He was not easily discouraged, and I was encouraged by his positive attitude, although I didn't like mustard sandwiches or the fact that that was all I had to look forward to in my lunch at school. But he was right that it was better than nothing.

At lunchtime, I'd sit at my desk with a lunch that did not satisfy my hunger and wish that the girl next to me would share hers with me. She always had twice as much food in her lunch bag than she could possibly eat, like that apple she'd take one bite out of, then put aside. I would have happily finished it, but I never would have humiliated myself enough to ask for her leftovers. *What a waste,* I used to think. Most of the time, she didn't even finish her cookies. Imagine that! How could anyone bring cookies to school and not lick up every last crumb?

Most of the other kids' lunches were on a par with hers, including the one boy whose family was poorer than we were. I used to feel sorry for him because he'd come to school with dirty hair more often than I did, wearing stained pants full of holes and ripped in the arse so badly that you could see he didn't have on any underwear. But even he had a decent lunch.

Carrie remembers bringing glazed buns to school one picnic day to share with the class. Dad had pulled them up from the depths of our freezer, as she was embarrassed to be the only one not able to bring anything in and didn't bother asking my mother to bake or buy anything because she knew it wasn't possible. The problem was that these glazed buns were bought off the sale rack and were way past the sell-by date; they had tiny black bugs sitting under the plastic wrap, snuggled into the icing. Carrie, determined to contribute to the class picnic, picked the bugs off one by one and brought the buns to school.

On mornings when there was no breakfast to be had, I'd be especially famished come lunchtime. But so as not to draw attention to myself, I'd eat my sandwich as s-l-o-w-l-y as possible—I didn't want to finish way ahead of everybody else. There were times when I felt sorry for myself, as well as jealous of the other children. To me, they seemed spoiled, which was probably unfair of me, as it wasn't any fault of theirs that they had something proper to eat for lunch. But I think it's safe to say that they were certainly fortunate.

One thing about not having much in the way of luxuries: you learn to become very frugal. I became skilled at rationing and appreciating every last morsel of food. For instance, I often took charge of pouring the milk in our cereal in the mornings to make sure it went around equally. One time I had a friend sleep over, which was allowed only when we had enough food to eat; during lean times, we wouldn't even invite children over to play, let alone sleep over. The girl was used to helping herself to as much milk as she wanted at home and was shocked when I almost slapped her hand away from the milk jug at breakfast. "I'll pour the milk in your cereal," I scolded, "to make sure we all get some." The possibility that there might not be enough was foreign to her. She was more accustomed to leaving a third of the bowl with milk in it after the cereal was eaten and couldn't imagine having to ration such a basic staple.

Even when we had enough to eat, we were conditioned to make it last. Even today, I am still very good at making just enough to go around with nothing left over. My ex-husband wasn't crazy about this, as he liked my cooking and loved leftovers, so I'll admit that my habit of always making just enough—nothing wasted, nothing left over—might have been a bit annoying. I developed a knack for judging quantity just right. The way I see it, why buy more than you need or make more than you need? Old habits die hard, I guess. I've remained resourceful, but I think it's fair to say that I learned these skills the hard way. I don't like being wasteful in the kitchen.

I became pretty good at hiding our financial struggles from other people, but it required a lot of thinking on my feet. To have to explain to my friends that I couldn't have them sleep over until we could afford to go grocery shopping would have been embarrassing. When we were outside during recess in twenty-five-below-zero temperatures, I insisted to my schoolteacher that I wasn't cold, despite my wearing worn rubber boots with plastic bags over my socks to keep my feet dry. Better to shiver in the cold than to have to explain that we couldn't afford winter boots, and my parents were too proud to get secondhand ones at the Salvation Army. I think my parents would have responded to our complaints if, for example, I cried to them about my cold feet or told them it was embarrassing to not have the proper winter clothing in front of my school friends, but I refrained from whining about things I didn't believe they could do anything about. I understood there was no point in putting pressure on them for things they couldn't change, and which would only make them feel worse. I just learned to manage with what I had.

Once you start getting into below-zero temperatures and all you are wearing are rubber boots, you are in trouble if you are outside for any length of time, as your feet will simply start to freeze. Of course, when we'd get back inside the building from the playground, my feet were aching. And once they started warming up, I'd be in agony, because thawing is very painful, believe me. But at least the plastic bags kept me dry and free from serious frostbite. (In fact, they were the same plastic bread bags I used to carry my lunch to school.) Most Northern Ontarians know this well, and it was my father's poor man's solution to not having proper winter footwear.

I seem to have inherited his resourcefulness. Friends of mine are always marveling at how I'm usually able to make things just . . . *work* somehow. I think to myself, *If you grew up the way I did, you'd learn how to make something out of nothing, too.*

One thing that baffles me today is that I sometimes meet families living below the poverty line who are overweight. After all, wouldn't you be skinny if you were hungry, not overweight? I naturally associated being poor with being hungry. Fattening, synthetic, refined foods were too expensive for our grocery list, so there was no risk of us getting fat, because we simply couldn't afford it.

Many of our cheapest foods today, however, are the packaged junk foods. Fast food is also very affordable, so many poor families are able to get their fill on empty calories while loading up on preservatives, colorings, saturated fats, chemicals, and "pounds" while remaining malnourished. They're full but nutritionally starving at the same time. In contrast, when I was growing up, the poor ate overripe bananas instead of packaged cookies, or drank a glass of water instead of a glass of soda. Nutritionally, we ate the better choices; we just didn't realize it then.

From as young as I can remember, I had big dreams regarding success in life. However, my definition of financial success was far more modest: I just wanted to earn enough money to live comfortably so that I never had to struggle through the humiliation of having less or not enough of the necessities in life. I would later find it difficult to adjust to the wealth that would come my way. How to manage it, how to share it responsibly, and how to enjoy it without guilt. Having more money than I needed was not something I was prepared for, since having more of *anything* than what I needed was just not my way of thinking. "Making it," to me, wasn't measured by having as much as possible but simply by having enough.

The feelings of anxiety and insecurity that not having enough money to eat or stay warm brought me growing up are painfully vivid, although from where I stand now looking back, they also feel incredibly distant, as though they might have happened in another lifetime or to another person altogether. So much has changed since then that it's hard to imagine it really happened. Time has allowed me the ability to talk about it with some acceptance and even amazement that we survived some of the more extreme situations. Most of all, I feel sadness for my parents for enduring the struggles and not living to see life get easier. I wish they could see that it all turned out okay. I wish I had the chance to share my life now with them. I'd spoil them with a nice house, a new car, vacations to places they've always wanted to go; take my mother shopping for fancy clothes; and sit with them in the audience during a Grammy night. I would certainly make sure they never had to worry about financial security ever again.

On Christmas 1977, when I was twelve, the best gift came from some relatives on the reservation who sent us a box packed with pre-cooked game, including rabbit, moose, fish, and partridge. It provided a welcome change from meager soups, bannock (similar to an American biscuit), and, of course, goulash. Despite our circumstances, Christmas felt festive after all. It was comforting to know that this food had been prepared by concerned extended family members who wished to share it in a spirit of goodwill and who knew what Christmas should be all about.

On the other hand, it brought home to me how bad off we must have been, because my parents rarely ever asked anybody for anything, so we didn't often receive anything. And this particular Christmas, the closest family with anything to spare was a four-hour drive away. Even during times when we didn't have enough, it seemed my mother always found it in her to bake for us at Christmas. Butter, sugar, flour, shortening, and a few other inexpensive basics allowed my mom to make something delicious and festive out of nothing. She made the best pumpkin pies, butter tarts, and shortbread cookies. I admired how she mustered enough cheer to put her heart into these small pleasures for us, and I am proud of her as I think of this; how she found the strength for our sake. This is a mother's love.

Another Christmas, my little sister asked for a Baby Alive doll. It was battery operated and could drink and eat baby food; it even needed its diaper changed. My dad was able to get one on sale, but it was an African American doll with curly black hair. Carrie, of course, had white skin and straight blond hair. He worried that she'd find it odd that her "baby" didn't resemble her at all and told her it was the last one on the shelf. But my sister was grateful just to get the doll she'd wished for and didn't seem to notice the color of its skin. I remember thinking, *And this is how the world should be: no prejudice, no judging who we love and care for based on the color of their skin.* Being raised in a racially mixed family, I was sensitive to this, and I said it to myself with conviction. Carrie's brown baby doll and her innocent blindness to color was beautiful to me, and I appreciated it. It made me feel good, and it made me feel like something was right about our poor, patchwork family.

That had been one of our happier Christmases. Getting back to the year 1977, we kids were all abuzz about what Santa was going to bring us. For my parents, however, who naturally wanted to give their children a postcard image of Christmas, the holidays often delivered serious stress, with advertising campaigns hard-selling the picture-perfect Christmas, with mounds of gifts under the tree, a feast on the table, and a healthy helping of milk and cookies to leave for Santa. This extravagance was simply out of reach most Christmases in our home. One afternoon I walked into the kitchen to find my mother sitting at the table crying. She'd just come back from town.

"Leeny," she said to me, sniffling, "pass me the lighter. I need a cigarette." I took a chair across the table to face her. My mother and I often sat at the kitchen table to talk about life, troubles, and music. She befriended me there; it was like our place to connect as companions, confidantes, friends. Sometimes the things she told me were beyond my level of comprehension, but I knew that my job was to listen and comfort her. With my heart breaking for her woes, feeling her fragility, I would often gently cup her face in my hands and say, "Mom, you are my angel." Not so much because she was guiding me but because she seemed too innocent for this world. A good person put in a bad place.

Sitting there, her face wet with tears and the tip of her nose red and sniffly, my mother began to tell me about her trip downtown. In a strained, halting voice, she proceeded to confess that she had gone Christmas shopping for us. When she got to the car in the parking lot, her shopping cart overflowing with gifts, "a policeman walked up behind me and said I'd have to bring everything back." I didn't understand at first. Then I realized what she was saying: she'd shoplifted everything in the cart. The officer was kind and didn't arrest or charge her; he just took the cart away and let her go. How pathetic she must have felt.

I had mixed emotions. Part of me was humiliated that my mother would do such a thing, yet another part of me appreciated her intentions; she didn't want her children to wake up on Christmas morning with nothing under the tree. Carrie and the boys were still young enough to maybe believe that they had been "bad," and that's why Santa skipped our house. But I think she was more likely to have thought we felt we weren't worthy of parents good enough to give us a proper Christmas. This weighed heavy on me, and I felt the guilt she carried of feeling like a failure to her children. It's no wonder Christmastime has such a high suicide rate. So much cheer that only reminds the unlucky of what doesn't belong to them, and that some parents have to explain to their children why Santa couldn't come to their house. The pressure parents feel to live up to giving a Merry Christmas they simply cannot afford.

Listening to her confess was painful for me. I didn't cry, though; I had to be strong for her. Another member of the family might have been in the kitchen with us; I really don't remember. All I know is that I felt alone with her, with her pain, and that she needed me to help make her feel better. I was relieved that the officer had let her go. Imagine if he'd arrested her: I would have considered the world officially cruel and callous if he had. That kind and sensible policeman did the right thing.

I thanked her in my heart for trying to do the right thing, even if she went about it the wrong way, and I honestly didn't believe that she should feel ashamed over the incident. But I know she did, both for having done something dishonest as well as for, in her mind, having let down her children. I looked at my mother with her knees curled up to her chest, shins pressed against the edge of the table, and her feet resting on the seat of the chair. This is how she always sat at the table. My tiny, skinny, sad, ashamed mother, helpless in her despair. And I, in turn, felt so sad for her.

My mother sat in this position at the table even when she wasn't in need of a role-reversal conversation with me. Sometimes she was laughing, scooping in her triple teaspoon of sugar and long pour of Carnation canned milk in her coffee, carrying on about what songs I should add to the song list of my performance repertoire, flicking her fingers up in the air, demanding a light for her cigarette. She needed anything to keep her happy and not focused on what there was for her to complain about. Anything to keep her from rightfully picking an argument with my dad about what was wrong.

The house on Proulx Court saw all extremes of the roller-coaster ride our family was on. Laughter, love, violence, fear, a family united, and a family divided. This house would be the last place in my youth where I would see such severe dynamics of dysfunction and violence in my childhood home life. The end of the days of watching my dad drag my mother along the slippery, linoleum floor by the hair and throw her down the stairs to the dirt basement, where the chickens ran around free, was drawing near.

Up the street lived a girl about a year older than me named Sue, who befriended us and had a heart of gold. Sue's kindness made these few intensely difficult years somewhat bearable through her generosity. When we were out of the basics, she'd sneak us sugar, milk, and bread from her mother's cupboard. Sue, a very athletic girl and a horse lover, enjoyed my mom's company and liked hanging around with us. She took care of some horses on the other side of the court, among them a pretty palomino mare named Angel. She had a golden coat, a platinum mane, and a striking white blaze down her face; to me, she looked like the kind of horse that Barbie would have ridden. I wanted to ride her, even though I'd never been on a horse before.

Sue taught me a few basics and let me give it a try. I had a hard time getting Angel to move any faster than a slow walk. About a half mile from the barn, I decided I'd better turn back, and as soon as we were heading home, the horse sped up and ran full tilt all the way back to her barn. I had no control at all, but I at least learned how to stay on and to enjoy the smell of horses. The horn on the Western-style saddle was a big help, as it gave me something to hold on to as she bolted for home. I grew to love being around horses even when I wasn't riding. In the winter, the roads were icy, and often we'd just barely make the corners without Angel's legs sliding out from under her. One time she took a shortcut and ran us straight into a deep ditch, sinking right up to her belly. She couldn't move with her legs stuck in the snow like pegs in four holes, so Sue and I had to dig her out by hand. Angel wasn't the easiest or kindest horse I got to know, but she taught me to like horses anyway. I took on the chore of feeding the horses in the morning before the bus arrived and would go to school with smelly mitts. I was embarrassed for anyone to smell them but didn't mind it myself at all. I liked sniffing them, since it took me out of school and back to the barn, which was where I really wanted to be. Besides, I was more embarrassed about going to school with no lunch than I was of smelling like horse manure.

One night my parents got into a spat, and once again, it got violent. As usual, money woes precipitated the argument. This fight was different, however, in a big way.

They started pushing each other around, and when things snowballed to where it became clear that my mother was about to really get it, I ran up behind my dad with a chair in both hands and smashed it across his back. I knew I was really going to get it for that one. I'd jumped on him before during fights between him and my mother in an attempt to pull him away, but he never did more than shake me off and warn me to stay back, which I did, as I was too afraid to do anything else. But I was getting a bit bolder around the age of eleven, and for the first time, I struck my dad. Before I could get away, he punched me in the jaw. Adrenaline pumping, I punched him back! It was purely a reflex action. He didn't put much force behind his punch, as if it was more of a warning tap for me to back off.

If my father was shocked, he wasn't half as stunned as I was at the fact that I'd punched him back. I didn't know where I hit him because I had closed my eyes, punched, and ran. Too afraid to face him after I hit back, I bolted to my room, hopped out the window, and raced down the street to the barn. I stayed with Angel and the other horses that night. No one came looking for me, but I worried about how things ended up at the house. Did the fighting stop after I left? Was my mother okay? And what about the other kids? I was too afraid to go back until the next morning to find out, and by then, things were calm. No one brought up the events of the night before, and we all carried on with just another day in the Twain house.

Part of growing up in Canada involves putting up with Old Man Winter year after year. The conditions can be extreme. At the end of our driveway on Proulx Court, the snowplow would leave us fifteen-foot-high piles of chunked ice and snow scraped from the street surface. Every night after the plow finished, my two sisters and I would head outside for about an hour to shovel the snow from our driveway so our dad could pull his car in when he got home from work.

Winter walks are beautiful, but when you're ten years old and walking miles in treacherous subzero temperatures just to get home from a late afternoon at school, it's not so fun. The town bus ran only on the main road, so the nearest bus stop was forty minutes away by foot. One cold evening, I was walking home wearing a cheap waist-length bomber jacket, running shoes, no mitts or hat, and only jeans on my legs. I would have pulled my hood up over my head for some protection from the biting cold, but it was too open and lightweight to give any warmth. As a preteen up North, it was cool to walk around underdressed in winter, despite the freezing temperatures, and it was common to see teens wearing running shoes to school even through the coldest months, as a fashion statement. They wouldn't play outside without proper clothing, but going from home to the bus, to school and back, it was better to look good than to feel comfortable.

The temperature can drop quite low once the sun goes down, and in my case this particular night, I was getting home later than expected, and the temperature had dropped lower than what I was dressed for. When the temperature gets down to where even five minutes of exposure begins to literally freeze your skin, fashion becomes the last thing on your mind. About fifteen minutes from my house, I just couldn't go on; the pain from freezing was unbearable. The joints in my knees and hands cramped and ached. My hands and feet were totally numb, and I started to cry, which is not wise when you're freezing, as your tears can literally freeze on your face. I hesitated for a long time, questioning whether to knock on a stranger's door for help. I wanted to make it all the way home and was so close, but I was too cold to carry on. Very few houses still had lights on, as it was getting pretty late in the evening. But I finally saw a house where it seemed someone was still up. I asked if I could come inside to warm up for a while, and the family was very understanding and let me sit long enough to thaw out before I set off again.

I finally made it home, but I can tell you, there were many close calls like that growing up in such extreme weather conditions. My youngest brother, Darryl, once came home from a night of playing hockey with both his earlobes severely frostbitten. He'd been wearing just a tuque on his head, which angles down over the ear but leaves the lobes exposed. Over the next few days, his earlobes turned red to blue, then a purple-black, and they drooped unnaturally low. The skin peeled away in layers until the dead, frozen lobe fell away. I worried that Darryl might end up like our grandpa Twain, who had only a jagged edge left to his lobes, as if they'd been chewed off by

Jack Frost himself. My grandpa's earlobes had frozen and fallen off so many times that eventually they never came back. Fortunately for Darryl, his lobes did.

My two sisters and I loved going public skating during the winter months, and the rink was about a forty-five-minute walk from our house on Proulx Court. We were fine on the way there, but on the way back, the temperature had dropped quite a bit. Yet in true Canadian spirit, we stepped outside the arena, took a deep breath, probably muttered something like "It's cold!," and carried on toward home.

Just recently, my sister emailed me a slightly rawer version of that same sentiment that made me laugh hard. It's quite a typical thing Canadians would share between friends to help get one another through the long, cold winter with a good sense of humor. I get this poem every winter, and every winter I love rereading it. It's beautiful—*very* well written—and I thought it might be a comfort to you on a cold day, as it was to me:

> "Winter in Canada"
> So appropriate and heartwarming!!
> Fuck!
> It's cold!
> The end.

The trail between the arena and the house block where we lived was a thirty-minute stretch of walk, wasn't lit, and there were no houses along the way. Just bush and field. Two brothers of about twelve and thirteen years old who lived in our same direction were making the walk home with us. Jill would have been eleven, me nine, and Carrie seven. Halfway down the trail, Carrie started to cry that she was too cold to go on. One of the boys generously offered to carry her on his shoulders. I looked her in the eyes and told her she had to be brave and that we were going to make it. As I spoke to her, I could see the tears in her eyes were actually crusting into ice. She was literally crying ice flakes. I know it's hard to picture, but believe me, her eyes were glazing over with ice, and I yelled at her to stop crying. I was panicking and felt that we were really in trouble.

Winter wasn't all a near-death experience, though; it was fun, too. Sometimes the snow would pile up so high that we could climb up it onto the roof of the house and jump off into a sea of clean, white snow. We used to knock off icicles from the roof to see who could get the longest one intact. Icicle harvesting tip: the poorer the insulation of the roof, the longer the icicles you get. Ours, it goes without saying, had plenty of great icicles.

One rite of passage for anyone from Northern Ontario is getting your tongue stuck to frozen metal. Any Canadian who insists "Never happened to me!" is just too embarrassed to admit that as a child he tempted fate by touching his tongue to the zipper on his ski jacket and then couldn't pry it loose. It's a strange and panicky feeling, but if you don't jerk your head back and have the presence of mind to exhale hot air out your mouth, the metal will thaw just long enough to release you. With a lot of skill and a little bit of luck, you can escape without leaving any flesh behind. Another winter hazard was going outdoors with wet hair on a frigid day; I once heard of someone's frozen ponytail snapping right off. Unfortunately, around our house, a hair dryer fell into the "luxury item" category, and so my sisters and I had to improvise. We figured out that if we took the vacuum cleaner and attached the hose to the end where the warm air blew *out*, we'd be able to dry our hair. The only hitch was that the jet of air stank from dog hair, dried bits from indoor accidents, stale food crumbs, and whatever else got sucked up the Electrolux that week. Consequently, our hair smelled accordingly—mostly like old dog poop, though. One alternative was to hang our heads over the heating vents in the floor, but this took much longer. On most mornings, when we were running late for the school bus, the smellier but speedier Electrolux was the better choice.

Sometimes, though, even that option wasn't available because either the hydro (electricity) had been turned off or the furnace was out of oil. It seemed as if there was always some utility threatening to cut off service if we didn't pay the overdue bill. My parents tried to make sure that at least one of the two would be functioning at all times, because in the heart of a Canadian winter, you couldn't manage without electricity *and* heat.

So, for instance, if my dad knew that we couldn't afford to get our oil tank refilled, he'd bleed the water pipes so they wouldn't burst from the cold. This called for us sleeping with our winter clothes on and cocooning ourselves in heavy sleeping bags. In the morning, we'd get up and huddle around the electric stove. It warmed us, cooked breakfast, and heated our socks and boot liners. Warm feet, hot porridge, and dry mitts were good enough for us to get by. Conversely, we'd have to do this when the hydro company turned off the power. Once it got dark, we used flashlights to see around the house. This type of situation typically lasted a day or two and, thankfully, occurred only about once a winter.

If the washing machine broke and we couldn't afford to have it fixed, doing the laundry became a very labor-intensive chore for a family of seven. As it was, we didn't have a dryer, and if it was still winter, we had to go to the Laundromat for hours to dry and fold everything. Our mom had relinquished this task—and most everything else involved in running the household, including cooking, cleaning, and taking care of the kids—so consumed was she by her depression.

If the washer didn't work, though, we had to wash everything by hand in the bathtub at night, then take it to the Laundromat for drying. Or, if it was summer, we'd hang the clothes outside, so that they'd be dry by the morning, just in time to take them down and hang up the next load. We had the whole process down to the precision of an assembly line, because if we didn't get it done by the end of the day, the damp clothes that were sitting around waiting to be dried would get all funky smelling and need to be rewashed. Every so often, we'd cram so many clothes onto the line that it would collapse from the weight and fall to the dirt ground, sending us back to the bathtub-slash-washtub to wash everything all over again. I'd spend hours kneeling at the side of the tub, scrubbing clothes against a scrub board or between my knuckles, like a pioneer woman. For that reason, I could relate very well to programs like *Little House on the Prairie* and *The Waltons*. None of my friends had to wash laundry by hand, but I kind of accepted it as no big deal. The way I saw it, if the Ingalls family could do it, I could do it.

In the winter, of course, there was no using the clothesline, so my father would drop us girls at the local Laundromat with an average of nine large, black garbage bags bulging with dirty clothes. We'd dump them all out on the floor, separate the loads by color and texture, start up the machines, and wait.

In our boredom, we'd sit out on the front step and play a game we'd invented called Cars. You'd flip a coin to determine who went first, then wait for the next car to drive by, because it "belonged" to that player. We'd cheer whenever one of us inherited a cool red Camaro and crack up anytime a rusty old clunker came puttering down the street.

Whizzing Carrie around in a laundry cart was another fun way to pass the time. I'll tell you, it spun really well! This game could only be played once we were the only people left in the Laundromat, although with so many clothes to wash and dry, we were inevitably the last ones to leave every time. If we weren't all finished by the time the guy with the key came by to lock up for the night, we'd throw whatever clothes remained back in the bag and fold them once we got home.

Believe it or not, I remember our weekly evenings in the Laundromat fondly. Even though we were little kids doing adult chores, we learned to make our own fun. We managed.

# 5

# Music Became My Savior

t was while living on Proulx Court that I started writing my first
songs. From the age of seven I'd been tapping out melodies on a
cheap electric keyboard purchased at a bargain department store,
but I picked up the acoustic guitar at eight and finally attempted
music and lyrics together. As I explained earlier, I first started writing songs in the backyard on Proulx Court at age ten. One of my first
sets of lyrics was a song called "Won't You Come Out to Play." It was
about a child playing outside, watching her mother watch her from
the inside of the house through the window. The child can sense that
her mother wants to be outside playing with her, enjoying the air, the
play of a child, but doesn't have the courage to do it, so the child
prompts her with "Ma, won't you come out to play?" This was how
I really felt about my own mother, and the song was a literal expression of my true feelings at the time. I felt she spent periods of her life
behind the window looking out, wishing she was more confident to
come out, but she didn't have the courage. I also wrote a song called
"Just Like the Storybooks," and it went, "Just like the storybook says,
like little girls when they lose their boys, then they cry." It was all
about lost love; sad girls crying with broken hearts.

My parents managed to buy me a microphone and Carrie a snare
drum. This cost money we did not have to spare, and my dad was
upset at my mother's insistence on buying us this equipment. Along
with my microphone were two Peavey amplifiers: one for the mic and

one for plugging in the guitar. Carrie and I sang in harmony while I strummed, and she kept time, tapping on her drum. We were eight and ten years old as a sister duo, and I think my mother had high hopes for us.

Although my dad was reluctant to put any money into our music interest, he was still very enthusiastic about music and our own passion for it. He played guitar a little bit himself and showed me my first chords: A, D, and G. But my main musical mentor was my older cousin Kenny Derasp, my dad's first cousin. Kenny had blue eyes and was more fair skinned than most on my dad's side of the family, as he had white blood mixed in on both his mother's and father's sides. To me, Kenny was so cool: he was seventeen, played electric guitar, had shoulder-length hair, and was allowed to drink and smoke. I enjoyed hanging with him, as he had an easygoing personality and a quick sense of humor.

Kenny took an interest in my musical ability and taught me more advanced hand positions and major and minor chords. He eventually moved in with us for a time on Proulx Court, as he was having trouble finding work in Timmins and had better luck in the area where we were now living. With Kenny around, the house was always full of live music, and I joined in more openly, hiding less in my room or in the backyard with my music. We'd sit around the living room, singing and strumming to songs by the Eagles, Linda Ronstadt, and Waylon Jennings.

However, when I was twelve, he and Jill left home together, which created a lot of tension in the house, as Jill was so young to be leaving home at fourteen. I remember my mother being worried sick, and Kenny now talks about how disappointed and angry my dad was with him. I worried about being left alone in the house as the oldest child. Jill and I had always shared the responsibilities of running the house when our mother was depressed in bed for stretches of time, and Kenny was a good mediator between my parents, helping to keep the peace. I was scared to no longer have my older sister around, and heartbroken that Kenny was gone, too. Most of all, I was jealous that they'd escaped the house. *Lucky them,* I thought.

Part of my childhood performing experience came from adult house parties. These happened a few times a year during holiday times such as Christmas, New Year's, and Easter, and the odd birthday or funeral gathering—usually at my Twain grandparents' house. When it was time for the kids to go to bed, my mother would pull out my guitar and ask me to sing. With everyone feeling good, the spirit was fun to be around, and it was musically very relaxed for me, with Kenny often there singing and playing along with me. But as it got later into the night, and the adults got more drunk, things just got too weird for me, the kid. I'd sneak off into the bedroom to join the other kids. The parties got pretty wild sometimes outside of the room where we slept, and we kids would get scared and huddle together, wishing things would just quiet down. This was especially true if a fight broke out, which wasn't uncommon.

The next morning, once most of the adults had cleared out and the ones remaining were still sound asleep, we would get out a bucket of hot water mixed with Javex and clean up the house. There would be sticky drinks spilled everywhere, cigarette ashes and butts on the floor, half-eaten food between the furniture cushions, and loads of beer bottles and empty glasses to pick up. The bathroom was always the worst because drunk people "miss" a lot, so you can imagine the toilet and the floor—never mind if someone got sick in there, which, of course, did happen. We kids were the morning cleaning crew. It was a bit like cleaning up after a Friday night in a seedy bar. We didn't like waking up to this mess and just wanted things back in order.

Besides having me sing at house parties, my mother was active in finding me places to play on a regular basis. My childhood career energized my mother and seemed to lift her out of her bouts of depression. During these lows, she had no spark for everyday life, for maintaining the household and taking care of the kids, but when it came to my music, she was a ball of fire. This caused problems because she would blithely spend money that we certainly didn't have on supporting her ambitions for me to be a successful artist. It became an obsession, in a way. For instance, she'd spend hours and hours on the phone trying to book me gigs, making long-distance calls to hotel managers and booking agents. My mother pushed the limits, especially when it came to spending money on my music.

My poor father, stressed over money issues as it was, would peruse the phone bill, hiked up with long-distance charges, and do a double take at the amount. "We can't pay this!" he'd shout. The bills were too high for him to pay, so the telephone company would cut off our service until he did. I don't blame my dad for losing his temper over things like this. My mother acted as if she was addicted to my career; she was certainly aware of the consequences of angering my father and the inevitable cutoff of our phone service, but she still wasn't able to resist anything to keep my career going, as if her life depended on it. I believe that she did, in fact, live for my music during the times when she felt most defeated by life, on the days when the only reason she got out of bed was to get on the phone to find me places to sing. The only way my dad could stop her from spending on her habit—my career—at the expense of the rest of the family's welfare was to rip the phone line right out of the wall. Her obsession with my childhood career drove my father nuts. He reminded her often that she had four other kids to raise, and those words made me feel so guilty. I knew he was right, that my mother was spending money on me that took away from the rest of the family. I didn't want the grocery money, for example, being spent on anything to do with my career, and I wished my mother would stop her nonsense: the wishful thinking that it would pay off someday, that I was going to make it. I wanted her to just be my mom, not my career manager.

One time, my mother took me to see Merle Haggard perform in Sudbury. I'm not sure if her hope was that I'd get to meet him, like that time she got me backstage at a Mickey Gilley and Loretta Lynn concert. She managed to get me on the tour bus and introduced to Mickey Gilley, but I never got to sing for him, even though my mother introduced me as a singer, hoping that's what would happen.

Everyone was very nice and said it was a pleasure to meet me, wished me luck, and that was it. I was not to be discovered that night.

The night my mother took me to the Merle Haggard concert, there was only enough gas in the car to get my dad to work the next morning. Going out for music on a recreational level was something we couldn't afford, and even when I was out performing, it didn't always pay. When it did, I'd get maybe a $25 or $50 tip, but I was usually a guest singer, and as my mother saw it, they were giving me a break by giving me the public exposure. Paying gigs required a full weekend commitment from Thursday or Friday night through a Sunday matinee, or the full week. I had to miss school to take those gigs, which I did, but I had to spread those out in order to manage both school and performing. On the particular night my mother managed for me to meet Mickey Gilley, it was not just for a gig in a bar, though. It was a chance to meet a star who might think I was talented and take me under his wing.

The reasonable thing to do the night of the Haggard show would have been to stay home, of course. But my mother decided that we would go anyway because, from her point of view, music was worth almost anything, and she was adamant about never losing an opportunity that brought her closer to her dream of getting me discovered. My mother and I worked out a scheme to escape without being noticed. I went to my room as if I were going to bed for the night. When my dad wasn't looking, my mother snuck out to the car, and I crawled out my bedroom window at the back of the house, hopped in the car, and off we went. Kenny, who was still living with us at the time, went along with the plan and came with us.

We got home late that night, around two o'clock, to find my dad angrily waiting for us. He grabbed me by the pant leg down at my ankle, swirled me upside down—suspending me in the air with my head dangling just above the floor. I put my hands out to protect myself, thinking about how I'd crash down once he let go. I was also thinking how mad my dad was to be able to hold me with one hand and hit me with the other, but I was small for my age and would have been easy for a man to lift—especially with the added force of the angry adrenaline he had raging through him. I remember Kenny intervening, thankfully; I fell to the floor and ran off to my room. That was the end of it, but I knew very well it could have been much worse if Kenny hadn't been there.

By the time I was ten, I was giving some of the neighborhood kids guitar lessons for a few bucks here and there. I understood basic theory and enjoyed teaching. I was lucky enough to have had a few lessons at the Sudbury Royal Conservatory of Music, which gave me a firm foundation in understanding how music was really its own, unique written language, with marks and symbols to indicate accent, sound expression, punctuations, and the overall delivery of how the music is intended to be translated through voice or instrument.

Of course, musicians understand all this, but I'm explaining it for those of you who might take for granted how complex and specific music theory is. There is so much detail to the language of music: like how long to hold a note, when to cut it off, and how sharply or gently. Every beat, note, and pause has a precise purpose and is written so. There is no room for improvisation, especially with classical pieces, which are taught to be played exactly according to the written music. Although my heart was driven more by the joy of making things up as I went along—creating, changing, improvising—I appreciated learning more about how music can be recorded on paper and be played back by being visually read like a storybook. I was impressed that music could go from black strokes and marks on a page to the sounds of a symphony orchestra. This was a wonder to me. I was fascinated by written music.

It would have taken some convincing from my mother to get my father to pay for these lessons, but it was around paycheck time that she would start on how important it was for me to develop my musical skills, and how was I ever going to make it if I didn't learn from professionals? She had a whole list of things she'd carry on about as to why it was so necessary. Because my dad also believed in me, although he knew it wasn't the practical thing to do, he had his own soft spot for my music and gave in to paying for a series of about four or five one-hour sessions. From that point on, I was able to teach myself, with the help of some books, how to read and write music. My skills in this area were very basic, but the knowledge soon proved very useful once I started playing in bars and other venues.

Many of the clubs had house bands. Most of the musicians and backup singers sight-read music, or charts. When I would come in to rehearse for the performance, I'd bring my own chord charts. After all, I played mostly my own songs, which the band members had never heard before. It made it fast and easy for them to learn the songs. Looking back, I can only imagine how funny the musicians must have found it at first for this scrawny little girl to walk onstage and hand them songs she'd written at the age of ten. These were grown men who made a living from touring the live club circuit. But usually they were impressed by my efficiency, that I was so prepared and professional, and so grown up for my age.

Maybe a little *too* grown up. Some of the guys would comment that they had kids my age at home and that I seemed so much older in comparison. I sensed that my maturity caught them off guard, and although they took me seriously once I started to sing, I could tell that some of them didn't feel that performing in the bar scene was appropriate for a kid. They were kind to me, but they would sometimes remark on how awkward it was to hear a ten-year-old sing about divorce, love, betrayal, seduction, and temptation in songs like "Golden Ring," "Blanket on the Ground," "Ruby, Don't Take Your Love to Town," "Somebody's Knockin'," and "Help Me Make It Through the Night."

The charts worked well for country music because the chord progressions were usually pretty simple, which suited my basic-level guitar playing and music theory. But when I was about nine years old, my mother brought me to my first *disco* band audition. That one didn't go so well. First of all, neither of us even knew what disco was, only that there was a goofy duck somewhere in the mix of its image, the "Disco Duck." It was a new danceable style being played more and more in the clubs, and my mother thought there could be work there for me, so she pulled an ad from the paper for a disco band looking for a lead singer.

I remember we walked into a basement apartment in Sudbury, where a guy sat waiting for us at an electric keyboard, fiddling with synthesized sounds and preprogrammed drum rhythms that were very foreign to me. He seemed a bit taken aback by my age, but he humored us and asked me what songs I knew and if I could sing something for him. I didn't know any disco songs, as it was still so new. Even if I had heard disco songs on the radio at that point, I didn't associate them with a genre specifically called "disco." Much to my embarrassment, I actually asked him, "What is disco?" He couldn't *believe* that I hadn't even heard of it. He was polite, but the audition ended quickly. I never did sing for him.

Although my mother was always backstage, she had no musical ability, so I was totally on my own once I walked out there with the band. A guitar bigger than me was strapped around my shoulder with the neck balanced in my one hand and my charts clutched in the other. I wasn't a performer at all in terms of stage presence, like dancing or chatting up the audience. I simply walked up to the microphone and introduced myself in a very rehearsed and almost rigid way: "Hello, my name is Eilleen, and the song I'm going to sing for you today is called 'Blue Eyes Crying in the Rain' by Willie Nelson." Then, looking back over my shoulder, I'd gesture to the band to set the tempo with my strumming, turn back to the mic, my eyes focused above the audience's heads, and start singing.

I was *petrified* being up there, and often it was all I could do not to pee myself just before I'd start to sing, or worse, as they'd call me to come out onstage during my introduction. It was incredibly hard to hold in my pee while walking from the side of the stage out to the center; much easier if the pressure was on when I was already standing at the mic and able to squeeze my knees together. Just the thought of this makes me sweat. I'd heard of people vomiting from stage fright, but for me it was my bladder, shakes, and sweats. Still is.

If I was doing a whole night's worth of three sets, I had the chance to warm up as the night went on, but if I was a guest singer with a band that already had a female lead vocalist, I would do only one song. It was scary being so on the spot, the do-or-die feeling of having just the one shot. I don't know if it was my mother's nervous edge rubbing off on me that made me feel as though I was singing for my life, but my understanding was that you never knew who might be watching. There could be a talent scout in the audience, and if I was good enough, he might take me under his wing, as my mother put it. I wasn't sent up onstage by my mother to have fun and enjoy myself—I was out there to impress people, to be noticed, and maybe discovered.

I had the feeling that I was singing for my mother's life more than for my own. It was her happiness, her dream I was trying to fulfill. I was uncomfortable under all this pressure and much preferred playing music in the backyard by the fire, but I put on a brave face for her. I also believed in her conviction that I would make it, because she was my mother, and my mother had to be right. I wanted to make it so that we didn't have to struggle financially anymore. This is what I saw success bringing us: enough to pay our bills, feed the family, and ease the tension in our home life.

I came across very few other child music artists during this early phase of my career. It wasn't a child's world. In fact, it was highly inappropriate a lot of the time, since the music world education system meant being around drinking, smoking adults, many of whom flirted openly among themselves. Understandably, many places didn't allow kids. My mother got around that most of the time and even managed to get me a Social Security card when I was just eleven. This allowed me to legally work underage, and it came accompanied by a formal letter of sorts granting me permission to work in premises that served liquor. I was now a real "professional."

I went through a long period where I lived some of the time in an adult world and some of the time in a child's world. But other kids my age wouldn't have understood a lot of the things that I experienced in the clubs and bars, surrounded by grown-ups, so I never shared with them. These worlds were separate and didn't belong together. Adults go to bars where they are free to do adult things, after all, behavior they save for when their kids are not around.

Over the years, my mother pulled me out of school on the odd Friday when I had a weekend gig, as well as for a full week every few months. Then there were the one-off gigs for television or a festival, where I would miss only one day of school. I was in and out of school throughout the year but never enough that I had to be pulled out for an extended period. When I got my license to play where liquor was served, my mother explained to the school principal that I was a professional singer and asked for their cooperation to help me balance both school and "work." I never sensed resistance from any of my schools, and, in fact, the principals and teachers seemed more enamored by the fact that I was a performer than by the fact that I would miss a bit of school here and there. I do remember being asked to talk about my career voyages in the principal's office upon returning from time off school, which I felt was partly to ensure that I was actually doing what my mother told them I was doing—out pursuing my career—and also out of curiosity for what it must be like being a stage performer.

As you can imagine, being in bars exposed me to a lot of drinking, naturally. Now, my parents weren't drinkers—they'd pretty much drink only on holidays and other special occasions—so there was rarely alcohol in the house and no casual drinking at home. I think it might have been Easter the first time I ever got drunk. I was twelve. My parents were aware that I'd become curious about drinking. A friend of mine up the street had a fifteen-year-old brother who snuck his parents' homemade wine from the stash in their basement on weekends. He told us stories about how he and his friends had so much fun drinking, staying up all night, laughing, playing pranks, and skinny-dipping while camping at a nearby lake. I wasn't intrigued by adult behavior when they drank, as there wasn't much mystery left in that for me by the age of twelve, but based on the bragging of my friend's older brother Steve, I was unfortunately more tempted to try it. Since I was exposed to it all the time in bars, I guess they thought it would be better for me to experience it under their supervision; my mom and my dad knew that it was probably just a matter of time before I would take the plunge and indulge my curiosity.

One night Kenny and I were sitting around the kitchen table playing guitars and singing, and my parents were nursing their whiskey and Cokes. "Could I have a taste?" I piped up.

My father smiled, almost to say, "Okay, Sharon, we need to let her dig her own hole and find out what it's all about. She wants to drink, we'll let her drink." "So," he said to me, "you want to see what alcohol tastes like? You want to have a drink of your own?"

"Okay!" How cool was this!

He poured me a whiskey and Coke, which didn't seem to amount to much: a couple of caps of whiskey to a whole glass of Coke. "That's *it*?" I pouted. "This is mostly Coke!" But since this was my first time drinking alcohol, I hadn't paid attention to the proportions of a powerful alcoholic drink; nor did I understand the potency of even one cap of whiskey and that a couple were more than sufficient to get me drunk.

"You want a bit more?" asked my dad. Feeling brave, I said, "Sure!" And he topped off my glass.

I was having a *great* time laughing, singing, joking, and generally acting like a total idiot. By the time I began stumbling around uncontrollably and bumping into things, my parents decided to put me to bed. My dad hoisted me up to the top bunk. I can still remember how the second my head hit the pillow, the room began to spin until I was dizzy. That's when I heaved a gush of warm, sugary liquid. I didn't feel it coming. I was just lying there on my back, trying to work out how I was going to stop the room from whirling around. The fountain of vomit pulsed up into the air before surrendering to the effects of gravity and splashing right back down all over my face. It soaked my hair and dripped into my ears. I called out meekly to my parents till they finally heard me, thank goodness. What ran through my spinning head were stories I'd heard over the years of people choking to death on their own vomit while drunk. From that experience, I can see how this can easily happen. If I'd eaten anything too solid just before, this could very well have happened to me, because I wasn't even able to turn myself over on my side, from what I can remember. I was only twelve years old and was at the mercy of my parents hearing me call out.

In hindsight, I'm pretty sure my parents had an ulterior motive in letting me have a drink at such a young age. What better way to check the lure of alcohol by allowing me to experience the pleasurable sensation of inebriation only to suffer payback in the form of getting sick. I have to say that their strategy was pretty darn effective. I felt horrible the next day, with all the classic symptoms of a hangover. I now knew what it was like to be intoxicated and to feel the effects of the morning-after headache, dehydration, and overall yuckiness. Drinking alcohol was not something I wanted to do anytime soon after that. Although that experience didn't prevent me from *ever* drinking again, it really did make me aware of the regrettable effects of overdoing it. I believe that as a direct result of that first exposure to too much alcohol, I remained more cautious throughout my teens and aware of what a reasonable limit was for myself. I understood how it felt to have no control over my own body and behavior, and that it was dangerous not to know when to quit.

With Jill and Kenny now gone from home, the whole world felt as if it had landed on my shoulders. I was overwhelmed and angry that I was on my own with all the responsibility of the house. In earlier years when the boys were still in diapers, if my mom was in a depressed state, it was Jill and I who changed the diapers and wiped the dirty bums. When one of the younger kids needed a dentist or a doctor, again, it was often one of us girls who took them. Much of the basic, parental care of the younger kids was shared between us. Now with

Jill gone, I was on the brink of teenhood, and with the curious anticipation of being a teenager, I wanted to socialize more and be with friends. I didn't want to babysit, clean the house, and do the laundry because my mother was too depressed to get up. I resented having to get out of bed on Saturday mornings to feed the younger kids and forage the cupboards for something to cook, during the times when there was so little. Why did I have to wake up an hour earlier on school mornings to iron my dad's clothes, be his alarm clock, make his coffee, and then get the other kids ready for school? All this responsibility was too heavy for me as an adolescent, and I didn't want it. But I did it anyway because I had to. Who else was going to do it?

Sometimes lying in bed at night, I'd say out loud, "I hate my life." I'd speak to time very deliberately, asking it to please pass as quickly as possible so all this could just be over with and behind me; it would tell me not to worry because it promised to keep moving forward. I spoke to time like this as if I were speaking to God Himself. I was pleading with something greater than me, a force I knew I could rely on as the one in control. I knew that tomorrow really was another day, that change meant "different," and even though different didn't necessarily mean better, change was a relief in itself. I'd heard countless songs refer to time in the same way that I saw it: that "time is a healer," "time heals all," "it will all be good in time," and "time changes everything." Those phrases had found their way into many songs that I knew, with prolific lyrics that spoke of how we can count on time to change and for it to change things. These songs were proof that I was not alone in my thinking. Others also had the same confidence in time, and so time was like a supreme essence, something I could pray to for change.

I spent every free moment listening to, playing, or writing music as a way to escape my home life. Music became my passion, freedom, discovery, comfort, and savior. I needed it. It was my drug. We had a turntable and a radio in the house. I also had a small cassette player, and although all these systems were inexpensive and of poor quality—often secondhand, given to us, or something we picked up at the dump—they allowed me to listen to the music just the same. It was almost as important as my mom having her cigarettes, so my parents made sure there was music in the house.

Very soon after first learning to play guitar, I developed thick, dis-colored calluses on the fingertips of my left hand. That's the hand that caresses the neck of the guitar and forms notes and chords by dancing over the frets. At first I didn't like these ugly, hard things on my fingers and would chew on them to keep them from getting too bulgy. I didn't realize that calluses protect the fingers, enabling you to press down hard on the metal strings without pain. One time I decided to trim one of the thicker calluses with scissors. I cut off the top, which left a circular area of tender, pink, and sensitive flesh exposed underneath. It was raw and sore, and it took a week for it to heal so that I could get back to playing. Needless to say, I never cut my calluses again.

Even with calluses, sometimes I'd practice for so many hours straight that my fingers would bruise purple anyway. It's amazing how much I played, yet I never became any good. Perhaps it was my lack of desire to become a great technician on the guitar; for me it was strictly a tool for composing songs. I was a singer-songwriter who used the guitar to accompany myself, not a guitarist per se.

I'm grateful for music and the many roles it played during my childhood and teen years. As much as I gave to it in terms of time and effort—exemplified not only by bruised fingers but well-exercised vocal cords and pages upon pages of lyrics—it gave tenfold in return and even saved me from getting caught up in trouble during a time of adolescent vulnerability.

My mother's wary eye also helped in that regard. She constantly reminded me to never leave my glass of soda untended, to prevent anyone from slipping something in it. (Or drinking out of my glass and giving me something else!) I was pretty safe from being exposed to anything harmful other than the thick secondhand smoke that clouded up the barrooms I frequented on weekends or the slobbering drunks tripping over me. As for the usual hazards, like bar fights that inevitably erupted around closing time, I just stayed out of the way. Besides, license to perform or no license, I wasn't allowed to hang in the bar between sets, as I was under the age of eighteen. Many of the places I played featured female strippers between band sets, and I felt uncomfortable being around that. I only saw strippers dance to recorded music and was never in a band that played live during the stripper set. I guess my mother or the bar manager would have drawn the line there in allowing a child to sing while the strippers were taking off their clothes.

I was ushered out after my set and would cross paths with the half-naked girls on their way to the stage. I remember thinking how beautiful they were: fancy, feathery costumes, sparkling necklaces, bright, shiny shoes, and amazing figures. My first impressions of a woman dressing up for a man's sake came from movies like *Cinderella,* where the concept was for the girl to look as pretty as possible. I didn't connect that strippers stripped as a profession, not to find a husband. I was confused as to why a woman would get herself all dolled up and looking so attractive if she wasn't trying to attract someone. Why would a girl try to look so good if she didn't want the man to be with her? In fact, while a dancer was stripping, she often came so close to the men at the edge of the stage that they could slip bills under the strap of her thong.

In my waiting area between my sets, I could often still see the stage from an outside hallway or a room off to the side that was officially not in the lounge but had a view of the stage from a distance. Sometimes I'd hear a dancer lash out at the men, "Don't touch me, you bastard!" The men were allowed to place money in her underwear but not touch her in any other way, and this confused me. It was hard for my child mind to understand why this was such a one-way street. The girl gets attractive only to be paid, not for the men to actually be attracted to her? This was not at all why the ladies in *Cinderella* dressed up so pretty. They were all looking to be asked to dance and to be kissed by the prince. "Look as close and as long as you want but don't touch" was part of the grown-up world I didn't understand. I felt very much out of place there, which, of course, I was.

# 6

# The Wrong Train

Even though I was independent and very mature for my age, there was one time when my parents certainly overestimated my ability to be on my own. At around the age of eleven, I was booked on one of Canada's national lottery TV shows that featured live guest performances. It was either *Wintario* or *Lotto Canada*—I can't remember which one—but it was being shot in Toronto. Gas was expensive—at least for us it was—so my mom and dad decided to have me travel by Canadian National Railway. It was an overnight trip, but it sure beat spending thirteen hours on a bus each way.

For a small-town talent like me, this was a big deal. My mother worked hard to get me on national TV as an amateur.

Just over an hour into my train trip to Toronto, I was settled in comfortably: homework out, guitar stowed above my seat, ticket in hand. My mother had arranged for a chaperone to pick me up in Toronto, and I felt confident that my first train ride all by myself was going to work out fine. What could go wrong?

Um, this:

The conductor glanced at my ticket, and his smile morphed into a frown. "Oh, this train isn't going to Toronto, young lady," he informed me. "You're on the wrong train." I remember feeling more annoyed than panicked, mainly because I didn't really believe him! How could it be possible? All the planning, the time my parents had spent on the phone, the process at the station buying the ticket, and he's telling me that this isn't the right train? It had to be!

"I'm sorry," he said with a disquieting certainty, "but this train is going to British Columbia."

Not only was I going in the wrong direction, I was headed about as far in that direction as a traveler in Canada could possibly go.

"W-what?" I stammered. "It can't be! I have to be in Toronto by eleven o'clock tomorrow morning for a TV show, and I can't be late—I have to be there!" My tone of voice was very adamant, like I expected this poor conductor to be able to do something about this, and *now*. "You have to stop the train right now," little eleven-year-old me demanded. Looking back, I'm surprised that he didn't pick me up and toss me out the door while the train was still moving.

"Isn't there another train going to Toronto I can get on somewhere along the way?" I knew that geographically the lines would run parallel for a while until they split to either continue south or turn east or west, and I figured it had to be possible for me to "switch" trains somehow.

The man thought for a moment, then said, "I will make a call; wait here," and hurried up the aisle. *Wait here?* I thought to myself. *Where can I go anyway?* I felt trapped, and every second that flashed by, with mile after mile of dense, northern bush speeding along outside the passenger car window, was taking me farther away from where I needed to be. All I knew was that I was getting the heck off that train and definitely not missing my big show. I didn't care if they let me off in the middle of nowhere and I had to walk to the nearest train station and find my own way. It amazes me now how I was so full of determination at that age. Nothing was going to prevent me from singing on national television. I scurried to pack up all my things and pulled down my guitar from the overhead rack. Just then the conductor returned with welcome news: sure enough, they were going to stop the train so that I could get off. But to do what, exactly?

"You wait by the side of the tracks," he instructed, "and within the hour, another train will come by and pick you up." I got off that

BC-bound train—and it *was* in the middle of nowhere, as a matter of fact—and stood there in the bush with my backpack and guitar, looking just like a little hobo. All I needed were a walking stick and bandana, and the scene would have been complete.

There was no sign of civilization anywhere, but I was fine with this. I had the presence of mind to know that train tracks always ran along the outskirts of towns, so if worse came to worst, I could always start walking back along the tracks to the nearest town and find a pay phone. Being all alone in the bush did not really concern me; the only thing that I was afraid of was being late for the biggest break of my career so far.

I didn't have a watch, so it was hard to gauge the supposed hour's wait until the other train came by. *If* it came by; for all I knew, I'd still be standing here come the next morning. To help pass the time, which just crept along, I pulled out my guitar, sat on its case, and starting singing. I waited patiently for about ten minutes, beside the tracks, then started to wonder if maybe I should start following them to the nearest town to try to find another way to get to Toronto. Maybe there was a bus I could catch or someone already driving down that I could hop in with. After this long, ten-minute wait, I was sure the BC train had just washed its hands of me, knowing there wasn't going to be another train to pick me up after all, knowing that once it was gone, there was no holding it responsible for abandoning me here. It was no longer their problem; I was on my own. Every ten minutes felt like an hour.

At last I heard a rumble in the distance. I hurriedly packed up the guitar and waited for the train to stop. Stop? It didn't even slow down. My hopes flagged as the cars thundered past. I couldn't believe it. *Maybe it didn't see me,* I thought, half in shock. But how could the engineer not have seen someone standing beside the tracks? I strained my memory to see if I could work out how far back the last town was that I saw from the BC train on my way here to nowhere. I guessed it would take me way over an hour to walk it, but at least I'd get there while it was still daylight. This was now my new worry, to get somewhere civilized before dark. I had no matches, and the mosquitoes would be out soon. I really wasn't looking forward to that, as a fire would at least help smoke them off and give me some warmth once it cooled down.

Just then I heard another rumble from down the tracks. Another train. This time it did start to slow down, much to my relief. As the train was coming to a stop, a man leaning out of a door asked, "Are you the little girl going to Toronto?" "Yep," I replied brightly, and hopped on with my things. Once aboard, I asked him how I could have gotten on the wrong train to begin with. He explained that in order to have caught the Sudbury-to-Toronto train, I'd needed to have taken a bus connection from the station. My parents, not being experienced travelers, didn't know that.

It must have been a hoot or, if not funny, at least an extraordinary event for the conductors on these trains to message each other about some little girl and her guitar with a determined attitude train hopping along the Canadian railway. It's not like these were subway trains or streetcars, these were massive passenger-cargo trains crossing the vast, wild landscape of Canada. They couldn't just stop anywhere, and they normally did so only at designated locations.

Amazingly, I made it to Toronto right on time. My chaperone was waiting for me as planned, totally oblivious that his young arrival could easily have been practically to Manitoba by then. At eleven o'clock, I was walking through the doors of the TV studio, ready to rehearse as if I'd had a perfectly restful trip. Just another page in the life of a child whose mother lovingly called her "my gypsy."

I'd already appeared on TV before, but those were charity telethons on local television and were nothing like the lottery shows, each of which claimed a huge viewership all across the country. I eventually made my way onto *The Tommy Hunter Show* as well, in 1980. Tommy Hunter, known throughout Canada as "the Country Gentleman," was a country music performer and radio-and-television personality. His TV show debuted in 1965 and would air for twenty-seven years, making it the longest-running weekly program of its kind in the world. I'd been a faithful viewer from the time I was about six years old, watching it on a black-and-white screen; in fact, I grew up watching Anne Murray and a long list of other big stars he'd presented.

*The Tommy Hunter Show* was the big time in Canada, with real dressing rooms, professional hairstylists and makeup artists, an elaborate set, producers, directors, and, of course, a celebrity host. I sang "Walk On By" by Leroy Van Dyke.

I felt quite legitimate and professional being led to the glam chair in the hair and makeup room to be fussed over like I'd seen in behind-the-scenes films of movie actors: with combs and brushes tugging and wafting hair, and faces being powdered and glossed, dabbed and blotted. I felt like a movie star.

The show's house band was the slickest I'd ever played with, and I even had backup singers. I couldn't believe it. I felt like a music princess with so much production behind me. It was daunting having to remember all my cues: when to enter, where to stand, when to walk, when to stop, which camera to face, and so forth. But I was excited by the buzz of the live television experience, and the adrenaline was pumping. It's too bad my mother couldn't be with me. It was obviously a time when money was too tight for her to be able to make the trip, as I know she wouldn't have missed it for the world.

My mother pushed everything to the limit in order to keep me developing musically. The more time, effort, and finances she devoted to my career, the greater the strain between her and my father. From most people's point of view, music is little more than a side interest or a hobby. Not to my mom. She was determined for me to make it, and was entirely convinced that I would. This belief was deep in her soul, and there was no hurdle too high for her when it came to my music. My father, I should emphasize, was very supportive of my music, too, but he was always more practical about things.

Well, my mother wouldn't listen to his common sense, and her fierce drive for my success often drove the whole family crazy. I al-

most felt that she wanted it more than I did. Actually, it's more accurate to say that she *needed* it more than I did. I've noted how music
was a great escape for me throughout my childhood, and I suppose
that was true for her as well. It preoccupied her mind, helping to
keep depression at bay, and it provided hope, which she clung to like
a drowning person clutching a life preserver.

That was great, but I increasingly felt the pressure to fulfill the
dreams that she was living vicariously through me—regardless of
what real talent or potential I did or did not possess. Imagine what
a burden that is for a young girl. I just wanted music, not necessarily
a music *career*. But because I felt obligated by her dedication to me,
her singer, I never had the heart to consider exploring anything else
in life, even though I'd dreamed of maybe becoming a veterinarian. I
also developed a passion for design and architecture that continues
to this day. In fact, that's probably what I would have pursued had
my mother not been so forceful about music. She dismissed those
and any other ideas that were outside of music as if *they* were silly
things to consider as a career. Her perspective was the polar opposite of most parents' point of view. What parent wouldn't be thrilled
for her child to show interest in a commitment that would require a
university education? My mother was convinced that music was my
destiny, and I was too young to argue.

I felt pushed into my music career as a child, but I don't say all
this feeling sorry for myself. I am happy that I was able to make my
mother happy, and smile at the conviction she had that I would make
it. She was right: I *would* make it. The road was not easy, but I have
no regrets and am very grateful for her persistence and belief.

My mother had contacted Ian Garrett, a voice coach who'd been
referred through Toronto's Royal Conservatory of Music, which I attended a few years earlier in Sudbury for guitar lessons. A fantastic
classical singer and a kind, enthusiastic voice teacher, Ian would
prove to be helpful more than once in my youth. My mom had
dreamed of sending me for voice training at the conservatory, but we
simply couldn't afford it. How could we? But Ian generously offered

to give me vocal lessons for free, so long as she could get me there. We're talking a *ten-hour* drive, one way.

Yet my parents gladly took me out of school for several days and drove me to Toronto for vocal lessons with Ian. He had a large, elegantly appointed house and a new car, and was well dressed. Wow. I figured that even if my mother was wrong about me making it as a singer, maybe I could at least teach music for a living someday.

Ian had a beautiful black grand piano in the room where he gave lessons. There was always another student waiting in the hallway for the next lesson, and knowing that that person could hear me singing through the door made me a little self-conscious at first. Ian taught using all kinds of interesting and perplexing techniques, many of which required you to do these ridiculous-sounding, freaky voicings that reminded me of Jerry Lewis imitating a person in painful agony. Not Jerry *Lee* Lewis the rocker, Jerry Lewis the actor and comic. I was shy, so some of the exercises felt awkward to me, to say the least. One of the most embarrassing was a technique that teaches you how to control your exhalation of air by putting pressure on your diaphragm. That's the dome-shaped muscle that acts as a bellows on the lungs.

Ian instructed me to stick out my stomach, then inhale as much air as I could without raising my shoulders, so the air went down and out. From behind, he would slip his arms under mine and wrap them around my abdomen—his ample belly pressing against my back—then lock his wrists and proceed to squeeze with an even, steady pressure against my rib cage.

All the while, I was instructed to purse my lips chicken-butt style, as I released as little air as possible, *slooooowly* but steadily. Ian would tell me to make a slight sound while doing this, so he could be sure that I wasn't faking it. The idea was to continuously exhale while conserving and extending the breath for as long as possible until you eventually ran out of air, completely emptying the last bit with one last flex of the diaphragm muscle. Then you'd be ready to take in the next deep breath. At least if I felt faint, which I often did, he was ready to break my fall should I collapse from lack of oxygen. These exercises were a strenuous workout, but they helped train me to sustain and carry long notes with a solid, even flow of volume and projection. It was the resistance against the abdomen that built strength and control in the muscles—sort of like vocal Pilates. Strange position, but it worked.

This type of vocal training left little room for creative expression and had me bored within the first fifteen minutes of the lesson. I preferred to improvise. One exercise after the other, drill after drill of scales, breathing combinations, interval gymnastics, pronunciation repetition, and contorted mouth formations, and I was physically exhausted after every lesson. I wasn't having fun with this, as I didn't want to be a classical singer and therefore didn't understand how it would help me. But my parents had sacrificed a lot for me to be there, and Ian was being generous to teach me, this self-taught child singer that the cat dragged in, which was how I saw myself. The other students were always well dressed, nicely groomed, and obviously not poor like me. They could surely afford to pay for their lessons, unlike me. I felt out of my league in regard to class. That was obvious.

I was not formally educated in music and had little theory; most of what I knew, I'd learned by ear. I was musical and could pick things up quickly but relied on feel. I had adequate sight-reading skills from the few prior guitar lessons I'd had, enough to work out melodies. With the help of Ian playing the piano, I'd follow along, straining my eyes on the sheet music while keeping my ears attuned to what he was playing. I faked it mostly, but managed. He never let on and spared me any embarrassment.

At the end of each lesson, Ian would relax the mood, I think sensing my itch to sing with less instruction and allow me a freestyle vocal exercise for which I could choose a song from a pile of his sheet music. It encompassed a variety of styles. I came across the music for Minnie Ripperton's 1975 number one hit "Lovin' You," a dainty, almost childlike ballad that showcased her five-and-a-half-octave range. I liked this one and chose to sing it. I already knew the melody from the radio, so I would just read the words and sing along, pretending to be reading the notes, too. I loved the challenge of the range—especially that really, *really* high glass-shattering part at the end of the "la-la-la-la-la" chorus—and Ian always seemed impressed afterward. Maybe he was just being kind to make me feel good. I was happy with myself in any case, but figured that I could probably hit those notes because I was still a kid with the natural high register of a child, not something I'd earned from intense, technical training.

One of the lyrics went, "Making love to you is all I want to do." The words meant nothing to me at that age, and I don't remember Ian reacting at all. But I laugh now, wondering if it had been uncomfortable for him to hear those words sung by an eleven-year-old. I know when my son sings songs with mature themes that are beyond his level of understanding, I chuckle, but I try not to let on in order to spare myself from having to explain the meaning to him. I just wipe my brow and say, "All righty then!" I suppose Ian must have done the same.

My parents and I were able to make the ten-hour trip only a few times over the course of a year. Still, my lessons with Ian were worthwhile, and I am forever grateful for my parents' sacrifice in making it happen. What a stress it must have been to go so out of their way, both financially and with their time, when they had four other kids at home. I don't remember who stayed home with my siblings when we made these trips, but it was most likely my dad's sister Karen, who was a few years younger than him, or even Kenny, as he was six years my senior and old enough to babysit.

My mother sent me to Toronto by myself a few times after that to meet with a manager she'd found for me who she thought could take me to the next level in my career. Kelly Kramer (already a pseudonym) was his name, and according to my mom, he would be able to promote me in all the right places and work up to getting me a recording contract. Kelly was a tall, imposing guy with long, black hair and long legs that clopped with every widely spaced step he took in his hard-soled boots and ankle-length fur coat. The first time I arrived at his house, I was so hungry from the trip that I devoured every last nut sitting in a dish on his coffee table. He asked his wife to get me something to eat, and she brought me a bowl of a very exotic, white, fleshy, oval-shaped fruit that I now know are called lychees. I didn't want to eat them at first, but I was so hungry I bit into one. Delicious!

The next time I visited Kelly's home, however, the wife was gone, replaced by a girlfriend. Undoubtedly, there was some cause and effect there. There were no canned lychees, either, although the girlfriend, assigned to be my guardian when Mr. Kramer was out, was the one who taught me, at age twelve, how to roll joints with a pencil. Worked pretty well, too, but I soon learned how to do it freehand. The funny thing is that I had no interest in smoking pot, not even out of curiosity. I understood that marijuana was illegal, and I worried about getting into trouble with the law. Also, I was very serious about being kind to my voice and knew that smoking of any kind can damage the vocal cords.

So I would take satisfaction in rolling "a good one," but I'd add it to the pile of joints on the coffee table. I was more interested in what record we were going to put on next, which song we were going to jam to—stuff like that. I had a one-track mind, and the only destination was music. Boys? Drugs? Not a distraction for me even as a preteen, a time when girls are usually developing their first crushes and getting all goofy in the company of boys. I was intent on developing myself as a singer-songwriter. My mother's passion was the music career, while mine remained creating the music, but she had been grooming me to be the performer since I was three years old. Now, ten years later, as if crossing a threshold of acceptance, I resigned myself to being what she wanted me to be, the whole package. I became determined to be the best I could be at that, and actually grew impatient to join the world of music entertainment professionals, and just get on with it.

Kelly decided I needed a stage name, so he renamed me Elly—without the Twain, I believe. But before anyone ever knew me by that one name, our professional relationship was over. To this day,

I'm not sure if he lost interest or if my mother had the sense to get me out of an unsavory situation. But my description of the fur coat–clad manager and my education in joint rolling would have fit several of the adults in my world. I'm not sure whether my mother didn't understand the music world outside our little Northern town scene to any realistic degree and was just too naïve to know what she was sending me to, or whether she figured that I could handle myself and kept her fingers crossed that it would all turn out okay. Probably a bit of both.

This being the mid-1970s, drug use was omnipresent. Mostly, I saw people smoking pot and hashish; some were taking acid. I never saw cocaine or heroin around me, and pill use probably would have been too discreet for me to really notice, I suppose. Of course, alcohol flowed freely in the places I played. But in a private area where the manager and entourage would gather, there was usually a table designated for joint production. Those who wanted to indulge would gather around to twist and roll cigarette papers with a thin layer of hash oil spread across them, then a sprinkling of weed, tobacco, or small hash chunks crumbled onto the paper as well. Twelve-year-old me would join the assembly line of joint rollers. But, again, I never smoked with these adults. In fact, I puffed a joint only once several years later, at a girlfriend's house. After a few choking puffs, I decided it wasn't worth all the fuss everyone made over it. I mean, it did make me dizzy and giddy, but at that age, so did having a good laugh over an unexpected, loud fart.

I was afraid of drugs more than alcohol at this age mainly because they were illegal and because I really didn't understand the effects all the different drugs had on the mind. I wasn't interested in experimenting to find out. Life had enough highs for me in my youth, without me relying on either drugs or alcohol. I can't say I feel I missed out on anything by not using drugs, especially as a teen. It was entertaining enough watching everyone else getting high and just letting the music take me away. Thank goodness I felt that way, because with all the independence my parents afforded me at such a young

age, I easily could have gotten into the drug scene without them noticing until it was too late.

Now that Mr. Kramer had unceremoniously departed, my mother
picked up the reins again as my manager. I felt a bit as though I'd
gone one step forward and two steps back by no longer having a professional manager. Now, I'd never consciously set out to become rich
and famous; my goal in music was to please myself by loving the
music I sang and wrote, and if I should ever make it, I hoped to be
respected as an artist and worthy of a place among the greats. I didn't
yearn to be famous just for the sake of achieving celebrity. Performing
wasn't even so much the main interest for me, as I was still painfully
shy onstage. If I had to be up there, I'd have preferred to be a backup
singer, not out in front. For instance, my debut on *The Tommy Hunter
Show*, while a very positive experience, brought home the reality that
I preferred huddling with the band and singers rather than standing
in the bright, hot spotlight alone. I wanted to write songs and sing
them to myself and around the campfire with my friends and family;
the dream was not to be the "star." The star would perform my songs,
and I would sing background vocals. This was my genuine childhood
dream: to be behind the scenes, which was clearly where I felt more
comfortable, creative, and happy.

My mother, however, insisted that the only way I was going to
make it was to be the singer and to get out there and sing anywhere
that would have me. Talent contests, local bars, music festivals, telethons, senior citizen homes, community centers—you name it, she
set up the gigs, plugging away toward the next opportunity.

# 7

## The Worst Year of My Life and the Pursuit of Happiness

declared 1978, the year I turned thirteen, the worst year of my life. At night, before I went to sleep, I would tell myself, "You will never have another year as miserable as this one. From here, things will get better." They *had* to, because they sure couldn't have gotten any worse, from my adolescent point of view. I had the feeling that a mix of emotions were fighting for air, stuck in the neck of a bottle that wouldn't give. If there could have been a message in that bottle, it would have read *"Heeeeeeelp!"* It was as if life had welled up in my gut and gotten clogged on its way up through the narrow of my throat, wanting to explode out the top of my head, but instead it was blocked and choked from moving up and out. I wanted out. I wanted to be free of my family life, the fatigue and stress of our dysfunctional home. I was mentally tired and my spirits low. Sometimes as an adult looking back on experiences of our youth, we can see with more clarity and perspective that our feelings about certain moments were dramatic, that we made more of them than was perhaps necessary, that the situation was not as bad as it seemed at the time. However, looking back on that period of age thirteen, I realize I wasn't being dramatic but realistic about how hopeless my position genuinely was at that point in my life.

Even the enjoyment my mother derived from handling my career was no longer enough to offset her more chronic state of depression from too much fighting with my father and our Twain family's never-ending financial struggle. She stayed in bed more than ever, and I was just tired of being left to run the house. It was a lot of responsibility for an adult, let alone a child.

I'd get home from school to the exact same mess that we'd left from the morning rush. Mom, too, was exactly how we'd left her: in bed. I saw my mother much like a bird in a cage: she was fragile and delicate, easy to break, and she sat at the bottom of her cage with her eyes closed, defeated. She'd abandoned her dream of one day flying to her potential. A bright, passionate, energetic but broken bird. My white, anglophone mother was unusually open-minded for a woman of her generation, coming from a small Ontario mining community but still speaking French and having had the courage to marry inter-racially to a Native. The French and English didn't fare well socially then, and mixed marriages between whites and Natives, especially when the woman was white, were very rare and openly were consid-ered unacceptable by most. It took brave souls to face the criticism that came with it.

I made my mother coffee and lit her a cigarette in an attempt to get her up and moving before my dad got home from work, because if she was still in bed when he walked in the door, he'd get upset, and from there the tension would build and possibly end in another night of fighting. It was not unusual for him to physically drag her out of bed by whatever he could grab—an arm, an ankle, her hair—or he would just clutch the sheet in both fists and yank off the bedding with her still wrapped up in it. I knew this was coming when he'd tell me to shoo the boys outside to play. My dad would proceed to drag my mother along the floor from the bed to the kitchen as she kicked and screamed, cursing him to hell: "Let me go, you fucker! I hate you, let me go!" My father let her go once they got to the kitchen; then he'd scold her to get up and take care of her family. My mother was in a bad state, half dressed, not showered, pale and frail. My heart broke to see her like this. Sometimes her reaction to this assault was one of submission, and she would sit at the table in her usual position with her knees curled up to her chest and just cry. I would comfort her by placing my hand on her back and saying, "Don't cry, Mom, it's going to be okay." Then I'd make her a coffee and hand her a smoke. "Dad's right," I'd say firmly. "You need to get up, Mom, and take care of us. You can't just sleep all the time. We need you. We have nothing to eat."

If all of this commotion went on for too long, an alarmed neighbor might call the police, who appeared at our door regularly. Most of the time, my mother would calmly tell the officers that, yes, there had been an "argument," but now everything was fine—when in reality, she'd probably be pretty bruised and battered from the spat, especially those times when she decided to fight back and not retreat to the table. At least the police's presence served to subdue her and my father, putting an end to the conflict.

I hated my life. I went to sleep feeling helpless at night and woke up angry in the morning. What amazed me most about the new day was the fact that not only one but both my parents were still alive and hadn't managed to kill each other during the night. This was a period when we were living the farthest distance from both of my parents' families. Hanmer was several hours' drive from Timmins, where most of our relatives lived. Consequently, we got to see them only on special occasions such as Christmas, about two or three times a year.

Extreme poverty and marital violence marked our years on Proulx Court, and I'm not sure why no one offered to help—at least not that I was aware of. It wasn't a mystery to those who knew us that my parents had a troubled relationship and that we had financial woes, but I really don't think anyone understood the degree of crisis we experienced at times. Ultimately, and somewhat remarkably to me, we would survive these especially turbulent four years, but in the summer of 1979, something had to give.

One particular morning after another long year had gone by, I was more convinced than ever that this was it. It was now or never. My mother had attempted to break up the marriage several times over the years, packing us up and going off to a friend's for shelter. It was never the same friend, for some reason; and sometimes it was someone we hardly knew that my mother would call on. I don't know the logic behind who she chose for refuge, but my sense is that my mother wanted to make sure we went someplace where my father wouldn't look, in order to avoid more drama should he find us. These attempts to leave never lasted more than a few days, however. She did get serious about leaving him once, going so far as renting us an apartment in a nearby town, but that lasted about a week. Then we were right back home with the same cursed cycle of ups and downs spinning us all dizzy. I couldn't count on my mother to make definitive decisions for our family or herself, for that matter; by this time, I couldn't even coax her out of bed at the end of my school day. So I made my own plan to break free of this cursed cycle we were all in. This was a defining moment for me. The "now or never" feeling is exactly how I said it to myself internally at the time.

School had just let out at the end of grade nine for the summer. One morning I simply made up my mind: *today is the day*. The minute my dad was out the door for work, I zipped around the house, packing a few clothes for us kids. Meanwhile, I tended to my mother as if it were just another day: coffee and a cigarette in bed. Next I herded Carrie, Mark, and Darryl into the car and told them to wait. There was a time when my dad took turns driving to and from work with a coworker to save on gas, which explains why the car was at home. In any case, we had a car that day, and I took advantage of the opportunity. I crammed it with as much of our belongings as I could. Whatever didn't fit, we left behind. The one possession I would not leave without, however, was our grandmother Eileen's grandfather clock. After everything else had been packed, I carried it out by myself, despite it being about three feet high and made of heavy wood and metal internal mechanics. I knew my mother would find comfort knowing her mother's clock had come with us. She was still very attached to the memory of my grandmother, and this clock meant something to her. I laid the heavy piece across the kids' laps in the backseat, along with my grandmother's crucifix, which my mom had hung above the entrance door of each place we'd lived since my grandmother died. This was obviously something that my mother would not want to leave behind, either.

Finally, after I'd spent the morning organizing the kids, packing the car, and rolling around in my head how I was going to break the news to my mother that we were leaving, I pulled her out of bed. "Mom," I said with some urgency, "you need to get dressed. We're in the car, all ready to go. All you need to do is drive." The usual routine of luring her to the kitchen table with now a second cup of coffee, and a light for her cigarette waiting, did get her up, but I felt I needed to pressure her for time, for fear that she might overthink what was happening and just go straight back to bed feeling overwhelmed by my plan for our escape. With her depression, spending most of the last four years in bed, it was as if she was disconnected from the rest of the world. I wasn't really surprised that she didn't argue; she merely asked, "Where are we going?"

"Toronto." Her only response was to nod numbly, understanding that what was happening was somehow inevitable and out of her control. She went through the motions like someone defeated, hopeless, under command, and I remember the feeling of guilt coming over me, knowing I was taking advantage of her in this vulnerable state of mind. She displayed no resistance to what I knew was a radical situation. I didn't feel good about it and resented the pressure of having no alternative.

Just as she was about to back out of the driveway, my mother paused. "I have to go back inside," she said. "I forgot something." I was so afraid that she'd lose her courage and wouldn't come back out, but, much to my relief, she returned in a couple of minutes, climbed back into the driver's seat, closed the door, and off we drove to Toronto.

I asked her what she forgot, and she said, "Oh, nothing. I just wanted to leave him a note."

"What did you say in it?" I worried that she'd be absentminded enough to tell him where we were going, but no. "I wrote him a note saying that I'm sorry things didn't work out." I was sad for her and still feel sad today that she felt so defeated at that moment; that she was so discouraged and empty of hope. And yet she still had the compassion to apologize to the man who had abused her. She truly loved him, and I could feel her heartbreak in letting him go, as well as her acknowledgment that it had been a two-way street: that life had been unfair to both of them, to their relationship, making it too difficult to live together in peace. She was taking responsibility for her part, by apologizing to him in the good-bye note. At the same time, though, I thought to myself, *Man, Mother, what do you mean you went back in there to write him a note of apology? Your four kids are sitting in the car feeling afraid, confused, and insecure about what's next, waiting for you to take them somewhere away from this hell so they can feel safe and secure for a change, be fed and protected, and you're moaning over the end of your relationship with the man who beats you?* I didn't get it at that moment, being fourteen, but now I see it quite differently. I didn't understand how excusing a man for violence could be acceptable under any circumstance. But she loved my father and appreciated his devotion to four out of five children that weren't his own. There were other things to love about Jerry, too, like the way he did his best to provide for us and how he always retained his sense of humor, even in the bleakest of times. He lost his temper under the pressure, but she surely saw this as forgivable, since it was a lot for anyone to take.

She must also have recognized her role in provoking him when she was upset. She had a way of carrying on, not knowing when to quit, when to shut up and let the mood settle so things wouldn't get so out of control. She was a passionate, fiery woman who would not stand down once she got going. This high-strung behavior fueled the fire between them, and I believe she knew it and regretted that she had contributed to the chaos. I saw all of this as well and felt compassion for my father, recognizing that, of course, it was not all his fault. I believed he'd done his best, but things had gone too far, and I'd reached my limit and desperately needed to flee. We were all dying in our individual ways, and the only way to survive was to run.

We drove in silence for a long while after pulling away from the drive of the green bungalow on Proulx Court. I glanced over at my poor mother. How deflated and disappointed she seemed when she got back behind the wheel. Life had let her down so badly, kicked the shit out of her, and left her to fend for herself and four children, with nowhere to go and no one to turn to. I shouldered some of the emotional burden of guilt myself. After all, it was my idea for us to leave. I was the one who walked my zombie mother through the steps of leaving the man she loved, to save herself and her kids. In a way, I guess I blamed myself that she was going through this torture. But we both knew there was no other choice; what's more, we couldn't turn back.

Imagine being a thirty-three-year-old woman in a beat-up old car, driving toward a big city where you barely know a soul, and with four kids in tow. She had no plan, no address there, and no money. She was in a daze, following the instructions of her adolescent daughter to get in the car and drive off to a new life. Who knew what kind of life? None of us did. But she knew that at least there would be a shelter or a YWCA for refuge and that I could continue with music there more easily than anywhere else in Ontario.

Ten hours later, we reached Toronto. Mom got out of the car to use a pay phone while we sat and waited in the car, returning a few minutes later with a piece of paper on which she'd scribbled the address of a homeless shelter.

That night, the five of us slept in a crowded, sweltering place on cot-like beds spread out along the walls of a series of spacious, open rooms designed for large groups. Our room held several families. I could barely sleep, it was so hot. Obviously, you had no privacy; everyone shared the bathrooms, and in the morning we ate at long, bingo-style tables, cafeteria fashion. Being surrounded by so many strangers was uncomfortable for me; I felt small and lost and wondered if maybe we'd made a mistake coming here. But then, at least we had someplace to go. And on the plus side, my first breakfast at the shelter was Rice Krispies cereal. I could have as much as I wanted—and no limit on the milk. This was new. We were eating with the down-and-out, but there was food to spare. We were soon placed in a smaller facility, a multistory house that had been converted into a women's shelter large enough for about five families and staff. The food was good, the staff members were attentive and helpful, and I felt safe and finally had a sense that things were going to get better.

There were strict security rules in the shelter. The front door locked automatically behind us whenever we went out, and we were told to never tell anyone our address or to speak to anyone about the other people in the house. Mothers were warned not to tell anyone on the outside, such as friends, family members, and especially husbands, where they were, under any circumstances. After all, one violent man showing up at the front door demanding to see his wife and kids could put everyone's safety in jeopardy. With this concern in mind, the residents were not allowed to answer the door or the phone. Counselors advised the women to not even call their abusers on the phone until the staff was confident that the person in question posed no danger. I could see how easily this protection protocol could be compromised with so many kids in the house, as it's hard for children to understand the necessity of so many bizarre rules, like not answering the door or the phone where you live.

Everything we needed was provided for—the women were even given an allowance for miscellaneous items, plus pocket money. If you had a birthday, the staff threw a party, and when the weather was nice, we'd have barbecues out back. What a blessing! The shelter provided a true refuge of safety, order, and security.

During the day, I used to go out for a walk by myself, just to get away from having so many people around me. Usually, I'd head up to a huge discount department store on Bloor Street West called Honest Ed's, to browse around. It's like a privately owned Dollar Store. Everything was so cheap! Now and then, I'd "splurge" on something for fifty cents or a dollar, like a new pair of flip-flops or a change purse.

I also liked to play basketball, and across from the shelter there was a basketball court. Although I was never much good at maneuvering, I was an accurate shot. I had wanted to play back in middle school, but my father couldn't afford the gas money to drive me back and forth for practice and games, so I had to pass on trying out. I was able to walk to another school closer by, though, where I could practice my aim and play a game called twenty-one against other kids. It turned into a constant pastime for me, and I became good at it. After a lot of practice, I was able to win. I went up against boys exclusively, too, simply because there were never any other girls at the court. Needless to say, losing to the short, skinny girl was frustrating to athletic teenage boys.

Although 1979 was a year that brought relief by breaking the dysfunctional cycle in our daily home life, there was still much un-certainty as to what would come next. It felt fresh to me, this shift in the direction of our lives. I was grateful that my prayers to Father Time had been heard, that my faith in it was not in vain. It knew I'd had enough, and change was granted. "I knew I could count on you, time," I sighed with relief. I bid farewell to the worst year of my life, coming from a deep sense of hopelessness only months before, to feeling hopeful. I was looking forward to better things.

Songs have a way of marking time, and "Sailing" by Christopher Cross does that for me. I first heard that song near the end of our stay at the shelter. The lyric "Just a dream and the wind to carry me, and soon I will be free" made me feel better about not knowing what the future had in store. The song inspired me to accept that as long as I have dreams, elements that are beyond my control can actually help me reach them.

Just before the start of school, the shelter arranged for us to move into a town house that we would share with just one other family: a mother and two gorgeous little blonde-haired girls. It was in Jamestown Etobicoke, a residential area northwest of the city, with blocks of attached housing and parks on either side. If you include the basement, the place had four bedrooms. Upon moving in, we were given weekly grocery coupons. My mother and Sherry, our town house roommate, went to a depot of some kind to collect our groceries each week. Each family received a box full of staples, such as bread, sugar, butter, and milk. It even contained one of my favorite cereals, Shreddies. Mom also received an allowance check based on the number of children she had. If we needed anything else, we might make the odd stop at the Salvation Army. It still didn't seem like much or even enough at times, and my mother realized that she had to get a job.

She managed to find a night job cooking at an Irish supper club called the Conception Bay Club, which was more like a hall. Owned by an accordion-playing recording artist from Newfoundland named Harry "His Nibs" Hibbs, it featured home-cooked East Coast food and Irish music and dancing. Mom hadn't given up on her little singer and quickly arranged for me to go with her there on weekends. She worked the kitchen standing over huge pots of boiling pigs' feet and cabbage, and I sang country songs on and off throughout the night for extra cash. Then I'd wait around for my mother to clean up after the crowd was finally gone, and we'd go home together. I liked the atmosphere at the Conception Bay Club, and the food, too, although *everything* seemed to be boiled; salty and boiled was how I figured the Irish liked it.

This was another one of those nightlife atmospheres where, although I was now fourteen years old and no longer a child per se, I was still out of place in this adult world. I remember a regular talking my ear off between songs one night, complaining to me about his supposedly bitchy wife. He told me he was going to leave her, that she was too uptight and superficial for him, and he just didn't love her anymore. "It's like living with a stranger," he grumbled. I told him I thought she was pretty and that I liked the way she did her makeup. She was very precise about it and quite glamorous. He hated her makeup, he said; in fact, he hadn't seen her without it since they married several years before.

"Wow, you never see her without her makeup?" I asked. "How can you be married to a woman and never see her without makeup?" Surely at night when they went to bed, he'd see her natural face then? He carried on to say, "Nope, she sleeps with her full makeup on, lipstick and everything."

Although I was just fourteen, my conclusion was that this man obviously drank too much and was flirting with me; meanwhile, his wife was unhappy and lonely and too insecure to ever take off her mask for fear that her husband would judge her without it and not love the real her. I also figured that she had to have been a very complicated person to allow a man to make her feel so insecure to the point of never being seen without her makeup, even by her own husband. The more pressing question on my mind was, Why is this man even *telling* me this stuff? Like I said, I was once again back in an adult world where I didn't belong, asking myself, *What the hell am I doing here?*

I made only a few bucks from singing, and my mom wasn't making much more than that slaving over the steaming pots. Therefore, she took on the extra job of selling club memberships, with me as her helper. By then, school had started, so I'd make my calls in the evenings and on weekend afternoons. About one out of every fifty people on my calling list even listened to my sales pitch, and maybe one in every one hundred considered it. We only had a dial phone at the time, and it took so long to dial each seven-digit number. By then I had my first boyfriend, Daniel, who lived just a couple of town houses down on the same attached block. His family owned several push-button phones, the more expensive kind. He let me borrow one, and, wow, did that make a difference. Not in terms of sales, mind you, but at least I was able to rack up more rejections per hour. I'm sure his mother found it very odd that one of her phones was being borrowed by the teenage neighbor. Sure enough, the next day she demanded that it be returned, so it was back to doing phone soliciting the old-fashioned way. Boy, did my index finger ache.

I met Daniel in 1980, when I was still fourteen. He was a very generous, bighearted guy. Despite being my age, he was mature for a boy and understanding and sympathetic toward my family's hardship. Being such close neighbors, we got to talking outside our gates when my family first moved in—just hanging out, without having to go any-where, still within earshot of our mothers' calls. All very innocent. For my fifteenth birthday, he took me to the Canadian National Exhibi-tion to see Van Halen. The CNE, founded in 1879, is an annual tra-dition in Canada. The two-and-a-half-week late-summer event is like a country fair but on the scale of a world's fair, with lots of rides, parades, sporting events, and entertainment. I happened to *love* Van Halen. Eddie Van Halen was such a heartthrob, and his guitar sound made me nuts. I thought he was a genius.

Daniel and I had fun before the concert going on rides and eating cotton candy. When we got back to our housing block, he kissed me politely and said good night. We soon fell in love and stayed together for the better part of two years. He was a fantastic person and will always have a special place in my heart as my first love.

Daniel attended a private Catholic school, while I went to the larger public high school. Every day after dismissal, we ran straight to each other and were together every chance we got. We were insepa-rable. My mother was pretty open when it came to discussing sex and had no problem explaining the hazards. With the overall awareness about AIDS still a year or two away, the foremost concern back then was to avoid becoming pregnant. I was pretty mature for my age, hav-ing grown up too fast too soon, and I decided to go on the birth con-trol pill to protect myself against an unwanted pregnancy. I felt safe and confident in my relationship with Daniel, so experimenting with sex didn't scare me, but I also didn't want to be caught off guard the way my mother told me happens with so many girls. She explained that in the heat of the moment, things can get out of control and just "happen," and before you know it, you have a baby on the way. The thought of that scared me. On my own, I made an appointment with a doctor, and Daniel and I went together to his office. Although my mother was open to talking about such matters, I wasn't comfortable sharing this with her, so it remained between me and Daniel. The doctor gave me my first vaginal exam, after which I explained that I wanted to go on the pill. He agreed that would be the best choice of contraception for me, and off I went with my prescription in one hand and Daniel holding the other.

I knew only a little bit about intercourse itself, such as the fact that the first time would probably hurt. I approached the whole experience fairly levelheaded, as Daniel was kind and patient, so I felt no pressure or stress from him, and my hormones weren't driving my decision to have sex, curiosity was. Without the heat of the moment fogging my brain, there was time to plan and think everything through. I have to chuckle at my methodical thoroughness in planning this, as there was nothing spontaneous about it and I really can't say that it was a physically satisfying first experience. But more important, from an emotional standpoint, I felt reassured knowing that I was learning with someone who cared about me as much as I cared about him. Looking back, I think that I was very lucky to have had a loving first sexual experience that initiated a positive association for me between physical and emotional partnership. I know that's not always the case for teenage girls. From then on, it remained an important personal value of mine that no sex was worth it unless the person was someone with whom I shared a mutual respect and consideration.

All in all, our life in the town house on John Garland Boulevard was tranquil, with no concerns about having empty cupboards. Still, having grown up with domestic violence, I sometimes worried that this comparatively *normal* way of living would prove to be just an interlude. What if my father eventually found us and came to bring us back home? Would we return to our old life, marked by periods of happiness shattered by horrendous arguments and physical brutality? I had no reason to believe we wouldn't, since that had been the pattern for as long as I could remember.

I had good reason to be concerned, since I was the one who had inadvertently given my father a clue as to our whereabouts. The counselors at the first shelter we'd stayed at really instilled in us the idea that you couldn't be too careful and should never divulge too much information to the physically abusive person. This made me feel paranoid and brought on a sudden, new anxiety. For quite a while after we moved to Jamestown Etobicoke, we never called my dad from our home phone; instead we'd walk to a pay phone a few blocks away, as he couldn't trace the pay phone in those days. The only thing my father knew was that we were somewhere in Toronto. One day I was talking to him on the phone, and without thinking, I mentioned that we lived near a street called Kipling Avenue.

The moment I hung up, I was scared. *Now he'll find us!* I thought. Intellectually, I realized that Toronto was a huge city, and for him to try tracking us down would truly have been like searching for a needle in a haystack. But logic is no match for a frightened young girl's emotions, and I ran right into the arms of absolute fear.

That night I started having nightmares, as I was so frightened he would find us and that it was all my fault for saying too much about our location. However, to my surprise, my mother told me not to worry so much about it, that she was going to give him our home phone number soon anyway, though not our address, yet. She was becoming more relaxed and comfortable about reconnecting with him, but I wasn't ready to accept that we were safe. Didn't she take the counselor at the shelter seriously? Wasn't she worried that he was just acting nice so she'd let her guard down and give away our whereabouts? My mother's newly lax attitude made me feel anxious and my fear launched me into a nightmare that even today remains vivid in my memory.

The town house we lived in had three floors. At first I'd slept in the basement, but after a year, Sherry and her two daughters moved out, allowing me to share a room with Carrie on the top floor. Like old times, we slept in bunk beds, only with Carrie on the bottom bunk and me on top. In my nightmare, my dad was standing at the foot of my bed, throwing dishes at me. I sat up and began waving my arms, crying, "No, no, stop! No!"

The plates shattered against my body, cutting my skin in clean, long slices. I had cuts everywhere, even on the soles of my feet, and it hurt like hell, although, strangely, I wasn't bleeding much. After a time, the throwing stopped. That's when I woke up.

I sit up in my bed, breathing heavily with my eyes open, keenly aware of where I am. The nightmare is still rolling, though I'm no longer sleeping. *I have to get out of bed to check on the others!* Although I'm awake, I'm still in the clutches of the dream. As far as I'm concerned, my father is coming for us. I have to warn everybody. What if he's hiding in the house? I'm expecting him to be.

I attempt to get down from my bunk, but my whole body aches. When I try to brace myself with the palms of my hands, they hurt, from the cuts—yet I don't see any cuts. It feels as if I have razor-thin slices all over me. When my feet touch the carpet, I can barely stand the sensation of the cut skin grabbing the knit of the carpet. I have to walk on my tiptoes, but I pad around to each bed in the house and check on my mother, my sister, and my brothers, certain that I will find them dead. Much to my relief, all four are still breathing and fast asleep.

I gingerly make my way down to the main floor, to check that the front door is locked. Yes. Good. But what if he is waiting for me in the basement? If I turn on the light, he might see me, so I creep downstairs and feel my way around in the pitch dark. Another surprise: no one there. I am sure, however, that my father will certainly be coming to get me. After all, it was *my* idea for us to leave him. It was *me* who convinced my mother, mired in depression, to climb out of bed, get in the car, and drive all of us far away. It was *my* doing that he came home from work that night to an empty house, to be greeted only by a pathetic one-sentence note of apology dashed off in a minute: "I'm sorry things didn't work out." I was responsible for his abandonment, and I was going to get it.

I am shivering from the pain as I crawl back upstairs and hide underneath the kitchen table. From here I can see every window and door on the ground floor. The cold touch of the metal chairs hurts so much against my cuts, and my feet are in agony. It's three in the morning, and this is where I will stay, frozen and wide eyed, until dawn. I've been scoping the house for an hour. I know this because it was two o'clock on the digital clock beside my bed when I woke up from my "dream."

I huddle beneath the table for hours, knowing that any second my dad is going to bust through the door with a shotgun. I've seen him in action, I've heard his roar, my mother's screams, our cries, the banging, the punching, and the yelling of two people entangled in violence. I am ready for the worst. I'm worked up and ready to take him on if he comes through that door trying to hurt my family. But he never comes. Around six in the morning, the sun streams through the window. My father never came. A warm sensation washes over me; I am all of a sudden no longer stiff and in pain. I'm back to normal. I shake my head and ask myself aloud, "What the hell are you doing here under the kitchen table?" I know the reason, but I can't believe it. It's as if someone had walked me there in my sleep, and now I've woken up, only I was awake the whole time. I crawl out from under the table with no pain, trudge up the stairs, and flop into bed like nothing ever happened.

A few hours later, my mother was shaking me awake. "Your father's on the phone," she said urgently. "He needs to talk to you."

"I'm too tired," I mumbled.

"He says it's very important."

I came downstairs and picked up the receiver.

"Eileen, are you all right?" he asked breathlessly.

Hesitantly, I answered, "Yes, I'm fine. Why?" I was anxious at his adamant concern for me, especially after what I'd experienced the night before.

He persisted. "Are you sure? Tell me you're okay." I reassured him that, yes, I was okay. Why was he asking me this? Was this part of the dream? I was utterly confused.

"Well, it's just that I had a bad dream about you last night, and I wanted to make sure you were okay," my father explained. Then he went on to describe his dream. "You were at the foot of my bed, waving your hands and shouting, 'No, no, stop, no!'" He'd woken up startled. The dream was so realistic, he told me over the phone, that he was worried about me and wanted to make sure I was okay. I believed that his concern was genuine. I also believed that he must have really been with me during those hours, in some way, and felt the power of whatever it was that happened. Our dreams were so parallel. He added that *his* mother woke him up around three o'clock because she'd heard him stirring and moaning in his sleep, obviously entrapped in a nightmare.

I couldn't believe my ears. Even the times matched. I was freaked out—who wouldn't be?—but I didn't say a word to him about my dream. "No, everything is fine," I said, and left it at that.

The summer I turned sixteen, in 1981, my mother went back to my father. She had become less dependent on me emotionally over the course of that period in Toronto, which had allowed me more time with Daniel. My communication with my mother diminished, and I wasn't included in her decision to move back to my father. She did openly allude to the fact that the boys needed their dad, though, and I could sense that she was growing weary of trying to support us on her own through working and collecting welfare. So it wasn't surprising to me that she would eventually decide to move back up North to a more familiar environment where there was some family, even if not to live with my dad. The fast pace of city life in Toronto wore on my mother, too. She was intimidated by the city dwellers'/peoples' less friendly attitudes.

I let it be known that, plain and simple, I wasn't going! I would not leave Daniel, and that was it! I was so set in my decision that my mother had no choice but to leave me behind, taking Carrie, Mark, and Darryl with her. Naturally, I couldn't stay in the town house anymore, now that my mother had given it up to move back. I packed up a trunk of belongings, pages of my song lyrics, stuffed animals, pictures, a diary, and a host of other personal trinkets to send on with the family. The only thing I kept with me was a small suitcase of clothing and a few functional items for my daily needs. I decided I could squat in the old house some nights to stay close to Daniel and ride the bus through the night as another solution for lodging. Did you see the movie *The Pursuit of Happyness* starring Will Smith, which was based on the true story of a man who was homeless for a time but went on to become a wealthy stockbroker? When I watched the scene where he and his young son ride the bus all night because they have nowhere else to go, it brought me right back to Toronto, 1981.

Squatting in our old town house wasn't very practical, as the electricity, phone, and water had all been turned off. Ironically, I guess you could say that in some respects I'd had ample training in roughing it under similar circumstances. My parents continued to try to talk me into coming home, as they knew I was bunking in the vacant house. Eventually they tracked down a distant relative of my dad's, an aunt who lived about forty-five minutes away, but I was reluctant to stay there, as I felt it was too far from Daniel.

I remember being alone in the empty town house one night when lightning lit up the sky, and with no curtains, it brightened the room in flickers. I was frightened, as the setting felt a bit like a scene from an Alfred Hitchcock movie. I was uneasy being alone there in the dark, but it was never as scary as the dream—was it just a dream?— I'd had when we were living there as a family. I had no bed, but the carpet was cushiony enough for me to sleep on. I was okay and would manage, I told myself. Daniel had asked his parents if there was any way either they or a neighbor friend could take me in, but no one wanted any part of housing this little small-town hobo. It made me feel like a tramp, embarrassed that no one wanted to get involved, but I also understood that it was an awkward imposition to expect anyone to engage in the drama of a teenage girl who wasn't with her own family because she refused to leave her boyfriend.

By the end of the summer, right around my sixteenth birthday, I realized I couldn't make it on my own anymore. Even though my father did eventually convince me to go to his aunt's, I was able to stay only a short time in her already cramped apartment, and there was no long-term solution that would enable me to remain in Toronto. I wouldn't be able to support myself working part-time at, say, McDonald's, and manage to get through tenth grade at the same time. I was gutted, but it was either drop out of high school in order to be with Daniel or go back to Timmins to live with my parents and continue high school there. Dropping out was never an option. As much as I loved Daniel, I knew that I had to finish school.

I reluctantly got on the Greyhound bus for the fifteen-hour journey back to my hometown. I knew my family would be happy to see me, and I was looking forward to reuniting with them as well, but leaving Daniel felt like a death—I was being ripped away from my best friend and first love!

# 8

## A Teenager in Timmins

t tore me in two to have to leave Daniel behind, as well as my independence, but just in time for my sixteenth birthday, I was home with my family.

Except that we weren't *home,* exactly. After my mom, my siblings, and I had fled our house on Proulx Court for the battered-women's shelter in Toronto, my father let the house go. From what I remember, he simply stopped paying the mortgage, so it was repossessed by the bank. He then went back to live with his parents in Timmins. I recall my parents later talking about how forfeiting on the mortgage had damaged their credit and made it very difficult for them to obtain loans for their future tree-planting business and a mortgage for another home once we rejoined my father in Timmins. They decided that while they were getting back on their feet financially, we would all move into my grandparents' house on Maple Street—one of the many streets in Timmins named after the local trees: Balsam, Birch, Cedar, Spruce.

Our family of six crammed into my grandparents' tiny six-hundred-square-foot home, making for a grand total of eleven people living under the same roof. There was my grandfather Gerry; my grandmother Selina; my dad's younger siblings, Uncle Timmy and Auntie Karen; and my cousin Lorie, who was my age. Now add in the six of us: two young boys, two teenage girls, and my parents. Needless to say, things were pretty tight, especially with just two bedrooms and one bathroom.

Once again, a basement served as my bedroom, except that this time our entire family lived there. The floor was all dirt, except for one small area covered with wooden floorboards that was just large enough for my parents' bed. Mark and Darryl shared the small space with them, sleeping all in one open room. As for Carrie and me, our bunk beds were squeezed into what used to be a cold storage room—built for preserving root vegetables during the winter—only the door was missing. Did you ever read the Gothic horror novel *Flowers in the Attic,* in which four children are coerced into hiding for years in the attic of their grandparents' mansion? Well, a book based on the Twain kids during this time would have been titled *Roots in the Cellar,* only, thankfully, our grandmother wasn't trying to kill us.

The basement had no bathroom; however, since the washer and dryer were down there, we had access to a couple of large, square laundry sinks, and I used one as my bathtub. I was a pretty tiny teen-ager, so I was able to crouch down with my knees pulled up tightly to my chest to have a soak. I was more than used to bathing like this from the years of rustic bush camping, having to sponge bathe by dappling open-fire-heated lake water from a metal bucket with a rag or coffee cup—so more like a bushman's shower than a bath, really.

Still, being a teenager, seeking acceptance, I was too embarrassed to bring a friend over or admit to anyone that I was living like a bush-man with my family, right there in town. Anyone visiting me in our basement dwelling would have been more likely to leave with their shoes sandier from our dirt floor than when they came in from out-side. I would have felt uncomfortable having to ask a friend to keep her shoes on rather than take them off when she entered. It was dark and dingy down in the basement, with meager peeks of natural, out-side light and only a few naked lightbulbs that dangled from exposed electrical cords off the unfinished two-by-four timber framework of the floor above. I could jump up slightly and easily touch the rough-cut timber over my head, as the ceiling was low. I was probably only a couple of inches over five feet at that age, to give you an idea of the lack of headroom down there. The basement was not finished as a living space, only as a storage, laundry, and utility area.

The cold storage room where my sister Carrie and I slept had a tiny ground-level window, no more than two feet wide by one foot high, with the bottom frame at the same level as my mattress on the top bunk. My sister was on the bottom bunk bed, and I'm not sure which of us was colder once winter came. Carrie's bed was closest to the only bit of "finished" flooring in this basement, as it was the cold storage corner, so it had a concrete slab. Concrete with no heat is cold, and having this under her back couldn't have been very healthy. My upper bunk, however, was like being pushed up against an ice block. I remember scraping frost off the inside of the window at night while trying to fall asleep. I'd draw shapes and doodles with the edge of my fingernail till the tip of my finger would sting from the cold, then I'd change fingers and carry on until I was ready to close my eyes.

This lone window came in handy as more than my bedtime doodling pad, though. Sometimes in the middle of the night, I'd throw on my clothes and slip outside just to escape reality for a while. Sneaking out was easy; the tricky part was easing myself back inside without getting snow all over my mattress.

Sometimes my little escapes from my cold storage bunk were with a high school friend of mine named Brian, who I met playing in the school orchestra's horn section. He was first trumpet player, and I was second trumpet. Brian was a good year older than me and had his driver's license. More important, he had a car to drive: a little stick shift with narrow wheels and no front- or four-wheel drive. It skidded all over the icy winter roads as we drove around together for hours in the back bush, having fun listening to music on the radio and pushing his car places it really wasn't built to go.

I never got caught coming and going from the window of my grandparents' basement, as my parents rarely checked on us once we were in bed, lucky for me. I'm sure my father would not have taken well with me secretly driving off in a car with some guy in the middle of the night. However, Brian was very nice and decent, and we never had a physical relationship, so there was no reason for my parents to worry about my possibly getting pregnant in his backseat. But certainly it *was* dangerous to be out spinning wheels in winter conditions without anyone knowing where we were.

The whole time we lived with my grandparents, I couldn't help but feel as though we were imposing on them. Not because of anything they said or implied. In fact, the two of them couldn't have been more welcoming, and I think they enjoyed having their son closer again after his being gone from Timmins for the previous eight years. There'd been a void of regular communication between them after we'd moved away to Sudbury, then Hanmer, before coming back to Timmins once I was sixteen. With all that time apart, I almost felt as though I needed to get to know my father's family all over again.

I rediscovered that I liked the Twains. They loved cards, joked and laughed a lot, and my grandfather was particularly funny, even though he was quiet and didn't speak much. But when he did, it was often to say something that made us laugh. My grandfather Twain had an obvious stutter—the result of a mishap in which he'd fallen and wound up with a stick jammed down his throat, leaving him with this broken, stalled speech. Sometimes he really struggled to get the words out, and between his stutter and several missing teeth, it could take a bit of a trained ear to follow what he was saying. Plus, he also had quite a strong Ojibway Indian accent. I was very fond of my grandfather Twain, whom everyone referred to as Jerry Senior. He was attentive toward me as the little singer in the family and cried every time I sang his favorite song, "Never Ending Song of Love for You."

Grandpa Twain had worked odd jobs in the bush his whole life, the bush being pretty much all he knew, as he grew up on the reservation of Bear Island, also in Northern Ontario. He spent his life trapping, hunting, fishing, bushwhacking, and claim staking for prospectors. He was fast and efficient in the bush, and I learned a lot just watching him walk through the dense Ontario forest while trying to keep up with him. His fingers were strong and well worked, with layers of calluses and scars healed over several times. He had the hands of a true bushman, and it seemed he always smelled of evergreen trees and fire smoke. He had the hands of a man who'd worked for many years with snare wire, animal traps, rawhide, open fires, fishhooks, jagged knives, chainsaws, and machetes, and had been thawed out of many bouts of frostbite from the bitter Northern cold.

My grandfather preferred to eat with his hands, right off the bone of the game, and often talked while he chewed. He'd sometimes spit out bits of food through gaps between his front teeth while trying to get his words out, and this would make me quietly smile to myself. Grandpa Twain also had a distinct, sharp angle to the bridge of his nose due to a severe break incurred during his youth that was left to mend crookedly. It only added to his charm somehow, and he was nevertheless still very handsome.

He'd lived so much, but I always felt older than him in some ways, even as a smaller child. Not that I felt more mature, but I just understood that I was more comfortable with "town life" than he was. He barely had a primary school education, having been pulled out of school to work in the bush. Grandpa Twain had an endearing naïveté about him that charmed me and made me respect the life he'd lived—a way of life that I understood was now gone from the Native youth of my generation. A life of simplicity, wilderness survival, getting around by dog team or snowshoe in winter, and by canoe and foot in summer. It all gave him a sort of innocence that I could see even from my childhood perspective. He felt more comfortable out in nature and with his Native community, as did I, and I understood him in this way. I still long at times for the solitude of the bush, the smell of my grandfather's wilderness scent, and the simple pleasure a little song from a tiny girl brought to him.

Although my grandparents had lived much of their adult lives in towns off the reservations, both of them were still very much of the Canadian Native culture. Grandma Twain, much like my grandfather, also maintained a long list of Native and bushman skills. For example, she is the one who taught me to track and snare rabbits. She also spent much of her life working with her hands in the bush and was a resourceful, handy lady who could make meals out of nothing and mend anything. My grandmother made a few of my childhood buckskin stage outfits that were displayed in the Shania Twain Centre in Timmins for several years, and she hand beaded several other articles of clothing for me, like my favorite mukluks that I wore every day through two winters of high school till the soles wore out. They'd been hand tanned over an open fire and never lost their smoky smell, which I loved.

Later, after we'd left our grandparents' home for our own place on Montgomery Avenue, several blocks away, a girlfriend of mine remarked on how she couldn't stand the campfire stink to my bedroom, like, "Ugh, what's that awful smell?" It was the smell of my mukluks filling the room that she found so revolting. I was a bit offended. Dolly Parton's classic "Coat of Many Colors" leaps to mind: the song she wrote about her dirt-poor childhood in the Tennessee mountains and the coat that her resourceful mother lovingly sewed together from discarded rags. At school, kids who were better off made fun of the homemade garment, but, she sings, "I felt I was rich. And I told them of the love my momma sewed in every stitch." I felt the exact same pride in my handmade moccasins, although at first my friend's display of disgust for the way they smelled made me feel ashamed and embarrassed. But I loved my Native connection, and I continued to wear the mukluks anyway, even though they were not very waterproof in the town slush, and I had to wear plastic bread bags inside of them to stay dry during my daily walks to and from school.

Grandma Twain was an excellent game cook and often sang old, traditional English folk songs in Ojibway, which had stayed with her from her youth. My grandmother was a Luke from Mattagami reserve near Gogama, less than an hour outside of Timmins. She looked very Native but had dark brown hair rather than jet black and some freckles on her cheeks. Unlike my grandfather, she took much more easily to town life, especially bingo night!

All of my father's family was quite attractive, with beautiful, smooth, tan complexions, strong bone structures, and thick, wavy, jet-black hair. I imagined them in their youth as resembling Elvis Presley's relatives. My uncle Timmy was particularly handsome, and Lorie had the most beautiful skin and hair I thought anyone could possibly possess.

Just a week after rejoining my parents and siblings, I started eleventh grade at Timmins High and Vocational School, the same school my dad had attended. Way up in Timmins, located practically four hundred miles north of Toronto, the beginning of the school year heralded not so much fall as it did winter: before you knew it, the days would grow shorter and temperatures would already plummet below zero at night.

I was back to leading a typical teenage life, more or less. I grew up following hockey and although Timmins didn't have a pro team, I used to watch games between our local junior league teams. Junior hockey is loaded with adrenaline, and once introduced to it, I got hooked. The atmosphere could get pretty wild: beer spilling, fists flying, people's dental work being rearranged. And that's just the spectators in the stands, never mind the action on the ice!

I made a few friends hanging out at the rinks, including a hockey player named Luc, a short French Canadian one year older than me. After one game, he invited me to take a ride on the back of his street bike, which is basically a souped-up motorcycle. *Very* cool. I'd never been on one before, only the much more rugged dirt bikes we rode over the punishing bush trails back in Hanmer. His street bike was sleek and white, with a motor that purred, and it had been painstakingly polished to the point of blinding. Since I knew how to handle a dirt bike, Luc let me drive it. I guess he was flirting with me, but I was totally devoted to Daniel and enjoyed the ride and only the ride.

A few days later, Luc asked if I wanted to go with him to a party at his older brother's place. I was cool with it and said sure. It started with a late-afternoon outdoor barbecue, but soon the weather turned cold, so we all went inside. The music got loud, and the booze was flowing. It wasn't the kind of party that normally appealed to me, but, to be honest, I'd been feeling a bit out of place since coming back to Timmins and was open to mixing with a new crowd. Despite my age, I'd been around alcohol probably more than anyone else there, but I wasn't drinking. As the night wore on, I began to stand out as one of the few sober people still standing. Maybe the only one!

Luc was in no shape to drive his bike, and since he was my ride home, I resigned myself to spending the night. I could have called my parents for a lift, and I know they would have picked me up without complaint, but I just . . . didn't. I'd been feeling a bit disconnected from them, to be honest. For one thing, I'd never wanted to leave Toronto (and Daniel), and for another, I was doubtful that the two of them could avoid backsliding into their same old pattern of violence. Plus, I didn't much like sleeping in a cold storage room, either, and, well, I was just plain angry at my mother and father *for my life*. Like most teenagers, I suppose.

Now: where to sleep? Everyone was passed out in chairs, on couches, on the floor; it was a messy home with dirty clothing left wherever it landed. Luc was sprawled out on a couch in the living room; I curled up on the floor. I was relieved that he didn't pressure me to lie down with him, as it would have been awkward, considering that I was in his "territory" and didn't know a soul there.

Luc's brother must have given up his bed, because he and his girlfriend ended up a few feet away from me zipped up in a double sleeping bag on the floor. I could hear her panting quietly in a curious rhythm. *Oh!* I eventually realized. *They're having sex!* How strange, I thought, that people would "do it" so openly. To me, making love was a private act, and I felt both embarrassed as well as shocked.

I especially felt bad for the girl. It never occurred to me that maybe she was drunk, horny, and quite happy to screw her boyfriend no matter who was looking on. All I know is that at the age of sixteen and being so new to sex, I just assumed that she was being controlled and that he was an arrogant, disrespectful, selfish pig, because what girl would possibly consent to being so exposed? I certainly wouldn't let any boy decide for me when, where, or if we'd be intimate. But maybe she was a totally willing partner. Or even the instigator! One thing was for sure, I was confused and uncomfortable.

I stopped hanging with this crowd immediately after the party, realizing that I was probably lucky to have escaped without being taken advantage of. Thank goodness that Luc had been so cool; another guy might have been much more insistent. I knew not to tempt fate, though, and decided that I'd better find some new friends.

I got a job at the local McDonald's, which happened to sit along the same highway that my sisters and I regularly walked to the Schumacher pool ten years before. I started on "windows," taking orders and making change at the drive-through, then soon moved up to being a crew trainer. Carrie-Ann began working there as well, and sometimes we used to have a bit of fun while manning the drive-through window late at night. There were big helium tanks in the back of the store. (I have a feeling you already know where this is headed.) My sister and I would suck in the gas, then get on the microphone. Customers would pull up and be greeted by what sounded like a pair of Munchkins from *The Wizard of Oz*: "Welcome to McDonald's' drive-through; can I take your order, please?" Some were amused, others confused. The two of us would also ignore the carloads of people waiting to order and chat over the speaker about boys, sing songs, crack jokes, and generally engage in more giddy nonsense. Looking back, I'm amazed that no one ever complained to the manager.

With the time apart starting to wear on us, Daniel and I agreed that we'd take turns traveling to see each other to share the financial strain of a round-trip bus ticket. Remember, there was no instant communication such as email or Facebook, so we relied on slow mail and the rare long-distance phone call if we'd saved up enough money. The first time he came to Timmins, I was so sick with anticipation/ excitement/impatience that I drove everyone around me *nuts* with stories about *my boyfriend from Toronto* who was coming to visit. I just went on and on and on. It usually would have been weeks since I'd seen Daniel, probably even as long as three months. This felt like an eternity at sixteen.

By then my family had moved into our own small second-floor apartment in a house that had been divided into four separate apartments. It was a humble setup, but brighter and cleaner than the dirt-floor cellar accommodations we'd been living in at my grandparents'.

This apartment had just one formal bedroom, which was where all four of us kids slept. We somehow managed to fit both sets of bunk beds in there, with about a four-foot space between them. I took the top bunk and Carrie the bottom, right across from the two boys, each of whom had his own bunk against the opposite wall. I was a little uneasy over the fact that a second door in the room led to a public hallway. Not only didn't it have a lock on it, but it was one of those flimsy hollow wooden doors. As a precaution, we kept both bunk beds jammed against it, but it wouldn't have taken much for anyone to force his way in.

The apartment consisted of just two other rooms: a caper-sized kitchen and an open living room, the far end of which became my parents' makeshift bedroom. Between them was a space just large enough for our kitchen table; it was the only place big enough for us to all sit together. The bath and shower were in the public hallway, to be shared with the other tenants, although at least we had our own toilet and sink.

During Daniel's first visit, my father refused to let him sleep on the floor. I don't mean the floor of my bedroom (shared with three siblings, I should point out, so what was likely to happen? I'll tell you: *nothing*). No, my dad wouldn't even allow him to sleep *anywhere* in the apartment. Finally, after much lobbying from me, we reached a compromise: Daniel could spend the night on the floor, out in the hallway.

Hey, it was better than sending him back to Toronto on the next Greyhound. And unbeknown to my father, I was able to leave the door to the hallway ajar a few inches—just enough for us to be able to touch fingers and talk quietly. I laugh about it now, but, really, how sad for us to be treated like a couple of silly kids in puppy love, when the reality was that our affection for each other was deep, mature, and anchored by a mutual respect. Daniel and I understood, though, that neither his parents nor my parents would ever be persuaded otherwise, not when we were only sixteen.

Eventually, the circumstances proved too much of an obstacle even for a love as genuine as ours. Between being separated by hundreds of miles and expensive long-distance phone bills (if only email and Twitter had existed back then!), we both had to accept that we would have to let go. The heartbreak would leave me mourning for a long time, and I was bitter and angry at life for taking my love away.

Even though Daniel and I never disobeyed my dad's strict rules regarding sleeping arrangements during his visits, my father started exhibiting a strange side to him that I'd never seen before.

As long as I could remember, it was my dad who tucked us all in at night, rather than my mother. He was more nurturing in certain ways than my mom. Whenever my legs ached from athletics, he'd sit on the edge of my bed and rub ointment on them for me. In hindsight, I can say without a shred of doubt that there was nothing inappropriate about his behavior. In fact, I looked forward to these times because we would get a chance to chat. So it makes what I'm about to tell you all the more confusing to me, even today.

Starting when I was sixteen or so, on more than one occasion, he would seem to just suddenly appear in our bedroom at night and stand silently by the head of my top bunk. Then he'd whisper in my ear disturbing things like "You're a bitch, you're nothing." "You slut." I acted like I was fast asleep, and there probably were times when I was initially, until I was awakened by his whisper of dark, disturbing insults. Not knowing what to do or how to respond, I just pretended to hear nothing.

Some nights, I'd get a double dose of his abuse. After he'd hissed in my ear, he'd linger against the door before leaving and start up again. "You filthy slut." "You disgust me." All in the same hushed voice. Then he'd walk out of the room and disappear into the dark. It was only a few years ago that Carrie and I were reflecting on our childhoods, and the subject came up.

"I used to hear him say these terrible things to you at night!" she confided. I assume that my brothers did, too, but I could never be sure and have never brought it up since. I personally coped by playing possum and had no idea that my sister was aware of these nocturnal visits until now.

Strangely enough, the next day, things with my dad would be back to "normal." I'd come home from high school to fry up my usual afternoon snack during that school year of bacon and eggs with toast, and my father and I would sit and talk just like we always did. It was as if these abhorrent episodes had never happened. God knows that I was more than happy to pretend that they never did.

As for my father, I honestly wondered if he was even aware of the twisted things he'd said to me only the night before. Could he have been sleepwalking? The way he spoke to me, almost in someone else's voice, it seemed like he was out of control. In a trance, almost. I know for sure that he wasn't drinking. And although I couldn't explain what might have provoked such behavior, I concluded that something was seriously wrong with him. I found myself actually feeling sorry for him. This went on until I left home at seventeen.

Still, from then on, I tried to avoid my father as much as I could without being too transparent about it. And our tuck-ins at night, which had once been a source of comfort for me, were now received with suspicion, anxiety, and dread. I couldn't think of anything worse than to be assaulted verbally, almost feeling verbally raped, by someone I'd trusted and respected as the father who'd taken me in as his own. I didn't want to know why he was acting this way, I just wanted it to stop. I resolved to remind myself that there was something wrong with him, not me. My goal was simply to survive it until I could get away.

# 9

## Avoid Open Ice

With Christmas approaching, my dad took on some bush work as a way to make extra money. "How about coming out to the bush and chaining on one of my crews?" he asked. I had three weeks off from school and jumped at the chance to earn a little pocket money myself.

*Chaining*, or taping, is a term used to measure the distance between stakes planted on a grid that has been claimed by mining prospectors. We did this often during the winter, when the ground is cloaked with snow and the trees are bare, for greater visibility. Men known as cutters cut the lines so that, come springtime, the prospectors are better able to access and visibly identify the grids where their claims have been outlined on maps. They then explore their marked areas with special mining exploration equipment used for gold and other minerals. They take advantage of the frozen surface of the lake in winter, using it as an anchor so they can drill down into the bottom of the lake.

It takes two people to chain efficiently. One other guy on the crew and I would each take an end of long measuring tape and mark off the distance between stakes by one hundred feet, or as they measure it now, twenty-five meters, then number them for identification. We rode through the forest on a Ski-Doo snowmobile, which pulled a sled loaded with stakes, markers, and other tools. The snow was deep, the temperature typically hovered around thirty below—colder still in January and February—and we were in the middle of nowhere.

Naturally, I loved it. I had a stubborn pride in not being some girly-girl; I was a Northern Canadian girl! The work was purely physical, so I could shut off my mind and feelings and just soak in the peace and tranquillity of the forest in wintertime. Just to wade through the hip-deep drifts took exertion, as you'd have to lift your legs up high with each step. Despite the cold, I'd get so hot and sweaty that I'd unzip my one-piece snowsuit to cool off or even let it fall off my shoulders to drag behind me until Jack Frost started pinching me again.

I loved growing up in the North from the mid-1960s to the 1980s. Where else in the world could a teenage girl drive a snow machine without a license, with a flask of whiskey slung over her shoulder, light a campfire to warm up, anywhere in the vast, empty forest she felt like, and exercise every four-letter word in the dictionary while trying to maneuver the machine through deep snow to prevent getting stuck, and still make it home alive by dinner? Your cheeks all red, your insides warm from the whiskey, bracing fresh air slapping you awake, liberty on your tongue, and a powerful engine under your ass. This was teenage fun for me and my friends, but working out in the winter bush was another story. Chaining out on the open lake was especially dangerous. It was necessary to follow the grids on the map, and if that meant crossing a lake, then that was what we did during the winter season, while there was a surface to mark and a line to be followed from shore to shore.

While crossing a wide expanse of ice, we had to be very careful to avoid open ice. Sometimes the ice cracks and leaves gaps. Sometimes you see them as you approach. But other times, blowing snow camouflages the hole or it gets covered by a thin sheet of ice that isn't thick enough to support the weight of a person, let alone a snow machine.

One late afternoon, around three o'clock, my father, a bunch of men, and I were wrapping up a day's work. In January darkness descends by three thirty, maybe four. We'd run out of stakes, and my dad asked me to ride back to the van—parked all the way on the other side of the lake—and bring a batch over before we went home. That way, we'd have plenty of room in the sled the next morning.

It was a good ten-minute trip across, and I wasn't sure I'd make it back before dark. The Ski-Doo had a headlight, but snow began falling, obscuring the shoreline in the distance. What's more, the thick flakes were covering up my tracks behind me, so I wouldn't be able to rely on following them on my way back. I needed to hurry, while the sun still lingered on the horizon. To be honest, I was a bit afraid. But I was determined to act brave in front of the guys and not be a whiny girl.

My dad had affixed a long pole made of poplar to the front of the machine—sticking out several feet on either side—so that if the Ski-Doo did fall through the ice, the unusually pliable wood would keep it suspended just long enough for the rider to at least clamber onto the surface before the machine sank to the bottom of the lake. This pole was specifically poplar, as any other kind of wood would have snapped instantly. I wasn't sure if having the pole provided a measure of comfort or if it only reinforced the potential dangers of piloting heavy vehicles across ice-coated lakes. Let's just say it was a necessary precaution.

I managed to make it to the other side, but with the stiff wind and swirling snow stinging my eyes and blinding me—I didn't have any "fancy" snow gear like goggles or glasses of any kind—the trip took longer than I'd thought it would. I also had to take it slow because I was heading for a clump of white birch trees. On a clear day, even at dusk, they would have stood out against the backdrop of dark evergreens, but not in the middle of a blizzard, which was picking up with every passing minute. White on white made it almost impossible to see the landmark from where I'd left.

We had only the one machine, though, so I had no choice but to return for the guys. Worst-case scenario, they actually could have made it back to the van by hiking their way back across the lake through the snowdrifts, but after a long day of working out in the bitter cold, they wouldn't be too happy with me. This was a large lake and walking around instead of across it would have taken three times the amount of time and was totally impractical, as the snow would have been very deep and made for an exhausting, slow walk, as opposed to tracking back over the machine tracks through the center. I pulled up next to the van, quickly filled up the sled with stakes, and wasted no time in heading back. As I sped along, I was grumbling aloud, "What the hell am I doing?! This is crazy! Eilleen, you can't even see where the hell you're going! Shit, it's dark enough to need the headlight already, and you still have to go back across the lake." Since I couldn't see my tracks anymore, I had to guess where I was going. I figured that if I just followed my nose and kept a straight line, I'd eventually get close enough to the other side that I'd be able to see the shoreline at least, and then make my way from there. This logic turned out to work, although I must tell you that, at the time, I wasn't at all confident it would. It is very disorienting being in a whiteout and extremely difficult to travel in a straight line with no reference point to help guide your direction.

By now, the sun had set completely. At last, I could make out, through the near impenetrable curtain of white, a faint black haze in front of me. My dad, realizing that I must have lost my sight line, was standing by the water's edge. As soon as he heard the growl of the motor, he started to wave his flashlight in my direction. The flickering light caught my eye. I'd made it! Ironically, what had been a potentially life-and-death drama for me went entirely unnoticed by the men, who were probably wondering only "What the hell took her so long?"

In the North, most people do things like this, even though we all know the risks involved. In that rough environment, you develop survival skills and attitudes that get you through; your senses seem to sharpen, too. Being out in hazardous weather teaches you to become resourceful and mentally tough enough so that, when confronted by situations like this one, you just carry on. It wasn't as if we didn't respect the power of Mother Nature; I mean, God knows, every winter you'd hear about people who'd died from exposure in the North. I guess we just never thought it would ever happen to us, and so there were no shortage of stories about close calls, usually shared around a warm fire with plenty of laughter.

Not my mother's brother, Uncle Don, though. One time he and my cousin Roger cheated death by the skin of their teeth.

It was a cold December morning. Now, with a temperature of twenty degrees below or so, you might assume that a frozen lake would be as hard as concrete. Not necessarily. If there hadn't been enough cold days in a row, you might encounter some weak patches of ice. My uncle and his twenty-four-year-old son, riding tandem, were the last in a small party of snowmobilers crossing the lake together. The other machines left a slushy trail behind them—a sign of brittle ice—so my uncle, who was steering, veered off to the side a bit.

Before either of them knew what was happening, the back end of the snowmobile plunged through the ice. Roger managed to jump off and scramble onto solid ice, but my uncle, in heavy boots and bulky winter gear, fell into the water. Don swam over to where his son was lying on his stomach. The first thing he said to him—and this will never cease to amaze me—was a reminder to place their helmets on the ice as a courtesy to other snowmobilers, to warn them of the danger.

Roger attempted once, then twice, to pull his father out of the water. But my uncle is a big, tall man, and between his size and his waterlogged snow gear, it was impossible to rescue him alone. My cousin turned and looked longingly at the lodge in the distance; there simply was not enough time for him to run there, fetch help, and get back to save his father. Not only that, but now the ice beneath my cousin was starting to crack. My uncle Don was getting weaker and weaker, and gasping for breath.

"Go on! Leave me!" he blurted. Later my uncle would tell me that he couldn't bear the thought of his poor wife having to bury both her husband and her son. But Roger, something of the family rebel, wouldn't hear of it. "No!" he shouted. "If you go, we both go!"

It's hard to explain what it's like to be soaking wet in twenty-below-zero temperatures to anyone who's never experienced it, but it is physically painful to endure and very scary realizing that your time is ticking down irrevocably.

Don, who had reached the end of his strength, had a last-resort idea: he removed his long snow gloves and handed one end to Roger. This would give them a few additional inches of leverage. Despite the numbness in his fingers, my uncle gripped on as tightly as he could. "Pull!" he instructed. Both of them knew that this was probably their last chance.

"Kick, you fucker!" my cousin screamed. "Kick!" According to him, it was the first time he'd ever sworn at his father.

Maybe it helped. My uncle pumped his legs enough that Roger was able to pull him out. But the two of them weren't out of danger, by any means.

With the shelf of ice still cracking beneath them, they inched forward on their bellies for some time until the surface was thick enough to support their weight. When they got to their feet, they hugged each other tightly, shaking violently from the cold.

My uncle's first words to Roger? "I will never call you my rebel son ever again," he said solemnly. From that terrifying experience, father and son formed a bond that would never be broken and developed a newfound respect for each other. In the name of love, neither of them was willing to give up on the other.

Three weeks later, my uncle's snow machine was recovered in twenty feet of water.

In the spring, the Twain family got into the reforestation business. Our apartment now doubled as an office. I can remember my parents and my aunt sitting around the kitchen table, which was covered with maps held open with coffee cups. While I prepared an after-school snack, the dog barked at the mailman, my brothers dashed in and out of the front door on their way to play street hockey, my dad tossed out ideas, my mom studiously jotted things down, and Aunt Karen calculated all the figures, trying her best to keep up with them.

From being present at so many of these kitchen sessions, I came to understand the principles of tree planting. Since I was good at reading maps, loved being in the bush, and was both physically fit and a tomboy, my father decided to let me try being a crew boss, which entailed being in charge of twelve or thirteen grown men.

My parents expressed their confidence that I could handle the responsibility, which is what really gave me the courage to go do it. The men in my crew, however, were a different story, and the moment I arrived on the job site, I can tell you that I felt very out of place. Not only was I just seventeen years old, but, as usual, I was the only person in the entire company who was missing a Y chromosome.

To be blunt, the men didn't take me seriously at all at first. And I certainly didn't help matters any when, on the first day, I basically treated them like schoolchildren, lecturing them as if I were their teacher. Never mind that this was *my* first tree plant, not theirs. I can only imagine what they thought of this inexperienced, skinny little white girl; they probably regarded me as almost as much of a nuisance as the ruthless black flies that infest the bush at certain times of the year, swarming around your head. (Know why they do this? Because they're attracted to the carbon dioxide that we exhale.) They leave bites that are similar to a mosquito's, only more painful, and they make you drip blood.

Basically, my crew humored me, no doubt for two reasons: one, I was the big boss's daughter, the importance of which should not be underestimated. And, two, like every one of the workers, the big boss was a Native, like themselves.

The first planting proved to be a harsh introduction physically as well as mentally. Tree planters, you see, are paid according to the number of trees they plant and need to meet their daily quota. If you're too slow, you're not going to stay on the job long. That should be obvious.

But also, we base our tree orders on how many we estimate we can plant within an allotted time. If we order more trees than we can plant, we lose money, because the Ontario Ministry of Natural Resources stipulates very clearly that trees must be planted as soon as possible and no later than a few days after being delivered from the nursery. The reason is that in order to ensure the highest success rate, trees need to be planted promptly before the roots begin to lengthen and grow together, and they must be kept cool and damp. Therefore, the ministry closely monitored not only the quantity of trees planted but also the quality of the job. So there is a lot of pressure on private contractors like my dad to plant the trees in good shape as well as quickly.

The first part of my job called for me to review the map indicating the areas my crew had been assigned to plant, and which trees went where. I would mark off these sections using colored flagging tape, then dispatch the men to their designated jobs, preferably without getting them lost. There's no surer way to dent morale than by sending men from the base camp to the place where a cache of fresh trees supposedly awaits planting, only for them to arrive forty minutes later and find nothing there. Or, worse, having them lug one of these heavy bags full of trees to a patch, and it turns out that you inadvertently pointed them in the wrong direction. Understandably, planters get pretty pissed off whenever this happens.

With experience, I became quite good at deciphering the maps and getting my crews where they needed to be. I also learned to judge my expectations of each crew member based on his average as well as the space and ground type. Ricky, for example, could plant 1,500 trees a day, and 1,700 if it was white pine with sandy soil, not too gravelly. But he might be reduced to under 1,000 a day if his job was to plant black spruce, for which the soil is swampy and stumpy and hard to maneuver.

Even when everything goes right, though, this is a difficult job. Think about it: you're working out in the exposed elements over long hours, subjected to temperamental weather, those unforgiving black flies, mosquitoes, and a host of other things that can make you uncomfortable, such as planting in a prescribed burn patch where the ground underneath you is still smoldering in places. Sometimes you step into dangerous hot spots of smoldering coals, the black soot coats your nostrils, and you feel like you've been working in a coal mine. The trees are prickly and uncomfortable to handle, the bags are heavy, and did I mention the bears, let alone moose during rutting season? They are particularly dangerous at this time of year, the fall, when they are mating. The bull moose are especially aggressive and will charge and trample you, if agitated, much like most people know the black bull to do. Only moose are several times a bull's size!

Tree planting is just a *hard job,* plain and simple. It wouldn't take much for a planter to decide that he wasn't up to it today and, in order to meet his quota, hide, bury, and double plant his trees. Consequently, part of my job consisted of supervising the men and being on the lookout for this. I'm sure that some of them tricked me, but all in all, not too many, as we always covered the projected amount of area according to our allotted number of trees. For example, as trees are planted six feet apart in all directions, it's not hard to work out on a map how many trees go in each plantable area. The Ministry of Natural Resources often awarded my crew an excellent 98 percent projected success rate, which means that each tree we planted was more than 90 percent likely to live long enough to mature into something flat, stamped, and green—namely, money. Sometimes I felt sad that the forests we were replanting were only being planted to be cut down. Like farmed animals, their only purpose for being brought into the world is to be killed in a very specific way at a very specific time. Our trees, depending on the type and what soil terrain conditions they were planted in, were scheduled for cutting in anywhere from fifty-five to seventy-five years, once they were mature enough to be cut for lumber. I do believe that well-managed reforestation is a very intelligent way to produce a supply in demand, so that wild and natural forests can remain untouched and protected.

I'm sure that the advent of the cell phone has made the crew leader's job somewhat easier these days. But when I was working in the bush, we had to rely on hand signals and a lot of bellowing over long distances. We'd pass messages from one man to the next as if playing the children's game telephone, only louder: "Where does Remy go next?!" "Chuck's shovel is broken! Bring him a new one!" The cache, as we called it, where the trees were stored till planting, was our communication hub, so I tried to keep abreast of everyone's position and to be there when each man came back to fill up with trees.

Back at camp at the end of the day, we'd all sit around long, bingo-style tables in a big, rectangular canvas prospector's tent to eat. A typical meal consisted of potatoes, frozen corn, and sausages stewed in canned tomatoes, and usually cake for dessert. I typically saved my cake for breakfast, because during the hot summer months, our days began at three in the morning, and who could eat a full breakfast at that hour? Just cake and black tea for me, thank you.

After dinner, I often went right back to my trailer for the night. No playing cards, the usual camp pastime, or socializing. Are you kidding? I was *beat*! I would brush my teeth, take off my boots, hang up my socks on a nail in the wall to air out, and fall into bed with the rest of my clothes on. It wasn't unusual for me to go for days without taking a good look in the mirror, which, to be honest, was quite liberating. In the morning, I'd throw on a fresh pair of underwear, a bra, and an undershirt, and I was good to go. My outer gear got washed every several days, on average. This may sound odd, but it's true. No deodorant, no shampoo or soap, but no body odor. Not just me, but everyone. Any perfumed products attract black flies, which is a hazard, so you go au naturel, and everyone just smells like the forest. We all know that if human adults do not shower for days at a time with deodorized products, they will be rank, but our camp diet was so basic, little junk food and no chemical products. I believe that once you sweat out the initial crap in your system after the first week of hard bush labor, your odor starts to blend in with nature. This is my theory, at least from my personal experience of being in a camp with a large group of men and no showers.

My personal way of bathing was to head off to the bush; I'd often fill a tree container with water and leave it in the bed of one of my dad's pickup trucks to heat in the sun all day. When I'd get back in the late afternoon, I'd put on the lid to avoid spilling and drive up the road to someplace where I could bathe in private. I would stand against the dropped tailgate and dip a large coffee cup or small pot in my tub of sun-warmed water and douse myself.

Once I got used to the routine, I came to enjoy the solitude of working in the bush and didn't miss living in town at all, not even the conventional shower. Out there, you knew your place, your purpose, your job, and what you should and shouldn't do. Knowing that bathing with fragrant shampoo and soap resulted in getting eaten alive by insects, I understood that if I was respectful and worked as hard and as fast as the guys, I'd earn their respect. If I ate or drank more than I should, I'd be too sluggish to make it through the long day; likewise, if I didn't go to bed right after supper, I'd regret it the next morning. Bush camp life offered few conveniences, yet at the same time, it gave me the luxury of more freedom from the burden of too much decision making over menial things.

My sister Carrie, who was then fifteen or sixteen, decided to join me in order to make some extra money. After all, the pay was much better than at McDonald's, where she worked after school and on weekends, but then, the work was a lot harder. Boy, was she ever in for a surprise. On her first day, we agreed that she would plant on my crew until she got the knack of everything. I would teach her how to plant the trees, how to maneuver the shovel, and so on.

Well, the black flies were out that day in numbers. Nothing attracts them like the sweet smell of someone fresh from town, all showered and wearing machine-washed clothing. Unfortunately for my sister, she'd joined the camp smelling of Wella Balsam shampoo, hair gel, and deodorant. The flies had a *feast*! Not only that, but although the trek from the tree cache to the planting patch wasn't far, the terrain was full of logs and giant roots to climb over, so that Carrie was exhausted before she'd even had the chance to plant her first tree. Within the first hour, my sister was threatening to leave, yelling, "I've had enough!" I couldn't help but laugh. I understood how awful she felt, but as I'd been there and survived, it now just seemed funny to me. Happily, I convinced her to stay for the season, and it was great to have my little sister as a roommate.

For privacy, our puny, run-down camper was parked up the road from the guys' camp. One morning I looked out the window and saw a big moose grazing lazily just outside. I walked out to take a better look. It just gawked at me and went back to eating. Moose are kind of goofy looking; they have oversized heads shaped like a peanut and a giant rack of antlers between their ears.

I thought, *Here is my big chance to bag a moose!* I ran back inside the trailer and grabbed a gun. We kept a few around the camp for scaring off curious and hungry bears. It was a .33-caliber rifle—a bit heavy for me, but I'd had lots of practice with it from years of joining my dad target shooting.

I crept up on the moose until I was about one hundred feet away, and as it was not rutting season, it was actually very docile and nonaggressive. Moose will often look long and hard at you if you approach and eventually decide to run off. Once I got as close as I could before sensing his urge to turn and run, I cracked open the barrel to pop in a bullet. There was already one jammed in the chamber, so I closed it back up, aimed, and pulled the trigger, figuring the gun would fire with the bullet already there. But there was nothing. I tried pulling out the jammed bullet, but it wouldn't budge. Now I'm getting frustrated: *I can't believe this! I'm out here alone, I have a big, fat moose standing a stone's throw from me, and I can't get the gun to shoot!* I angrily threw the .33 to the ground (probably not my greatest idea ever; what if it had discharged?) and started stomping on it and yelling at it, "You useless, good-for-nothing son of a bitch!" I guess for fun I could say "gun" in this case, although that's not what I said at the time. If my father had been a fly on the wall, he would have found the scene comical. But it was just me and the moose, who stared at me with puzzled eyes. His lack of concern made me feel foolish, and after a while, I gave up, at which point my erstwhile victim slowly sauntered off into the bush.

To tell you the truth, I was secretly relieved. I mean, I would have shot it, since in the culture of the North that's what you do when you've grown up on moose meat, you have a moose standing right in front of you, and you have a rifle, but I sure wouldn't have felt good about it afterward. With all the gun carrying through the bush during the hunting treks with my father and my grandparents, I'd never personally shot anything before, and for such a majestic creature to fall at my feet just because *I felt like it* would have bothered me deeply. Although I'd snared rabbits with my grandparents and I enjoyed the bonding and the learning of their ways, I felt uneasy, making the connection that in order for us to eat these cute, fluffy animals, they had to choke in our wire. Hunting was an integral part of our way of life, but I realized, having been able to reflect on it at this moment, it didn't sit right with me.

A full season's planting was divided into three parts: spring, summer, and fall. Depending on what I was doing with singing, I would join the plant for any one of the three or the entire season. During each of the stretches, we'd get only one excursion into town. Personally, I never had any interest in going, but it was my duty to take my crew, who were, as you might imagine, anxious to leave the confines of the camp. Besides, having Carrie's company, as she was now in her second season, had me looking forward to the two-hour van trip.

The food in camp was tasty enough but was limited to stews, soups, and very basic, repetitive dishes. Like most teenagers, I was craving a fast-food hamburger with an order of fries, a chocolate milkshake, and cherry pie right about then. So a stop at my sister's usual place of employment, and my former workplace, the Golden Arches, ranked first on our itinerary.

Of all the guys in my crew, my favorite was a sixteen-year-old named Berny. Among his many fine qualities, he was the hardest and most honest worker. No matter what the weather, Berny wore

The very first picture of me.

My father, Jerry, age twenty-two, with his three newly adopted daughters: Jill, Carrie, and me, in the backyard on Bannerman Street, 1971.

My mother cooking in a makeshift kitchen in a typical bush cabin. My father's winter boots are drying on the wood stove.

Timmins, 1970.

With Carrie, Jill, and Mark in
the stroller on Bannerman
Street, Timmins, summer 1972.

With my sisters, Carrie and
Jill, in the backyard of our
house on Bannerman Street,
Timmins, Halloween, 1972.

Carrie and me,
Timmins, 1973.

My and Carrie's first snowman of
the winter, Proulx Court,
Hanmer, 1975.

At the age of ten, singing with Lawrence Martin, a Native Canadian singer from
Ontario.

Class photo,
1972.

Redwood Acres School, Hanmer, 1976. I'm the one in the middle holding
the sign.

Singing in a bar in
Sudbury, 1976.

Singing in a bar in Sudbury, 1976.

With my mom and Brent
Williams, second from left,
after singing in a bar in
Sudbury, 1976.

Performing at an old-age home in Sudbury, around 1977.

Singing in a club in Ontario at the age of twelve.

My sixteenth birthday, just after leaving my boyfriend Daniel in Toronto and going home to Timmins.

On a four-wheeler with my mom, working on the tree plant, summer 1982.

Carrie stuffs my shirt with a pillow; goofing off on the tree plant.

At the tree plant, at
the age of seventeen,
with two of my crew
members.

Tree-planting crew
having a rare beer
at camp to celebrate
the end of a tree plant.

The tree-planting crew.

With Longshot onstage at J.P.'s Lounge, Timmins, July 1982.

Onstage with
Longshot at
Hollinger Park.

One of the last photos of my parents, a few weeks before they died, October 1987.

Last photo of my parents alive, October 1987.

My parents' headstone in Timmins cemetery.

My writing cabin in the forest on the bank of Kenogamissi Lake.

Writing a song in the Kenogamissi Lake cabin.

At my spot in
the dressing room
at Deerhurst.

The early years in Nashville, with PolyGram's Harold Shedd (left), Billy Ray Cyrus (middle), and Luke Lewis (right). *(Courtesy of Mercury Records, a Division of UMG Recordings, Inc.)*

Promo shot for the Four Winds Bar at Deerhurst.

Nashville studio. From left to right: Joe Cotton, Norro Wilson, my friend Laura, Harold Shedd, and Joe Scaife.

Triple Play with Toby Keith (left) and John Brannen (right). *(Courtesy of Mercury Records, a Division of UMG Recordings, Inc.)*

With my team of supportive Timmins friends at Fan Fair in Nashville 1993. In the background, my first booth, made by my friend Cynthia's father.

a T-shirt layered with a long-sleeve wool sweater. It could be sixty degrees out or eighty, he always wore the same thing, no more and no less. When it rained, he wore a plastic garbage bag over his shoulders. His English was as poor as my Cree, and so he rarely said a word. Nevertheless, the two of us always seemed to understand each other. I gauged my fairness toward the crew by Berny: If he was hungry, then I knew it was time for everyone to eat. If Berny was tired, then I knew everyone else was exhausted, and it was time to take a break.

Like a number of the men, Berny had teeth in need of dental care. They were stained black and brown; clearly, the concept of tooth brushing was foreign to him. One morning on our walk to work, I'd asked him point-blank if he brushed his teeth. He shook his head no. "You need to brush your teeth, Berny. They're going to fall out if you don't. If I get you a toothbrush and some toothpaste, will you use it?" "Uh-huh," he answered. Berny lived up to his promise to brush his teeth and before too long, I could actually see his smile. It turned out that he had nice, straight, perfectly formed teeth. Hopefully, now he would go on to keep them, I thought.

Anyway, we pulled into the McDonald's parking lot for our fast-food fix. I took everyone's orders—all fourteen of us—and asked Berny to come inside with me and help me carry everything back to the van. He just looked at me, then stared down at his shoes.

"Come on, Berny, let's go." He shook his head vigorously. No.

"Why not?" I couldn't understand why he was acting this way. Now Berny was starting to get agitated. Slowly and very reluctantly, he came to the open back door of the van, and I could see that he had tears in his eyes.

Finally, someone piped up, "Berny *can't* go in. He's too scared. He's never been into a McDonald's before, and is too afraid to be among so many white people."

*Of course,* I realized, chastising myself for being so insensitive. In fact, it wasn't unusual, at least at that time, for some Native North Americans from the more remote areas of Ontario to have little exposure to "town" life. I immediately apologized and took along another guy more familiar with being the minority. I felt really bad about pressuring Berny, but it was unintentional.

A trip to town always included a stop at Angelo's, a small, family-owned corner grocery store located several blocks away from our home on Montgomery Avenue. We had a tab there that my dad paid throughout the year, both for our family and for the planting crews. Angelo, the owner, was a supernice man, accommodating and non-racist. If I brought a dozen or so unshowered, unshaven Native bushmen into most grocery stores, I could count on them receiving glares and being watched with suspicion. Personally, I was offended by this attitude and would have none of it: I was offended by the prejudice.

Angelo, to his credit, was one of us and always welcomed the planters who accompanied us into his store. We loaded up on necessities to get us through another few weeks of isolation, such as magazines, gum, cough drops, and aspirin. Afterward, I dropped the men off at a local bar, then went off to a sauna for an advertised deep-cleansing treatment. You have no idea how out of character this was for me! I actually loved the smells of smoke, bush, and fresh air on my skin and usually cleaned only the essential parts, leaving the rest "natural." After several weeks in the bush, the typical girly regime of shaving my legs, applying moisturizer, using hair conditioner, and so on seemed like a real nuisance. Nevertheless, I *was* a civilized town girl who, now that I was back in town, should be freshly showered and groomed. So I splurged on the sauna.

I walked out of there as red as a lobster, with my eyes all swollen from the dry heat and my face irritated from the soap and hot steam. I felt strange and sleepy, unaccustomed to the chemicals in cleansing products and superficial heat, but I needed to find the guys.

They weren't in the bar where I'd left them. Or the next one, and it wasn't even dark yet. I ran into two men from Carrie's crew, and they didn't recognize me at first. "Hey, guys!" I called to them. "It's me, Eileen! Where's the rest of the gang?" They stared at me like they'd never seen me before in their lives.

After clueing in that it was actually me, their normally scruffy crew boss, who looked so radically different cleaned up, one said, "You look . . . different."

"Yeah . . . different," his friend repeated. The two of them were so nonplussed by my cleaned-up appearance that it didn't occur to them that I might take offense when they added that they *didn't like me as well this way!* Gee, thanks, guys! Actually, I just chuckled about their reaction. They pointed in the direction of where the others had gone, and we set off in opposite directions.

I soon found the guys in yet another bar, and already half drunk. The music was loud and the atmosphere a bit rowdy. They ordered me up a shot of something, I slugged it down, and we were off for a fun night. We stuck together as a crew and we were often glared at by onlookers who found it odd to see thirteen Native men out with one white girl, and it often provoked racist remarks. I have no tolerance for racism and especially as a teenager, it was hard for me to bite my tongue when it came to such small-minded attitudes.

Sometimes the tension would build pretty high and it became clear that it was time to go. I hated to be a party pooper but even on our night on the town, I was still the crew boss, and I had an hour-plus drive ahead of me back to the bush camp. "Let's go, guys," I announced. We had to plant the next morning at five o'clock, and it was already *way* past our bedtime. I wanted to round up everyone before someone there got into a fistfight, lost a few teeth, or possibly wound up cast in a drama with the local police. It was not an unlikely scenario.

Now, I should tell you that in all the years I spent around older men as a crew boss, no one had ever acted inappropriately with me. In fact, only once did someone even acknowledge my femininity. Hmm, maybe I should have been insulted! I was helping the men load one-hundred-pound tree bins in the back of the truck when one of them remarked very matter-of-factly, "You have a nice body." I took it as a compliment and didn't feel threatened or uncomfortable at all, as it was said innocently and not in a leering manner or anything like that.

Before we hit the road, I needed to grab something from the back of the van, which was piled high with provisions from Angelo's. The men were strewn around the metal floor like throw rugs, using their jackets as cushions. As I turned around to exit out the back door, Berny impulsively grabbed my arm and tried to kiss me. I pulled away, caught off guard and totally surprised.

"Berny! What are you doing?"

He didn't release his grip, and his lips were about to attempt another landing. This time, I jerked my arm back, and he let me go. Before I could climb out, Berny's father, John, spun me around and started screaming in my face, "He wants to marry you! You have to kiss him! Kiss him now!" he demanded.

I could not believe what I was hearing. I told the older man very firmly that I had no intention of marrying his son, but this only set him off further. His face reddened and his voice grew louder as he accused me of insulting Berny and humiliating the entire family by not submitting to the demand for a kiss and for turning down his . . . marriage proposal?

I was still in shock that any of this was happening, although as the guys were pretty inebriated, I suppose I shouldn't have been. As John was the oldest, the men felt awkward stepping in and it took a few minutes for them to break it up. All the while I'm thinking, *Uh-oh. What have I gotten myself into?* I struggled some more with John, who by now was completely out of control, until finally the other guys broke it up, realizing that I was physically not capable of holding my own. A couple of them calmed John down while I slipped out of the van, closed the doors, and climbed into the driver's seat. The incident had shaken me, but I knew it was essential that I keep my nerve and be strong. I was just glad I wasn't as drunk as the crew and able to get back behind the wheel to drive us the hell out of town. I'm amazed at how we managed those town outings after weeks on end of isolation in the bush. It was as though the safe place for us to be was out in the wild and town was the more dangerous.

I paused, exhaled deeply, then told everyone to settle down, and with my foot on the gas and hands firmly on the steering wheel, off we drove.

Berny, his father, and his older brother, John, couldn't have been more silent that day. Ordinarily, John Jr. was very accommodating and communicative with me. Now he wouldn't even make eye contact. In his judgment, I'd committed an unforgivable transgression by humiliating his baby brother as well as the family. That was just the way it was.

The rest of the crew was understanding, but from that moment on, the easy rapport I'd had with Berny, his brother, and his father vanished. Over the last weeks of the summer, the atmosphere was awkward and at times confrontational, as when I had to do my job as foreman and perhaps correct either Berny or John. This saddened me, because they were such decent people, and I'd admired them for their work ethic and sincere natures. I'd felt a bond with all of these men, despite my being the only woman in the crew. I'd worked hard to gain the respect of the men. Now I felt like I'd lost that with Berny and his family, and it hurt. I rejected one of them, and they were unforgiving about it.

It can be difficult for a teenage girl to read a man's sexual intentions, or to recognize when a man is about to cross a boundary with her, sometimes until she's already in a tight spot. The incident with Berny just happened out of the blue, but I suppose that since I was the only girl working with these men for several months at a time, alone in a remote area of the wilderness, it's not surprising that there was the potential for something to get out of control. Looking back now, I wonder why my parents weren't more concerned and watchful for my sake, but I suppose I gave off such an independent, "Don't worry about me" attitude, they just genuinely didn't worry.

But the brush with Berny ended up being less disturbing than another encounter with a man that year. Some months later, at home, I was taking an afternoon catnap on the living room couch. Nobody was home but me and my father. I was lying on my side, with my back toward the TV set. Suddenly I felt a man's hand cupping my right breast from behind.

In my grogginess, it took a few moments for it to register. Am I asleep? Then my eyes opened, and as I realized where I was, my dad pulled away. I wasn't quite sure what to do so I continued lying there for a minute or two, feeling very weirded out.

"Dad?" I called out meekly. "Dad? Do you need something?" trying to act as if nothing had happened. What if he was standing behind me? I froze and didn't want to move. A few more minutes passed. I tried his name one more time. Silence. He must have left. The living room floor had thick carpet, so he was able to tiptoe out as silently as he'd come in.

I consigned the incident to the back of my mind, just so that I could face him the next time we saw each other. I never said a word to him or to anyone else, figuring that no one would understand or believe that my father was capable of crossing such a sacred line with me.

# 10

## From High School to Hitting the Road

Since I'd had no choice but to follow my mother and siblings back to Timmins in order to finish high school, I spent grades eleven and twelve at TH&VS: Timmins High and Vocational School. It did have better music and drama classes, but I put in a halfhearted effort during my last two years of high school. I skipped a lot of classes, showing up regularly only for music period, gym, English, World Religions, and drama. It wasn't that I had no interest in learning, it's just that I was utterly consumed by music and bored with everything else. Most kids, when cutting class, ducked out of the building for a cigarette. Me, I'd blend in with whatever class of students was filing into the music room and barricade myself in the soundproof music-practice cubicles in the back of the class. Close the door tightly and you couldn't hear or see a thing from the outside, so I was free to sit there with my guitar and write and sing for as long as I wanted, unnoticed. The inside walls of these three-by-four cubicles were soundproofed with thick fabric and a layer of padding, just like you'd find in a recording studio.

I'd brought my acoustic guitar to leave in the classroom for this purpose, along with a small tape machine to record my writing. These cubicles were the perfect hiding place for a class-skipping teenage songwriter. They were a place you could go to isolate the sound and prevent driving everyone crazy with loud, bad notes.

This soundproof hideaway was my music refuge. I think it's possible I got more accomplished in the soundproofed cubicle than I ever would have in class. Much of my writing skills was honed here in my private place. To prevent getting caught, I'd keep an eye on the time and work it out just right to file out with the flow of students from the class at the end of the period or sometimes even stay for two periods. It was tricky when there wasn't a music class during the period I was skipping, though, as there was no student crowd to blend in with as I attempted to make a clean exit.

Occasionally, the music teacher spotted me, in which case I'd emerge from my inner sanctum brandishing a textbook and a ready-made pretext for being there. "Oh, hi! I left a book in the cubicle from earlier today. Well, gotta get to class! See ya!" He always let it go or let on that he was wise to my scheme. For the record, I also excelled at forging notes from my parents, as missing a class required a parent's or doctor's note explaining your absence. Since my parents weren't paying attention, no one ever questioned this, and I simply got away with it. Naughty me.

But I counted the days through those two years until I could finally make it back to the city of Toronto. I knew that if I was going to reach my long-term goal of becoming an adult professional in music, I would have to leave my hometown and head back to the city. Toronto was the obvious next step for me after high school, and at this point I'd already made the decision that while my other friends would carry on with their educations at college and university to prepare for their futures, my future was going to be in music, even though I really didn't know where it was going to lead.

In both grades eleven and twelve at Timmins High, I played second trumpet in the school orchestra. As part of a band exchange program, we were scheduled to perform at a high school in Ottawa. Each of us would stay with a local family of band kids from the exchange school for a few days leading up to the concert. Although I'd been to

Toronto several times, Ottawa was our capital city, and I was excited to be away from home exploring somewhere new. I got to stay with a nice family that was a notch above your average "roast beef family," with a bigger house and just more of everything. They were decidedly *not* dysfunctional: everyone was well mannered, everything was orderly, cooking aromas filled the air, and it was just . . . well, normal. The way I perceived a home should be.

Mr. Tony Ciccone, my grade-twelve music teacher, knew that I wrote my own songs and asked me if I would sing one of them at the concert, accompanying myself on guitar. Before I could stop myself, I said yes. Despite the fact that I'd been singing in public regularly since the age of eight, I was still self-conscious about performing and used to suffer terrible stage fright, torn between wanting to keep music as a private and personal experience, and feeling compelled to pursue it as a career. If I was surrounded by other musicians, I usually relaxed into it after a song or two. But the prospect of standing onstage all by myself scared the living shit out of me.

Sometimes I would get so stressed-out about having to perform that a day or two beforehand I'd develop a tight, sore throat. Now, my mother-manager wasn't about to cancel a gig due to nerves, so she would nurse me with what she called hot toddies: a cocktail of hot water, honey, and whiskey.

My inflamed throat would sometimes develop into full-blown bronchitis, and I was regularly on a cycle of antibiotics all through my primary years. My mother wasn't canceling anything, however, and hot toddies got me through. "Let's give a warm welcome to . . . Eileen Twain!" A nudge from my mother, and I'd walk onstage very stiffly, because the fact was that I was ready to pee my pants. And I don't mean figuratively. It was a perpetual nightmare trying to get from the wings of backstage to the microphone, my lower abdomen feeling like a knotted-up garden hose about to burst.

I was to be highlighted as a soloist during the Ottawa high school student exchange concert. I prepared something I'd written and accompanied my vocals with my acoustic guitar. I cringe at the thought of how awful that performance must have been considering I was such a weak guitarist, let alone the nerves in my voice. The most memorable part, however, was not the quality of it, but the sheer fear of the whole experience. After that performance, I was forever clear on why never to share my musical world with my peers. It was also the most glaring example of how pronounced my stage fright was.

As soon as our orchestra finished one of its classical pieces, I set down my trumpet and thought, *How did I get myself into this?* Time for my solo performance, in front of this huge high school, much bigger than ours. The emcee's booming voice—"Please welcome from TH&VS: Eileen Twain!"—startled me, and I swallowed hard as I got up from my chair. That's when I felt a warm stream running down the insides of my legs. Shit. I was used to stage nerves bringing me some close calls in the past, but this had never happened before. Now what?

I'd set a tall glass of water by my seat to wet my throat before singing. Thank goodness, I had the presence of mind to accidentally on purpose kick it over, so that I could yelp, "Damn! I spilled my water!" As far as the trumpet players on either side of me knew, the puddle pooling at my feet was nothing more than $H_2O$. Way to go, brain! Quick thinking!

In a second stroke of luck, we were wearing our band uniforms of gray bottoms, with skirts for girls. If I'd been wearing pants, there'd have been an obvious wet spot for the whole school to see, and I'd have bolted from the stage, mortified. Now that the burning in my bladder had been relieved, all I had to contend with was the anxiety from having to face all the pimply strangers sitting in front of me. I plunged into the song, doing my best to appear at ease, when in fact, my underwear, nylons, and even my shoes were soaked with pee. Much to my surprise, the audience was extremely appreciative, applauding loudly when I finished. I realized then that my stage fright stemmed totally from within and that my peers weren't as critical as I'd feared they might be. I just wanted to get the hell out of the spotlight all the same. I was proud I'd followed through with it, but filled with relief that it was over.

While still in high school, I joined a local rock band called Longshot. It was a big change for me musically, since up to now I'd performed mostly country and folk music professionally. Of course, I grew up singing soft rock and pop music around the house, but never in bars where I actually got paid. I've always loved country and learned about songwriting through the genius of many a country artist, but now I was free to explore other music, live.

Longshot consisted of me and four musicians: Rick Dion on guitar, Guy Martin on piano and vocals, Mike Mitchell on bass, and Mike Chabot on drums. They were all finished with high school, except for Rick, who was in his last year. We rehearsed at his house, which was practically around the corner from where my family lived on Montgomery. We were a cover band, performing the hits of the day—Pat Benatar, Journey, Foreigner—as well as some Beatles and other rock classics mixed in. Bar audiences weren't much interested in a local act's original material, if it even had any; people came to drink, dance, and have a good time listening to songs they knew, period. They wanted to hear the commercial Top 40.

After several weeks of practice in Rick's basement, we'd built up enough of a repertoire (consuming boxloads of pizza in the process) to invite club owners down to audition us. J. P. Aube, the owner of the most happening nightspot in Timmins, J.P.'s Lounge at the Escapade Hotel, was impressed and booked us to play Thursday, Friday, and Saturday nights. A steady gig!

The nights typically didn't end until one in the morning, so we amassed quite a lot of material. As a singer, I was enjoying the creative freedom of covering such a broad range of styles away from the usual country song list I'd stuck to for years. I was also finally starting to feel comfortable fronting the band, although it was a difficult adjustment to be up there when I first started leaving my beloved guitar behind. When you're clutching a guitar, even if you're not particularly playing it much, it functions as a shield between you and the audience. It's something to hide behind, and you don't have to think about what to do with your hands.

Without it, I felt completely awkward—maybe *naked* is a better word. I'd never been much of a dancer, and I was still somewhat self-conscious about displaying my body. You know, you're singing songs mostly about love and romance and longing, plus you've got this gale force of sound behind you, and you're losing yourself in the seductive rhythm. It's one thing to sway suggestively in front of a mirror in the privacy of your own room, and quite another when a whole club full of strangers is watching your every move. It took me a while to lose my inhibitions onstage, but I gradually became more comfortable in that role by mentally involving the audience and not isolating myself as the center focus. I developed the outlook of throwing a house party, where I was hosting but not alone. We were all having fun together, and this made me feel less in the spotlight.

I related best to female singers such as Pat Benatar and Ann Wilson from the band Heart, as they weren't dancer-singers. They weren't choreographed or staged, but they put the singing first, and their body language followed as a secondary, natural part of the performance.

June 1983 marked my graduation from high school. Given my spotty attendance during the year, it seems fitting that I didn't make it to either the graduation ceremony or the senior prom. Nope, I was out on the road with a new band called Flirt. I passed the exams but didn't attend the ceremony.

I'd heard Flirt at J.P.'s on a night when Longshot wasn't booked, and they sounded pretty good. Certainly they were much louder than we were, with their more sophisticated gear; they also boasted elaborate arrangements of songs such as "Africa" by Toto and "Wind Him Up" by a popular Ontario band called Saga. The lead singer, Diane Chase, was tall, blonde, and very pretty, much more so than me, and she could sing quite well, too.

On the eve of a regional tour, she suddenly quit the group. Flirt needed a replacement and fast. Its agent knew me as the lead singer of Longshot and asked if I'd be interested in filling the spot. Seeing as how I already knew many of Flirt's songs, I said yes. Twenty-four hours later, following an audition, I was in. We'd be leaving in two weeks.

Unbeknown to my parents, I asked my high school principal, Mr. Andrietta, if I could take my exams early, and he agreed. As for the prom, I wound up giving the white, lacy dress I'd bought with my savings to a girlfriend of mine. While she and the rest of the kids were dancing and drinking punch and presumably having a great time at the prom (I really wouldn't know for certain; after all, I wasn't there), I was off on the first road gig of my music career.

My whole life, music has been a passion rather than what I would describe as an ambition, and at the age of seventeen it was my passion for music that overpowered my desire to go to my prom and pretend to enjoy wearing a pretty dress for a night. Instead I was much more interested in joining a rock band and going on the road— the far less glamorous of the two and much more daring, but I felt no anticipation about prom night and was incredibly restless to get started, finally, as a full-time music professional. I was looking forward to singing over a big sound system and spending my time learning songs, parts, arrangements. I just wanted to be busy doing music.

My mother, long since used to granting me my independence, had no qualms about me being out on the road playing sweaty bars with a rock band or with me missing my prom. No, what upset her was that I'd be singing rock instead of country; whereas my father preferred it when I sang R&B. I was a free bird in that sense, balking at the idea of being caged by any one style of music. I liked good songs, regardless of what genre they were in. In particular, I was a sucker for ambiguous lyrics, since that would allow me to interpret the words however I wanted. If the song contained minor chords, so much the better, and vocal harmonies were always a big plus in my book.

Although I was Flirt's lead singer, I was not the bandleader. The song choices were pretty much set in stone before I'd joined, so on a musical level, the group wasn't all that fulfilling for me. But what a great experience to be independent and working professionally in music, even if that consisted of touring Ontario crowded together in the front bench seat of a small moving van, our amps, drum cases, and other equipment sliding around in back with every sharp curve. Nice bunch of guys, though, and it was a pleasant experience for me overall.

In August we played several weeks all the way on Canada's East Coast: New Brunswick, Prince Edward Island, Nova Scotia, and Newfoundland. Getting from Nova Scotia to Newfoundland required a thirteen-hour overnight ferry ride. I'd never seen such a large ship: the open vehicle ramp to the cargo bay reminded me of a giant whale's gaping jaws, and here we were driving right into its belly. I looked at all the cars, trucks, campers, and cargo containers parked around us and simply could not believe how much the ferry could swallow.

I was hoping we'd spot some real whales during the crossing, this being the first time I'd ever seen an ocean. In fact, I'd never traveled on a body of water so large that you couldn't see land in any direction. Nor had I ever been off the mainland before. As we pulled out of the port, I was so excited. I paused at every opportunity to listen to the exotic accents around me, which were sort of a musical cross between Irish and French Creole. I barely understood a word.

Being an inexperienced traveler, I made the mistake of assuming that Newfoundland and Northern Ontario shared the same climate. At home, August temperatures usually average around twenty-five to thirty degrees Celsius during the day. I packed accordingly, but it was much too cold for the shorts and T-shirts I'd brought along.

This hunk of metal was not a fancy boat. It was very much a transport vessel and not something you would take for any other reason other than to get from point A to point B. It was a grim gray color, with chunked and lumpy layer after layer of paint that had obviously been washed on over salt and rust. I'm glad I hadn't seen the movie *Titanic* yet, as I would have imagined that if a ritzy, expensive prize like the *Titanic* could sink, surely this mass of metal could without much trouble. Especially in iffy weather, which is what we were in.

The journey turned out to be safe, but it was not fun. We were only a couple of hours out to sea, and we had eleven to go. "Frigg," I moaned out loud. I was thinking like a four-year-old who asks repeatedly, "Are we there yet?" The other passengers started scuffling off the outer decks to go to sleep for the night, and I was ready to go, too. Only I wasn't sure where one was meant to sleep! There were no designated seats like on a Greyhound bus or an overnight train, just general tickets. "General" meant that you could spend your time anywhere on the upper or middle deck. The upper deck was an open-air free-for-all, but in the rain, it was not an option for me, and the middle deck, although covered by the upper deck above, was only half shielded with Plexiglas to keep out the elements.

I wasn't very savvy about thinking ahead and claiming my spot for the night, not knowing how the whole thing worked and figuring that surely there would be at least somewhere dry, if not a seat for every passenger on board for an overnight trip. Much to my dismay, this was not the case, and once I caught on to the fact that the more experienced ferry travelers had already staked their claims on all the dry spots on the boat, there was no room for me. The bow deck with no sides had room, but rain and sea mist were spraying in, although if you stayed in the center just a bit, you'd get damp but not soaked. I tried this for a while alongside a few other poor suckers who'd obviously also boarded with "I'm a Dumb Tourist!" written all over their faces.

I was so uncomfortable that I finally gave up and accepted that I'd have to just stand all night. I was feeling sorry for myself—cold, damp, tired, and pissed off. I felt I'd been tricked, not knowing what kind of ticket I'd bought, and if I'd known ahead that I'd have nowhere dry to at least sit, let alone sleep, I would have changed it. Of course, now I realize I probably had the ticket I had because that was all I could afford.

In the hopes of warming up a bit, I headed down a floor to the bathrooms, and I could see from a distance a line of women queuing up outside the ladies' room. What else is new? But there was a funky odor drifting up as I walked down the stairs, and soon it became clear that it was vomit I was smelling. I hated that smell! Now, I admit that's a pretty witless comment. I mean, who doesn't? What made it worse, though, was that I had no choice but to go down there at some point no matter how revolting the stench was, since eventually I would have the urge to pee, and I couldn't just walk up the street to find a cleaner public restroom. This was it!

Finally, I was so exhausted that I was ready to sleep *anywhere*. *Where was the rest of the band this whole time?* I wondered. I was the new one in the group so at this point we were pretty much still strangers, but I still felt a tinge of *Thanks for looking out for me, guys!* Having done the trip before themselves, knowing the every-man-for-himself routine, they most likely had the savvy to secure their spots for the night, while I was milling around looking for the best spot to take in the view.

The trip got better once we were back on land and I had the chance to encounter the friendly locals. Happy to be back on land, I wanted to explore some of the local beaches. I could just picture myself lounging on the warm, sandy, sunny shore, listening to the gently lapping ocean waves. However, this was the Atlantic Ocean off the eastern coast of Newfoundland, not Florida. Although the beaches were stunningly beautiful, they weren't at all what I'd expected: rocky, not sandy, with loud, crashing waves of inky black water. And, needless to say, cold. Nevertheless, I was determined to take my first swim in salt water, no matter how overly idealized my vision of the ocean had been. I squealed and screeched as I inched into the freezing, frothy water, but it was so ominously dark, and the undertow tugged me so insistently, that I was afraid to go in over my head. When the water reached my waist, I quickly submerged my whole body, then dashed out as fast as I could before hypothermia set in. I was used to subzero temperatures at home, but not swimming in icy water.

I turned eighteen during Flirt's East Coast leg, and it was as if my world was starting to expand exponentially. If I was back home for the summer, I'd be in the bush planting trees with my dad. He wasn't thrilled with me for missing the plant, and in phone conversations he sometimes intimated that I'd let him down.

I have to admit to carrying a little guilt along with me during that tour. Certainly, I worried about my family while I was away, since I wasn't just going off for a short period, then coming back. I had made the decision to start my own life and that made me feel selfish. As I didn't only feel I was leaving them, but that I was leaving them *behind*.

I felt especially anxious about my mother. Was she okay? What if she and my father were fighting? But then I'd tell myself that I was an adult now and needed the chance to follow my dreams and be out on my own. After all, my parents were adults; they were supposed to be capable of managing life and the family without me. Maybe I overestimated my family's need for me to carry so much responsibility, and perhaps they were perfectly fine without me there. But I had deep concerns that stemmed from the years of being under the Twain roof, and it was hard for me to let that anxiety go.

A few weeks into the tour, my father called me up, frantic. "Where are you?" he demanded gruffly, the implication being that I wasn't where I was supposed to be. I reminded him that I was on the road, performing. It turned out that my mom had suffered a miscarriage. She and my dad were asleep when he was awakened by something wet. When he peeled back the covers, he discovered my mother unconscious. Her blood soaked the sheets. He rushed her to the hospital.

My father scolded me for not being there and for the fact that he'd been unable to reach me during the night. Well, the accommodations we stayed in were pretty funky, with no one at the reception desk to man the phones after hours.

"Your mother could have died, you know, if I hadn't woken up when I did!" he said accusingly. Although I felt he was being unfair, part of me was pleased to hear him sound so shaken up by the prospect of losing her; it meant that he still loved my mother. Maybe this would serve as something of a wake-up call for him, reminding him how much he needed her.

Before we hung up, my father tried pressuring me to come home at once. "Family," he lectured, "is more important than being in some bar band." It seemed to me that I'd always shown how important family was to me. As I pointed out to him, my mother was in good care at the hospital and didn't really need me. Besides, I was something like 1,500 miles away; I couldn't just pick up and come right home. Overall, though, my father succeeded in making me feel extremely guilty.

Furthermore, I had an obligation to the guys in the band, who were always good to me, although I pretty much kept to myself. On Canada's East Coast, it was common for bands to stay in "band houses" paid for by the bars that featured live music. Act after act passed through. If the walls could talk? Personally, I wouldn't want to hear all the lurid tales of what probably went on there. Nonstop booze, sex, and drugs. Never mind what secrets the bedsheets could have divulged. *Ew.* I observed a few ground rules in these places: (1) never walk around barefoot; (2) always check to see that the sheets have been washed (although burning them probably would have been preferable); (3) shower with the plastic curtain pulled open so that it never comes in contact with my skin; and (4) put lots of towels on the floor so the soles of my feet never touch it.

One good thing about these band houses was that they had kitchens. After a while on the road, you can get real tired of eating in restaurants, so I relished the chance to cook for myself. I'd shop for groceries (and disinfectant), using my own money. I usually ate only one meal a day, around noon, as our nights typically didn't end until three in the morning, but what a meal: pancakes made from scratch, drenched in maple syrup and melted butter; a tall glass of milk, *al-*

*ways;* bacon, fried up crispy; two eggs, cooked in the bacon grease, done over easy; and toast for dipping in the yolk. And for dessert? A bowl of cereal, usually Honeycomb, Cap'n Crunch, or Froot Loops.

I was tiny, but, boy, was I stuffing myself like a pig. I loved these meals. The liberty of eating what I wanted, when I wanted, and however much I wanted was an experience of independence I'd never had before. As a vocalist, you don't want to eat just before it's time to perform, as it's hard to use your diaphragm properly if your tummy is full, taking up space you need to fill up with a good intake of air, so I'd usually skip dinner. I was so gorged anyway, it's little wonder that I didn't need anything else.

The guys in Flirt and I lived like roommates in these band houses. One day I needed to borrow a pen. I went out into the hall and, forgetting to knock, opened the door to one of the rooms and was about to ask "Does anyone have a pen I could borrow?" But I never got the first word out.

One of the guys was lying in bed with the covers pulled up to his neck, and there was a curious pumping motion going on around his groin area. Of course, I realized he was masturbating. Crimson with embarrassment, and hoping to God that he hadn't noticed me (he seemed to be pretty, um, engaged), I silently backed out of there, closed the door, and tiptoed back to my room, petrified that at any moment I would have one angry musician screaming in my face for having invaded his privacy.

I *knew* that men masturbated; stumbling upon him in the act just caught me off guard, that's all. However, I have to admit that I was a late bloomer—make that latecomer—to the concept of masturbation. Even though I'd been sexually active since the age of fifteen, I still didn't know that girls masturbated, too. I only discovered this a bit later when I was chatting with a girlfriend on the subject, as she was so open about it, and sex in general. I admitted to her that I was surprised she did it and that I didn't even know a girl could. She couldn't believe it and told me she'd been masturbating since she was thirteen. She was amazed that I was so new to this awareness, exclaiming, "Where have you been?!" I wasn't really sure. It had just never dawned on me.

I would still say that in most ways I grew up fast, the result of singing in bars from the time I was eight, as well as growing up in a harsh family environment that demanded uncommon maturity from me, and now, at eighteen, touring with a rock band. But in many other ways of the world, I was still naïve.

# 11

## On My Own

From the time I reluctantly moved back home from Toronto in 1981 at sixteen, I had told anyone who would listen that I intended to move back there once I was out of high school. And as soon as Flirt's East Coast leg was over at the end of summer 1983, I did exactly that. My father, having more or less accepted that his eighteen-year-old daughter was now an independent adult, and not moving back home, packed the contents of my bedroom in the back of a van and drove me to the big city. Toronto was the hub of the Canadian recording industry. If I was to achieve my long-term goal of making music for a living, this was where I needed to be. It's no different from the would-be starlet from Anytown, USA, getting off the bus in Hollywood, hoping to break into the movie business. Toronto is Canada's largest city, with the greater Toronto area having a population of 5.5 million. It's the fifth most populated municipality in all of North America.

Probably because I'd been around the bar scene so long, I harbored no illusions about how hard it would be to sing professionally full-time. Believe me, I'd seen many women performers in their thirties still playing dive bars, painfully aware that they had long since passed the point of becoming the next Tanya Tucker. I accepted the reality that the same fate might await me. Part of the reason that I was so restless to get on with this next phase of my life was to see if I could, in fact, support myself as a musical artist. One thing I knew for sure was that I had no intention of becoming marooned in clubs for the rest of my life. At some point, if things didn't pan out, I would quit to go do something else—although I hadn't decided exactly when and what that would be.

I shared a one-bedroom apartment with two girlfriends of mine who were starting college in Toronto: Laura, from Hanmer, and Michele, from Timmins. Having the company was great, as was getting to split the rent three ways.

Of course, in the music industry, there's no academic ladder you can climb. As for exams, I suppose you could say that every time you walked out onstage, an audience was grading you. The same was true if you recorded a demo tape of yourself and submitted it to a record company; if you received a recording contract, you passed. Then it would be up to radio station programmers, the still relatively new video channels such as MTV and CMT (Country Music Television), and a national or even international audience to determine whether you received your gold or platinum diploma in the form of millions of record sales. But pursuing a career in music is really unlike pursuing any other field.

So while my roommates were in class during the day, my college education took place in the living room of our tiny apartment. My professors consisted of a long list of artists from a variety of genres. To a great extent, an amateur performer is left to assess the quality of her own work and whether it fits in—or doesn't fit in—with what's going on musically at the time.

I spent hour upon hour alone with my guitar, tape recorder, records, and pen and paper. At eighteen, I didn't allow myself to worry too much about where this might take me; my sole focus was to get good. I would analyze how my singing and my songs measured up against my favorite artists. It was lonely and daunting, but not discouraging.

All these hours of self-motivated education reflects a theory I read of recently and believe has some validity. In his book *This Is Your Brain on Music*, Daniel J. Levitin, a cognitive psychologist and neuroscientist at McGill University, as well as a musician, explains that in order to be a world-class expert in anything, be it audiology, drama, music, art, gymnastics, whatever, one needs to have a minimum of 10,000 hours of practice. No one has yet found a case in which true world-class expertise was accomplished in less time. It seems that it takes the brain this long to assimilate all that it needs to know to achieve true mastery. He writes, "We find this with music all the time. Some people may have a biological or genetic head start in music. In fact, we know that people, and children in particular, may all start at different levels when they get interested in music, but without 10,000 hours of practice, they probably won't achieve world-class status, regardless of their innate ability. So on a pragmatic level, it takes about three hours a day over ten years to acquire 10,000 hours. So the time spent at the activity is indeed the most important and influential factor. Of course, this is consistent with what we know about how brains learn new tasks and skills. In other words, learning requires the assimilation and consolidation of knowledge within neural tissue. As the experience is repeated and enriched through practice and skill development, the stronger the memory and learning of that experience becomes."

Over the course of the first eighteen years of my life, I most certainly had spent at least 10,000 hours in concentrated time on my creative development in the way of music. So much so, that I spent much of my youth isolating myself.

Had I lived by myself at eighteen, I might have become a hermit. Fortunately, my roomies, while hardly party girls, were sociable and introduced me to their new, interesting friends from school. Among these was a flamboyant guy from Trinidad named Sheriff, who was attending college in Toronto with a small group of friends from his home country. My understanding was that he came from a well-to-do family that had set him up comfortably, even with his own car.

Sometimes on a Friday night, we'd go out to gay bars with Sheriff and his friends. They'd come over to our place first, and we'd all dress up and put on dark eyeliner—the guys included. Madonna had just hit it big, and everyone was copying her look. We'd dress like her, back-comb our hair until it was too big and all spiky, then head out on the town. This was an adventure for me, as it was all new. Gay bars had the best dance music and the most impressive dressers. Another benefit, from a young woman's perspective, was that you could dance with your friends without having to fend off guys trying to pick up chicks.

Being inexperienced at applying makeup, I marveled at how artistic and glamorous some of the men were. They looked so gorgeous, with features that had been defined and exaggerated with blushes, liners, shadows, and accessories. My fascination with this initial introduction to men transforming themselves into beautiful women likely sowed the seed of inspiration for a song I would write years later: "Man! I Feel Like a Woman!" Not everyone got all dolled up, and I saw men who did not seem identifiably gay at all. Most of the clubgoers, though, paid incredible attention to style and aesthetics from top to bottom, taking obvious pleasure in and having fun with fashion and flirting. Looking great was part of the entertainment, it seemed. I was personally more interested in dressing to dance rather than for style: comfortable shoes and clothes that I could move and sweat in, basically. Not being in a club as the performer was novel to me, so when I was there socializing with my friends, I was there to dance, not worry about how I looked.

We had great, innocent fun on these nights out to gay bars, and I can remember jamming the dance floor shoulder to shoulder, getting lost in songs like UB40's pop-reggae hit "Red Red Wine," Madonna's "Material Girl," "When Doves Cry" by Prince, and Culture Club's "Karma Chameleon." For me, alcohol wasn't necessary to get high on the magical sound of "Red Red Wine," especially because that particular record pumped through the club sound system so loud that you couldn't hear the person dancing next to you and because it resonated through me like a drug anyway. Afterward, my roommates and our Trinidadian friends hung out laughing and talking into the wee hours of the morning. They would regale us with stories and descriptions of their beautiful country, especially its annual winter Carnival festival. It all sounded so exotic, and people and places far away intrigued me. Toronto was a real teaser in that sense, with such an intoxicating mix of cultures from the huge influx of immigrants flooding into Canada. Our colleges and universities attracted young people from all over the world. As a small-town girl who'd seen precious little of the world, I thrived on this exposure and was lapping it up.

Unfortunately, my funds lasted only until the spring. Much to my father's delight, I returned to Timmins to work the entire tree-planting season, from May to October. I earned sufficient money to go back to the city with enough in the bank to last me through the winter. This time I roomed with yet another college student originally from Timmins, furnishing the place with my things and some throw-away furniture.

But just one month later, I came home one day to find her gone and her things cleaned out. No note, no explanation. How would I swing the rent on my own? What really pissed me off, though, was when the phone bill arrived a few weeks later with $300 in charges that she'd run up without telling me. I didn't know how I was going to make it financially, but no way was I going to go back to living with my parents and lose my independence.

It so happened that my apartment was a stone's throw from Ian Garrett's house, where I'd taken voice lessons seven years earlier. I asked him for help in finding work, preferably in singing. He couldn't do anything for me on that score, but once again, Ian made a deal: if I cleaned his house, he'd let me use his piano room. He'd even throw in some vocal lessons as well. As a songwriter, I was thrilled to compose on his grand piano: a real, black lacquer grand piano. It may have been a baby grand, but it was grand, that's for sure, with a big, round sound and brass foot pedals. The scale of the piano was hard for me to judge, as the room it was in wasn't very spacious, and it's possible that the piano seemed larger than it was considering its proportion to the size of the room. I especially loved pumping the pedals to create a lingering effect on the notes, allowing them to overlap one another. Although I don't know how to play per se, I've always been quite productive in plunking and tinkering my way around the keys to create melodies and chord progressions that were different from what I wrote when playing guitar. The piano set a fresh territory for me stylistically and definitely propelled my writing into a new direction. Guitar prompted more of a rhythm-based feel to my writing, whereas piano inspired less structure, and the melodies tended to meander and be more complex.

Money woes were a constant source of anxiety, however. I can recall sitting in Ian's piano room humming melodies while watching the activity on the street corner below. I noticed a trio of attractive young women dressed provocatively in miniskirts and tight pants, stiletto heels, and fur coats. They always seemed to be coming and going, getting into one car and being driven away, then returning to the same spot a short time later. This urban drama also starred a pair of male characters, who seemed to orchestrate everything on the stage before me. It was like watching a silent movie through a window. After a few days, I finally caught on: *these girls are prostitutes!* I felt sorry for them having to sell their bodies for pay. Then again, they probably made good money, I guessed. I never would have considered going that route, but I could understand the desperation that can drive people to do things that they wouldn't do otherwise. I was anxious about my ability to feed myself, but I slumped back over the keys and carried on with my music.

During this songwriting phase, I wasn't very productive in writing songs I can even remember today. It was more of a developmental period of toying around with ideas that just lingered in my creative subconscious until eventually they worked their way into real songs. For me, song ideas remain unidentifiable until they are eventually placed somewhere into a song format and under a title. Until then, they roll around in my head, like so many of the bits and pieces that came to me while sitting at Ian's grand piano.

For extra money, I resorted to taking odd jobs singing in bar bands that were sometimes contractually required to feature a female vocalist. As was usually the case, the repertoires reflected whatever was in the Top 40, which made it easy enough for me to wing it. The pay was feeble, and it was a creative and professional dead end, but it did help get me through the winter, so you heard not a word of complaint from me!

Correction: actually, I did benefit from the experience artistically in the sense that the pop and rock songs I was singing demanded a more dynamic stage performance, which had never been one of my strong suits. With practice, I got better at commanding the stage and interacting with the crowd—although I can't say it ever came naturally. I began to come out of my shell with more and more experience, but if I'd had the choice to sit with my back to the audience on the floor, my legs crossed, hovered over my guitar, and still get paid, or to earn a living remaining a backup singer or recording commercial jingles in the studio, I'd have taken that above having to face an audience to perform. Just like when I was a kid, I loved harmonizing with other singers and enjoyed the challenge of coming up with individual vocal parts that would blend together seamlessly. Believe it or not, I used to imagine myself happily sitting on a stool in some out-of-the-way coffeehouse, strumming my guitar and singing my own tunes while people chatted quietly and sipped their coffee. I may have ended up in the spotlight, but I actually *aspired* to be in the background, where I felt safer and more reassured. You see, I didn't enjoy music for the fact that it brought me attention; I enjoyed it because the music itself brought me pleasure. It took me somewhere else: in my own world within the real world. But as a female singer who was a very average guitarist, the only job I could get making money in music was to be in front as the lead singer. This forced me to be up front, center stage, if I intended to make a living in music.

Of course, that's not exactly the ideal attitude for becoming a "star." Stars are supposed to brim with confidence; they're bold, beautiful, and shameless. At least, that's what I thought it took to become a star. That certainly didn't describe me; nor did I want to become that person. Therefore, my career plan—if there is such a thing in music—was to succeed based on my songwriting and vocal talents, not on my performing ability.

In the end, neither studio work nor coffeehouses worked out for me. I didn't have the background in music theory to sight-read well enough to break into the exclusive network of studio regulars. Those singers were *fast*. Let's say that you walk into a session for a commercial jingle or to lay down backing vocals on a record. The sheet music is placed in front of you, you run through it a cappella one or two times, the engineer rolls the tape, you nail the part in one or two takes, and you're out the door. And bear in mind that this is for a piece of music that you've never heard before. I was too amateur as a studio singer to have a chance.

As for playing coffeehouses, I wasn't a good enough guitarist to cut it on my own. I thought about hiring an accompanist, but the gigs didn't pay enough to make it feasible financially. So I stuck to the night gigs on weekends. I would have preferred something during the day, because the subway ride back to my apartment at one or two o'clock in the morning made me nervous, being a young woman at night alone in a large city. Like any big city, Toronto had its share of crimes reported over the news, and being a small-town girl, I was leery of being out alone after dark.

I did reluctantly take jobs outside of music, which made me feel like a failure, because my goal was to be able to support myself as a musician. But I didn't have a choice. I was hired at the McDonald's across from the Toronto Eaton Centre shopping mall, right in the heart of the city. The biggest perk of working there was that you could eat for free, although only the food that had "timed out"—that is to say it was past the sell-by time and could no longer be sold. But for someone pinching pennies, I was grateful to be fed.

I took pride in doing a good job there, especially when it came to serving up McDonald's famous fries. (Historical note: this was when they were still fried in artery-clogging beef tallow, not today's vegetable oil.) Now, promise you won't laugh, but I was a stickler about how the fries were arranged in your scoop-shaped cardboard container. To the eighteen-year-old me, it was critical that they be presented exactly as they appeared in any McDonald's advertisement: standing as tall and straight as a platoon of soldiers, of a uniform height, and, for God's sake, no broken or squished ones! I learned how to position the scoop and angle my wrist in such a way while cupping the fries that they slid into position precisely, thereby achieving a photo-perfect serving every time. Obsessive? Maybe. But I was just trying to live up to the photo ad. I do tend to be like that with most things, just wanting to do my absolute best at whatever I do.

So went my life for the next three years: winters spent in Toronto, writing songs, working odd jobs, and taking sporadic bar gigs, followed by five-month stretches supervising tree-planting crews back in Northern Ontario with my family.

I still needed to share accommodations during the months in Toronto, as money was tight. Laura had just moved into a new place when our paths crossed again a year later. She was in a basement apartment of a large, old house where there was a small six-by-ten room filled with stored junk covered in webs and dust. The stuff piled in this space couldn't be very valuable, as it looked obviously forgotten. Laura said the owner never came down to the basement, so I asked her if she thought I'd be able to move this abandoned junk to another spot farther down the hall. My idea was to be her new roommate, pay her on the side, and we'd both be safer living together, as there had been a recent warning about a rapist in the immediate area.

I would move everything myself, clean the large "closet" of its layered insect habitat and grunge, cleaning nonstop almost the whole day. Then I bought a cheap can of white paint and painted the bricked walls to brighten it up because when it was empty, it looked like a prison cell. I found an end-cut carpet somewhere to cover up the cracked cement floor and was ready to move in. There was still the odd giant centipede zipping by and grossing me out, and there were lost spiders wondering where the hell their pad went. But this was my place now, and I wanted them to get lost after all the hours and sweat I'd put into making myself a home in this hole in the basement.

But somewhere between my brilliant plan and my move, Laura told me that her landlord came downstairs for some fluke reason and discovered our secret. She was furious and warned Laura that everything had to be moved back where it was, or else! I was not happy about this, as my paint went on those walls, my sweat cleaned and moved everything, and I felt like it was mine to use now. If anything, I figured she should be happy that the place had at least been cleaned and the junk stored safely, after all. I'm not sure why I felt this sense of entitlement to live somewhere secretly, without permission. It wasn't like me to help myself to something that didn't belong to me. Looking back, it's strange observing this about myself now, but I believe my immaturity allowed me to abandon logic. Not to excuse my behavior with youth, but my thinking was I needed to solve the problem of where to live, and my solution was to take it upon myself to create something out of nothing; and when I was criticized for it, I felt put out.

That spring of 1987, I took my annual sabbatical to help oversee my parents' tree-planting business. Based on what I observed of the state of their marriage, the tension between them seemed apparent.

We had a young, pretty girl with long, strawberry blonde hair who came around the camp regularly that summer, an employee of the Ontario Ministry of Natural Resources, whose job was to monitor the tree-planting operation on the ministry's behalf. My father made it pretty obvious that he noticed her. She was a university graduate, a nature lover, single, and way too friendly with him. I have no idea whether or not the two of them had an affair, but just the presence of this flirty bush flower was upsetting to my mother. Further complicating matters, my father insinuated to me one time that my mother had engaged in an inappropriate liaison with one of the crewmen. He didn't provide any details, and I didn't ask any questions. The way I figured it, he probably deserved it after having sent my mother into a jealous frenzy all summer over his flashy-haired hottie.

Shortly after the plant ended that season, I went back to Toronto to sing at a few corporate gigs that Mary Bailey organized for me. Mary Bailey was the professional name of Eveline Kasner, a dear family friend. We met a man by the name of John Kim Bell, an American, part Mohawk Indian, who'd recently relocated to Toronto from New York City. Not long after we met, Kim and I started dating and quite hastily moved in together to a house on Indian Grove, located right near beautiful High Park, the largest park in Toronto.

Kim was a talented orchestra conductor and serious classical pianist. He was several years my senior, so it was awkward taking him home to Timmins to meet my parents, who were only a few years older. My mom and my dad tried to talk me out of the relationship. "He's not for you," they insisted. When my father scornfully referred to Kim as an "apple," I didn't know what to say. That's a derogatory term used to describe someone who seems like an Indian on the outside but whose core is "white." It's the equivalent of calling an African American person an Oreo.

I argued with both my parents that night, defending Kim and my right to choose my own personal relationships without their criticism. Later, I would regret that this upset my parents, as it would not be long into the future that I would never see them again.

I woke up one morning in the Indian Grove house from a terrible dream, dazed and covered in sweat. It took me a few minutes to realize that it was just a dream, but nonetheless it shook me up enough that I had to step outside for some air. As much as I wanted the dream out of my head, I sat down on the front step and reviewed it, like rewinding a video.

In my dream, my mother had taken a taxi home from the grocery store with the car full of bags. There was a crash, and she was cut from head to toe, bleeding everywhere. She was dead when I saw her, yet she was alive in a strange and different dimension and still able to speak to me. She told me cryptically, "You have to take care of things." Then she was gone. Just dead and gone. For a few moments, I felt as if I was in shock and had a hard time accepting that it was just a dream. The images and conversation were so vivid and felt so real that I truly had that hollow feeling in the pit of my stomach that you get when grieving for something or someone. It was very upsetting and left me ill at ease for the rest of the day.

I've often experienced real emotions through the events in my dreams, as I'm sure many people do. It's such a relief when you discover that you were only dreaming, but it is wrenching to be forced to feel such deep and disturbing emotions through the events intense dreams can drag you through. You may not have *lived* the events in the dream, but the feelings are real, as this dream was for me.

Strangely enough, that same summer, my mother called me from a pay phone. "I need to see you," she said in a pinched voice. It turned out that she was calling from Toronto—just down the block, in fact. Once again she'd left my father. "Can I stay with you?" she asked, explaining that she had no clothes, no money, and no shelter. I was stunned and a bit surprised that she hadn't called before to tell me of her plans. I felt Kim's resentment toward my parents, that they did not accept him as a man with the heart of an Indian. This was my parents' perception of him, and I doubted very much he would take in my mother with open arms, considering her opinion that he was bad for me.

I felt terrible not being able to help her when she needed me. I suppose that was as good an indicator as any that this man couldn't be very good for me if I didn't even feel comfortable welcoming my own mother. But after all, it was his house, and under the current circumstances, the best I could do was to help her find a room in a boardinghouse up the street. It was dirt cheap and extremely spartan, but at least she was a stone's throw away and not in a shelter, for heaven's sake.

I pulled together some clothing from my closet for my mother, and then got on the phone to my father. "You need to send Mom her clothes," I told him. "And I think you owe it to her to send her some money, too. She's supported you all these years and has been a big part of the success of your tree-planting business." On and on I went, feeling like a mediator negotiating for my mother's rights.

He responded, "Whatever she left behind stays here. If she wants anything, she'll have to come and get it herself. Her home is here, and this is where she belongs." This possessive behavior was his way of saying that she was his: his wife, his life partner. That's what I sensed in his voice. A sad longing for her to come back home, back to him. He was dramatic about it, and I could detect an underlying, sincere pain in his voice.

The fact that I was supporting my mother by trying to at least get her some of her things until they worked something out between them made him feel as if I was taking sides, and this angered my father, only making him more stubborn and defensive. Then he blurted out something that almost made me drop the phone: according to him, she'd left him *for another man,* one of his own employees. "She can pay the price and suffer," he said, clearly hurt by the betrayal. As far as he was concerned, she was on her own.

After hanging up with him, I confronted my mother. "What the hell happened?" I asked. Although my father had exhibited some jealousy over the years, there had never been any evidence to support it. I was in shock. My mom told me that she and my dad had grown distant, and that she'd fallen in love with one of the guys from the tree plant. Through sobs, she explained how this man had planned to join her in Toronto. But he never called, and never would. She was humiliated and heartbroken, too, as I really think she fell for this guy. He obviously got cold feet. My guess was that my father had likely put a scare into him—the Native tree-planting world was small—causing the man to reconsider hooking up with the boss's wife.

I felt sorry for my mother—my father, too, for that matter—but at the same time, I didn't like being caught in the middle of this awkward dance. For once, I wanted the two of them to grow up and just get it over with, one way or another. I was tired of playing referee to the people who were supposed to be my caretakers in life, not the other way around. As much as I loved them and felt selfish for feeling impatient with their behavior, I had resolved that I would not be pulled back into their dysfunction.

In a familiar pattern, after several weeks of separation, my mom went back to my father. It became increasingly evident to me that her courage to start life over again on her own was weakening. Her lover-slash-boyfriend had abandoned her, my father refused to help her unless she came home, and there was also the matter of two adolescent boys still at home. When she left for Timmins in the fall, I hurt for her, but at the same time, I was relieved to be free of the relationship complications between my parents.

As I said before, I'd been on the periphery of the music business long enough to understand I was in for an uphill climb. I was now twenty-two years old. While other people my age were graduating from college and moving closer to their professional goals in life, music was the only thing I knew how to do. It was time to figure out my plan B. I decided to take an introductory course in data entry at a community college five mornings a week. This was back when computer monitor screens were still black with green characters. Imagine! Several of the other students were immigrants whose English was so poor that the instructor asked me if I'd help a couple of the other girls along. One was from Ghana, the other from Ethiopia. Communicating with one another wasn't easy, but we managed, and besides, I was intrigued hearing about what it was like to live in another part of the world. I enjoyed exchanges with people from faraway places, and it was far more interesting to chat with them than learning how to use F6, highlight, underline, and cut and paste text.

Much as I felt the necessity to have a backup plan by learning functional skills such as computer keyboarding or data entry in case my singing career didn't pan out, my attention to practicality did not mean that I was giving up my dream at all. I wanted to be able to pay my own way and not depend on anyone to take care of me. I didn't want kids early in life, I had no intention of being supported by a man or living on welfare, nor did I have any desire to work menial jobs and live hand to mouth for the rest of my life. Not only did I want to be monetarily comfortable, I was driven to earn it myself. I'm not sure if this fierce desire to be independent came from believing that there was no such thing as being able to rely on anyone else. I suppose that was part of what I'd learned to accept as reality, and the other part was based on my father Jerry's consistent example to not look for the handout, the sheer principle that unless you earn what you have, having it doesn't hold the same pleasure of reward or accomplishment. For me, this was where the motivation to strive to better myself came from.

# 12

## Together Forever

November 1, 1987. It's a quiet Sunday evening at home with my boyfriend, Kim, when the phone rings. I can tell by his tone that it's for me, so I step up to take the receiver from him, only he doesn't hand it to me. He gets very serious and signals for me to sit down. I feel worry straightaway, as I sense it's someone I know and that the call is for me, and I don't understand why he isn't just passing the phone.

I try to interrupt him a couple of times, asking, "Who is it? What's going on?" but he's concentrating hard on what's being said, as if straining to comprehend what the person is saying. I'm getting upset and can't sit still, anxious to know what's happening, as I can feel something's wrong. I'm restless and beginning to pace as I wait for him to respond to my anxious string of questions.

At last Kim hangs up the phone and reaches for my hands, and we sit down on the sofa, facing each other. I'm bursting at this point with a rush of anxiety over what I want to know but realize I'm not going to be able to handle. I can feel it coming on, and I just know it's going to be bad.

Kim began to tell me very quietly but clearly that my parents had been in a terrible car accident. I jumped in with total panic. "Are they okay? What's happening? Tell me!" This must have been incredibly difficult for him, to have to deliver such devastating news and answer my panicked questioning. He began to explain, but with several interruptions from me, Kim couldn't get it out fast enough for my racing thoughts. My mind was spinning, and I needed him to hurry up and tell me what I didn't want to hear but had to know. I was a wreck waiting for news I deeply sensed was going to shock me. I probably could have guessed just from the somber sound of his voice and the strain in his eyes that the worst thing possible had happened.

When he finally said, "They were killed," it was as if something burst inside of me, like an emotional explosion. I'm not sure how I appeared on the outside, but on the inside, I was erupting. My insides were rushing to empty out. Pain, rage, fear, confusion, and a crushing sadness deflated me as I sat there feeling it all drain from me. I remember very little from that moment on, but I was faintly aware of pounding Kim's chest with my hands, shrieking that this could not be true. My mind was going to resist reality for as long as it could. Surely he would tell me that this was nothing more than a cruel joke, but he didn't because it wasn't.

I have no idea how long it took me to settle down enough to speak coherently. *My brothers. My sisters.* I needed to hear their voices, to know more. I managed to find my breath long enough to call my parents' house on Montgomery Avenue, where Jill and Carrie were together. They passed the phone back and forth between them with me on the line as they tried to fill in whatever information they could. But we were all in shock and hysterical, as the conversation lurched back and forth, punctuated by wails and sobs.

Suddenly they whispered, "Darryl just walked in the door. He doesn't know yet." Poor Darryl, who had already lost his mother to suicide when he was just a baby. Seconds later, the most agonizing wail you can imagine pierced through me, the kind of haunting, wounded cry that rips your heart out and, though wordless, expresses utter despair. As I heard his cries, I couldn't help but feel that the world was an awful place, that God couldn't possibly exist, that compassion and goodness were gone forever.

Sitting four hundred miles away, with just a telephone receiver in my hand, I had never felt more helpless or alone. My desperation to be with my family at that moment and knowing I couldn't be overwhelmed me. I was grieving from a place so deep within that I could not bear it, crying inconsolably, like an abandoned baby. I did not know that it was humanly possible to hurt so viscerally and feel so empty.

Reflections of that night after the call to my sisters exist for me only in flashes: There I am in the Toronto, Indian Grove, house, sitting at the kitchen table—*How did I get from the living room to the kitchen?*—with the lovely girl from the apartment upstairs gently rubbing my back in large circles, encouraging me to drink the tea she had made me. But I just keep sobbing, lost in a haze of shock and disbelief.

Next I'm in the backseat of Kim's car, hurtling through the night to Timmins. My friend and ex-roomie Michele sits up front with Kim so I might get some sleep across the backseat, but the minute I close my eyes, anxiety's hands start choking me until I cannot breathe. Too terrified to be alone, I climb into the front seat.

The days back home in Timmins for the funeral are a blur, although I do remember placing a copy of one of my demo tapes in my mother's coffin, so that she'd have my music with her wherever she was going. Oddly enough, calmness enveloped me once I viewed my parents in their caskets at the funeral home before the service. The coroner's report noted that my mother died instantly from the impact of her forehead striking the dashboard. But other than a sizable lump and a gash, which had been partly covered with makeup, she bore no visible signs of having been in a fatal car accident. It came as some solace to know that at least she had not suffered.

My father's injuries, too, were not apparent. According to the coroner's report, he had suffered massive internal damage because of the steering column crushing his chest. The force from the collision had pushed in the vehicle's front end on the driver's side like an accordion, so that the steering wheel was left almost touching the back of the seat. Unlike my mother, though, he was still alive when the ambulance arrived and calling out for help. The medics rushed my father and two other injured passengers, both Native North American can employees of my parents' reforestation company, to the hospital. It has always upset me that they decided to leave my mother behind. I understand their reasoning—she'd been declared dead at the scene, and the ambulance was already at capacity—but the image of her being left there alone in the bush, hunched over the dashboard, bleeding and lifeless, haunted me for a long time.

The details of the accident tortured me over and over again, as if the horror scene were stuck on repeat and I couldn't find the remote to turn it off. It took quite a while before I finally found the off button, although the graphic images still flash in front of me from time to time, and the scene plays itself out as well.

My father died from internal injuries while on the way to the hospital. Apparently one of the injured workers regained consciousness long enough to ask, "Where's the boy?" I can just imagine the medics wondering, *What boy?* "The boy," he repeated. The fourteen-year-old son in the backseat. The medics promptly turned right around and raced back to the accident site. By now the sun was dipping below the horizon, and it took a while before they came upon Mark lying unconscious, quite a distance from the demolished vehicle. Upon impact, my brother had been thrown through the windshield of my father's truck, landing out of sight, well off the side of the road. His injuries were not fatal, but if they hadn't hurried back for him when they did, the bleeding and cold November air would have compromised his chances of survival. We were told that he was lucky.

Whatever peacefulness I felt in my parents' presence at the funeral home might have been numbness more than anything else—and possibly some lingering denial—but I felt as though they were still with us, though in a different state. The permanence of their separation from us hadn't sunk in. Not to be morbid, but I can remember thinking to myself very matter-of-factly, *Why can't we just preserve them somehow and take them home?* I actually imagined setting up their caskets in the living room so that they could remain with us in this state of permanent sleep. It seems strange to me now, but at the time, I was absolutely serious. It had all happened too fast, and I just was not ready to accept the finality of losing them forever.

Together we kids discussed what to have engraved on our parents' tombstone. It's surreal sitting around making a decision like this. How do you encapsulate the lives of two people and what they meant to you in just a few words? Even more challenging: how do you refer to two people who died together but barely lived their lives together without killing each other?

From the time I was little, I'd always worried that my father would someday kill my mother during one of their violent struggles, or that my mother would actually live out her contemplations about killing my father as the only way she felt she could escape their destructive relationship. I never took her seriously, never thought she would ever *really* kill him, but it was twisted, I thought, that she would go into detail about what method would work best. I warned her that if she ever killed him, it would be considered murder, and she would go to jail for life. I reminded her that we'd lose her forever. I recall genuinely feeling that fear, even though the intention of telling her that was more to calm her down and shake her back to reality. It was all crazy thinking, in my childhood point of view, and I tried to talk her out of thoughts that scared me and that I believed she was saying out of desperation, not sincerity, and that she wasn't actually capable of it anyway.

So I couldn't help but be struck by the irony that they had died together in the end as the result of a car accident. It was as if, despite everything, they had been destined to be together for eternity. So "Together Forever" were the words we chose to have engraved on their headstones.

After the funeral, I thought back to something my mother had told me only months before, when she was living near me in Toronto after having left my father yet again.

We were having one of our woman-to-woman talks, which I'd found so heartwarming, because it was as if our relationship was entering a new, richer dimension. We were laughing about something when suddenly my mom turned quiet.

"I have to tell you something," she said hesitantly. I wasn't at all prepared for what she was about to reveal.

Apparently, my mother had visited a fortune-teller/palm reader recently. "While reading my palm, the woman said that my husband would die this November, then suddenly told me that she could not finish my reading and closed my hand," said my mother. Neither she nor I read anything too deep into this at the time, although we both thought it was peculiar and a bit creepy. My mother believed in fortune-tellers enough to go to one in the first place and she was uncomfortable that the woman had so abruptly stopped the reading, as though alarmed. I brushed it off for both our sakes, in an attempt to dampen any worry by saying, "Ah, superstition, that's all this stuff is about. It's really nothing to take seriously, Mom." You can imagine my feelings when I reflected back on this after the accident, as exactly what the palm reader had foreseen had happened. My father did die that November, on the first. What the fortune-teller could not bring herself to say out loud was that my mother was fated to die along with my father. It was incredible to me that this palm reader could be right, that she must have been for real. I was impressed by the reality that the phenomenon of clairvoyance really existed. This lady did see something that freaked her out, causing her to not finish reading my mother's palm. Today, rather than being impressed with this skill, I'm more wary of its reality, and personally prefer not to know my future, the future of the ones I love, or even of the world I live in or of mankind. That doesn't mean I am passive regarding the welfare of others or my role as a citizen of the world, but I believe that ultimately our Creator has it all planned out perfectly, whether I agree with the plan or not. Regardless whether I'm aware of what that plan is, it is not for me to alter it in any way, and I would therefore not want to experience unnecessary suffering and anxiety over potentially devastating information I cannot change. *Why do that to yourself if you genuinely have faith in God's ability to manage what He created?* is my thinking.

In the weeks after our parents' burial, I remained in Timmins with my siblings to help with the family responsibilities and my parents' personal and professional affairs, which were beginning to build up with each passing day.

Kim returned to the house on Indian Grove after the funeral, and as it soon turned out, I would not be joining him anytime soon. One day, feeling overwhelmed by everything I had to deal with, I called Kim seeking a little moral support.

"Why are you calling me?" he asked icily.

Huh?

Then he simply told me never to call him again. The end.

His ruthlessness and, frankly, his timing blindsided me. I was so mired in grief and wrung out emotionally that all I could manage was a meek "Okay." Under ordinary circumstances, I would have felt humiliated—and probably irate at being treated so shabbily. But now I had heavier burdens to bear than a bruised ego.

Jill was the oldest sibling, but she was engaged to be married and had moved out of town. Being the oldest left in the house, I assumed the role of handling the grim details of my parents' estate. They had left no will. The most pressing issues facing us were establishing guardianship of Mark and Darryl, the business affairs of Sharont Enterprises (the name of my parents' company: "Sharon" plus the *t* for the first letter in "Twain"), and paying personal and corporate taxes. There was also the distressing matter of having to sit and review with attorneys the coroner's reports and details of the accident, because, technically, it was my father's fault. *That* was a hard reality to process.

My father was driving a Chevy Suburban truck, a forerunner of the sport-utility vehicle. It had front and backseats and a covered storage area as big as that of a pickup truck. In all, a large, heavy

vehicle, with room for nine plus gear. He and my mother were trans-
porting two of their men along the Trans-Canada Highway to a town
called Wawa, about 170 miles west of Timmins. The men were to
meet a helicopter there and bring food supplies to the bush camp.

About two-thirds of the way en route to the helicopter site near
the town of Chapleau, my father was driving along a winding gravel
road, into the sun, which was low in the sky. As best as the police
could determine, the glare most likely blinded him just as he came
up over a slight ridge. He saw the oncoming transport, but too late.
It's probable that he overreacted and braked abruptly, which sent the
Suburban skidding head-on into the other vehicle. Brake marks in
the gravel determined that he did in fact see the transport and reacted, but it's very difficult to stop abruptly on a gravel surface, which
is slippery like ice.

The concept of the cycle of life and death, and the realization of
how my parents were a part of it, resonated through me with a deaf-
ening ring, like the sound of crashing metal, I imagined, that echoed
through the bush when the two vehicles collided. It rattled me to
consider that while they were still alive that summer and fall, my
parents were replacing the very trees that would soon be loaded and
transported by a truck they crashed into only weeks later. *Out with
the old, in with the new,* I thought, was life's cruel way of cycling and
recycling. They planted new life to replace the old trees that would
kill them. It was a twisted way of thinking, but my mind was in an
unusual state of confusion. I didn't know whether to be angry or sad,
who to blame, if there was, in fact, anyone to blame, and I had no answers to anything other than the police report stating that my father
was technically at fault.

I don't remember how it came about, or even what the gentleman's name was, but there was a lawyer representing my parents' case
regarding the accident, and the estate and legal matters associated
with my parents. I asked the lawyer to explain how the accident could
have been my father's fault. Naturally, I was defensive and wanted to
be able to blame it on the transport driver, who survived, as his ve-

hicle was bigger and tons heavier than my father's, and, considering the sheer size of it, it was no wonder the collision killed my parents. The notion that my father had been responsible, on top of everything else, was just too much to bear. But as the attorney explained, although he didn't exceed the speed limit, my father would have been expected to be driving at a speed appropriate for the slippery road conditions. Further irony: had he just continued driving and not applied the brake, the two vehicles would have passed each other harmlessly like ships in the night, as there was ample room between them. Braking or not braking is all that determined whether my mom and my dad stayed alive.

For me, being just twenty-two, it was hard to take: sitting in an office, surrounded by total strangers, and having to relive my parents' final moments, which had been reduced to several paragraphs and black-and-white diagrams. But it was necessary for an immediate family member to know and understand the circumstances as part of the procedure regarding the various insurance issues at hand. I had to sign that I understood what had been explained to me and that I accepted the accident report to be true. I wished I could deny it all, but there it was, right in front of me. I signed my name.

It was explained to me that my father's being at fault meant that his estate would most likely be sued by the insurance companies representing the two employees and the transport driver. The company that owned the truck would no doubt sue as well for damages. I couldn't help but think to myself, *Who cares about the other vehicle? My parents are dead, and you guys are worried about a few thousand dollars' damage to your truck? Your driver is alive; what more do you want? Hasn't the Twain family paid enough, with two lives?* I was really torn, because, on the other hand, I freely if painfully acknowledged that my father *had* been at fault. Which made me angry at him! But how could I be angry with my own father, when his simple error, which anyone could have made just as easily under the same circumstances, had cost him his own life?

To this day, I am still not sure how I found the strength to go through all of this. My mind was overloaded with information I could not compute, leaving me feeling vulnerable, lost, and very sorry for myself. At one point, the lawyer started discussing my parents' mortgage on the family house, and I actually had to ask him what a mortgage was! I had no clue about banking, loans, credit, debt—any of that. My knowledge of personal finances consisted of depositing cash in the bank and withdrawing cash from the bank. That was it. Now I was having to make decisions about how to liquidate my parents' business assets, what to do with Sharont's current contracts with the Ontario Ministry of Natural Resources, and so on. I would walk out of these meetings mentally and physically exhausted and ready to run away from it all. In fact, I came seriously close to doing just that, I was feeling so suffocated by all the legal and business affairs and weighed down with too much responsibility and decision making.

My mother's brother, Uncle Don, told me during the initial period after my parents' passing that he'd promised my grandmother Eileen on her dying bed to be there for us kids after she was gone. He reminded me that he was there if we needed anything, and I should have taken him up on that after my parents died. I was lost in a world of legal protocol and jargon that I knew nothing about, but I didn't feel right about burdening anyone else with our problems. I needed help but didn't know how to accept it. There really wasn't anyone else I felt I could turn to, as it was my parents whom most of our other relatives depended on. So I got through this legal affairs aftermath alone, but not without being overwhelmed and feeling the urge to flee at certain moments.

I'd heard of student groups going on missions to third-world countries. In my youthful idealism and naïveté, I figured that volunteering to do relief work in a crisis region of the world would not only take me far away from all my pain and suffering, but would put me among people in much deeper despair than I was, so that, by comparison, I'd realize how lucky I was just to be alive.

I visualized a lone child lost, dazed, and sitting by herself in the middle of a fly-pit dust bowl with her entire family dead and no relatives to help her, her fate sealed with no help no matter how hard she cried out for it. No one was coming. This was who I felt I needed to be with to help put things in a different perspective: a child whose suffering was so unimaginable, I'd actually consider myself lucky that I had lost "only" my parents and not my whole family, like this poor girl.

I imagined my only responsibilities on this mission would be carrying supplies, aiding nurses, hauling water, feeding babies, cooking meals, and living in possibly uncomfortable but manageable conditions while fulfilling helpful but functional duties that took no education or expertise. These were all things I could do, things I could manage without pressure. Understanding my parents' estate, how it functioned, and how it would have to be dealt with over the months to come, handling their taxes, resolving the insurance issues, inheritance details—it was all too much. My role in the "no will" process of settling my parents' affairs took many stressful and painful months to resolve. Advice to any adults out there with children: write a will so that your children never have to go through this logistical nightmare should you die unexpectedly. You will save your loved ones a lot of anguish.

In this state of mind, I was on the phone one day with a dear family friend by the name of Eveline Kasner. She, too, was a singer, known professionally as Mary Bailey. Mary was my mother's age, and they'd become friends after having crossed paths backstage from time to time during the various shows we played together. My mom and Mary stayed in touch by phone over the years, sharing music industry stories and discussing how best to nurture my career. Mary could relate because she had been there, and my mother was, well, my mother, obsessed and passionate about her dream of her little girl making it. I got to know Mary in a more personal way after my mother died; in some respects, she became like a surrogate mother to me.

I was telling her over the phone, as Mary lived more than an hour's drive from Timmins, how overwhelming everything felt and that I was considering flying to Africa as part of some humanitarian aid mission. I knew that I could not just abandon my younger siblings at this difficult time, but I was so beaten down that I questioned how much good I could do for them. I mean, I didn't even know what a freaking mortgage was! Plus, I was no less in need of comfort and support than anyone else.

I remember saying to Mary, "What good can I be to them anyway, when the only professional thing I know how to do is in music? And I'm still at the bottom of the box in the big, bad world of the entertainment industry." The most pressing concern at the moment was how to provide for me, Carrie, Mark, and Darryl, because no life insurance money had been released to us yet, and it was caught up in a lengthy logistical process, so it wouldn't be for a while. What was I to do in the meantime? The idea of having to support an instant family was terrifying. My younger sister worked full-time and was very independent with regard to her own personal needs, but what about keeping up the mortgage of the family home we were all living in and covering the daily living needs of two adolescent boys, let alone electricity, heat, and phone bills?

I had no formal education and could not imagine singing in a local bar in Timmins to make my living for the next several years until Mark and Darryl were grown. That was just too depressing a thought. Not only would it derail my hopes of having a career in music, but also it wouldn't even come close to meeting the bills. The only way I could make a decent living singing would be to travel in a band. Except how could I care for my family with two minors if I was on the road all the time? The remaining options were unacceptable to me: seeing my brothers taken separately by relatives—which was a possibility but by no means a sure thing—or, if no one could or would take them, placing them in foster care.

I could not imagine the boys being separated. They were crushed by the loss of our parents, and it would have been cruel to have taken them from each other. In fact, I believed strongly that all four of us staying together was the most emotionally supportive choice for everyone. I was barely old enough to qualify for becoming Mark's and

Darryl's guardian, but I felt naturally obligated to step into that role. I was convinced that we needed to stick together, and I felt they were counting on me for this.

So, I rambled on to Mary, either I would commit myself to assuming the family responsibilities or run away to Africa. Whatever I decided, however, I would have to quit music. When you're twenty-two and have just lost your parents, logic becomes a relative concept.

Mary listened quietly to this young woman she'd known from childhood unraveling. When I finished talking, she kindly but firmly encouraged me not to quit music—and certainly not to run away. As I said, just as I'd had the role of protector thrust on me, Mary willingly found herself playing surrogate mother to me, and as so often happens between mothers and daughters, I didn't regard her advice seriously at first, because how could she possibly understand the enormous pressure I was under? She did, of course. I gradually began to put more stock in what she had to say regarding my future and that of my siblings.

One day Mary called to tell me of a golf resort called Deerhurst that she had just been to, located about an hour and a half north of Toronto, on the outskirts of a town called Huntsville. "They have a Vegas-style production they run there featuring various styles of singers and performers," she explained with a bit of a sparkle in her voice. "Before you go ahead and quit music, please promise me you'll go there with me to see what it's all about, okay? Then you can make up your mind." I wasn't sure how this prospect solved anything, given that it was so far away. Not only did I feel it was essential that my brothers remain together, they needed to continue to live in their home, amid familiar surroundings. So even if there was a job for me at this Deerhurst place, how could I possibly accept it?

Mary has an infectious positivity to her personality, so although I was feeling entirely discouraged about knowing what decisions to make next, Mary motivated me to at least consider checking out Deerhurst. So with a bit of gentle coaxing, I agreed, albeit reluctantly.

# 13

## Wind Beneath My Wings

It took a while to make up my mind, but in May, just as the snow was melting, Mary picked me up and drove me to Huntsville. I had never heard of the town, but as we drove south along Highway 11, I realized I'd passed it many times on my way back and forth between Timmins and Toronto.

Several kilometers past Huntsville, a winding road took us around countless bends and up and down a few hills before depositing us at a golf resort overlooking tiny Penn Lake. Deerhurst was not nearly as developed as it is today. The centerpiece of the complex was a charmingly rustic main lodge (which is still there but modified), set amid rolling acres of greenery. The stage featuring the resort's musical production *Viva Vegas* was in the lodge showroom, which at the time was the property's original, main reception building. Quite a few condominiums surrounded the main lodge, though only a third of what is there now. I was impressed with the place—my perception of the resort was that it was an exclusive rich man's retreat. Way out of my price range, that was for sure.

Mary and I met with Brian Ayers, the producer of *Viva Vegas*, which ran there six nights a week. Brian was tall, soft-spoken, and friendly, and he explained a little bit about the small production and suggested that I stay to watch it that night to see if I felt it would be the right fit for me, and vice versa. He also gave me an impromptu audition in the piano lounge. I was nervous, to tell you the truth, but

I must have acquitted myself well, because after just a few songs, Brian offered me a role as a lead singer in the main show. I was flattered but didn't really know what this meant. I had never been in a produced stage show before.

The *Viva Vegas* production had me squirming in my seat and sweating at the prospect of becoming a cast member. It bore little resemblance to rock or country bar stage setups and was patterned after the type of show most commonly seen on the Vegas strip, or a mini version of Le Moulin Rouge, with topless dancers in rhinestone bikini-type costumes and fishnet stockings. (Only this was Canada, and topless dancers were restricted to performing exclusively in licensed strip clubs.) A six-piece band that included a small horn section backed two lead singers: a handsome gentleman in his fifties named Sam, who looked years younger than his age, and a tall, wiry-haired woman with a wide smile. I'll call her Sheila.

Sam was a great entertainer and sang beautifully. I always enjoyed watching him perform. He was very cool and charming onstage—an old crooner type, in the manner of Dean Martin, with a voice incredibly similar to Johnny Mathis's. A second man, Frankie Vogol, served as the show's emcee. Also a very smooth and fluid entertainer; you knew right away that he had been doing this for years.

Sheila, with big, lashy eyes and a round, pretty face, was also very talented. Her voice had a lot of power and range; she was a fine comedienne and a reasonably good dancer. She projected confidence with a dynamic stage presence. It was intimidating for me to imagine that I was going to share the stage with such an all-rounder. She reminded me of one of those versatile entertainers who'd just walked out of a performing-arts academy à la the movie *Fame*. In fact, all the younger members of the cast gave me that impression. In contrast, my musical education consisted mainly of learning as I was earning, singing in bars, community centers, old-age homes—pretty much anyplace that would have me. My only formal training, with Ian Garrett, amounted to but a fraction of what these performers obviously had under their belts.

I explained to Brian that the only way I could take the gig was if the pay supported my family's needs. If I was going to leave our family home in Timmins, I would have heavy monthly rent, as with my younger sister, two teenage boys, and a dog, we would need a house. Brian, sensitive to the situation with my family, offered me a generous salary that would enable me to afford a decent rental while still meeting the expenses back home. Although the style of performing required of me was *totally* outside my comfort zone, and taking this job would mean relocating my family at a fragile time in our lives, I took a deep breath and signed the contract. It was a big decision to make, as I was taking the responsibility of moving my family and imposing change on everyone due to my limited access to work and ability to provide. I felt trapped by the lack of options and was nervous about plunging into so many unknowns. The world felt too big for me at that moment. Every step felt gigantic, like I had to stretch beyond my reach to get from one footing to the next.

My contract required me to perform as a lead singer in the main production six nights a week and, afterward, entertain in the piano lounge or the Four Winds dance bar. Some nights I appeared in all three. I enjoyed the variety, since each venue called for a different genre of music. Over the few show seasons I spent at Deerhurst, a typical night's performance would take me through numbers like the Village People's "YMCA," the Supremes' "Stop! In the Name of Love," a solo ballad like "Somewhere over the Rainbow," the old French song "La Vie en Rose," written and sung by the great Edith Piaf, then perhaps a Latin medley—whatever the show's producers suggested for me.

The Four Winds featured whatever was popular on Top 40 radio, which I preferred, along with the same musicians and a few of the dancers. I especially liked working the piano bar, which was called the Cypress Lounge, probably because it came closest to my earlier desire to play in the more intimate setting of coffeehouses after years of loud, smoke-filled bars. Instead of slinking around a stage in some curve-hugging costume, I sat demurely on a stool, accompanied by a guitarist or a piano player, and sang material like Roberta Flack's "Killing Me Softly with His Song" and Rita Coolidge's "We're All Alone," along with a list of yesterday's and today's Top 40. Great atmosphere in that lounge, I thought: the patrons actually listened appreciatively some of the time.

The main show was a different story. Up until this point, I had worn mostly comfortable outfits designed for moving freely and wore either flat shoes or went in bare feet onstage. Setting foot in the dressing room at Deerhurst was like culture shock for me. Picture ten girls crammed into a space about the size of a large closet, a long, narrow space with a tabletop, a bench, chairs, and lit mirrors that ran the full length of the walls on both sides. Rhinestone-embroidered garments hung from the walls and the ceiling, along with feathers, headdresses, scarves, wigs, and drapes of every fabric and color dangling overhead.

The girls glued tiny rhinestones on the outer corners of their eyes, which looked odd close up but gave off a pretty sparkle from under the stage lighting. I really didn't want to glue those things on my face. The same went for the false eyelashes. First, I did not know how, and I was extremely awkward at working with these fussy, messy things, and, second, I thought for sure that I would get a rash or something from the glue irritating my skin. I felt a bit ridiculous about putting on the showgirl-style stage face, as it seemed tacky and over the top to me, but I soon got into the spirit of the glitzy look and became efficient with it.

I'd never been a makeup-wearing kind of girl: only blush, a bit of eyeliner, mascara, and lip gloss for me. Foundation? Never wore it, only ever used it the times I applied it to my mother's face on special occasions. The first time I tried it myself, it felt as if someone had coated my face with pancake batter, like a mask, and I could not wait to scrape it off.

The costumes I had to wear were also alien to me. During fittings, I probably looked like an astronaut getting into her spacesuit for the first time. The outfits were amusing in the sense of making me feel like I was playing a game of dress-up, but was I really going to have to walk out onstage half naked in these? The whole thing felt so weird: tits perked, belly button bare, and lots of legs—either high slits or everything short. If I did wear anything that covered more skin, the fabric was flashy and glitzy. The way I looked at it—maybe the way I *had* to look at it in order to go through with it—I was no longer going out onstage as myself, I was performing in character. For example, one act had me playing a member of the Supremes; in another, I played the American Indian member of the Village People. (In the interest of historical accuracy, the real Villagers had been an all-male fivesome.)

Then there was the footwear. Sheila wore three-inch stiletto heels. I had probably never worn anything higher than an inch in my entire life. How on earth was I going to stand in these stilts, let alone walk and sing in them? Adding to my discomfort, the fishnet stockings itched like crazy, as the professional-quality ones were coarse and scratchy.

Brian introduced me to the cast of about fifteen, six of whom were dancers. They were all lovely, patient girls and, thankfully, were considerate toward me even though my hiring prompted extra rehearsals for everyone in order to prepare me for the show. Coming in on weekends could not have been fun for them, but they did it graciously. The dancers, primarily two girls, Kelly and Karen, spent extra time teaching me how to walk gracefully in those giant heels as well as to memorize the complicated choreography. This wasn't like singing in a club, where you do what *you feel* onstage.

Nothing was freestyle or ad-lib. All group performances were staged exactly, with different colored Xs and strips of tape, each color indicating different people and their positions, all over the floor of the stage. For example, there might have been two white Xs for my and Sheila's two center positions, our "home" X for the spotlight position, then maybe three red Xs to indicate a vocal group number off to one side of the stage so that we were properly spaced and centered downstage for that number. The tape was a stage-blocking guide. Marking the stage surface with tape for this reason is common in all stage productions, but for me it was completely foreign to even have to think about where I had to be and when. Even the mics had colored tape labeling them so that there were no mix-ups. Sheila's always had a thick, red-colored coating that caked between the meshing of the microphone cap. The soundman, John Noble, cleaned our mic caps, but her lipstick never seemed to come out, so there was no mistaking hers. It was daunting to have to think about so many details when performing, as before I'd only ever thought about the music and communicating it to the audience and performing by feel. I was in way over my head here. But I had to press on and learn this stuff, or else I was out of the best possible job I could hope for at the moment: with a decent salary and no traveling, so that my siblings and I could be together. And I was still getting to carry on musically, even if not exactly in the way I had envisioned. I had several weeks in which to rehearse, and by the time of my opening show in the ballroom, I had managed to get everything down.

The moment I was hired, I explained to Carrie, Mark, and Darryl that I had found a steady music gig to support us and that we would all be moving to this place none of them had heard of. As you can imagine, they were anxious about leaving Timmins, our parents' home, and everything familiar. I was asking a lot of them, I realized.

After rehearsals, I would look around Huntsville for a place to live. My brothers were still in school, of course, so although it was only early summer, I wanted to give them as much time as possible to adjust before September. I found a newly built bungalow just outside of town, about ten minutes up a dirt road in the middle of the bush. This suited me just fine, and I knew that the kids would like it, too, being in the bush. The house was far from ideal, but it was the best I could do on relatively short notice—and still being relatively short of funds. By the fall, I figured, we'd find something better. We'd have to, as the bungalow had no running water and therefore no functioning toilets, either. That meant hiking down to the river to haul five-gallon jugs of water back to the house, while baths consisted of lathering up on the riverbank, then diving into the water. And since the toilet couldn't flush without plumbing, the bush out back had to suffice as the loo and poo. As for laundry, I'd carry baskets of dirty clothes down to the river, and—in a flashback to our days living on Proulx Court in Hanmer—resort to my hand-washing skills, only with no hot water or my dad to help me wring out the big things, like jeans. This was more like camp: hand washing, soaping, and scrubbing everything against the rocks. I was as discreet as I could be because I didn't want anyone to see me putting laundry detergent in the river; I knew I'd be told off or reported to the ministry. But I was getting by, and at the time, I would have been likely to tell them where to stick it unless they had a better idea of how they thought I could get the laundry done. Because that was my reality: I had to get things done with what I had. I had a cold, black river, some detergent, and my two hands, so this was my laundry room, period.

Until my family got there, I slept on the carpeted floor with no mattress and brushed my teeth in the small creek that crossed the driveway and ran down to the river. If I heard a car coming, I'd quickly stand up and hide the brush behind my back, looking nonchalant, so as not to let on what I was doing. It would be rather embarrassing for anyone to know that I was paying to *camp* in a rental home.

Now, this was real backwoods country, the kind of remote place where cousins married each other, your uncle was also your grandpa, and so on. I'm exaggerating, of course, but you get the idea. This rental house came with no locks on the doors, and being a young woman all alone out here was—understandably, I think—a little nerve-wracking. But I'd brought our family husky-shepherd cross, Sadey, with me from Timmins, not so much for protection as for company.

She was also a comforting reminder of my mother and father. In the days after their deaths, poor Sadey laid down on my parents' shoes, which were on the floor mat by the back door. She did not move from that spot for days. It wasn't like she had ever done that before; Sadey was expressing her grief in this touching way, trying the only way she knew how to be close to them in their absence. It meant a lot to me to have her with me in Huntsville. She was used to wandering around outdoors, so I could let her roam free to sniff and scout the bush.

The two of us had a routine every night when I'd get back from work, often as late as one in the morning. I'd pull up the drive, roll down the window, and call out to Sadey. At that time of night, sound would carry far into the woods. Wherever she was, she would hear me and come racing back home. Sometimes it would take her a few minutes, so I would just wait in my GMC Jimmy truck until she trotted out from the tree line of the bush surrounding the house. Since the bungalow didn't have any locks on the doors, I always felt better having her by my side, given the late hour.

The nearest neighbor lived about ten minutes away in any direction. Unluckily for me, one of them was a guy named Norman, who used to stop in whenever he felt like it. He frequently had alcohol on his breath, regardless of the time of day. I would hear his long white, rusty car barrel up my driveway and then screech to a halt.

I was afraid of him, as he spoke with his face directed toward the ground, making only occasional eye contact. It didn't seem like he was all there; something was just not quite right about his behavior. I'd hurry outside, to cut him off at the pass, so to speak, before he could make his way inside. I acted friendly enough, calling out, "Hey, Norman, what's up?" but I was always wary. We'd stand there making chitchat about the weather and other superficial topics for a little bit, then I'd try to help him on his way. (One good thing about half-witted drunks: they are often highly suggestible.)

"So, where are you off to?" If that didn't work, sometimes I would flat-out lie and tell him I had a friend waiting for me inside or that I was on my way into town to meet someone. I always had to think on my feet with Norman, and whenever he *finally* left, I felt as if I'd just squeezed out of a tight spot.

Considering that the Deerhurst cabaret-type review did not really conform to my natural style of singing, I think I adapted pretty well, musically speaking. Fitting in socially, however, posed a much harder challenge. I felt bullied by the other female lead vocalist, Sheila, right from the start. I was warned by other cast members upon joining the show that there had been other singers before me who'd come in one door and gone out the other after Sheila's surly treatment. She apparently didn't like sharing the spotlight. Now, professional competitiveness and cattiness are as much a part of show business as feather boas, but the resentment I felt from her, I was told, also stemmed from the fact that, apparently, I'd been hired at a higher salary than most of the other performers, some of whom had been there for some time. I say "apparently" because I had no way of knowing what anyone else was paid. Brian named a figure, and I took it.

How did Sheila find out how much money I was earning in the first place, right? I'll tell you: unbeknown to me, every payday, our paychecks would be left in an envelope at our spots in the dressing room. I'd rushed out after the show on paycheck night, and although I was expecting to be paid, I wasn't aware that our checks were left on our spot each week. I guess I assumed we picked them up at the office, for example, so at the end of my first week, my check sat there unopened till the next show, when I realized how the pay routine worked. When I found my check sitting at my spot, the envelope had already been opened. I was told that Sheila helped herself to it, didn't like what she saw, then shared it with everyone. When I walked into the dressing room the next show day, the atmosphere was thick and cold. I felt so alone, but I didn't bother to say anything; they couldn't have made it more apparent that I was not one of them.

Here I was just months after my parents were killed, trying to make a new start for what was left of our family. I was in a strange town, surrounded by strangers, and trying to get a handle on a job that was very intimidating. I was pushing myself to the limit in every way. Frankly, I did not need this added complication to my already overburdened life. But I was too emotionally wrung out to react. My method of coping was to just get on with it and roll with the punches, because I needed to keep this job, plain and simple. I was in the middle of putting my family through a big change, and I needed to forge ahead, regardless of the mean-spirited nonsense Sheila was creating for me.

She would humiliate me in small ways here and there over our time together in the show, and I would tolerate it through clenched teeth. To make matters worse, someone had started a rumor that I was having an affair with one of the resort owners. Aha! I suppose that would explain my handsome salary. It was humiliating to think that anyone might have believed this bald-faced lie, but, of course, there's never any way for a person to defend herself against those types of whispered accusations, and so I didn't even bother trying. It was such an immature attempt at sabotaging me, I just let it go. In fact, the person in question was always kind toward me and never made an advance—which would make him something of an anomaly in the entertainment world.

The resort's bar manager, on the other hand, was much more representative. At first, he, too, seemed like a nice guy. Around the time that my teenage brothers were to arrive from Timmins, I asked him if he would consider hiring them as busboys in the Four Winds on Friday and Saturday nights. I explained that there was no one at home to watch them while I was performing from seven o'clock until one in the morning. This way, they could earn some money, then we could all drive home together. The manager seemed very empathetic and said he would be happy to help.

Everything was working out nicely. But just a few weeks later, he cornered me in the small, dark coatroom tucked away in the back at one end of the bar. I'd gone in there to hang up my jacket, and he'd followed me in, closing the door behind him. He pushed his body up against me, pinning me against the wall, forcing his weight on me. I shoved back and told him sharply, "Get off me!"

"Aw, come on," he said slyly. "I think I've been pretty good to you and your brothers. Don't be such a bitch." Then he threatened to fire them as quickly as he'd hired them. Again I demanded that he let me go and started to struggle physically with him. Finally, he backed off, but the sneer on his face told me that this was the kind of person who would exact revenge. It came as little surprise when both of my brothers were let go the following week. Incidents like this made me feel so alone that I wanted to cry, but I fought my tears and marched on, like I felt I had to. There was no time to break down when I had siblings relying on me, and no one for me to rely on in turn. I had to be strong against the Sheilas, the overwhelming burden of managing a family, and assaults from abusive men.

I was never one to take personal relationships lightly, and casual affairs were not my style. Not to sound like a prude, but not only did I never sleep my way to anything, I very distinctly avoided it. I simply was not interested in flirting with men as a pastime or for any other reason other than to have a meaningful relationship. I've learned not to take such accusations to heart, since it is such a common tactic that jealous people use as a convenient way to hurt those they envy, but it still ticks me off. It's cheap, trite, and just plain immature.

One night after work, I pulled up to the bungalow, called out for Sadey, and waited the usual couple of minutes. Fifteen minutes went by, with me calling her name, and she still didn't come. Between being upset that she might be lost, and feeling extremely vulnerable sitting there by myself in the darkness, my mind conjured up a frightening scenario in which my unhinged neighbor Norman—*of course,* he'd have to be named Norman, like Norman Bates in the movie *Psycho*—killed Sadey so that he could be waiting inside for me without any warning from the dog.

No way was I even going to get out of my truck. I turned around and zoomed the hell out of there, heading for town. *What am I going to do for the night?* I thought. The only place I could think of was Pierre's, the drummer for the house band; we'd had a little cast get-together at his house not long before, and I remembered his address. At three in the morning, there I was, knocking on his door. Thankfully, Pierre answered. He was a very nice, mild-tempered guy. I explained my situation, that I was afraid to stay in my bungalow, and could I please crash on his couch until morning. In his thick French accent, he invited me inside and set me up in a side room to sleep.

The next day, I saw Pierre backstage. His face was scratched and his lip was cut, as if he'd been in a fight. "What happened to you?" I asked. He took me aside and explained tersely that another band member, who lived right next door, must have seen me either coming or going from Pierre's house and spitefully shared the big news with the cast. Not surprisingly, the story that I'd spent the night there promptly found its way to the drummer's girlfriend, who then got all upset, confronted Pierre, and freaked out on him. My first reaction was to chuckle, as I figured he either gave her an embellished story about why I stayed over—maybe in an attempt to make her jealous, and it backfired—or poor Pierre simply had a nutcase for a girlfriend. I did feel badly, though, as he had done me a favor, after all. The obvious bad intentions of the neighboring musician made me feel unwelcome and outcast. All this drama because my dog didn't show up. It was a bit much trying to get my head around the stage cast mentality and its petty dramas. It was all just silly, really. Making the whole situation sillier still, when I returned to the bungalow in the morning, guess who was there waiting for me, happily wagging her tail? Sadey had probably been out chasing a deer the night before. Go figure!

I decided to get Sadey a buddy, a big, beautiful six-month-old German shepherd that I named Roman. He had good instincts: from the get-go, he did not like my creepy neighbor. Anytime that Norman pulled up in the drive and climbed out of his truck, Roman would block him and bark incessantly.

Carrie, Mark, and Darryl joined me midsummer. One hot summer morning, we heard a car skidding and sliding on the gravel road just out front of the house, then stop abruptly. It was the sudden stop of the car that caught my attention from inside the house. I ran out alarmed, as it was odd that a car barreling down the road would just suddenly brake. Norman had struck and killed Roman. I can't say whether he hit him on purpose or if it was an accident. Accident or not, all I knew was that all the grief I'd suppressed over the past half year or so trying to keep everything and everyone, including myself, together came rushing back to me at that moment.

I didn't know what to say to Norman. I know I felt like kicking the shit out of him. I wanted to take all my anger out on his car, jump up and down on the hood till it caved in, smash his windshield with rocks, and spit in his face for killing my dog, frightening me with his creepy drop-ins, for being behind the wheel half cut after having one too many, and for being a menace. But all of this was just me fantasizing about what I wanted to express but couldn't. It was locked inside me, all of this emotion. I didn't know how to let it out without feeling anxious about losing control.

I wanted Roman buried as soon as possible and called to my brothers to grab shovels and start digging. I was at the end of my rope and ready to snap, and they didn't move as quickly as my patience allowed. "Get off your asses and dig that hole!" I yelled at them, clutching my pink robe tightly around me. "If you don't get out there and dig that grave *right now,* I'm going to throw your damn hockey trophies out the door!"

I was losing it on my brothers, and they made the mistake of not taking me seriously. I marched into the bungalow, snatched the trophies off the shelf, and proceeded to hurl them onto the front lawn one by one. *That* got their attention, and they started digging. I instantly felt terrible about breaking the trophies. I'd put my pent-up emotional energy into my throwing arm that day, and those trophies went flying, but much of it still remained unleashed. It was hard for me to find outlets for my feelings when I was so concerned about maintaining a level head as the "responsible one."

It was very sad hoisting Roman's limp body into the grave. Only eight months before, we had watched our parents being lowered into the ground, and now another burial. This was too much for me, and I cried deeply at the sadness of love and loss, and at the brutal beating life seemed to be dishing out to us kids. I regretted freaking out on my poor brothers; they had only just met Roman, but I'm sure they must have felt the significance of what had happened and the reminder that grief was right there on the tips of their shovels. The death of our parents was still so fresh.

Around this time, I wrote a sad song called "Hallelujah," a song later finished with Mutt Lange and titled "God Bless the Child," which I recorded on *The Woman in Me*. I was standing on the gravel road in front of my unfinished rental house in a numb, mourning kind of state, staring out into the forest hills, and I just started to cry and sing the words and melody. I was on my way back up to the house from the river when I heard the agonizing cries of a bear off in the distance. It carried on for so long, and my heart was breaking for him. Normally when this happens, it means either someone shot a bear and didn't finish the job, and the bear managed to get away wounded and was now roaming in pain, or it was caught in a trap waiting in agony until it either bled to death or the trapper came back and finished it off. It always made me upset when people who had no skill with a gun shot at an animal, wounding it and then giving up on it. I say shoot to kill the animal the first time, or don't hunt. I think hunters should have to go through annual courses before each hunting season to make sure that their shooting skills are up to snuff, as with the time lag between seasons, one's marksmanship can get rusty and the "practice shooting" ends up being on live animals. That's just barbaric, in my opinion.

I did hunt with my dad and my grandparents growing up, and it was emphasized strongly that the goal was to always kill your prey swiftly to avoid as much pain as possible for the animal. It is very difficult to shoot any animal without actually causing it some pain, unless you are extremely accurate and kill it instantly with a direct shot to the heart or brain. I much prefer being a vegetarian and avoiding any association with this today, to be honest. We hunted our common Ontario forest foul, partridge, often on the tree plants, and as we didn't always have a gun with us, we did this by hand. Partridge like to stay cool and close to the ground in low bushes—often several of them together—so if a couple of people pounced on the cluster at just the right moment, you could often grab two or three. A quick twist of the neck did the job even more swiftly than shooting them. I hated this hands-on method, and it was a skill I can't say I acquired with any pleasure or pride, but it was quicker for the bird than bullets. I hunted partridge into my twenties, as they were easy to get just off the side of the road. I'd clean them right there and then, as it's much easier to do when they're still warm, by stepping on their wings with a foot on either side of the breast, pulling on the feet, and out slides a clean bird ready for the pan or freezer. There's not much meat on a partridge, so once I had accumulated a handful, I'd make a meal with them.

I don't judge anyone who hunts or eats meat, as I believe it's a very personal choice, but I have a hard time imagining that I ever killed and cleaned any animal with my own hands. This all seems like another lifetime to me now, as I haven't eaten any animal parts in about twenty years, let alone killed any animals.

The Deerhurst musical productions changed periodically. One of my favorites, from my third and last year there, was a spoof of the musical *Cats,* called—but of course—*Dogs.* I played a pink poodle that tiptoed around the stage, half singing, half acting, and mostly feeling silly the rest of the time. It was actually fun to do, on account of its queer sense of humor and the fact that it took me about as far away from my singer-songwriter background as you could go. I enjoyed the opportunity to stretch myself musically and viewed it all as part of an ongoing education.

However, tackling every style under the sun except for my own began to slow my progress as a songwriter as well as my quest for a record deal. Sometimes a steady, stable gig can be detrimental to an artist; it's nice to be comfortable, but not *too* comfortable.

Beginning around 1990, when I turned twenty-five, I refocused my sights on my ultimate goal and began writing songs in earnest. The death of my parents prompted a song called "Send It with Love":

*Whenever I think of you, it seems so unfair*
*That I have to close my eyes, to see you there.*
*I know I'm makin' it now, but it's tough.*
*I can't begin to tell you enough, the pain is too much.*
*And I give my heart in a prayer, and send it with love.*

Obviously, that song was personal to me. I made a rough demo of "Send It with Love," but I never got back to finishing it or making a proper recording of it. It was eventually released against my wishes by the producers involved during the demo stage once my career began to pick up.

"No One Needs to Know" was another song I wrote during the Deerhurst period, but it was eventually finished and produced by my future husband, Mutt, and released on *The Woman in Me* album. There was a more playful, cheerful sentiment behind that song, which I often used in my writing in the immediate period after the loss of my parents in order to take myself out of my sadness and into a more make-believe world where things were happy and ideal.

After shows at Deerhurst, in the wee hours of the morning, I got to work recording rough versions of my original material. The guys in the band were night owls, so I was able to enlist a couple of them for these demo sessions. The recordings were pretty basic—amateurish, I'd have to say—but, then, we were taping in a makeshift studio that a friend had set up in his basement or sometimes at the lodge venue after the audience left. The soundman John Noble recently reminded me of how we also once used the basement bathrooms below the lodge stage as singing booths. He ran cables from the mixing board to the lower level to get some sound separation for the voice. Maybe we thought the acoustics were good in there, or maybe that was me. I often find that bathrooms have great vocal room sound. Singing my heart out till four in the morning after a night of belting out songs on-stage for two hours would have given me an interesting vocal sound, at any rate!

Mary Bailey, my manager at this point, had arranged for a promi-

nent music business attorney named Richard Frank to travel all the
way to Huntsville from Nashville, Tennessee, to see me perform.
Music lawyers were well connected with record company executives
and producers. Knight, Frank and Lion, Richard Frank's law firm,
consisted of music attorneys who played matchmaker for promising
artists. What's funny is that the review we were putting on at Deerhurst at that time bore no resemblance whatsoever to the music that I
was interested in making or that Mr. Frank was interested in hearing.
Nevertheless, it served as my showcase for the recording industry.

My big solo song was to be the dramatic ballad "Wind Beneath
My Wings," which Bette Midler had recorded for the soundtrack to
the movie *Beaches* and took to number one in 1989. Under the circumstances, the song had a special resonance for me. Here I was
on the verge of finally realizing the dream that my mother and I had
chased since I was little, and she would not be in the wings nodding
her approval. It was then and at other noteworthy moments in the
future that her loss often hit me the hardest. I wished so badly that
she was alive so she could have been able to bask in my success. *Our*
success.

Although I'd always imagined my mother dying young, I'd believed that it would be from something related to her abused, battered, and tattered life, or at the very least, from the effects of chain
smoking. I prepared myself from a young age to lose my mother, but I
never imagined I'd be robbed of her in such a common way. A car accident wasn't worthy of taking my mother's life, I thought.

Between the distraction of feeling so empty and alone in my
mother's absence and the pressure of feeling that I was about to sing
for my life, I was nervous. Screw this up, and I might not receive
another opportunity to prove myself to the record industry. Not only
that, but I would have just minutes in which to change costumes and
catch my breath before singing "Wind Beneath My Wings."

I ran down a mental checklist of what I had to do: rip off the
previous costume, squeeze into a sleek, floor-length gown and high
heels, chic up my hair, and then literally run—in the heels—from

backstage down a flight of stairs, through the service hall, up two flights of stairs, along the side of the indoor tennis courts, up a ramp, and into the back of the ballroom, just in time for the spotlight cue. *And* I had to strike a statuesque pose and look completely poised because the song opens with a low dynamic, when, in fact, my heart was racing from the combination of nerves and having just sprinted from one side of the theater to the other.

Somehow, I managed to get through the number without passing out or without getting choked up on lyrics like "You were content to let me shine," "I would be nothing without you," and, of course, from the chorus: "Did you ever know that you're my hero?" It could have been a letter from me to my mother.

This performance would be my first and last showcase. Luckily, I impressed Richard Frank enough for him to play my demo tape of original material for a well-known record producer named Norro Wilson, who'd helmed records by the likes of Reba McEntire, Charly McClain, John Anderson, and Charley Pride, to name a few. Norro, an accomplished songwriter himself, had sharply tuned ears and a sincere love for music. He was enthusiastic about my voice and songwriting, and he relayed his excitement about my potential to Mercury Nashville Records A&R man and close friend Buddy Cannon, playing a key link in the chain of events that led to the making of my first album. Buddy, in turn, thought that the label head Harold Shedd would be interested. He was right, and I was signed. I was told many years later that Buddy was reported as saying about me, "She got signed and I got my picture taken." He was right about that, too, as other than my own personal recognition of him for his support during that time, he didn't receive official, professional reward from the company or industry for being connected to my success story, although I'm sure that Buddy's association with me as a new artist with Mercury Nashville is well known within the industry. But in the end, Buddy was not included on the production of my first record even though he was a big believer in me.

Within a matter of months, Harold and Richard Frank had hammered out the details of my record contract, and just like that, I went from being a small-Northern-town girl with little chance of ever making a career anywhere outside the borders of my own country to signing an international recording contract at a record company that sat smack dab in the middle of Nashville, Tennessee. Nashville! Home to giant singing stars, top record producers, megastudios, hit songwriters, world-class musicians, and, basically, the crème de la crème of the music industry. This was it—the big time—the only place to be if you were trying to make it as a country recording artist. My mother's dream was coming true at last.

# 14

## My Little Corner of the Wild

But first, I quit Deerhurst. PolyGram Records at the time, later becoming Mercury Nashville, hadn't advanced me any money yet, and I couldn't afford to move to Nashville. Before knowing I would land a record deal, out of necessity, I managed to get a mortgage at the CIBC Bank and bought my first house after leaving the remote, no-water bungalow rental. Winter was approaching, and we needed the minimum of a hot water shower and flushing toilet. We moved to Melissa, a small district just outside of Huntsville. Our new pad was a one-bedroom bungalow made into four bedrooms, with two-by-two divider-type walls to break the one existing bedroom up for each of the boys and two makeshift bedrooms downstairs for Carrie and me. The house was one story with a walk-out basement and one bathroom. We squeezed a washer and dryer underneath the stairs to the basement and called it a laundry room.

Although I was technically the house "elder," responsible for the bills and running the household, the place probably had more the feel of a clubhouse overrun by a bunch of kids. Carrie, Mark, Darryl, and I were in a new town, trying to make our way alone together.

My boyfriend at the time, Paul Bolduc, also from Timmins, moved in with us and helped man the house. With a mortgage, two teenagers, a house that needed maintenance, and a winter's worth of firewood to chop, Paul was a tremendous support, and we made a good team. I'd met him in Timmins not long after my parents died.

He was only eighteen, four years younger than me. We would be to-gether for more than five years.

My sister Carrie's new boyfriend, whom she would eventually marry and is still married to today, was also around to help out with the boys at times. Jeff reminds me now of the heavy load that was on my shoulders during the first few years after our parents' passing. He sometimes talks now about his observations of my challenges at the time, of running the household at such a young age and trying to deal with my grief at the same time. Jeff, by the way, is the guy who inspired the lyric "You're one of those guys who likes to shine his machine / You make me take off my shoes before you let me get in" in the song "That Don't Impress Me Much." We all remember Carrie explaining that whenever Jeff drove her somewhere, she had to take off her shoes before getting in the passenger seat. He kept his vehi-cles sparkling at all times and was very impressive and a perfectionist in many ways for a nineteen-year-old, especially compared to us Tim-mins bushwhackers, who were definitely not worried about dragging in a bit of mud here and there.

Both Jeff and Paul were unusually mature, responsible, and cool for their age, and there were times when their presence was espe-cially comforting—such as when the police came to the door in the middle of the night with one of my teenage brothers in tow, picked up for underage drinking. I'm small in stature, and a strong, intoxi-cated male teen can be a handful. I'm just grateful that the police never knocked on my door *without* one of my brothers, as that would have meant the worst. It was moments like these that I was thrust into instant parenthood and the worrying that comes with the terri-tory; those sleepless nights when it's three in the morning, and the kids still aren't home. Sometimes I drove home from work at Deer-hurst well after midnight, hoping that when I got in the door, both boys would be safe and sound, asleep. These were my genuine wor-ries at the age of twenty-three, and I was relieved when they were where they were supposed to be.

My routine during the cold months was to stock up the stove with wood that would burn for about four hours before it needed to be fed again. At six in the morning, I'd wake up and refill it, then wake up the boys for school around seven once the house had warmed up again.

My brother-in-law, Jeff, says today, "I think back on those times, and I don't know where you found the courage." I'm not entirely sure myself, but a particular dream I had back then boosted my strength. It couldn't have come at a better time, because the weight of taking on two teenagers, working, homemaking, and trying to keep my career on track was beginning to seem too heavy for me to carry.

Here's the dream: my parents come to me, but only my father speaks. He floats close above me; actually, just his face. In a gentle voice, he tells me that he doesn't have much time, as my mother is waiting for him. I see her floating up behind him and want her to come forward, but she doesn't.

My father says to me, "She was already on her way out of this world and is just now waiting for me to come." He then reassures me that I am doing a good job, that everything is under control, and that I shouldn't worry. Both of them want me to know that they know I am doing my best, and this is exactly what I am meant to be doing.

In my dream, and after I wake up, I feel so relieved and encouraged by his words. I needed to hear them so badly, because I felt guilty that I wasn't doing a good enough job and that I was letting down my siblings after all they'd already been through. I'd turned my life upside down to keep us together, put a roof over our heads, and support us, but I still felt I couldn't make them happy, and I believed it was my fault. But *of course* they were still unhappy: our parents had been snatched from us, along with the life that they had known in Timmins.

Back to my dream: The whole time my father is speaking to me, my mother is telepathically tapping him on the shoulder that it is time for them to leave. I desperately want them both to stay and to not leave me alone with all of this pressure, but it is as though they are about to cross a threshold, and there is no time to waste. It's almost as if they have to catch a plane, and if they miss it, they will be stuck in some kind of holding pattern or purgatory. My father explains that if he doesn't go now, my mother will have to leave without him.

It was very symbolic to me that they both went on together, as it confirmed their destiny to me so clearly. Not only did they die together, my dream was implying that they really would be "together forever." That actually brought me peace as well, since they'd both suffered so much throughout their lives, and I felt energized to hold up the fort for them, to not give up and to provide their other children with a measure of stability. I felt that I owed my father something in that sense, considering that he'd taken on Jill, Carrie, and me as his own children, and although he was not perfect, he was sincere and selfless to have done that. My respect for him was profound.

The time came when we Twain kids would go our separate ways, and there was no reason for me to stay in Melissa. The boys were over sixteen and seeking out their own independence, and Carrie and Jeff were getting more serious as a couple. Besides, I couldn't afford it anymore, not without a job. I could no longer handle the monthly mortgage payments. Selling the house would take too long, so with Paul's help, as he was an amateur carpenter at the time, I gutted the basement by hand and renovated it into an apartment with a kitchen, bathroom, and living space. Renting out both the upstairs and the downstairs enabled me to cover the mortgage. But once again I was a gypsy, with nowhere permanent to live.

I couldn't help but find irony in the fact that I'd quit my well-paying gig at Deerhurst to pursue my career as an international recording artist—for free! That is, at least until I could prove myself. The odds of finding success in the music industry is said to be on the order of 0.005 percent. That's right: point-zero-zero-five, at best; if one does the math on the success rate of *American Idol,* it's even lower. One hundred thousand people audition for each season, so over ten years, that's one million people. Only one singer wins each season, making ten winners overall. Only two have gone on to have genuinely successful careers, which makes the percentage of success

0.000002 percent. Lucky for me, back then I had no idea how slim my chances were. You can't be discouraged by what you don't know, so ignorance truly was bliss in my case. I had optimism on my side, and with the newfound freedom from domestic responsibilities, I thought that I might have the opportunity to make up for lost time. I was in my midtwenties; it was now or never.

I had a recording contract, but with nowhere to live, I moved back to my parents' old house in Timmins for a short time. We were renting out both the downstairs and the upstairs until we could sell it, so I took the temporarily vacant upstairs apartment. As the family member responsible for managing my parents' estate, I really needed that apartment to be rented to cover maintenance bills on the property, but the short window between renters was a blessing during the pit stop I made back at 44 Montgomery Avenue. I was grateful for the chance to take refuge in the empty nest my parents provided for me even in their absence when I had no place else to go.

I spent those weeks holed up in the apartment, intently writing music and feeling sad and melancholy, for the house evoked so many family memories. Nothing had changed in the five years since my parents' death. I could practically smell and taste the past lingering in the air, and I could still hear everybody's voices. At times, I imagined their footsteps clunking up the stairs and half expected them to barge in through the door any second. My stirred emotions there produced a lot of songwriting.

Along with the sadness, however, I felt at peace. Unlike the other places where we'd lived, the Montgomery house hadn't been tarnished by violence. I've always maintained that financial woes accounted for most of my parents' fights. Well, things were looking up when they bought this place, and while my mother and my father may have squabbled, the arguments never turned physical.

Once I had to leave the apartment for the renters who were about to move in, Paul's parents, Larry and Helene, generously let us stay with them for a while. I was signed to the label and hoped it was only a matter of time before I would be more stable professionally, but for now, I was still in transition, with one foot in my old world and one in the new one. I worked part-time at Sears three days a week, and when Paul and I had time off, we'd head to his parents' camp on the shores of Kenogamissi Lake. There in the bush, we built a tiny ten-by-twelve-foot cabin made from scraps of wood and recycled bits from demolished homes. Paul was a skilled builder, and I designed the layout so that we could actually cook, sleep, bathe, and stay warm in this small space. With no electricity or plumbing, the cabin was the equivalent of a circus clown car; we squeezed a lot of living into it.

I enjoyed my time alone in the bush during the stretches when Paul was working in town and I couldn't get any shifts at Sears. He'd drive me out to the cabin with a week's worth of food supplies, then join me on the weekend. I loved the solitude, especially during the gorgeous winter. The road leading to the campsite would be snowed in and impassable by car or truck, so Paul would have to haul the Ski-Doo with a trailer pulled behind with supplies for a couple of miles off the main road. Once in the cabin, I felt isolated yet safe, and very much at home. I wasn't afraid of staying alone in the bush in the middle of winter. Bears hibernate in the winter, and road access is much more limited, so humans were nowhere in sight, either. I had nothing to worry about other than freezing to death if I ran out of wood. Wolves are no problem, as they are timid toward humans and they can't knock doors down, let alone blow a house down. A bear could have ripped through my windows or doors, but like I said, they were sound asleep at this time of year.

The experience stamped me with the joy of aloneness. By that, I mean the chance to dive into a space where time has little importance, and the divine right to feel, think, or say whatever you want is yours. All yours. Lost in the bliss and simplicity of less, with all the time in the world to reflect and turn those thoughts and feelings into music. I was very productive in my little corner of the wild and enjoyed every minute of it. I miss that cramped hideaway! The basis of many of the songs that I would eventually complete and record with Mutt Lange a few years later were written there. I still enjoy listening to my cassette tape recordings of my writing sessions from that time, as you can hear the wood stove fire crackling in the background.

I spent the days chopping wood, clearing snow from my door and path, listening to the silence of the snow, taking in the view, and writing music as it came to me. I had a well-organized routine to my winter days alone in the cabin. Before going to bed I'd prepare chips and slivers of wood and kindling near the stove for quick access in the morning. I'd load up the stove with large, dampish pieces so it would burn as slowly as possible through the night, then I'd go to bed wearing wool socks and a sweater, and a heavy down sleeping bag draped at my knees ready for pulling up over my head in the middle of the night once the fire died out. The wood stove wasn't airtight and the cabin not insulated, so it didn't take much time for it to get cold out there in the winter woods with the average temperature anywhere between twenty and forty below zero. I had no radio or communication with me, so I never had any idea of what the temperature would drop to at night, but I had a good feel for what was coming naturally. The stars, the color of the sky, the wind, and the snowfall all provide clues of what to expect. The calm and clear nights in Northern Ontario are often the coldest ones. Clear, crisp, and cold. I loved those nights but knew I had to be ready for an uncomfortable morning.

With my fire goods handy and my wool socks and sweater already on, I was ready (or as ready as I'd ever be) to leave my cocoon and restart the fire around four o'clock, then wriggle back into my sleeping bag to enjoy a few more hours of warmth before the cabin cooled down too much again.

For bathing, I'd place a pail of water on the wood stove. Once it reached just the right temperature, I'd stand in a basin on the floor and use a cup to douse myself with the warm water as I soaped and rinsed in my makeshift shower. Melting snow into water was an all-afternoon affair, as it evaporates to nothing. But I had the time, so I didn't mind.

Once Paul and his family got there on a weekend, they'd fire up the sauna near Paul's parents' cottage, and there'd be enough heat and water for everyone. I secretly preferred my cozy method and would often pass on taking my turn in the sauna. I'm sure they thought I was nuts, but I loved the rustic system I had going. It was exactly how my parents and I used to bathe in the large prospecting tents in the bush during tree-planting season once the cool of the autumn air made it too cold to jump in the lakes. The workmen used to hang out at my parents' tent in the evenings, but when it was time for my mother's sponge bath, she'd kick everyone out. I remember walking up to their tent one time to find a bunch of men standing outside, shivering in the cold. "What are you guys doing out here?" I asked. "Your mom's having a bath," one of them harrumphed, his breath forming a tiny cloud in the cold air. Not all the tents had stoves, so my parents' tent was the place to gather till it was time to go back to their own smaller tents.

My days were simple and happy at any camp, and the one on the shore of Kenogamissi Lake was special. Staying warm, clean, fed, and creatively productive was all I had to do every day that I was alone there. It was heaven.

# 15

## New to Nashville

As much as I loved living the hermetic life in a remote cabin in the woods, this was still an uncomfortably scary period of transition for me. I was involved in what amounted to a long-distance relationship with my new record label because I could not afford to move to Nashville. Yet I was expected to fly 1,500 miles down there whenever they wanted me to spend time finding the right songs. I needed to be there in person for the listening sessions, as they were literally at the publishing houses. I would get couriered packages with cassette tapes brimming with songs to consider as well, but much of the serious shopping for hit tunes was done in person. Today we're able to just email songs in seconds, and being somewhere in person or waiting for a couriered package in order to hear potential songs to record just isn't necessary. In fact, whole recording sessions are done over things like "source connect" on the Pro Tools recording program on the Internet.

It came as a great relief when PolyGram finally advanced me $20,000, a fortune to me at the time, enabling me to rent a one-bedroom apartment in a newly built complex called the Landings, in the suburb of Brentwood. I'd fully expected to live in another dive, given my limited finances, but this was *nice*: brand-new range, a balcony off the living room—even a washer and dryer. No more scrubbing clothes on rocks down by the river! The grounds had a swimming pool and a circuit around the buildings that made for lovely evening walks. I could not believe that the rent was so reasonable; to me, this was living in the lap of luxury. I felt like I was moving up in the world.

In the summer of 1992, I packed my Jimmy to the roof with every household item I owned. The rear window and the side windows were completely blocked, but I made the two-day drive from Timmins to Nashville safely.

By now, I even had my first credit card. To be honest, I was surprised by how easy it was to obtain one in the States. In Canada, card companies were far more discriminating about extending credit to people without a full-time job. And you'd have thought that my not being a U.S. citizen would have made it even harder. Nope! I wasn't complaining, though. Having credit really helped me to cover my butt during the dry months to come.

Harold Shedd and Norro Wilson were the producers of my first CD. Harold owned a famous studio called the Music Mill, where countless gold and platinum records had been recorded over the years, and I was even lucky enough to meet Glen Campbell in the hall once. I always loved Glen's voice, so it was a big moment for me to see him in person and be recording in the same building that he was.

Although Norro believed in me as a songwriter, I think he felt I wasn't quite there yet and needed the support of Nashville's writing community to find hit songs. Nor was Harold Shedd satisfied with the caliber of my songwriting just yet. On my first several trips down to Nashville, and after I moved there, the number one order of business was to carry on shopping for songs for me to record. The term "shopping" might sound a bit funny, but this is how we actually refer to looking for songs. Although not exactly in the context of "Attention, shoppers. In aisle seven, we're having a sale on tear-jerking country ballads. That's aisle seven!" So of course you don't walk around pushing a cart, but the publishers push songs, and the producers and artists scan the choices till they're satisfied they've found just the right list of goodies to take to the studio.

Usually it was Norro and I, and sometimes Harold, who would

go down to Music Row, the hub of the country music industry. It's like one-stop shopping for becoming a recording artist. Within a radius of several blocks, you pass recording studios, record companies, and the offices of artist-management firms, public relations consultants, production outfits, song publishing companies—you name it. If this were New York City or Los Angeles, the other two major nuclei of the U.S. music business, they would all be housed in imposing corporate-looking buildings and skyscrapers. What makes Music Row so unique to me is its quaintness: the tree-lined streets are full of charming houses with wood-planked verandas and deep porches. The only way you would know that those *are* the studios, and headquarters, and so on, are the discreet plaques above the doors, bearing the businesses' names. There are more mortar, metal, and glass structures on Music Row now that have cut into the charm of the smaller converted homes, so the feel is different today.

Imagine my surprise the first time I set foot in PolyGram's Nashville office, which was in a large, inviting-looking three-story house with a white porch. It certainly made meeting the label head Harold Shedd for the first time less daunting than it would have been ordinarily. Music Row had an authenticity and warmth to it that just made it easier for a small-town girl like me to adjust.

That was true of Nashville in general. It was apparent to me right away that I'd been given a break by getting my professional start there. To be honest, if my introduction to the United States had come in the Big Apple or Hollywood, for example, I might have found it too overwhelming, at least at first.

The Music City of the early 1990s was less populated, slower paced, and more family oriented than other music industry hubs of the larger centers and certainly than it is now. When I first laid eyes on the surrounding countryside, I was charmed by the horse ranches that sprawled out in every direction, their miles of triple-rail fences framing vast stretches of pastoral, picturesque landscapes. I especially liked the Brentwood and Franklin areas south of the city, which called to mind country classics such as John Denver's "Take

Me Home, Country Roads" and Porter Wagoner's "Green, Green Grass of Home." (You're probably most familiar with the 1967 version by Welshman Tom Jones, but Porter had a big country hit with it two years earlier.) When I was growing up, those songs planted in my mind images of the Old South. Now they were coming to life for me: plantation homes, black-eyed peas, muddy rivers, watermelon wine. For quite a while after my move to Tennessee, I felt as if I were living on a movie set.

All in all, I think I adapted to my new home pretty well for someone who had never been outside of Canada before. There was so much I wasn't used to. But it was all good. Like, grocery stores being open twenty-four hours a day? Get out of here! I couldn't believe their size, either, or the fact that some of these so-called megastores sold everything from movies, to liquor, to tires—even guns. A completely new concept to me. If I needed to go out and buy milk at three in the morning, I could. *Whoa.*

In my international travels, I've found that Canadians are often stereotyped as being a friendly people with a good sense of humor. I found Southerners to be much the same, although more formally mannered, addressing a lady as "ma'am," for example. Southern people cursed a lot less than Northern Ontarians as well. When a Northern Canadian gets mad, it's not uncommon for a string of "Jes*s f*cking Chr*st!"s to come out of his mouth, and the French Canadians have some doozies, too. Sometimes, though, the friendliness of the South was misinterpreted by the likes of a Canadian girl, as when total strangers walking toward you on the street would smile and say, "Hello, how ya'll doin' today?" I didn't always respond, for the simple reason that I wasn't sure they were actually speaking to *me,* even though they looked right at me and seemed so sincere. *Why would someone I've never seen before in my life care how I'm doing today?* was my thinking.

You know what else kind of caught me off guard initially? The very American propensity to happily share personal information with a perfect stranger. A store clerk might say to me, "Well, hello there, how can I help you today? My name is Jennifer if you need anything, honey." Responding in an equally laid-back, uninhibited manner sometimes got me bombarded with personal questions as well as intimate secrets on the other side, whether I asked for it or not, and sometimes the information just kept coming, like, "You know, I tried that shirt on when it first came in, but my husband told me I was too fat to wear bright colors, so I decided to just stick to black instead. I think your color is red. You're a bright-color person, I can tell. Are you married? Does your husband like color or does he prefer more subtle tones? Sometimes I think we worry too much about what men think, don't you agree?" I was taken by this friendliness, and it made me feel welcome.

In addition to this warm, personal charm, among the many other things that I would grow to love about the South was its food, primarily since I was still a carnivore back then. "Meat 'n' threes," a local staple, became a regular thing for me because it was not only cheap but also home cooked. The components vary, but as the name suggests, you get one serving of a meat dish plus three sides. I fell in love with corn bread, which I'd never tasted before, and iced tea was new to me, too. In Ontario, when you ask for tea, you get hot tea. In the South, if you don't specify "hot," you automatically get iced tea.

Since I was from the North, living in the South took a serious cultural adjustment. When I saw chicken-fried steak on a menu for the first time, I was perplexed; I just could not imagine what on earth that could be. Didn't really matter: I was never able to wrap my head around the idea of eating steak coated in batter and deep-fried like Kentucky Fried Chicken, so I avoided it. I shamelessly became a pig for barbecue, though. Seeing this on a menu, I asked the waitress, "Barbecued *what*?" Was it steak? Chicken? She patiently explained that *barbecue* was just the way of cooking but referred specifically to pork meat smoked slowly on the barbecue, with a spicy sauce that was to die for. Thinking about my porking out on this Southern delight now makes me feel guilty, as it was not only very fattening, it was an animal, after all, something I wouldn't take any pleasure in eating now. One might wonder why, if I enjoyed these meat dishes so much, I would stop eating them. I became a vegetarian after reading a book called *Diet for a New America* by John Robbins, which Mutt gave me not long after my arrival in Nashville, nearing twenty years ago now. I'm sure my heart and waistline are now better off, too. My carnivorous days are over, and I say that with great conviction.

If only my adjustment to the music business had been as easy as my transition to my new home.

PolyGram's decision for me to record other people's songs and not my own was disappointing but not surprising. I understood when I got to Nashville that I would have to prove myself and that it was not all just going to fall in my lap overnight. I viewed my situation as a good start and continued to write constantly in my apartment. I fully believed that if I were patient and persevered, I would get my chance to shine as a songwriter in the not-too-distant future.

But I have to say, most of the music pitched to me for that first album was formulaic, cookie-cutter stuff. One thing, however, that did impress me of the countless listening sessions was the sonic quality of the recordings. They were only demos, but the musicianship and arrangements sounded *so good;* I couldn't wait to hear what my actual, finished CD would sound like when it was all recorded and mixed. But the songs just weren't there. Part of the reason for that had to do with my place in the Nashville artist hierarchy. In short, I was not part of it! I was this newcomer from another country and somewhat against the grain in every way. Artists are always looking for hit songs to record, and that includes country music stars, who typically got the pick of the choicest material. Hey, if you're a songwriter or the song's publisher, it stands to reason that you would give your strumming hand to have your pride and joy adopted by a megastar with platinum record sales. I was at the bottom of the first picks.

Likewise, I agreed with PolyGram's suggestion that I try collaborating with other songwriters in town. These writing sessions were booked like doctors' appointments: you sat in an office at a publishing company and had three hours or so to be artistically productive while the clock ticked down. I found it difficult to write anything worthwhile in such a setting and under time pressure. It's just not conducive to creativity. I did manage to place one song of mine on the first album, "God Ain't Gonna Getcha for That," but I think it was accepted only because I'd cowritten the tune with a proven hit maker named Kent Robbins, a future member of the Nashville Songwriters Hall of Fame. Our song was not a hit, but it was a pleasant experience writing with Kent, and I remember him fondly as being easy to get along with and kind to me as a newcomer. Tragically, he died in a car accident at only fifty years old.

Timed sessions booked by appointment were how I was experiencing the recording scene in Nashville. It harked back to the compartmentalization that existed in popular music prior to the early 1960s. Musicians played instruments, singers sang, and songwriters wrote songs, as if each were a specialist. Today many singers don't rely on songwriters for their hits; that is not unique to any period of music history. Some artists are performers only and others are on the other end of the creative process as writers, arrangers, producers, and vocalists as well. There were the exceptions, of course, those who were multitalented, such as Chuck Berry, Buddy Holly, and Johnny Cash, just three examples of stars who wrote their own material as well as performed it. But the Beatles, probably more than any other musical act, advanced the idea that a group could be a self-contained unit and record its own songs rather than rely on outside writers—much to the dismay of veteran tunesmiths and lyricists. However, on Nashville's Music Row, song-penning factories similar to Manhattan's old Brill Building still flourished.

Even the recording of the album itself fell short of what I had envisioned. I'd expected that the sessions would be crackling with energy and ideas, like what I'd seen in documentary clips of Elvis Presley. He would jam with his band in the studio for days on end, going over and over the same tune until everything felt just right, then cut the track. Same thing with the Beatles. Some of what they went into the studio with were songs they were regularly playing live already, but much was also worked out in the studio, experimenting with blends, sounds, grooves; many classic ideas were discovered by the live jamming itself, allowing room for the magic to unfold in its own time. This was what my perception of making a record was.

Recording my debut felt more like knocking out commercial jingles than record making. Given the limited budget, we zipped in and out of Harold Shedd's Music Mill studio in a few three-hour sessions, and that was it. Game over. The recording process was fast and efficient. The session musicians, to their credit, were quick to learn their parts, professional and slick, but they were booked tight, and so everyone's eyes were on the clock, with no time to play around. There was little room to experiment with musical parts or arrangements, as that would have interfered with the assembly-line approach.

As for me, I was afforded little artistic input. During playbacks, the engineers would ask me, "You happy, Eileen?" "How d'ya like it?" and I'd just nod, because it seemed pretty clear my opinion wouldn't change anything had I been candid and said that I wanted to try something different or even that I liked it but wanted to work on it some more. The budget drove the limit on our time in the studio, and the engineer's and producer's jobs were to stay within budget. It was pretty much like a waiter asking if you're finished with your meal after he's already cleared the plates. Still hungry or not, you're done as far as he's concerned. Overall, my fantasy of what the recording process would be was not to be. Nevertheless, we were recording in the Music Mill, where countless gold and platinum records had been recorded over the years and that, along with the friendly, warm studio gang of engineers and technicians, kept some of the magic alive for me.

When I arrived in Nashville, I was firm and bold about my creative ideas and career vision. It didn't take long, however, before I was warned that I'd better learn to keep such thoughts to myself. I have never been a complainer, but as my frustration grew throughout the recording process, I began to share my discontent over some of the material and explained that I was feeling trapped and disheartened by the rigid system of recording. I missed jamming with other musicians and just playing music. I felt that I was being treated like I was just some silly but decent-looking girl from the North who could sing pretty well, and here they were giving me my shot, and therefore I needed to shut up and do what I was told. I was disillusioned in thinking that I, as the artist, was supposed to be part of making the record, not just doing the vocals. I wanted to be involved, not only come in, sing my part, and leave the rest to the producers and engineers.

I was passionate about music but also pragmatic. When you are starting out, you usually don't have much choice. I wisely tempered my attitude to avoid being viewed as a troublemaker and being dropped from the label before my record even came out in the spring of 1993. My attitude was to view this as the first step of a long journey. If I played my cards right, I'd get another opportunity to make a record that was more artistically satisfying to me. So for as long as I could without getting myself in trouble, I kept my disappointment, and my opinions, to myself.

# 16

# Go Home, Small-Town Girl

As with many women who work in a man's world, such as the music industry, I've had no shortage of men trying to take advantage of me over the years. Throughout the time I was playing bars in Canada, I was usually the only girl in my immediate company of musicians, technicians, agents, and bar owners. Deerhurst Resort had a more balanced ratio of girls to guys because of the female dancers. Of course, as I learned the hard way there, working with other women can subject you to jealousy, cattiness, and drama, with the added dynamic of PMS, which men just don't bring to the scene. I learned to be the female minority among men from early adolescence and might have been more prepared for the male-dominated environment of Nashville than were some female artists.

With the frustration of having to bite my tongue rather often during the onset of my recording career, I had to talk myself out of losing my cool (*Keep your shirt on, Eileen*), all the while trying to contend with guys trying to take my shirt off. My pants, too, for that matter. Cripes! I'll give you an example:

I came across a songwriter who seemed to share my feelings about writing when inspiration struck as opposed to punching a time clock. He'd enjoyed some success placing a few of his compositions with country artists, and with a decent publishing deal, too, and I thought it was cool of him to agree to work with a newcomer like me.

For privacy's sake, let's refer to him as Dick. (I really did choose that name arbitrarily just now. Honest.)

The two of us had been working on songs together all day at his home outside of Nashville. Since it was very late and a long drive for me, we'd agreed that I would stay over. His wife had already gone to bed. I went off to my room and wasn't long under the sheets when Dick came creeping in. Bending down over me, he whispered, "Are you awake? Can I join you?" I guess he thought he'd just hop right on in and help himself. My reaction was sharp and abrupt. I reprimanded him as you would a pesky child, asking him what the hell he thought he was doing. I let him know that, firstly, I was surprised by his indecent proposal and, secondly, I was *soooo* not interested.

I wondered what in the world gave Dick the idea that I was attracted to him, but then I felt a dirty chill come over me when it dawned on me: that was just it, he didn't actually care if I was attracted to him or not. He saw me as a struggling singer-songwriter, far from home, new in town, vulnerable—and therefore available. I guessed his thinking was that if I gave him what he wanted, I'd fall for the trap of believing that he'd help me out professionally somehow in return. Yeah, right! I was so disgusted and discouraged about human nature at that moment. Weary, too. It seemed like a woman performer just could not avoid these humiliating encounters. Dick acted resentful and cold to me the next morning. I have never seen him since. Gross!

In those first few years of my adult career, I began to recognize a trend that I hadn't experienced as a child artist. The suggestion that a young, attractive girl gets to the top only by sleeping her way there was becoming annoyingly recurrent. Jealous women who create rumors that you've slept your way up and disrespectful men who attempt to make reality of it. I was quickly becoming fed up with this childish, spiteful attitude, but just as quickly, I had to learn to let it roll off my back and not allow such negative distractions to affect me too personally.

Another sweaty-palms experience involved an older gentleman

who, again for privacy reasons, we will call Henry. He was handsome, popular, and very well respected in the entire country music industry. Henry spoke softly in a soothing Southern drawl that exuded kindliness. I liked Henry. He was polite and fun, and he invited me to events and social gatherings as a way to help me get settled in the area. While enthusiastic about my talent, he advised me strongly to keep a tighter lid on my dissatisfaction. I appreciated his support and friendship.

One night Henry invited me to a party at his home. As with the previous events he'd asked me to attend, I expected it to be full of people from the music industry. However, I arrived to find only a few people there, and they would soon be leaving.

*What is this?* I thought to myself with great suspicion. *What am I doing here and why?* I'd never seen the other guests that were about to depart, and I got the feeling that they had been given some kind of signal to scram. They were a bit tipsy, and Henry was topsy-turvy. Before long, the two of us were left alone in this great, big house, which made me feel very small and vulnerable. But having had ample experience around drunken men in bars as well as fending off unwanted advances, I acted cool and didn't panic—yet.

Before I got out the words "Well, I think it's time for me to go, too," Henry was all over me. "Don't leave," he pleaded, slurring his words. "Why don't we go to my bedroom?"

"Henry," I said sternly, "I think *you* need to go to bed. You're drunk." He was staggering, and I think that even he was aware that he wasn't fit for much else other than crashing. Like a little boy who had been caught staying up past his bedtime, he agreed to go to bed. Alone. One problem: how was I going to get home? A friend had dropped me off, and there was no public transportation where Henry lived.

"Henry, is there a cab company I can call?"

"Don't be ridiculous," he said. "I'll drive you home." We both had a good laugh over that, knowing that he was in no shape to get behind the wheel.

"Here." With that, he tossed me his keys. "Take my car." I wasn't about to argue.

Never having been terribly interested in cars, I can't tell you what make and model it was, but I do know that Henry was very proud of his pricey, posh wheels. It was some kind of luxury sports car, maybe a Porsche or a BMW. Whatever it was, I'd never driven anything like it in my life. I slid into the driver's seat and I felt as if I were in the cockpit of a jet on wheels. All these buttons and knobs on the console in front of me. I didn't know where to begin. This vehicle needed a freakin' pilot!

It actually took me several minutes to work out how to operate this machine, with the biggest problem, other than actually starting it, being that I couldn't figure out how to adjust the seat. May I note that Henry was a very tall man, and I was simply too short to reach the accelerator.

I had a moment of near tears trying to maneuver my escape vessel. I felt like a useless, silly girl running to save her decency, trying to salvage her self-respect by scraping out of a compromising situation with some dignity still intact, and I couldn't even adjust the seat of the hunk of metal testosterone I was counting on to save me? How could I drive my dad's big, blue school bus on a bush road, a swamp buggy through a marsh, and pilot tin can vehicles of all shapes and sizes in winter with no four-wheel drive and not be able to drive this car that was so sophisticated that it gave the impression it could drive itself?

While I angrily pressed this button and yanked on that lever, I could swear that the fancy-pants car was taunting me: "Go home, small-town girl. Back to the simple existence you were born to. You're in over your head and way out of your league here." Maybe it was right. Maybe this world *was* over my head. At that moment, I might have considered giving up and going back home, except that I had no home to go back to. It was forward or failure. Whenever I hear the song "Good-bye Yellow Brick Road" by Elton John, cowritten with Bernie Taupin, I get emotional, as it reminds me of this time in my life when the society I was trying to make it in wasn't really *me*. The male dominance, the trophy value of a pretty woman on the arm of a powerful man, the dangling carrots, and integrity at stake every step of the way. Maybe it was time I woke up and realized that I wasn't made for the music business. It was tiring trying to keep it all together and not become so overwhelmed that I wanted to just give up and go back to what was familiar, the small mining town. As Elton sang so poignantly, "I should have stayed on the farm." This was *so* how I felt, only in my case, I should have stayed in the bush.

The truth is, I was as mad at myself for being in the situation in the first place. I'd let this guy set me up. How could I not have seen it coming? And how could I have let myself trust this man as a friend and not see his true intentions? "You should have known better," I scolded myself. "This is the *music business*, after all. This was a classic case of the casting couch, and you walked right into it."

*Finally,* I managed to tame the beasty bastard of a car well enough to make my way home. Although I wasn't able to move the seat all the way forward, at least my toes now *just* touched the accelerator and brake pedals. When I finally pulled into the parking lot at my apartment complex and got out of the car, I was right pissed off and ready to give it a good kick. Instead I just cursed at it a few times, figuring, why leave a dent or a scratch? Part of me was proud that I hadn't banged it up on the way home.

The next morning, I avoided having to speak to Henry directly by deliberately calling early and leaving a message on his answering machine, telling him where his car was (in case, in his drunken fog, he had forgotten all about it) and that the keys were under the sun visor. Henry was directly involved in the music community that surrounded me, so we crossed paths often after that, but he was never quite the same toward me. I later heard rumors that we'd had an affair, and although I resented it and wanted to smack him in the face for allowing this to be whispered around town, I didn't know if he was personally responsible for circulating them, so I let the matter drop. Hey, if Henry wanted people to think that he got lucky with the young

Canadian newcomer, good for him. By now I have some experience with this kind of crap and am able to just shake it off, although I still find it upsetting.

I carried on with my chin held high and focused on my music. Never did I sleep with any man just to further my career, which in the entertainment world can be risky. Certainly there are powerful men who, if a woman does not play along, will go out of their way to make her pay professionally. But I was confident enough in myself to believe that I could succeed without compromising my body or my integrity.

# 17

# New Country, New Name

My debut album was slated for release in April 1992. I felt that it was a pretty average record, to be truthful, but PolyGram was gearing up for the launch enthusiastically. Typically, a label, having invested in an artist, will support at least the first single with a promotional push. This means investing in photos and a music video, and arranging a string of radio and television appearances and magazine coverage. If the record is successful, you will probably get a shot at a second single, a third, and so on until that CD has run its course with public demand and radio interest. Then, if all goes well, the company will bankroll a second CD. My deal called for delivering eight albums, so I felt fairly secure, even though artists contracted for multiple albums have been known to be dropped unceremoniously if their previous public offering meets with indifference.

The CD was to be titled simply *Shania Twain*.

That I agreed to the record company's request for me to change my name should be sufficient evidence of my level of cooperation. To be honest, I had more qualms about the caliber of material being sent my way than I did about adopting a professional name. After all, even Mark Twain himself was born Samuel Clemens. The thought of picking out a stage name actually struck me as kind of fun. But I made it clear to everyone that under no circumstances would I change my last name, out of respect and loyalty to my father. He had sacrificed to raise me, putting gas in the car so that I could get to gigs when the money really should have gone toward groceries or paying the heating bill. To abandon our family surname would have made me feel like a traitor. But even I had to admit that *Eilleen* and *Twain* didn't make for a dynamic combination for a performer. My first name was too soft sounding. Great stage names often have hard consonants in them, something catchy like *Dol*-ly Parton or Nat "King" Cole. Alliteration also works well: *Loretta Lynn* (her married name) has a melodious quality to it and seems to roll right off the tongue. Or it is just unique, like Elvis Presley. That was a one-of-a-kind name.

What, then, to pair with Twain? I tried a long list of combinations. Then I remembered a wardrobe mistress I'd met at Deerhurst Resort shortly before I left there. She was about my age and, like me, had been raised in a biracial family, only her mother was Native American, and her father was white. The first time she introduced herself as Shania, I had to ask her to repeat herself. I had never heard such a beautiful, unique, and exotic name, which, unbeknown to me at the time, means "on my way." I just knew that the name had such a hopeful ring to it. I started rolling *Shania* around on my tongue, then *Shania . . . Twain.* Yes. Yes! They seemed to fit together perfectly. I ran it by executives at the record company, they liked it, and it stuck.

As the release date drew near, I was sent to media training. In addition to toning down my Canadian accent, I had to learn when to put the brakes on my naturally impulsive sense of humor and my tendency to express myself freely and, um, colorfully. Wouldn't want to unnecessarily offend anyone in, say, an interview for a newspaper or on radio and TV with political incorrectness or things that would have been considered derogatory in some areas of the States I wouldn't have thought twice about maybe saying "For Christ's sake" if being spontaneously expressive or maybe "No shit!" if caught by surprise by what was being said. With my unrefined Northern upbringing, four-letter words certainly made up a sizable portion of my vocabulary, and I was not raised in a religious environment, so I didn't understand the sensitivity to using words that would be considered offensive to some. I was ignorant in that sense, and an expression like

"Jesus effin' Christ" (used regularly by my father) is common where we're from. I mean, when you stub your toe, there is nothing quite as satisfying as a good old guttural curse word. That was not acceptable in my new environment, however, if I wanted to be respected and taken seriously, so the bushwhacker language had to go. Also, being naturally hyper and energetic, which on TV can look like someone in the control room accidentally sped up the videotape, I needed to speak slower and be less animated. It's not a matter of muzzling yourself, but sometimes comments that seem perfectly innocuous, or hilarious, when you're horsing around on the tour bus with people you know—and, just as important, who know you—just come out all wrong when you read them the next day in print or when you see yourself on television.

It's as though the in-person lens and the television lens can give off a different tone even when they show the same image. Have you ever listened to your voice on a phone message you left someone? You might find yourself unrecognizable or at least weird sounding. We have different ways of acting and sounding when we're being recorded or on the phone. I've even heard the term "the phone voice," for example. If you overhear someone speaking, you can pretty much tell if she is speaking to someone in person or over the phone, just by the tone of her voice.

PolyGram's Nashville office oversaw the label's country acts exclusively. Now, I had always considered myself a versatile singer and songwriter, and not tied to any one style of music. But, as with popular art in general, the recording industry needed to decide in which display case to put me in order for the marketing machine to work. The reality is that categorization exists in every aspect of the music business: a country artist's records will receive airplay on radio stations with a country music format, obviously, and not on stations that cater to fans of rap or so-called classic rock. Likewise, in which section of the record store will your CD be filed? And while there are general-interest publications and radio and TV programs that will cover anyone who's creating a buzz, you have others that are more narrowly focused and are interested only in artists belonging to a specific genre.

Without a doubt, my musical roots sprang from country music. Growing up, I related to musicians such as Dolly Parton, Waylon Jennings, Willie Nelson, and Johnny Cash. I still love their music. However, years of playing bars and nightclubs force you to juggle a variety of styles, which is a good thing for anyone's musical development. I thought of myself as a crossover artist in the mold of Elvis, Glen Campbell, Olivia Newton-John, and John Denver. They touched on multiple styles and did not restrict themselves to just one genre. They were in an elite group of artists capable of something called crossing over.

I developed my joy of singing from listening to a wide range of vocalists, some of whom did not necessarily leave a detectable imprint on my own approach to personal style and development of self-taught techniques. For instance, Stevie Wonder. He slides around notes with such ease. As a vocal exercise, I used to play his records and study every bend and nuance to help me develop more agility. His timing and pitch were so technically correct, yet he sang with enough soul to keep me musically high for life. Singing along with him was an intense vocal exercise. Gladys Knight is another voice I couldn't get enough of, as it touched me somewhere deeper than I could ever reach with my own voice. For me, Stevie and Gladys represent the epitome of vocal soul.

During my teenage years, every day there was something new to blow me away: Michael Jackson, Supertramp, Van Halen, Def Leppard, Whitney Houston, the Police. Different genres, to be sure, but each had a unique effect on me musically.

By the time I signed with PolyGram, it had been many years since I'd sung or listened to country music, and the whole scene had changed drastically. I wasn't familiar with any contemporary country singers—not even Reba McEntire! If you had asked me to name the newest female country artist, I'd have said Tanya Tucker, and she recorded her first record in 1972. I was obviously out of touch with what was happening in current country, but here I was signed to the country music department of PolyGram. I tried to convince Harold Shedd that I'd be best marketed as more of a pop artist, which would allow me to explore a more eclectic mix of styles. I made the same case to the people in the label's A&R department. A&R stands for artists and repertoire; it's the division of a record company responsible for scouting talent, overseeing the artistic development of the artists it signs, and acting as a sort of liaison between artists and the business side of the label. However, the powers that be insisted on keeping me firmly in the country genre for my debut.

I knew I'd better get up to snuff on things. I started watching CMT as much as possible, and it was a fantastic platform for seeing, hearing, and knowing all you needed to know about the "new country" that was monopolizing the country charts. It didn't exactly take me back to my roots: what I would consider *true* country. Occasionally the video channel reunited me with some familiar faces from my childhood who were still around and managing airtime, like the odd George Jones single, but for the most part, it was all new artists. Personally, I preferred the old country I'd grown up with, as I felt it had more depth and sincerity than the new batch.

Nevertheless, this was my world now. I had to understand the way it worked if I was going to give my label music it would get behind and promote actively. My intention was to be always true to myself creatively. However, all artists must contend with the reality that without the support of their record company, radio, music television, and to a lesser extent the press, the public will never hear their music. It becomes a bit of a balancing act, especially when you're trying to get your career off the ground. I started to feel pressure to fit in and to ignore my pangs to be a mixed-bag, original artist. To the industry critics and my label, I think the fear was that I would be considered unidentifiable and confused about who I was artistically. So they had to compartmentalize me.

When I first went to Nashville, I began to share my discontent with not being able to find songwriters in the league of writers I wanted to write with, who would write "after hours" and outside an office, away from the publishing house. I explained that I was feeling trapped by a system and couldn't be original that way. Although I was happy that my first record was well on its way to being produced and would soon launch, I was disheartened by the lack of creative control and input I had. It took some tight lipping to get through it.

What I heard and saw was assembly-line-type songs and music videos of imagery, artistic direction, design, and style, all seemingly respecting formula over creative freedom. Few videos stood apart from the rest, was my observation. Garth Brooks seemed like the only person setting an innovative bar visually for country music videos. I remember telling myself that when it came time to make the video for my first single, "What Made You Say That," I would see to it that we came up with something truly unique and interesting. I was determined to express my individuality.

The video was directed by a fellow Canadian, Steven Goldmann, who would go on to direct five more videos for me. Great guy, energetic, easy to work with. He had the perfect personality for working with someone who had never made a video before. I had no idea how to perform in front of a camera, karaoke style, trying to live the song with as much sincerity as possible while lip-syncing. I had never lip-synced before, either, and found it incredibly tricky to match my video performance to the record. Do you sing out during the filming, so that it looks as authentic as possible? Or do you just sort of "air sing" in order to hear the playback better and be more precise with your facial expressions and how you mouth the words? Thanks to Steve's patience and understanding, I eventually got the knack of learning how to act my way through the fake singing without losing my concentration. Although Steve had strong ideas, he was flexible and open to my input, so that I was involved with the direction and feel of the overall look, image, and story.

With little money behind us, the production was small. Nevertheless, Steve pulled it together and made it into something eye-catching.

We shot in Miami, Florida. He was skilled, especially at filming in natural light, and I can still say today that I am very happy with the way my first video turned out. Except for two things, starting with my thick eyebrows. I laugh so hard when I see those, as I had no idea how to pluck eyebrows yet. I'm not even sure that we had hair and makeup professionals on the set. Even if we had, I probably would have been too insecure to let anyone reshape my brows. I also cringe when I look back at earlier images of myself and see the kinked, frizzy look of my overpermed hair.

Steve and I went wardrobe shopping at a cheap department store. I fished through the racks until I found a few outfits that I thought were flattering yet also reflected the song's playful nature. And I had to be able to move comfortably in them. One thing I'd never seen on Country Music Television was a woman's bare midriff, surprisingly enough. You saw it everywhere else in popular culture, from a Cindy Crawford workout video to Madonna's latest video clip. I did not see any reason not to bare my midriff for a video set on a Florida beach in the hot summer sun. What's the big deal, right?

Apparently bigger than I ever imagined. CMT refused to air "What Made You Say That" at first, claiming that it was too suggestive because of the—and let's be honest, really modest—crop top I wore. I couldn't believe it. The three-minute video consists almost entirely of me and my studly fantasy boyfriend frolicking playfully on the beach, with a little innocent canoodling here and there. Two of the three outfits I wear in the clip cover my midriff completely. It's only a black two-piece that shows anything, and we're talking maybe four inches of skin from the navel on up. *Billboard*, the music industry's weekly trade magazine, referred to my dancing as "alluring," and while I appreciate the compliment, even that's a stretch. I would go so far as to call it quite tame even for that time.

Eventually CMT reversed its decision, adding "What Made You Say That" to its playlist, but the whole controversy left me wondering what had happened to country music. I'd turned my attention elsewhere for a few years, and it had gone all prudish on me! The performers I'd followed as a child were sexy, flashy, brash, bold, beautiful. Take Dolly Parton. She certainly wasn't shy about dressing to accentuate her stunning Barbie-perfect figure. Or how about Elvis, who was as beloved in country music as he was in rock 'n' roll, with his sexy, steamy image? Willie Nelson and the boys? They weren't exactly known to be clean-cut, law-abiding citizens, and they sang freely about their "outlaw" ways. Loretta Lynn sang about being a honky-tonk girl early on and later about deciding to take the pill (and many country radio stations refused to play "The Pill" when it was first released in 1975). All of this was the country music that I knew: real, raw, and relatable. So why on earth was the country music industry now bucking me for merely showing my midriff?

I'm standing on a stone-lined path, accepting that I have to take them one step at a time. The particular step of my first CD and the whole Nashville experience is proving to finally feel more solid. After this initial period of about a year, I sense I'm past the shaky transitional phase of leaving my country, a steady paying gig, the scrimping by of part-time clerking at Sears in Timmins, the temporary bunking from the Montgomery apartment, Paul's parents and the river cabin, to open a new chapter in my life. It's as though I'm about to graduate from a university of sorts. I finished high school in 1983, and it's now the end of 1992. Nine years of education between the cradles of hometown high school and the lap of the music industry giant of Music City. I can sense I'm poised to leave the Nashville campus, take what I've learned from the professors of legends, and apply it to my own entertainment career. My record is finished after several months of preparation and anticipation.

Soon after the single "What Made You Say That" came out in February 1993, I went out on my first professional tour, dubbed Triple Play because it featured two other PolyGram acts who were also readying their debut albums: Toby Keith and John Brannen. We were very different artists musically, with equally different images. The three of us got along pretty well considering we spent several weeks cooped up together on a bus. I came back from the promotional blitz having learned many things I didn't know before, like how to chew and spit tobacco—a curious but short-lived habit. I received frequent reminders that I should starch my jeans so that they had the appropriate center crease; furthermore, they had to be Wrangler brand or nothing. Also, my red ankle-strap, platform high heels were not really working, and I needed to get myself a pair of Ropers, which I was plainly told were the only legitimate cowgirl boot at the time. I also added a few line-dancing moves to my repertoire, which were quite fun. I understood the need to conform somewhat, but, again, I was feeling a bit like a puppet on a string. There was pressure to fit a certain mold if you hoped to gain acceptance in this industry. I always wondered just who, exactly, set these standards for how to look, act, and sound in the first place. And how could anything original ever have a chance to develop in such a one-dimensional, homogenized environment?

Just one single into my career, and already I was feeling trapped. I didn't think I could keep my ideas, opinions, and creative energy locked up too much longer. But the pragmatic me understood that if the record label began to view me as "difficult," there would be some other up-and-coming performer ready to take my place. For the time being, I had to suppress my dismay and just keep forging ahead one step at a time. Adding to my insecurity about feeling like somewhat of a misfit was the fact that Mercury Nashville had a new president, Luke Lewis, taking over the label's day-to-day affairs, and Harold Shedd had been bumped upstairs. Luke Lewis went on to head up Mercury Nashville for ten years. Although I felt that I had more to offer artistically than Harold appreciated, he was still the person who'd signed me to Mercury, showed me around town when I first got there, and coproduced my first record. I had heard stories about new artists sometimes cutting an album, then having it shelved for so long that it was outdated by the time it hit the stores; in some cases, the record never saw the light of day. At least that wasn't my fate.

Being an artist on a record label really is no different than being an employee anywhere else: when a new boss comes in, especially from outside the company, you worry about where you stand. Would Mercury purge its roster, as had been known to happen during times of managerial changes, and would this Canadian newcomer be a goner?

My concerns vanished once I met Luke, a calm, cool man with a deep, sexy voice and a straightforward way of communicating. He was firm but quick to laugh and didn't take offense at the edgy part of my personality. I knew right away that we'd get along fine, much to my relief.

The Triple Play tour provided great exposure and a crash course in what it is to be a performing artist in the States: the types of venues, the radio environment, the tour bus "thing" of living in your transportation, and the competitive nature of the business. While my single was doing okay, eventually ascending to number fifty-five on the *Billboard* Hot Country Songs chart, Toby's first record, "Should've Been a Cowboy," was on its way to number one. I was happy for him: he was a hard worker, a decent guy, and he'd come by his success honestly. But he really earned my respect because the song was his own, not the product of a Nashville tune factory. As the tour progressed and Toby's popularity soared, John and I receded into the shadows; wherever we went, most of the public attention was directed at Toby. The fans who came out to the shows would ask me and John for our autographs, too, but I think it was mostly out of interest in getting all three—like completing a place setting. At one point I wasn't sure I'd get another chance for a second single release, but I was happy for Toby and enjoyed the whole experience.

While still on the tour, I learned that actor Sean Penn was interested in directing my next music video. I still don't know how he'd even heard of me. Perhaps he watched CMT at the time? I was glad he did, in any case. Frankly, I'm not sure that Mercury had planned on a follow-up to "What Made You Say That," but to have someone of Sean's caliber interested in working with me might have made the label take me more seriously and agree to finance the production. The timing was great, and I felt I may have a second chance with a follow-up single, after all.

During a tour break, Sean flew to Nashville to meet me and discuss his concept for the video. He was very cool and fun, direct with his ideas but easygoing and open to my input. He took the project very seriously, so before I knew it, I was at a Los Angeles film studio shooting the video for "Dance with the One That Brought You." To be honest, the song, a midtempo number, wasn't very strong, and I regret that Sean's ability and enthusiasm were wasted on a track that I knew was never going to amount to much commercially, but the experience of working with him was incredible. He'd pulled in noted character actor Charles Durning to play the role of the overage good-time Charlie who goes out two-steppin' with his loving wallflower wife on a small-town Saturday night. I adored him as an actor and even more in person. He was such a sweet man and very gracious toward me.

Before shooting the video, Sean and I met in L.A. for a couple of days to work out some details. At one point, we went to get something to eat in his beat-up Mustang convertible. On the way back, he stopped off to see his wife, Robin Wright Penn. She came outside, and the two of them had a quick word while I stayed in the car. I'd always admired Robin's acting and thought she was so beautiful. I feared that maybe she'd suspected that I was some girlfriend tagging along for a while. Or even if Sean had explained that the girl in his car was a recording artist he was directing in a video, what if she had the impression that there was something going on between us? I would have hated for that to be the case, because Sean was a perfect gentleman every second I was in his company. Something in me wanted Robin to know that, even if it wasn't necessary.

One time when he was dropping me off at my hotel, this unassuming movie star pulled out a $100 bill and handed it to me. He didn't say anything, just gave it to me. I was still struggling to get by, because the meager advance from the record label was just enough to cover basic living costs, so when I traveled, I had little money left over for eating at restaurants, taking cabs, and so forth. I didn't say anything to Sean about my dire financial straits; I guess he just sensed it and felt sorry for me.

I was embarrassed to receive a handout like that. "Thank you," I stammered as I moved away from the Mustang. "I promise I'll pay you back." I never did do that, so I'll have to make a point of doing it now. Sean may not even remember, but I do, and I thought it was very kind of him. To me, Sean came across as someone who cared about the underdog. It seemed that he listened more than he spoke but was not afraid to speak his mind. A real straight shooter.

# 18

## Meeting Mutt

Shortly before the Triple Play tour ended, my manager, Mary Bailey, asked me if I'd ever heard of anyone named Mutt Lange. I hadn't but thought, *What an interesting name.*

"He's a record producer," said Mary, who had also never heard of him. "He's got your CD and asked if you'd sign a photo for him."

I did, only I spelled his name "Mut," with one *t* instead of two. Years later, he showed it to me, and we both had a good laugh. It was probably the first genuine "fan" autograph I'd ever signed, since all the others I'd autographed up to that point were on the coattails of Toby Keith!

Mutt initiated our first phone conversation through Mary, and the communication between us evolved quickly after that, with calls that would last for hours on end. I was now on my own but still touring in small country music bars across the States, singing "What Made You Say That," "Dance with the One That Brought You," and one or two other cuts from my debut CD. I wasn't out with a backup band, though: that would come a bit later into the release of the album, where I tried to generate some money by live club performances with a small group of musicians. The purpose of this particular road trip was primarily to meet and greet disc jockeys and do radio interviews during the day, then put on these abbreviated performances at night. With *Shania Twain* selling only modestly, PolyGram was not about to spring for supporting musicians and all the infrastructure that goes into mounting a full-scale tour, during a purely promotional tour. So, much to my chagrin, I had to stand onstage and sing along live to my own CD. That's right: Shania Twain was singing karaoke to Shania Twain. No band, no vibe, just me holding a live mic, standing in a spotlight. It was downright embarrassing.

Although it was humiliating, the way I had to look at it was that I was involved in a fight to keep that first single afloat as long as possible while the fate of my recording future with PolyGram was surely being questioned with each passing week. Would I get a shot at a second single? There was no certainty. Even though Sean Penn directing the video for my second single gave me hope of having better success at radio and more security with my record company, the song just wasn't strong enough for that to happen. I was encouraged that Sean considered me and my music worth his while, but I didn't have the song that would make the most of that break.

Afterward, I would return to my run-down hotel room around midnight and get on the phone with Mutt, who was in his studio just outside of London. Talking to him cheered me up, since he seemed to speak my language musically, only with the added charm of a South African–British hybrid accent. He sounded mature, and I guessed he was older than me. Over time, I developed a mental picture of what he must look like: a tall, pudgy man in his fifties, wearing a floral shirt, balding in front but with long, black-silver hair tied back in a ponytail. I have no idea how this image found its way into my head.

Our hours together were spent mostly talking and playing music. He'd either call me directly in my room or leave me a message to call him when I got in, then he'd immediately tell me to hang up, that he'd call me right back so I didn't have to pay for the calls. He knew I couldn't afford it and was considerate that way. He was working on a couple of original tracks at the time and would play me bits and pieces. Then it would be my turn to prop up the phone receiver on a pillow, pull out my guitar, and play Mutt some songs I was working on. He was very complimentary about my ideas and my voice, and it was refreshing to have someone so musical sincerely interested in me as an artist. Although he was born in Rhodesia (now Zambia), attended school in South Africa, then moved to England in his twenties, he had always been a big fan of American country music.

The first time Mutt played me what he was working on in the studio, I almost fell out of my chair. The sound was so outstanding. I was blown away by it sonically, the arrangement, and the whole gorgeous wall of sound pouring through the receiver. It was hard for me to hold in my excitement as I heard this incredible music. I remember thinking, quite naïvely, *This guy is really good! This stuff's going to be big!* I may even have made a fool of myself by saying something stupid like that to him.

Mutt, a very humble person, never name-dropped the many multimillion-selling artists for whom he'd cowritten many of the songs and produced (AC/DC, Boomtown Rats, the Cars, Def Leppard, Foreigner, among many others) or mentioned the hit songs he'd cowritten—including Huey Lewis and the News's "Do You Believe in Love," much of Def Leppard's 1980s output, and the Grammy Award–winning "(Everything I Do) I Do It for You," which he co-wrote with and produced for Bryan Adams. I never had an inkling that he was a big-time producer with millions and millions sold. The album *Hysteria* by Def Leppard alone moved twenty million copies worldwide.

My interest in him musically developed over many weeks of these transcontinental phone calls. By the time I finally discovered Mutt's iconic status in the music industry, we had already bonded on our own terms without the influence of too much information. The foundation of our early relationship was based simply on my wanting to hear more of what he was working on and his wanting to hear more of what I was working on.

The first time we met was in June at the 1993 CMA Music Festival/Fan Fair, an annual four-day event that the Country Music Association had been putting on since 1972. It's like an all-you-can-eat buffet for devotees of country music. Performers, ranging from

the most famous names to relative unknowns, play concerts, sign autographs, and, in general, rub shoulders with the most enthusiastic
fans you'll meet, more than 130,000 of them, on average.

I was scheduled to make my Fan Fair debut on the main stage; I
believe it was Tim McGraw's first appearance there, too. Mutt was
going to be at the Tennessee State Fairground to see Randy Travis
perform, his favorite of the country artists of that period.

We had agreed to meet backstage after my performance, and I
was so excited to finally see him face-to-face. I was also nervous to
know that he was watching me onstage, as I wanted to live up to
whatever his expectations were of me as a singer. Obviously Mutt
knew what I looked like; I was still expecting that tall, pudgy, balding dude with the ponytail. As soon as I walked around the back of
the stage, Mutt approached me and introduced himself. We hugged
like two long-lost friends, and out rang that familiar voice I had been
speaking to for so many weeks. But aside from being tall, nothing
about Mutt's appearance fit my image of him. He had curly blond,
shoulder-length hair, light blue eyes, and a slender, fit physique. He
was older than me but looked younger than his voice suggested. I
was surprised that he looked so different from what I was expecting. He was even warmer and more approachable in person. I loved
Mutt Lange at first sight. Not that I was *in love* with him, but I loved
him with a familiarity I could not explain. We had a connection that
I didn't understand and didn't question. It was natural and easy. Not
romantic; not yet. It was a love that felt innocent and comfortable,
just the way it was. I had not looked ahead or anticipated a deeper
relationship with him at that point.

I was excited at the thought of seeing him again and creatively
charged to be writing music with someone so musically incredible.

The next month I flew to London to meet with him, loaded
with a long list of song ideas, titles, and melodies I'd been banking
since Deerhurst, including those rejected by the record company
for my first record. We stayed overnight in a little area on the out-

skirts of London called Hind Head, where Mutt lived in a charming country-style cottage that sat at the bottom of a small valley with patches of ivy and spotted moss cloaking the exterior walls. It was very picturesque, this cozy home of Mutt's, I thought. On the inside, it was always very tidy and particularly quiet. He had stunning gardens that he'd designed himself and also planted much of with his own two hands. I related very well to his own approach of rolling up his sleeves and digging in, so to speak, when something needed to be done. The rooms in his house, with windows looking out on the gardens and framing them like masterpiece paintings, stopped me in my tracks as I took in the glorious views of fountains and pristine, carpet-like lawns framed in by flower beds of tremendous contrasting color and texture. Mutt was a gifted garden designer.

The next day we flew to his house in Spain, where he felt the change of scenery would be more creatively inspiring. I was already awed by Hind Head, but as he lived there, I could see his point, so off we went to his hillside retreat overlooking the Mediterranean Sea. It was a two-story house embedded in the side of a rock face, with a sun-and-sea holiday feel to it, creating a relaxed vibe, perfect for artistic inspiration. It wasn't an extravagant house, but I could tell Mutt had been thoughtful about the décor. I appreciated his sense of style and attention to aesthetic detail. Like in the Hind Head house outside of London, it was clear I was in the home of someone particular about his surroundings and sensitive to quality and personal taste. Mutt and I made great progress in the two weeks I was there, combining our collective writing. It was a concentrated time of all writing. We stopped for meal breaks but stayed focused on making the most of each day writing songs. I enjoyed this time indulging in being creative with no interruption. It was almost like a songwriting vacation. All I was required to do was sit around thinking of musical ideas. It was fantastic! It was reminiscent of the period when all my friends were at university and college all day studying, while I stayed back in the apartment working on music. Only this time, I had a partner, someone who was doing the same thing I was: living and breathing music intensely for an extended period of time until he came up with something satisfying.

There was never anyone around except for the two of us and the cleaning lady, who came with a whispered presence off and on throughout the weekdays. I remember very clearly feeling uncomfortable with her doing my laundry. I wasn't used to people doing domestic chores for me and felt guilty when she took it upon herself to add it to her other cleaning chores. I was more accustomed to rolling up my own sleeves to either do it myself or at the very least pitch in. I asked her how to use the machines and insisted on doing it myself. This was very odd behavior to her, I could tell, but she smiled and obliged. I felt awkwardly spoiled letting someone else clean my dirty clothes. Such luxury was for the likes of Scarlett O'Hara in *Gone with the Wind,* not for Eilleen from Timmins, Ontario.

Too soon for me, my songwriting holiday was over and I had to fly back to Nashville, pack my bags, and hit the road again to carry on promoting Shania Twain. The second I walked into my Brentwood apartment, I called Mutt and told him that I missed him already. I didn't feel coy about saying it, as I missed him in the way that you would miss a family member or close friend. At this stage of our relationship, Mutt never indicated that he was interested in anything other than creating songs together. He was a gentleman and never made me feel uneasy in any way.

I made a second songwriting trip to Mutt about a month later and the songs between us were really taking shape. But it was our third round of writing sessions that would change the course of my personal life forever.

I could sense that being with Mutt was awakening something else inside me other than friendship. My impression was that Mutt was a humble and sincere person, interested in music more deeply than anything else, but he began to reveal a sincere interest in me personally, which I was also feeling mutually. Mutt didn't concern himself with what I knew about "who" he was and what he'd accomplished. I appreciated this quality in him. Instead, we spoke about our music and our childhoods, and entertained each other with endless conversation about life overall. We were getting to know each other as people in this week and discovering that we wanted to spend more time together. We wanted to be closer. By the end of our Majorca writing session, I knew my life was changing before my eyes and by the second. Just being around Mutt gave me energy, and we had so much to talk about.

Although this time brought us to admit a personal affection toward each other, I wasn't certain what my feelings meant, and in this confusion, I tried to control my burgeoning feelings for him. Life would just carry on as before. I would go home to Paul, his family, and our little cabin by the river and ignore that something within me was somehow different. I wanted to sit around the campfire and sing my new songs, deny the realization that the person I'd spent the last six years in a relationship with was not the one I would build my future with. I was afraid to let go, as letting go of my relationship with Paul felt as though I would be letting go of stability itself. I was unsettled by the thought of leaving his companionship, his caring family, and the comfortable familiarity we'd developed between us over the years. We had a special bond that was painful to imagine living without. Paul made me feel safe and loved, but I could not hold on to something for the sake of feeling safe. I had to be honest with him and myself that I was not committed to marrying him, and holding on would be wrong. I knew I had to let go of one to have the other, and not when it necessarily suited me. My relationship with Paul had been too meaningful to abuse, so I left the security I had with him, his family, and our friends more abruptly than I was emotionally prepared for, and it felt as if I were flying from the nest and about to enter a whole new, scary world.

It was as though I'd come to the end of a volume in my life. Timmins, my family, Paul, Canada—none of it was coming with me. After saying good-bye to Paul, he went to our little cabin on the bank of the Kenogamissi Lake to be with his family; and I to my manager Mary's house in Kirkland Lake, two hours south. Emotionally drained, I pulled up to her and her husband Bob's log cabin, which they'd built themselves between a wide river and a white birch forest. I don't remember much about this brief interlude of mourning, as I was in a fog the whole time, but I do recall sitting on her basement sofa sobbing for three days straight and going through boxes of tissues.

I was gutted that Paul and I were over, even though I'd realized that he wasn't the one I wanted to spend the rest of my life with. After crying every tear I had, I left Mary's to head back to my new world of Mutt and music in Nashville.

# 19

# The Woman in Me, Married

"Shania, when are you coming back to Nashville? It's time to get your butt in the studio!" This was Luke Lewis, wondering where in the hell I'd been during the recent promotional tour breaks. The *Shania Twain* CD was petering out, and it was time for me to start on the next record and get it released while there was still an awareness that there had ever even been a Shania Twain, recording artist. Ironically, the first step was to go through the process of shopping for the songs. Of course, Luke had no idea at this stage that the entire song list for what would be my next CD was almost already completely written. With the few trips back and forth to Europe, writing these songs with Mutt, and the trip to Canada to say goodbye to Paul, I'd scarcely been in Nashville over the past few months, so I understood Luke's pressure for me to shit or get off the pot. They weren't giving recording opportunities away, after all, let alone second chances. I was grateful to him for another shot after the feeble sales of *Shania Twain*. Frigg, I was thankful just to have been kept on the roster; not all PolyGram's country artists survived the managerial musical chairs of the past several months.

Mutt and I agreed that label executives would likely be leery to learn that I was collaborating on songs with an Englishman by way of South Africa who also happened to be *that AC/DC–Def Leppard guy*. They might think I'd gone rock. You could just imagine them worrying that I'd be grinding my Spandex-clad body in front of skyscrapers of amplifiers while flashing the devil's-horns sign, or what- ever it is, at the audience. So we kept the news from Luke for the meantime.

Without going into detail, I did my best to reassure Luke that I was not just goofing off sightseeing in Majorca. "I'm working really hard," I told him. "I just need a little more time before I share it with you." I'm not sure I was all that convincing, as I sensed some skepti- cism from the other end of the transatlantic call. But as I was being vague in my attempt to avoid lying, I probably gave the impression that I was being unappreciative.

"I promise I'll come back next week and let you have a listen, okay?" Before Luke could press me for more details, I feigned not being able to hear him due to the poor connection (well, that part was true; the line was a bit static-y) and quickly got off the phone.

Believe me, I would have *loved* to have played Luke some sam- ples right then and there, because I knew these songs were magical, even in their raw state: just the two of us playing acoustic guitars and me singing with Mutt joining with harmony and vocal counterparts. Mutt and I were rockin'. I was feeling charged creatively and hav- ing the musical time of my life. Especially after the less than fulfill- ing experience of feeling like a ghost during the recording of my first album. In contrast, Mutt expressed that he appreciated the way my mind worked as a songwriter and genuinely loved the sound of my voice, commenting that the tone reminded him of Karen Carpenter at times. Whoa, that was a huge compliment to me, as I considered her style so exquisite. Mutt had sensitive ears, and it's not surpris- ing that her sound was a noticeable influence on my own style. Even with his track record of success and my lack of one, he respected me as a fellow artist and treated me as an equal.

His confidence in me encouraged me to push my own boundar- ies. He pushed me, too, challenging me again and again to strengthen melodies and tweak lyrics. "Good enough" did not exist in his vocabu- lary, and rightfully so. It wasn't good enough unless it was a hit. But when a song hit the mark, he'd say, "That's it, you got it, Woody." (The nickname, dating back to when we first met, is a joking reference to the fringe-cut bangs I wore at the time, à la Woody Woodpecker.)

There was no time to waste on ideas that wouldn't make the album, but something like "Man! I Feel Like a Woman!" was just there. I was inspired right off the bat with that one, for example, by a riff Mutt had going, and the lyrics and phrasing just came out of the blue. Mutt gave that one a thumbs-up, no questions asked. He could recognize a hit idea when he heard one. His groove flowed easily, and that song came together between the two of us, without any push and pull.

I knew during this songwriting phase that I was privileged to be working with such a genius as Mutt. He is a great writer and doesn't need anyone to help him craft a hit song, but he wanted me to make the material we wrote together my own. So he might come up with an irresistible chord progression, I would listen to it a few times, and then start shaping a melody that fit. We'd duel back and forth, adapting the melody and chords until everything just started to click and Mutt flashed a thumbs-up. Something that adds to the fun of songwriting is that every song comes together in a different way. Mutt was incredible with the feel and groove of a song, and my challenge was to write lyrics and melody to his phrasing for a lot of the time. We pretty much both did a bit of everything in the way of patching the songs together, and we'd often go off separately to write things on our own, then come together to see how we could combine our individual ideas. Some of our writing notes contain both of our handwriting, as we shared the same paper pad, taking turns jotting lyrics down as we went. Some of what we wrote together stemmed from what I'd previously written as well, and he'd morph his ideas into my lyrics, and mine into his. Some songs evolved from foundations we'd each had in storage for years, with the other person building upon the existing framework. I learned so much from Mutt about songwriting during this time, and I learned it fast.

I made good on my promise to Luke Lewis and flew back to Music City a few days before a meeting about my future. Let me tell you, was *I* a pack of nerves wondering how he would react to the news that I had run off with the "rock" guy.

Sitting across from Luke felt like being in front of your school principal, who clasps his hands on his desk and intones seriously, "So, young lady, what have you been up to in your absence?" I beat around the bush for a minute, squirming in my chair, restless and anxious as I tried to find a comfortable position and begin explaining myself. I felt naughty for being so secretive about things since I was signed to a serious contract, and I felt obligated to be honest with them about my plans musically. I was in a vulnerable position not knowing what Luke's reaction would be, if I'd be dropped from the label because of my careless decision to run off writing with a "rock" guy when I was supposed to be making country records. What if he expelled me? I guess I'd find out.

"First, I just want to say that I'm really excited about my new music, and I cannot thank you enough for giving me the chance to show what I can do as a songwriter." Of course, if he didn't like what I heard, the A&R department would be taking me shopping at the Music Row publishing companies again. Luke wanted to know what song direction I was interested in, so that A&R could match me with a suitable producer. Of the two producers on *Shania Twain,* Harold Shedd was no longer with the label. As for Norro Wilson, he was an obvious choice, but, Luke emphasized, no decision had been made yet.

I finally just came out with it.

"I've been cowriting for weeks with Mutt Lange, and we've pretty much finished a full album's worth of songs."

I was on edge waiting for his response, like the anxious feeling of waiting for an important test result. Luke's a laid-back kind of guy, and although he has plenty to say, he gets to the point and sums things up with few words. He sat up in his chair as his eyes widened slightly, and all he pretty much said was, "Holy shit, that's cool!"

You cannot imagine the relief I felt. However, I was not about to press my luck and start talking about my hope that Mutt would produce the album. It was enough to break the news that my intentions were to record my own songs this time around and more, that they were cowritten with the rock legend Mutt Lange. Actually, Mutt had not even raised the suggestion of producing me yet, since we did not know if PolyGram would balk at my recording our collaboration, and besides, he already had other projects on the go, so time was also an issue. Luke conceded that the news might be viewed unfavorably in some quarters of the country music field. Nashville wanted Nashville songs and Nashville producers, and Nashville musicians recording in Nashville studios. It was bad enough that I was a foreigner and pushing to record my own songs.

"Personally, I like the idea," said Luke. "A lot." Frankly, I could not imagine anyone offering a logical objection. Just look at all the popular songs that bore Mutt's name. Not only that, but in spite of his rock 'n' roll pedigree, the man was a lifelong fan of country music. And besides, wasn't a great song a great song, period, whatever the style? But then, record companies make illogical decisions all the time.

I was quick to phone Mutt to fill him in on the good news that Luke was on board. This was going to be a very controversial approach to making a record for a Nashville record company, and we were bracing ourselves for what was next, but with Luke behind us, we hoped Mercury Nashville might favor the collaboration and not kick me out of town.

We gained a second ally at the label when I played rough sketches of the songs to A&R man Buddy Cannon, who was known to have some of the best ears in the business, as they say, meaning that he knew a hit song when he heard it. Although I think he was surprised by my new direction, Buddy knew it was special and powerful. Norro also had a listen, and he perked up along with Buddy in his reaction. But I'm still not sure what was going through their heads, to be honest. I could tell they were caught off guard by something that sounded so different from anything else coming out of Nashville, but they seemed sincere about their support regarding the quality of the arrangements and the strength of the songs. My sense was that they had mixed feelings about their personal taste toward the music, but were experienced enough professionals to understand that it was special and powerful. At least, that's how I read their perception.

Overall, I felt that both Norro and Buddy supported what Mutt and I had done. I was over the moon to have them on our side, and I realized that it was especially important to have Buddy's support, as he was part of the label team. It meant a lot to me personally, too, as Buddy was also one of the sweetest people I'd ever met. He was so good to me when I first came to Nashville, treating me like a daughter. I used to go to his house for his lovely wife Billy's amazing Southern cooking. Afterward, out would come the guitars: me, Billy, and his girls tightly weaving our voices together on bluegrass tunes, playing, laughing, and just having a great time. I loved these blissful moments with the Cannons. My parents had been gone for seven years already, so I relished the comforting feeling of being part of a family again, with parents, kids, warmth, security, and sincerity. I will be forever grateful to have been invited into the Cannons' hearts and home. Their generosity and kindness were fulfilling, with me being so far from my Canadian life. The fact that their family was so musical reminded me of the times I'd sat with Kenny and Carrie in our family home as small children, singing in harmony.

From 1991 to 1993, the stage between my showcase at Deerhurst and the first signs that real success in the music industry was just around the corner was pretty quick. I was lucky to get the succession of breaks that kept the steady climb rolling: the signing itself; Luke giving me another chance for a second album; Mutt discovering my writing ability; me not being kicked out of "country music" despite the obviously controversial news that Mutt Lange had not only co-written my next album but had also produced it; and Luke putting his neck out to take the chance with it, as I think we were all pretty nervous about how radio was going to react. I'm not saying it was easy, but other than the temporary financial strain and overall adjustment to the recording industry during those two years, the struggle at that point was relatively manageable.

The two years between signing my deal and the promise of success actually seem short to me now in relative terms compared to the fourteen years that would follow. The next fourteen years would pose many more challenges and struggles than the first two did. It was with success that I would work the hardest and sacrifice the most. The transition between pre–record contract and the release of *The Woman in Me* was intense, and emotionally it was challenging as well. Too much was new, and as natural as it was for me to grow with the new life that was before me as a recording artist in America, I was sad to leave Canada on what I knew would now be a more permanent basis.

Mutt was now gearing up to produce the next album, and Luke Lewis was all for it, although he was still getting resistance from his team at the label and was concerned about the budget Mutt was proposing to make it. That record really happened largely because Mutt agreed to absorb much of the cost himself. It has been well documented that Mutt is a legendary perfectionist in the studio, but I see him rather as a man with a deep passion for the quality of his work, and my record would be no exception. He insisted on having the freedom to take whatever time he needed to make the music we both wanted to make, without having to be constrained by someone else's budget. He had a lot of faith in what we were doing and put his money where his mouth was. He also put a ring on my finger.

Marriage came on suddenly for us, to say the least, with Mutt and I saying "I do" only six months after we met. I had been in a couple of long-term relationships, especially with Paul, but had never felt like I was truly ready to get married. So I wasn't prepared for the powerful feelings that would take hold of my heart in such a short time. I think the same was true for Mutt, who was seventeen years older than me and had been married twice before. We were both sure of what we wanted, and that was a lifetime commitment to each other.

We were married on December 28, 1993, at Deerhurst Resort, for the convenience and proximity to my family and the familiarity of the place, which made a short-notice wedding easier to pull together. It was forty-one degrees below zero, yet there was no wind; it was sunny and bright, a dream winter wedding. I remember my wedding day as being the happiest day of my life. I giggled like a little girl all the way down the aisle. It was small and intimate, a beautiful start to our lives together. We were happy and sincere about the vows we'd written ourselves for each other. We chose our wedding song together, "Let It Be Me" by the Everly Brothers, my mother's favorite vocal duo. It went, "I bless the day I found you." My mother's only sibling, my uncle Don, walked me down the aisle to give me away. We had a few immediate family members in attendance from both sides of our families: the Twains drove up from Timmins and the Langes flew in from South Africa.

Mutt and I honeymooned on the Caribbean island of Anguilla, which was a great escape from the January cold of Canada. I was in heaven, especially because this was my first trip to that part of the world and couldn't have been more perfect as a romantic dream of a bride. I was very inspired for songwriting by the incredible atmosphere of sun, sand, and crystal-clear waters. We affectionately called ourselves a two-guitar family, as we brought two guitars with us no matter where we traveled together. Two guitars were necessary while songwriting, and we found it frustrating having to pass one guitar back and forth all the time. Marriage was so new then, and I enjoyed the novelty of being referred to as a "family." That unity was so meaningful to me in that sense that I took Lange as my new family name and left Twain now only as my professional identity.

A follow-up trip to our honeymoon brought us back to the sun and sand of the Caribbean to continue finalizing the songwriting tweaks on our song list for *The Woman in Me*. One of my more vivid recollections of songwriting during our honeymoon is of "(If You're Not in It for Love) I'm Outta Here!"—a warning to pickup artists everywhere, set to a pulsing rock beat, and embroidered with slinky slide guitar. This song would be a country radio number one.

# 20

## *The Woman in Me* Succeeds

With all the songwriting finished, it was time to start making the actual record. Mutt suggested we bring the production to a certain point before playing it for anyone at Mercury Nashville. Mutt was right about putting the stamp of our musical direction on it before opening it up for discussion to any possible naysayers or conservative attitudes that would take the wind out of our sails. I could see very clearly, from where I was standing as the artist, that Mutt did not need any influence or guidance on what kind of record to be making for me.

Listening sessions with label personnel during various points of a recording process were common then, in order to make sure they felt the record fit within some kind of acceptable margin that worked for the genre. That kind of artistic constraint was exactly what Mutt and I were trying to avoid. I was not experienced in the world of making records, but I was so in sync with Mutt's conviction not to necessarily make a genre-specific record, but to make a great record, period. Our idea was to create something unique, unlike anything else; something that would stand the test of time, groundbreaking music the listeners would turn their heads to when they heard it for the first time. This was Mutt's way of looking at making a record, and it rubbed off on me. The personal conviction it took to stand behind your own creative ideas took guts. I never witnessed Mutt wavering from outside pressure, and I admired this. I felt protected as an artist that my producer was going to make sure my record was the best it could be before anyone else got his hands on it.

It was only when we were in the final stage of mixing the tracks that we invited department heads from the label—eight altogether—to meet us at Morin Heights Studio, located just north of Montreal, for their first listening session.

Mutt set up a playback session, and from what I recall, it was outside the control room where everyone could fit around the sound system. I do remember, however, that the reaction was mixed. Mostly that it wasn't country enough or at least not familiar enough to what they were used to hearing. But even those who had reservations about the music acknowledged that we had achieved something new, different. In fact, that's the trouble some of them had with it: it sounded *too* different. That's all we needed to hear. We didn't need approval in regards to the standard of the record we had. I already had total confidence in Mutt as the producer, he had the same confidence in me as the artist, and we both believed in the songs. We were more concerned that the execs *got* what we were doing than with whether or not they *liked* it. Most important, the music provoked a big reaction, with lots of discussions taking place in the days that followed.

I personally loved my/our new album. This was a teamwork project between Mutt and me, and it feels awkward to say it was "my" record. Although I was the artist, Mutt was a very involved producer and cowriter and I saw the record as a team effort. I was excited about how it sounded so bold and dynamic and, as a style, almost unidentifiable. Mutt's own voice was layered in the background as backing vocals, with the unexpected arrangement blends of fiddles backdropped by concussive kick and snare drums, and steel guitars intertwined with the range and sexiness of distorted rock guitars. All this contrast was exhilarating, and sometimes I didn't know where to listen. It was as if I could almost watch the sounds and effects coming out of nowhere from all directions, similar to 3-D visual animation, only sonic.

As high as my opinion of the record was, and I think Mutt's belief in it was also very strong, no one could have guessed what the radio and public reaction would be. With Mutt's years of experience in the industry, he especially held no illusions of how impossible it could be to assume what would or would not fly, reminding me regularly that there were no guarantees of success, no matter how great a record might be. I think we were all pretty nervous about how country radio station programmers were going to react to the less overtly "country" sound, and we didn't want to assume anything either way. Not that I was asking to become a controversial artist among country music purists, but my perception of contemporary country music at the time was that it defined itself too narrowly—which would explain all those near identical songs pitched to me during the search for material for my very first record, which I did my best to avoid writing and had no interest in recording. My version of country music, with Mutt's personal stamp on the arrangement and sound, was the new album. Accepted or not by the industry, Mutt had produced a record I was proud of.

In the end, Luke Lewis stuck his neck out and decided to take a chance on *The Woman in Me,* regardless of the reservations or the concerns of others. In fact, he was more optimistic about its reception than I was. I can remember sitting in his office in late 1994, just before the album's release, and a bunch of people from the label were playing at guessing how many copies it would sell. At that time I didn't actually have a number in my head. I wasn't even thinking numbers yet. Later, although it was still in the earlier stages of the album's release (though it was showing exciting possibilities of being a big seller), Luke phoned me at home in upstate New York from his office in Nashville to share his anticipation of the record's realistic potential. He wanted me to take a guess at what I thought it might climb to in sales.

"Well, I know that Reba McEntire's last record sold three million copies; I would *love* to equal that." Come to think of it, I really didn't answer his question, did I? I was just daydreaming aloud about how many albums I *imagined* it could sell; I honestly did not think it could even approach such a huge number of three million, as that was giant for a female at the time and fifteen years later was still a big number. So I was pleasantly surprised when Luke said, as I imagined him shaking his head on the other end of the line, "I think you're aiming too low."

Whether we did or did not achieve platinum sales, or even gold-record sales of a half million, clearly my career was moving into a new phase.

Luke was open to new ideas and to going outside the box on all levels, giving me a lot of freedom with the art direction with *The Woman in Me.* My manager, Mary, felt brave and thought she'd approach someone completely out of the scene to take the photographs for the album cover. She asked John Derek if he was interested, and although he wasn't, his wife, Bo, took it upon herself to respond with a yes, and John reluctantly went along with it. John Derek was an actor, director, and photographer, well known especially for photographs of his gorgeous and famous wives, Ursula Andress, Linda Evans, and Bo Derek. He himself was a very handsome man, and although there was a thirty-year age difference between him and Bo, I thought they looked good together. Bo was stunning in every light and John, although in his late sixties when I met him, had aged well and was still very attractive. I was too young to have known of John Derek and his fame, but I knew Bo as the perfect ten on every man's scale of female perfection, most famous from her starring role in the movie *10.* Bo lived up to her movie-star, sex-symbol beauty in person. It was hard for me not to stare at her, in fact. I don't think I'd ever seen anyone so pretty in real life before.

When I arrived at John and Bo's ranch in Santa Ynez, California, they explained in a very frank and forward manner that they didn't normally do this sort of thing—that is, take pictures of other people. John warned me that part of the reason he no longer bothered to photograph any women other than his wife, Bo, was because no other woman could tolerate his severe honesty. I personally also got the feeling that he genuinely felt that there was no one more naturally beautiful who was worth photographing.

John continued with an example of how he would express this honesty by telling me that I was overweight and that he didn't like my crooked nose. Compared to Bo, I was overweight at 115 pounds and, yes, my nose is crooked, so he was right. It didn't bother me to hear things I already knew, and I didn't see any reason why that would make me not want to work with him. He went on to tell me that the last time Raquel Welch tried to get him to photograph her, she ran off crying. I believed this was probably true as, for one, he didn't seem like the type of guy who would bother bullshitting me, and two, most girls are sensitive to criticism, even if constructive, regarding their appearance.

Thinking maybe John misunderstood the intentions behind me wanting him to take my photos, I explained to both John and Bo that I wasn't there to be photographed as a model, movie starlet, or sex symbol. I was none of those things, and I knew it. I was there simply as a recording artist needing photos for my album cover and promotion. I wasn't selling my beauty, I was selling my music, and I needed some visual artwork for the packaging. I went on to say that if he made me look as good as I was capable of looking, that I would be satisfied, as long as he was willing to work with my looks, since it was clear they didn't meet his standard of beauty. I was a pretty straight shooter, and I think he appreciated that I could be as frank with him as he was with me. It was actually refreshing and appealed to my Northern Canadian lack of political correctness, which I was being told I needed to temper if I wanted to make it in country, but which John and Bo didn't seem to mind.

In our first shoot together, it took no time for John's character to become full blown. One particular shot got John very frustrated, as my nose was posing all kinds of beauty issues for him. He started cursing and swearing about it as if it were a person itself, like me, *the person*, didn't actually belong to it. He finally piped up to say something to the effect of, "Someone give me a goddamn knife so I can cut off that nose." Although not okay with him cutting off my nose, I was fine with the fact that he wished he could, and we just carried on shooting.

It was humbling to me that the real beauty, Bo, followed me around with light reflectors, trying to flatter me with the best light possible, while John snapped the photos. The photo of me in the water was actually done in their personal swimming pool, and the water was chilly. After an hour in cool water, it gets uncomfortable, but Bo was right in there with me, holding her reflector, taking orders from John. The pink hat I wore was hers, and she'd pulled it out as a prop since the wet hair wasn't flattering me so much. This photo is on the album cover of *The Woman in Me* and is one of my favorites.

We would work together on two more projects: the "Any Man of Mine" and "Whose Bed Have Your Boots Been Under" videos. Bo took photos as well, which we used for a few things. She had a great feel for candid shots.

I loved working with John and greatly respected and admired him very much. Both he and Bo were incredibly professional in their commitment to the work and took it all very seriously. I appreciated this, and it made me want to keep up and do as good a job as I could possibly do. They made me want to work for the best results. I matured a lot working with them, and I believe by being in their company so early in my career, I learned a great deal about my face, lighting, shooting, filming, and, maybe most of all, about tolerance and teamwork.

They also had a team that set a good example for me in this early time when I still had everything to learn about being filmed. I saw Bo and John as real partners, and Kerry, Bo's sister, was John's assistant photographer. Bo's mother did hair and makeup, and Ramon, who was their personal horse trainer, was the guy who rolled up his sleeves to do whatever had to be done. This was a close-knit group, a team.

I have always been incredibly impatient when it comes to waiting for something I can't do myself but wish so badly I could. To me, John also seemed impatient in a similar way, only he was a man of more experience who knew what he was after, with a strong intent to get it. Creatively, this is a very important strength to have if you expect to actually make your vision materialize. If you are leading the show, you have to be able to direct clearly with no wishy-washy fussing around. If you have capable people around you, there is a better chance of getting what you want from them if you know what it is *you* want yourself. John and I both knew what we wanted; however, it wasn't always the same thing. One afternoon in the middle of the "Any Man of Mine" video shoot, John kept directing me to do something, and I kept reminding him how I wanted it instead. He'd then tell me again what he wanted, and I would again remind him that wasn't the way I wanted to do it. So John came out from behind the camera, walking straight up to my face and telling me, "Look, sometimes I can be an asshole—" but before he could finish explaining that as a self-proclaimed "asshole," he insist I do it his way, I cut in, took his face in my two hands, and eye to eye said, "Right now, you *are* an asshole." I calmly but surely spoke my mind, and without letting on outside our nose-to-nose discussion, he let it go, and we carried on with the shoot. He respected my stance, and there was not another word said.

Unfortunately, it's a familiar story in the music industry that once promising young artists reach a certain level—typically when they're on the brink of stardom—the manager or management team that worked so hard to get them there no longer has the expertise and influence necessary to navigate the unfamiliar waters up ahead. The stakes become much higher than before, and the learning curve can prove too steep for the manager who excels at guiding artists through the early stages of their careers to follow through with the demands of this new environment. This was not the immediate case with me and Mary, however, as we found ourselves still together as Mercury Nashville was readying my second album for release. I also felt a loyalty to her, as our relationship transcended business. Although she had officially represented me since 1991, I had known her for years through her friendship with my mother. I think we both felt a lot of pride that the two of us—a couple of small-town girls from Canada—had made the bold, brave leap to Music City together. It definitely took some courage and a lot of faith.

I was forever indebted to Mary, and to her husband, Bob, who had generously advanced us some money to get through the tightest of spots until I was able to pay him back. Mary's faith in me was unconditional, but neither she nor anyone around us could possibly have known that day was just around the corner.

Eventually having to end our professional relationship was painful for both of us. Mary was like family to me. She also represented a connection to my mother, which made our bond all the more personal. I am happy to say that over time, we renewed our friendship beyond our professional association, and Mary remains a very precious friend to me today. At the time, however, the thought of carrying on without her by my side was scary. It dredged up feelings similar to when my relationship with Paul ended, and I felt a separation anxiety come over me, like I was leaving a part of myself behind.

Before even the first single was released from *The Woman in Me*, I set out on a tour to introduce the new music to radio. Prior to asking anyone to actually put it on the air, I sat with programmers in a listening session, just for the sake of letting them sample what we had. Some stations were open enough to just put me on the air in a live interview and even play one of the songs. I was out there representing the new music in what felt like the front line, while Mutt and the label waited patiently for reports of how it was going at the end of each day. I was meeting all hours of the day with radio programmers, one after the other, who in some cases didn't even want to listen to the music due to Mutt's involvement, and others who were big rock fans who'd spun many of the AC/DC and Def Leppard records in the past at previous stations, so they welcomed me with open arms.

It was a hot and cold experience with a bit of warm here and there. There was nothing certain about how things would go from that promotional period pre–single release. It was exhausting sustaining my energy and heart through the love/hate responses to the new record, and it was getting under my skin that industry institutions were even able to stand between an artist and the public, as time went on and the resistance grew. With the Internet not yet part of public mainstream media, radio was largely able to control what their local listeners heard. This type of monopoly could kill a record, if that was the desired effect. Instead of being dictated to, I felt strongly that the public should be able to decide for themselves what they do and don't want to listen to.

"Any Man of Mine" was the one song off the album that I was most anxious to play to radio during the promotional touring period, and it was equally the one I was most concerned they would reject me for, due to its radical twist of rock and country combined. During *The Woman in Me*'s introductory tour, I primarily played a choice of three songs for the programmers, "Any Man of Mine," "Whose Bed Have Your Boots Been Under?" and "(If You're Not in It for Love) I'm Outta Here!" If they were responding well, I'd play "You Win My Love" and "The Woman in Me."

My choice for the first single of the album was "Any Man of Mine," but it was true that programmers were showing mixed reactions to it, and the record company felt safer going with the more country-flavored "Boots." I wanted to hit them between the eyes with the true blend of genres that I felt best represented who I really was, the variety of childhood musical influences that had shaped my personal taste as a singer-songwriter. I agree now, though, that it was probably best to warm up with "Boots," so if the public liked what they heard and wanted more, we'd have less risk of losing "Any Man's" chance to reach its full potential. This was a very exciting time for everyone involved, as we could feel the friction behind the scenes, yet a positive, buzz-like commotion at the same time. It made it hard to make decisions about the release order of the singles, as it was too early and all we had to go on was radio, and it was like they were almost divided and confused as a whole.

As 1994 turned into 1995, Mutt and I celebrated three times within five days, beginning with our first wedding anniversary on December 28. We'd moved onto a private lake property in the area of Saint Regis Falls, New York, where the snow was plentiful throughout the holidays. Two days into the New Year, PolyGram released the advance single from *The Woman in Me,* one of the more straight-ahead, you-been-cheatin' kind of numbers, "Whose Bed Have Your Boots Been Under?" It was one of the real country-sounding songs on the CD, although still pumped with Mutt's signature layering and power production.

"Boots," as I always refer to it, had come to me during my time in the bush cabin by the river. Like ten of the album's twelve songs, it was credited to Shania Twain and Robert John "Mutt" Lange; the other two were solo compositions from each of us. What a contrast to my first album, which contained only one original, and an outside collaborative effort at that. Mutt had liberated the songwriter and recording artist I truly was, and I could not have been more satisfied.

"Whose Bed Have Your Boots Been Under?" would spend a total of seven months atop the *Billboard* country charts. But not right away. In fact, sales were modest at first. "Boots" looked like it would stall several times as the resistance from industry gatekeepers, who complained that the music was too "out there" and that I didn't belong in country, was managing to block the connection between artist and public. The listeners weren't hearing me because much of radio wouldn't play me. This is where radio programmers and consultants make choices for the public: they decide what they hear and take the decision away from the listener, not exposing them enough to form opinions and demands of their own. The democracy is killed, and the choice becomes industry-based and no longer the people's. I was frustrated and surprised by the lack of control the listener had.

I don't believe stations that refused to play my record were so much resistant to *me* personally, but more to changes in the style of country music they preferred. This new sound that was so different just seemed plain weird to them, and I heard comments to that effect quite regularly. I was hurt by these opinions, taking them personally. It offended me that they were insulting my music and trying to prevent it from reaching the ears of the listeners, the ones I was actually making the music for in the first place. I felt vulnerable by this lack of access to the people, and it made me feel disconnected from the purpose behind being an artist. There were genuine efforts to stomp out "Boots," and although they successfully did some damage to the song's momentum, in April it made it up to number eleven, giving me my first Top 20 hit. It wasn't a number one, or even Top 10, but "Boots" at least managed to reach enough of the public for the album to show signs of kicking into another gear. But much patience was required of me still, as my one-step-at-a-time climb in the recording industry continued.

On the heels of "Boots" (sorry—couldn't resist), we released "Any Man of Mine." This was my favorite up-tempo single off the album, a song you might consider as having a split personality. It was especially magical watching this one come together in the studio. As much as I loved Mutt as my husband, it's possible I admired him even more for the unique way his musical mind worked. I cannot claim to know how it worked, or how he came up with these unusual ideas; all I can tell you is that it amazed me, and things that sounded like they weren't going to belong all came together in the end to create hit music. But it didn't just happen "like that"—Mutt worked long and hard, painstakingly developing every single second of sound. It's just that it wasn't always obvious where it was going until it pulled together as a unified piece of work. It was as though the only person who really had the whole thing in his head all at one time was Mutt. With "Any Man of Mine," I witnessed as Mutt combined traditional country instruments with anthemic stadium-rock sounds. Raspy, throaty vocals punctuated my own vocal phrasing, and the switch from a groove reminiscent of Queen's "We Will Rock You" to the foot-stompin' Western-style chorus, which almost sounded like it came from another song, totally worked. This contrasting arrangement of styles Mutt pulled together made me crazy with curiosity to see how the listeners were going to react the first time they heard it. I was crawling out of my skin with excitement to share it.

In July 1995 "Any Man of Mine" went to number one on *Billboard*'s country singles sales chart, spending ten weeks up there. It was the first number one single on that chart by a non-American since Anne Murray's "Now and Forever" in 1986 and was my first Top 40 crossover hit on the pop charts.

# 21

## The Flip Side of Fame

Mountain climbers will tell you that the most grueling and dangerous part of their sport starts the moment they set foot on the summit. It's not unlike having your first hit record. In both cases, the ascent is physically and emotionally exhausting. You make it to the top, and your first reaction is more relief than jubilation, followed by the thought *Okay, now what am I going to do?* Chances are that you haven't given it much thought; people usually dream of reaching the top of Mount Everest, not navigating the descent. Consequently, the majority of serious accidents occur on the way down. Unlike for climbing athletes, however, the idea for at least a good number of entertainers once they get there is to stay there.

July 22, 1995, marked a career pinnacle for me when *The Woman in Me* and "Any Man of Mine" both went to number one. It was the culmination of two solid years of work, starting when Mutt and I began collaborating on songs for the album. And the groundwork for all of it, really, goes back to my preteen years, when I would slip into the woods near our house in Hanmer and sit writing songs on my guitar—not that I ever foresaw selling millions of records one day.

At least when a mountain climber scales a peak, he gets to take a nice, long break afterward. To continue the music-industry-as-mountain analogy for a moment, in the music business, you expend just as much effort, if not more, to stay on top.

"Any Man of Mine" was the second single from the album. Everyone involved believed so strongly in the quality of the material that as many as eleven singles were planned. That is a lot, even in the country music field, which differs from rock 'n' roll in that the hit 45—or, nowadays, digital file—still drives album sales. It's very much a throwback to the 1950s and 1960s, when recording artists routinely put out five or six singles per year: from Elvis Presley and Ricky Nelson, to the Rolling Stones and Creedence Clearwater Revival. Back then, the LP was practically an afterthought, released to provide an artist's fans one disc containing the two or three hit singles they probably already owned. Except for the Beatles, Bob Dylan, and a few other monumentally talented performers, sandwiched between the hits was mostly filler, consisting of pedestrian cover versions and maybe the artist's second-rate originals. But starting in the late 1960s, following landmark albums such as the Beatles' *Sgt. Pepper's Lonely Hearts Club Band* and Dylan's *Blonde on Blonde,* the LP began to take precedence over the 45—especially now that there were new rock radio stations on the FM band willing to play album cuts and not just the Top 40 hits that dominated AM music radio. The shift never came to country music, however, which still prizes the hit single.

In August, while "Any Man of Mine" was still riding high on the *Billboard* Hot Country Songs chart, Mercury Nashville put out the lush ballad "The Woman in Me (Needs the Man in You)." It became my third Top 20 hit in a row. The next three singles, issued like clockwork every three or four months, all went to number one: "(If You're Not in It for Love) I'm Outta Here!," "You Win My Love," and "No One Needs to Know." And there were two more minor hits to follow: "Home Ain't Where His Heart Is (Anymore)" and "God Bless the Child." Eight singles in all. This took us to January 1997, exactly two years since we had all kept our fingers crossed when the label launched "Whose Bed Have Your Boots Been Under?"

Traditionally, an artist promotes her new recording by going on tour. I chose not to, passing up millions of dollars in the process. But

I looked at it this way: *The Woman in Me* was only my second album, and, as you know, I was less than enthused by the material on my debut. So how was I going to entertain people for an hour and a half to two hours? Play my handful of original hits and lots of other people's songs? Tell jokes and juggle between tunes? I'd seen other new artists hit the road too soon, to strike while the proverbial iron was hot, and I squirmed in my seat watching them try to fill in and repeat their one or two hits at the end of the performance, in an attempt to redeem their credibility to go from being a cover tune act to being the original artist they wanted to be. That wasn't for me. It would have felt too much like my days playing the bar circuit in Northern Ontario, only with much nicer outfits, superior lighting, and a more attentive (and sober, I'd hope) audience.

I was now beginning to enjoy performing live, a long way from peeing my pants at age sixteen, but at this early stage of my recording career, I felt that my time could be better spent promoting the music I believed in so strongly. And, I was already looking ahead to the next album. Being on tour leaves precious little room in your schedule for sitting down to write. Many new artists fall into this trap. They're lucky enough to have a hit album, and so they spend the following year on the road. I've heard many a co-artist complain that when they finally return home, fatigued and half crazed, the record company, eager for a follow-up, strong-arms them right into the studio. Except that they don't have enough first-rate material. (And after a year of largely being confined to a tour bus and hotel rooms, the last thing they want is to be cooped up in the recording studio for the near future.)

It's well known in the music business that artists have an entire lifetime to write their first album, but less than a year to write their second. So what do you do? Hastily knock out some new tunes, like a teenager who's put off writing his English paper until the night before it's due? We all remember how well *that* usually turns out. Or you salvage scraps of what you wrote while on tour, which rarely yield any treasures, because it is hard to feel inspired when you're doing the same thing day in and day out. It's why so many new acts' second CDs meet with the so-called sophomore jinx. There is no jinx, of course, just a bunch of half-baked songs that probably needed more time and a clear head to develop.

I chose a different route for bringing *The Woman in Me* to public attention: an intense promotional blitz encompassing music videos; media interviews for radio, TV, and the press; photo shoots; and one-off performances like morning television (*Good Morning America*, for example) or entertainment talk shows such as David Letterman's. Eating up a lot of my time in the schedule was also my hands-on involvement with the art direction of photos, videos, and staging for live performances on both the production side and the performance side. I was constantly working directly with producers and designers for everything I did. I started editing my own videos, right from the beginning, which is a time-consuming, painstakingly tedious job. I was energized being on the production side of my projects, but it was also exhausting playing so many roles at once.

Then there were in-store autograph signings and special appearances, such as attending the Grammy Awards. Nothing I'd ever done up to then could have prepared me for the workload ahead: ten to fifteen hours a day, seven days a week. I was booked solid six months in advance and would barely have time to come up for air for the next two and a half years, because no sooner would I finish promoting my latest hit than the next one would be released, and the whole cycle would rev up all over again for another three months or so. Now multiply that times eight.

A typical day's work itinerary would look something like this, if we assume the stretch begins in New York City:

| 4:00 a.m. | Wake up! |
| 4:15 a.m. | Depart hotel for *Good Morning America* |
| 4:30 a.m. | Begin hair and makeup |
| 5:00 a.m. | Call time for sound check |
| 5:30 a.m. | Sound check |

6:00 a.m.    Continue hair, makeup, and wardrobe; have a
             morning juice!
7:30 a.m.    Performance!
8:00 a.m.    Depart *GMA* for hotel
8:15 a.m.    Arrive hotel; beauty/bathroom break!
8:30 a.m.    Beauty touch-ups
8:45 a.m.    Media interview "Round Up" at hotel
12:00 p.m.   LUNCH BREAK
12:30 p.m.   Depart hotel for meeting with video director
2:00 p.m.    Depart meeting for radio interview at station
2:20 p.m.    Arrive radio station
3:00 p.m.    Depart radio station for hotel
3:15 p.m.    Arrive hotel; beauty/bathroom break!
3:30 p.m.    Journalist interview at hotel
4:30 p.m.    Meet with sick children/fans
5:30 p.m.    Wardrobe meeting for Grammy outfit
6:30 p.m.    Prep for dinner with radio programmers
7:00 p.m.    Depart hotel for dinner with radio programmers
7:30 p.m.    Arrive dinner
10:00 p.m.   Depart dinner for hotel
10:30 p.m.   Arrive hotel—DONE FOR DAY!!

By now, I had a personal assistant, a super girl named Sheri Fo-bare, who had three times my energy. Sheri used to prepare my daily itineraries. I knew things were spinning out of control when I noticed that she had astutely started to insert "pee break" in the schedule, because otherwise the opportunity would not present itself, as everything was such a rush, and I'd be sitting in the car ride to the next destination with my knees pressed together. "Snack break" soon got added, too. Life got much more civilized after that. Thanks, Sheri!

I know, I know: it sounds ridiculous, how could anyone *forget* to eat and go pee? In the beginning stages of your career, when all the things you have dreamed of are finally starting to happen, you feel compelled not to let a single opportunity slip through your fingers by taking it for granted. We had all sorts of important bookings coming up: appearances on Leno, *The Morning Show,* and the Country Music Awards, a cover shoot for *Rolling Stone* magazine, my next music video. Because magazines and TV programs have long lead times, in some cases I'd agreed to do them months earlier, before I had any idea of what my limits were. Okay, so which of these great privileges do you cancel in order to buy yourself a little downtime? You don't, or at least I didn't. Each was essential to the success of the album. Also, I didn't want to come off as a prima donna and seem ungrateful. My jam-packed itinerary was a new artist's wet dream.

I just carried on like the Energizer Bunny, even long after I'd established myself. Looking back, I see now that I was exhausted for a good part of twelve years. My weight dropped, and I often became seriously lethargic from malnutrition and fatigue. One time, a journalist conducting an interview noticed me slurring my words and practically passing out. "Are you okay?" he asked hesitantly. "No," I replied, eyes glazed, I wasn't okay and really didn't want to be there. It was the only time I'd ever admitted to not being okay professionally when someone asked me. I would never have wanted to come across as being unprofessional by letting the façade down. I needed to appear "fine" at all times while in the public eye, as though it was a responsibility, an obligation to the privilege itself. He probably thought I had been drinking or was on something. The fact was, not only did I *not* drink alcohol or take drugs, I didn't even drink coffee or Coca-Cola. Maybe I should have—drunk coffee or Coke, I mean—in order to survive the grueling schedule with more ease. Once, while shooting a video in London at three o'clock in the morning, I broke down and blurted out, "That's it! I've had enough!" Kim Godreau, Sheri's successor as my assistant, assumed the worst; maybe I was about to pull a page out of the diva playbook and storm off the set.

"I can't take it anymore! I'm—I'm *having a Coke!*" She laughed with relief. To me, needing any sort of substance to keep going betrayed weakness on my part. I had always gotten by on natural energy or somehow managed to run on empty, but it was cold and late, and we had been on location since dawn. Kim kindly fetched me my Coke, and the kick from the caffeine and sugar carried me through.

And beyond, too. From the video shoot, which didn't end until daybreak, we headed to the airport to catch a plane to who knows where. For the next few hours, I talked a mile a minute, spewing ideas faster than Kim could write them down. Kim, who is still a close friend all these years later, was exhausted herself from two fifteen-hour days in a row and just wanted to drop off to sleep. At last, she fixed me with a stern expression. "Woody," she snapped, *"no more Coke for you."* We both burst out laughing—me probably a bit maniacally—at the absurdity of it all.

Just a thought: good thing that no snoopy reporter was within earshot, or else the tabloids would probably have been shrieking the news about Shania Twain's out-of-control Coke habit.

As my success began to build, I started to experience being recognized in public. I remember the first time I was at an airport and could sense people hovering around me. No one approached; everyone stood at a bit of a distance, but whispering and staring. I felt as if I was on display, and it was uncomfortable, as I was there for the same reason they were: to take a plane. This had never happened to me before, and I wasn't sure how to handle it. I'm sure you can imagine how awkward it would feel if perfect strangers started staring at you in public, especially if this was all new to you. You'd probably wonder, *Did I put my skirt on inside out? What's everyone looking at?* I decided to get up and walk to a pay phone around the corner, figuring that if I stayed out of sight—and, for good measure, pretended to be engrossed in a phone conversation—no one would bother me. It worked.

Although I gradually learned to deal better with my newfound celebrity, it comes with certain aspects that I cannot imagine anyone finding tolerable. As I said, I like talking to people. But there is an inherent imbalance in the relationship between stars and their public. Because of all the magazines and TV programs—cripes, even a whole network—devoted to chronicling the lives of those in the public eye, fans sometimes come to know more intimate details about their favorite performers than they know about members of their own families. Depending on the source, the fact that much of it is libelously untrue often gets overlooked.

But this worship of celebrities can fabricate an artificial sense of familiarity on the part of fans. A fan might approach a celebrity in public feeling very much like the celebrity is an old friend, and that can be very flattering. But the celebrity knows absolutely nothing about the person, making for an unnatural, one-sided connection. And because people may view you as someone with whom they feel a kinship, they can be demanding or just plain pissed off when you don't treat them with equal familiarity.

After a while, you start to feel as if everyone wants something from you, even if it's nothing more than an autograph, and you begin to question people's motives even when their motives are completely innocent. I'm writing this bit to explain my personal point of view as someone who at that stage of my career was new to celebrity and public attention. I'm not sharing it with you to complain about being a celebrity, but to shed light on the realities of being famous for those who may not understand it, or whose only exposure to it is through the media and not personal testimony.

I am friendly to strangers and would be whether or not I was famous, but as for anyone, appropriate boundaries are necessary. It's not always easy to be objective, but I'll give you an example of one attempt to transition to my new fame as Shania Twain from life as plain old Eilleen. I'm at an airport and a man approaches me at an uncomfortably close distance and starts asking a string of questions: Am I traveling alone? What time is my flight? Where am I going? He even wanted to know who I was meeting. A little too forward, don't you think? But I try to be gracious, while answering as vaguely as I can; believe me, I take no pleasure in offending fans, or anyone, for that matter.

The guy had one more question for me.

"So," he says, suddenly full of swagger, "what's your name?"

*What's my name?* I couldn't believe it. I realized then that this guy wasn't looking for an autograph or a picture, he was trying to pick me up! He didn't have a *clue* as to who I was.

The episode upset me anyway. It disturbed me that I'd let the fact that I was now a public figure override my natural instinct to get away from this person. It made me feel vulnerable and wonder, *Don't I have the same right as everybody else to decide for myself whether or not I wish to respond to a stranger who engages me in conversation?* The fact that I had utterly misread the situation also made me start to question my own judgment. I was in the middle of the transition period between the before and the after of fame. Throughout the rest of 1995, as album sales surpassed one million, two million, even three million, I would find myself having to squirm out of far tighter spots than that.

One time, in upstate New York, my sister Carrie and I hit the mall for a bit of shopping with her nine-month-old son, Dylan. We started off okay, zipping in and out of a few stores, but as more shoppers began gathering around us, our pace slowed until we were trapped in a crowd and unable to budge. Baby Dylan, looking up at the mass of people from his stroller, was getting antsy with all the fuss. For that matter, so were Carrie and I; this was still new for both of us, and we really did not know what to do.

A pen materialized, and I began signing autographs and smiling through it, but the more I signed, the more the size of the crowd just mushroomed until, finally, mall security came along to break it up. As they escorted us out to my car in the parking lot, I could feel whatever normalcy remained in my life slipping away. A simple outing to a mall with my sister and nephew was no longer simple; would it even be possible anymore?

To this day, I make every effort to be gracious, patient, and polite to anyone who treats me with the same respect. I do my best to live up to the public's expectations, but of course it's impossible to please everyone, all the time.

Before the promotional tour for *The Woman in Me* was over, I had to hire a security staff for being out in public. Maybe if you are born to royalty, you get used to that, but for me it was a very hard adjustment. It's pretty impressive, in an adrenaline rush kind of way, the first time you're part of it—like a paparazzi car chase, for example; you feel like you're starring in a James Bond spy thriller. The tension can get hairy and scary; after all, look what happened to Princess Diana. Things can get out of hand pretty fast. I can't imagine being president or the Queen of England. All I can say is that everyone at the beginning of her public career is faced with a transition from not famous to famous, which for some celebrities can come seemingly overnight. It's an adjustment and gets very little sympathy or understanding from the press or the public. Whatever that means to you; I'm just sharing my perspective based on my initial, youthful experience of having a public profile.

You know what's ironic? The whole purpose of making music is to connect with people, and yet the more your popularity grows, the less you are able to interact with your audience any closer than from the stage and through your records. Fame can be isolating. I know it was for me for a very long time.

When I'm making a public appearance, I consider it a pleasure to set aside time for the fans. If not for them, entertainers simply would not have a profession. But it can be frustrating when a line is crossed. Once, I was out at a restaurant, minding my own business, and a woman approached me to ask if I would mind wishing her friend a happy fortieth birthday. They were sitting in a private room nearby, and I obliged, following behind the lady. When she reached the doorway to the birthday room ahead of me, she held her hand behind her, signaling for me to stop, and then bellowed into the room, "Hey, everybody, look what I found!" This spoke volumes to me about what I truly represented to this person. I was an object, not a person. I was an "it," not a "who." This is the reality a lot of the time when you are a display item, as is often the case for a celebrity. If you are someone looking to be famous, make no mistake, this is all a part of that reality. Of course, today I personally accept that this comes with the territory and just go with the flow as much as the situation allows me to.

Earlier in my career, however, while still adjusting to this type of treatment, my way of coping was to walk with my head down, avoiding people's gazes. Because once you established eye contact, it was as if you had extended an invitation for someone to intrude upon your personal space. I also began to walk really, really fast, everywhere. I used to laugh watching the security guys in the cars ahead of me jump out practically before they'd come to a full stop in order to get a head start. Otherwise, I'd be halfway down the street, with these big bodies panting to keep up. What a pain I must have been for them!

Most of my communication was happening through things like interviews and work meetings, so all I ever talked about was career related. This was soul destroying, as conversation rarely went on to subjects not related to my professional life, and I never got to talk about the inspiration I drew from exploring and experiencing new things, like vacationing somewhere of my dreams and meeting new people who were interested in the real me and not the "Shania" me. After a while, you start to develop two very different existences. The private world of me, Eilleen, is safe for her to be herself, to swear, to drink too much, to wear the wrong clothes, to sing out of tune, to be late, to behave regretfully—the list of imperfections that I'm allowed to display without being judged or criticized goes on and on. As Shania, however, I've spent years being overly attentive to how people perceived me, at all times. I'm less concerned in this regard now than I was even five years ago, however. Not that I would say I don't care what people think; in fact, I'm less likely to pose nude for *Playboy* today than ever before, especially now that gravity is having its way with me. But I am more relaxed about criticism and sense I'm less affected by the things I cannot control.

Trying so hard to keep up with what I expected from Shania, I began retreating from people and keeping them at arm's length. This can get to become such a habit that it spills over into your personal life. I found myself feeling increasingly distant from childhood friends and even from my family. On the road, it was next to impossible to find a block of uninterrupted time to chat on the phone, and although I would invite friends and family to meet up with me, they could not just drop their jobs and families to come hang out. Not that we got to do all that much hanging out on the rare occasions when they could get away; mostly, they got to watch me work. It was wonderful for me, as I felt buoyed by their presence and moral support, but less so for them.

In a way, the people I was living with day in and day out—Sheri and Kim and publicist Patty Lou Andrews—traveled with me the most and became a surrogate family. Road siblings, I called them. We went through so much together and bonded quickly, kind of like a platoon of soldiers who'd served together and come home with war stories that only they can fully understand. Mutt's love was in the studio, not on the road, and we spent long stretches of weeks and sometimes months apart, as my schedule was relentless, and unless he came to me, we simply didn't connect.

I had moments of sheer desperation over these years, and although I never contemplated suicide, I was looking for an escape. I even wished I would catch the next bad flu going around, so that I could get a forced rest, or for the album suddenly to lose steam so it would be time to get off the road and pass my hours with my guitar just writing in peace with a few friends around the fire. I hoped for doom because a break was no longer optional. Rest was a selfish request that compromised the success of my work, and so many people were contributing to what I was doing: from my record company and my own staff to Mutt and every person related to the project who was relying on me to carry the torch until it burned out. I felt as if it was all riding on me. It was clear that when I stopped, the whole machine stopped.

I didn't drink alcohol at all, took no drugs, barely even a painkiller, let alone Ambien or other soothing helpers. I didn't turn to food to comfort myself, nor did I have a therapist. I was alone in this mess with seemingly no way out. I was meant to be a soldier and just stick it out in this prison of exhausting loneliness.

I remember speaking to Luke on the phone from a Las Vegas hotel room. It was a large suite and had huge floor-to-ceiling windows that spanned the width of the living room. I was way up somewhere on who knows what floor towering over what seemed to be everything else. Although it's hard for me to imagine my thought process in the moment back then, this was what I was experiencing. The living room was spacious, and as I was talking to Luke, listening with one-half of my brain and contemplating with the other, it occurred to me that all I had to do was move the coffee table out of the way, and I'd have a good, clear run at the window with enough force to actually break through and jump. It wasn't anything Luke was saying that brought this on, of course, as Luke was always very compassionate and sensitive to me personally. I may not have even told Luke more than that I was tired and could use more rest, but I wouldn't have expressed the true depth of my desperation that night. I was too strong, or maybe weak, depending on how you look at it, to burden anyone with my pain. It would have been more painful to do that than to jump through the window, in my mind. I was experiencing amazing success, and my thinking was that I didn't have the right to complain about it.

Over the course of these two years, my schedule allowed for pit stops at home near Saint Regis Falls only every two or three months, and for no more than a few days each time. During one trip home, while promoting "You Win My Love" in the early spring of 1996, the loneliness and sheer exhaustion of the past year caught up with me.

Still more singles were in the pipeline, and I just didn't feel like I could go on. I was soaking in a hot bath one night, feeling alone and very sorry for myself. That day I'd finally implored whoever would listen—a hometown friend, Mutt, or a road sibling—that I needed a break and wanted a couple of more days at home to rest, but everyone's response was the same: "Come on, Eileen, you can do it. You have everything going for you. Anyone would cut off their right arm to be in your position. Stop complaining." Breaking commitments could come back to hurt me in the future, was what I learned to believe. What's more, the team had worked so hard on putting the machine in motion for the new record, and it would be a shame to let them down. Basically, I felt pressured to suck it up and do whatever it took to make the most of the record's success. I should have leaned on my family at that point in my life, but I wouldn't allow myself to display what I considered weakness on my part. Being the self-sufficient, strong one was how I'd come to view myself, and I wasn't about to tarnish their image of me. *My* image of me. Besides, what good would it have done? I'd just sent out a distress call and was rebuffed.

I lay in the hot water a long time until it began to cool and I started to cry. But to myself. Mutt was taking a break from the studio for a couple of hours to watch a sports match of some kind on TV, and I didn't want him to hear me. I did not want anyone to hear my weak, pathetic breakdown. When the tears stopped, I went to bed alone.

I can imagine someone reading this and miming playing an imaginary violin. "Oh, boo-hoo. Your second album is selling millions of copies, you're doing all this cool stuff. Please, spare me." Exactly. I said the same thing to myself plenty of times. I felt guilty, because what right did I have to complain about anything? With all the good fortune that was coming my way, how could I possibly be unhappy?

# 22

## Life Among the Loons

It goes without saying that I was way off the mark when it came to guessing what *The Woman in Me* would sell. But then, even the most wildly optimistic predictions from people at my record company fell far short. One year after its release, the CD had sold almost 3.2 million copies, and it would eventually surpass 15 million, making *The Woman in Me* the top-selling album by a female artist in the history of country music. When you consider the immense talent of the women who paved the way for me—Patsy Cline, June Carter Cash, Tammy Wynette, Loretta Lynn, Dolly Parton; I could go on and on—it's beyond humbling. It is mind boggling.

*The Woman in Me* took other completely unexpected honors that I never could have imagined, including the 1996 Grammy Award for Best Country Album and Album of the Year at the Country Music Awards. The success of that period would also earn me trophies for International Rising Star (British Country Music Awards), World's Best Selling Female Country Artist (World Music Awards), and Top New Female Vocalist (Country Music Awards).

That sort of recognition helped to offset my fatigue as we set our sights on the next record. Good thing, too, because I would have only about four months to finish writing and recording in order to meet the targeted fall 1997 release date. It helped that I could do some of the work in Saint Regis Falls, roughly twenty miles from the Canadian border. I guess you could call it centrally located: about eighty miles southwest of Montreal and eight miles southeast of Ottawa. Yep, centrally located right in the middle of nowhere. Which was exactly what Mutt and I had wanted—and, more to the point, needed.

We both loved nature and wanted to keep a distance from public recognition. We were creative people who needed solitude, with no distractions, in order to focus on why we did what we did musically. We enjoyed living our days around being creative for no other reason than to create. The public only became a part of it once the material was ready, finished, and ready to be shared. Who wants to see a painting before the artist decides it's finished and the paint is dry, after all?

The idea was to restore some measure of sanity to our lives by limiting the amount of travel I'd have to do, especially since I'd planned all along to support this CD with my first full-scale concert tour. However, we did end up traveling quite a bit so that Mutt could capture certain musicians in their own environment, and so that they didn't have to travel. We also wanted to change up the scenery for ourselves as writers, to be in new places we could draw inspiration from. The Saint Regis Falls home was something we built with the idea of spending many creative years there as a base, as nature was all around us in the miles of forest that circled the house and the lake that was centered in the property. We designed deep porches all round the building so that we could sit outside and take in the sounds of the northern woods that echoed over the lake.

We named the secluded property Loon Echo because at sunrise and at dusk, the loons would call to one another. Hearing the large birds' fluty cries bouncing across the glasslike surface of our private lake reminded me of my childhood in Canada; I'd get positively giddy at the sound. The spacious office, the hub of all things in Mutt and Woody World, featured large picture windows that overlooked the inlet. Between the breathtaking view, a deep porch, and the aroma of Kim Godreau's masterfully baked apple pies wafting from the kitchen, it made for the perfect setup.

Kim came on in 1996, and for the next fifteen years, I felt I couldn't live without her! We developed a sisterly bond and loyalty over all the years of working together. I think that if I was ever in a room with other celebrities and we got talking about our PAs, I'd be very immature and make sure everyone knew that *my* assistant was better than their assistant.

Working out of the office at Loon Echo as part of the team was Stacy Smith. She'd been around from when Sheri began working with me in 1992 when I first moved to Nashville and started out doing some basic accounting for me. Her role grew to becoming full business manager. She has now been with me eighteen years and is another one of my most trusted friends who really has my back.

Patty Lou Andrews was also a gem of a friend on the team during the period of *The Woman in Me*'s success. She did the most traveling with me during the promotion of that CD. Patty Lou was dedicated to the project, and with Mary no longer there, she took on quite a load. She was handling the marketing and publicity in coordination with the record company, and it was a demanding post, being that I worked so heavily in the area of promotion and marketing.

Patty Lou had a husband and family at home in Ontario and managed to be a traveling professional, a loving mother of two preteen sons, and a dedicated wife to her beloved husband, Rob. She was a shining example of how to do everything well. She spoke of her family constantly and it was great to hear all about them, as it was a welcome escape from the reality of promotional road life.

Kim, Patty Lou, and Stacy essentially fulfilled the role of professional management for more than two years. I couldn't have gotten through the intense promotional period for *The Woman in Me* without them.

While working on *Come On Over* in 1997, I was introduced to Jon Landau and Barbara Carr, longtime managers of Bruce Springsteen. Jon started out in music as a well-respected rock critic; in fact, in 1974, shortly before Bruce's career erupted with his third album, *Born to Run,* Jon saw him perform in Boston and was moved to write the prophetic words "I saw rock and roll's future and its name is Bruce Springsteen." A few years later, he was rock 'n' roll's future's manager. As my comanager, Jon was extremely attentive and lent moral support when I needed his ear and encouragement, especially when it came to stage fright. He knew how to talk me through to the other side of the panic.

Barbara, a steady, no-nonsense lady with loads of management experience (Hall & Oates, among others) and a heart of gold, spent a lot of time with me on the road. Consequently, she saw me at my best and my worst, but she always handled either extreme well. Jan Stabile, another management partner at Landau Management, completed the trio with Barbara and myself. Both women possessed strength, brains, compassion, common sense, and know-how. They made my life easier, and even though we would part ways professionally after five years, I still feel a bond with them today.

The three of us spent loads of time traveling internationally, promoting *Come On Over* together. At the time my music was already well on its way to breaking many music industry records, but I was still an unknown in many parts of the world other than North America. I was starting from scratch in the overseas international market, and Jan and Barbara did the miles with me. They dug the trenches and dredged the ditches over and over again until finally I would have success abroad.

By the time I'd gotten through the rigorous period of *The Woman in Me* CD, I was already half burned out on promotion, but *Come On Over* would become an even bigger success and more demanding. I remember being in Scotland during the promotional tour for *Come On Over*. I was suffering sleep deprivation and getting desperate. The schedule was grueling, and jet lag didn't help. I needed to sleep but couldn't. I was waking up in the middle of the night in this insomniac state, having to be in hair and makeup in only a few hours. I could not continue this crazy workload with three to four hours' sleep for days on end. I was exhausted but wired with a crawling-out-of-my-skin-type energy. I asked Jan if she could organize for a treadmill to be in my hotel rooms, as the only way I could think of physically ridding myself of this excess energy and get back to sleep was to run it off. Barbara and Jan got me through it still sane and alive. I thank them for their patience, as there were times I was close to the breaking point, and although I was very good at controlling myself in front of anyone else, once the three of us were alone, my release would flow and it wasn't always pretty. Lots of good ole Northern Ontario, small-town girl came out in my language, let's put it that way.

Now that I formally had management again, Patty Lou Andrews retired and returned to her husband and two preteen sons, Michael and Matthew. Sadly, two years later Patty Lou died suddenly of a severe brain aneurysm. I cried like a baby when I received the news. She was truly a special person, one who kept me laughing when I was grumpy from too little sleep and too many commitments. Her ability to remain calm and gracious under pressure was an inspiration.

Not long after Patty Lou's passing, I received a package containing a beautiful pearl necklace that had belonged to her late mother. She'd left it to me in her will. With my mouth open in disbelief, I clung to the pearls as if they were the tips of Patty Lou's very own fingers reaching out to touch me. She did touch me that day, and deeply. I could not help but wonder when she had made out a will, not knowing, of course, that she would soon face death so prematurely. And why would she have left these to me? I literally fell to my knees, humbled by her thoughtfulness—but not surprised. I miss Patty Lou.

*Come On Over* was written in bits and pieces over the course of the two years since *The Woman in Me* had been released. Mutt and I connected periodically when he'd join me on the promotional touring. We wrote while dining out, driving, even at a soccer game, where the bulk of "From This Moment On" was written. I was a bit bored with the pace of soccer compared to the lively games of ice hockey that I was more accustomed to, and it started flowing out. This is one of my favorite original songs. The writing sessions between Mutt and me were scattered, and no one specific place or time alone represents that songwriting period.

Mutt and I spent a lot of time apart as I was promoting and touring, and he was in studios working on tracks and arrangements as we wrote. It's surprising that we were able to write all this stuff with so little time together. We wrote independently and merged ideas when we joined up. I remember feeling very excited about the counter line sung by Mutt as backing vocals in "You're Still the One." As I sang the chorus melody repeatedly while working out the lyrics, he kicked in with the counter line "You're still the one," and it gave me chills. All of a sudden we had a hit chorus. It was a magic moment.

That song crossed over to pop and international success. I passed Elton John while I was coming and he was going from a radio station visit, and as we approached each other in the corridor, he started singing "You're Still the One." I was so flattered that this legendary songwriter extraordinaire, who I was seeing for the first time in the flesh, honored me with such an incredible compliment as to address me by singing my own chorus. "You're Still the One" brought us nominations for four Grammy Awards, two of which I took home.

"That Don't Impress Me Much" was the seventh single released from the CD, and it kept the momentum going. It's extremely difficult for the average album to sustain itself even after the third single, never mind a seventh. This was rare in the music industry and still is. "You're Still the One" had opened the world of international and crossover success to my career, and "That Don't Impress Me Much" kept it going. It won several pop, country, and international songwriting awards.

"Man! I Feel Like a Woman!" was the eighth release, and it ensured even more longevity to the life of Come On Over. Phew, I was exhausted, and although I was thrilled by the success, I feared it would never end: the work, the travel, the loneliness. I am so proud of that record, the songs themselves and all that was achieved from scratch to finish. I feel a huge sense of accomplishment now, but at the time, I was too tired to appreciate it. Every time I'd get news that it just kept selling, and the demand for more singles continued, I wanted to collapse at the thought that normalcy, rest, recharging my batteries were all yet another single away. It was an incredibly bittersweet experience to be enjoying the success and feeling a pang of almost resentment toward it. I considered myself selfish, feeling this contradiction of emotions, but I was confused about what to feel. I didn't know whether to be happy or sad. I was losing touch with what I wanted. There was no peace. "More pain, more gain" thankfully applies to the experience of *Come On Over* for me, and today, I am able to look back on it with great pleasure and satisfaction. I saw my day-to-day reality then as a struggle with no end in sight, though of course I now appreciate that this was a rare blessing that very few recording artists are ever gifted with experiencing. I saw it then as well, but it was a blur, as I was standing too close to see it clearly.

Even at home—even a haven like Loon Echo—I still felt constricted by my newfound fame. This may seem hard to believe, but after a while, you start to miss the mundane stuff of daily life, like walking into a drugstore and buying yourself a toothbrush. Granted, not the stuff that dreams are made of, but when *you never get to do it*—at least, not without first having to mobilize your security detail—it just becomes less of a hassle to ask your assistant to make a tampon run, you know?

Not only that, but you never seem to have time because there's always something more pressing that needs to be done yesterday, and it typically involves other people. So if it's a toss-up between my wanting to iron but having to lay down a vocal overdub in the studio, or else I will be holding up Mutt, the recording engineer, and who knows who else, the simple chore at home is going to take a backseat. I cannot very well delegate lead vocals on my own record to someone else while I get the ironing done. You don't even have to say it: "So what's so bad about that? I'd *love* to have someone do those things for me." Well, whether we're aware of it or not, we all derive a measure of satisfaction just from being self-sufficient and feeling competent in the world. I was starting to feel as if I'd lost my chops at life's fundamentals—and I'd been someone who could survive on my own in a cabin in the woods with no running water or electricity in subzero temperatures and snow up to my butt. Now, with a skilled full-time staff at home to handle every domestic and personal chore for me, I felt . . . useless and inept.

I used to come home after being away and feel like a houseguest. For one thing, I could never find anything! *Where are my rubber boots?* For that, I would have to ask the cleaning lady. *Damn! I forgot how to program the oven!* For that, ask Kim. It seemed like my being there disrupted the graceful efficiency of my own household. When I'd want to do things for myself, it would throw everybody off.

Cooking in your own kitchen, for example, where your cupboards have been arranged by someone else in your absence, can be discouraging. A cook has to know her way around her own kitchen, otherwise a lot of the fun is taken out of it, just in trying to find everything. "Why don't you relax? What do you want to *cook* for?" I heard that all the time. Why? Because I wanted to feel normal again! I didn't want to be waited on hand and foot like spoiled royalty; I wanted to do the things that kept me real and gave me some sense of control over my life, like folding my own towels, making my own bed, and putting my socks away where I wanted *so I always knew where to find them.*

Here is how much I began to crave normalcy: One Friday afternoon, not long after Kim began working for me, I asked her about her plans for the weekend. "Oh, nothing special," she replied. "Tomorrow I'm off to the Walmart to pick out some paint."

I perked right up. "Can I come with you?!" You'd have thought she'd said, "I'm taking the Concorde to Paris to go shopping on the Avenue des Champs-Élysées, and all the stores there are having a hundred-percent-off sale." We had not gotten to know each other well yet; she probably found my enthusiastic request off, if not just plain sad. But she came around the next afternoon in her beat-up truck. "Excuse my rattletrap," she said apologetically. Are you kidding? I grew up riding around in rattletraps. I had a great time hanging out with Kim that Saturday doing something that I am sure most people would file under "drudgery."

There was one activity around Loon Echo that I could call my own: tending the horses. I had wanted to own horses ever since I was twelve years old and caring for my friend Sue's palomino, Angel, when we lived in Hanmer. Now that I finally had the money and a little time between albums, I rewarded myself by purchasing five of these noble and proud creatures. I love everything about horses: their power and grace, the balance and weightless motion of their massive, athletic frame, their elegant silhouette, the energy and fiery passion that flows through their veins, the way they carry themselves with breathtaking beauty. I am in awe of them. How could such a powerful animal possess so generous a temperament as to carry man obediently and thoughtfully through the ages?

I visited several farms in the Nashville area looking for my equestrian friends. Once they finally arrived at Loon Echo, I spent every chance I could with them. The barn became a refuge where I could mentally escape show business. The smells of the sweet hay and the animals' musty coats, the *clip-clop* of their hooves on the wood floors, their snorting sighs of contentment—I loved it all. Every now and then, I would have what I called "salon day." One at a time, I would pamper them with a deep clean while grooving to the radio. Suds and conditioners, finely combed manes and tails, sleek 'n' shiny coats, dressed hooves, lots of hugs and kisses, and they were ready to roll out in the paddock. Horses never stay clean if you let them have any fun outside, just being horses. The point of the salon days was more the hands-on contact and communication that keeps their manners and patience in line while standing tied and being handled. It was a chance to check closely for cuts and bruises and just give them a good once-over from head to toe.

I even enjoyed mucking out their stalls; there is something very satisfying about leaving your friend's bed clean and ready for a good night's rest. I took pride in my horses' health and happiness. Just as they depended on me, I looked to them to listen to me when I was sad and to teach me patience; act impulsively around horses, and you'll most likely get hurt. Horses demand respectful, calm, and gentle handling if you expect them to be respectful, calm, and gentle in return. A horse that does not behave is dangerous, because if her will is not in sync with yours, she'll likely overpower you and either injure or kill you. One kick'll do it, in fact. So being around the horses was always humbling. I hugged them often and took comfort in their willingness to let me, and when they had the chance to just walk away and didn't, I knew I had a friend.

In winter, my favorite time of day with them was the dinner feed, around five o'clock, when it was already dark. I would go out to the stable and fill up the hand wagon with enough hay for all five of them. Then I'd line up their piles on the snow, making sure to place them far enough apart so that they would eat in peace and not spend the time scowling at one another and posturing with their ears back to defend their grub. There is something so peaceful about watching a horse eat. All bundled up, I would plunk myself down in the deep snow and sink into a perfect, soft, custom-contoured chair. I felt warm and cozy in the silent night, staring up at the stars and just listening to them chew contentedly. It was magical. Later in the evening, I would come back out to put them in for the night and give them their grain.

I loved each horse in a unique way, but one was particularly special to me: Dancer, an eleven-year-old Andalusian gelding with a kind face and an all-white coat that made him resemble a unicorn. I first discovered this Spanish breed at John and Bo Derek's ranch when we were shooting photos for the album cover of *The Woman in Me*. They were breeding Andalusians at the time. I fell instantly in love with the horses' arched necks, bold and confident characters, and consistent temperaments. That was in 1994.

Three years later, the Dereks' horse trainer, Ramon Becerra, the same guy who trained the spotted horse you see me riding on the back cover of *The Woman in Me* CD, was passing through upstate New York with his traveling horse show. He asked if he could stop off at my stable so that his ten horses could graze and rest a few days. I was thrilled at the prospect of having horse company and having a riding partner for a few days.

I learned a lot from Ramon. His life is training horses, and he's particularly specialized in working with classical riding, the type you see at the world-famous Spanish riding school in Vienna, Austria. Dancer was an Andalusian, a Spanish breed of Iberian horse. Dancer's training was extensive in *haute école* movements of classical dressage. Ramon also taught Dancer to stretch out low to the ground so the rider could mount easily. He could also bow with one knee to the ground and tilt his head down as if to tip his hat. This was one fancy horse.

Ramon and I went riding the horse trails on our property. He was on Dancer, whom I'd remembered seeing while touring John and Bo's stable. "Would you like to try riding him?" he asked me. To be honest, I was afraid to. The gelding was impressive but intimidating, with a bit of an attitude around the other horses. He moved purposefully—veins popping, nostrils flaring, mouth frothing—his powerful legs pounding the ground.

"Uh-uh," I told Ramon. "This is too much horse for me."

"No, you can handle him," he insisted. Just then, we came up to a wide puddle across the trail. Dancer refused to go through it, forcing Ramon to work hard to get him to move. The stubborn horse dodged side to side, then got up on his hind legs and pawed at the air, vigorously shaking his head as if to say "No way!" The corners of his mouth became red and raw from the pressure of the bit. All this over a *puddle*.

At last, Dancer tentatively set one hoof in the muddy water, then quickly yanked it back. It occurred to me that this handsome white horse didn't want to get his pearly white socks dirty! The only way he would cross the puddle was to tiptoe through quickly, like a fire-walker on a bed of hot coals. He looked so prissy, I could not help but laugh, and at that moment, I fell in love with Dancer. So he *did* have a vulnerable side.

I told Ramon that I was interested in buying the horse and asked if he could leave Dancer with me for a couple of weeks, to see if we got along. If things did not work out, in two weeks the trainer would pick him up on his way back home to California.

We did not get off to a smashing start. Dancer was hostile toward the other horses, so I had to keep him in his own paddock. He could see the other horses, though, and became agitated. I figured he would gradually calm down and left him for a few hours. When I walked back to check on him, I could see from a distance that was wrong: Dancer's neck and shoulder area were red with blood. Horrified, I ran to him as fast as I could and inspected him. Apparently, the horse had been running back and forth along the fence and cut himself on one of the post edges. Blood still seeped from a foot-long gash that ran diagonal across the front of his neck. Despite my state of panic, I put his halter on him and led him quickly back to the stable, shaking the whole way. Thankfully, the vet was able to close the wound using two layers of stitches, which, miraculously, left Dancer with only a hairline scar. The cut had been deep, though, and I shuddered to think of what might have happened had I left him overnight. Probably, he would have bled to death. It was awful feeling that I had exposed this beautiful animal to harm while he was under my care, especially considering that he had been entrusted to me.

Through that terrible experience, Dancer and I bonded. In the days following his accident, I stayed with him in his stall for hours at a stretch. But the Andalusian didn't like anyone in his stall, which he made clear by backing away and turning his butt to you when you entered. Nor did he like being patted, hugged, or kissed. He was indifferent to such nonsense, it seemed, and potentially dangerous enough that I left the stall door open partway just in case he became ornery and I needed to make a quick getaway. I did not quite trust this unfriendly horse, and he obviously did not trust me, either.

We probably resembled a miserable old couple who'd just decided to get a divorce: me, squatted down with my back against the wall and my eyes glued to the floor, humming along with the radio and twiddling straw, just waiting. As for Dancer, every once in a while, he'd stop sulking in the corner, turn toward me, lower his head, and sniff—but then he'd go right back to being his sullen self. And no sooner would I leave than he would poke his head out the top of the door, eagerly surveying the scene. This went on for days. Gradually, Dancer started sniffing me more regularly and curiously nipping at the straw between my fingers. He was finally communicating with me—but only up to a point. Any time I reached out to touch him, he jerked his head back and returned to facing the corner.

When Dancer had healed sufficiently for me to ride him, I took it cautiously. To my surprise, everything went very smoothly. Out on the trails, alone with each other, we began to connect, to the point that he started to accept me being in his stall. We were becoming friends. Good friends. So after a few weeks with Dancer, my confidence had built up enough to buy him and give him a permanent home with us.

When I told Ramon and Bo Derek about the progress that Dancer was making and his revealing a sweet disposition, they were both taken aback. According to Bo, most people had found him too scary to ride because he was disobedient and a dominant bully; on group rides, Dancer always had to push his way to the head of the pack. In fact, she told me, Dancer could be such a bugger at times that they'd taken to calling him Maniac.

He never acted that way with me. Once we had established a bond, the Andalusian even tolerated my insisting that he walk calmly through the dirty puddles he hated so much. "Dancer has become a different horse with you," Bo marveled. He was my trustworthy, gentle companion. My prince.

The stable was where I fit in best. I often dreamed of how fabulous it would be to live in the loft above the horses. That's where I wanted to be. I could always find things where I had left them, the smell was heavenly, the horses didn't care how I looked, I had fantastic company, and I always had a soft nose to kiss.

# 23

## Taking My Show on the Road

The *Come On Over* CD, due out in November, was just about finished. While Mutt practically moved into the recording studio full-time, tweaking the final mixes, I turned my attention to assembling the band for my first concert tour. I sat on the floor in the home office, sifting through piles of demos, cassette tapes, and résumés sent in by musicians seeking an audition.

I knew I had a lot to prove in the live concert arena. Because I hadn't toured behind *The Woman in Me,* several critics jumped to the conclusion that I must have been a product of the recording studio and not a capable singer onstage. I guess they weren't aware that I'd already put in more time playing in front of audiences than many artists rack up in their entire careers.

But I understood the skepticism. For one thing, my strategy of focusing solely on promoting the album *was* unorthodox, to say the least. For another, recording technology had advanced to the point where studio trickery *could* enhance a mediocre voice. Just multitracking the lead vocal can lend heft to an otherwise thin set of pipes. An even bigger breakthrough, if you want to call it that, has been the advent of Auto-Tune, an audio pitch corrector that absolves artists of having to sing on key. Too sharp? Too flat? No problem! If you ask me, it seems a bit like cheating. I mean, you're billing yourself as a singer, right? Well, then, don't you think you should be able to sing? On the list of job requirements, I'm pretty sure that's at the top of

the list. Or maybe not so much anymore. This trend of better singing through science has been prevalent mainly in the pop and dance
music fields, however; the country music audience still expects its
musicians to have the goods, and rightly so.

I admit to being quite critical about live singing ability, but that
attitude came back to bite me later on. As my career built, so did
the pressure to be what I was on the records. Before I was a recording artist, there was nothing to be compared to. I just sang my best
and didn't worry about being held hostage by my own studio performance. I prided myself on being accurate and consistent, with good
pitch, control, and stamina. It was almost as though my childhood
stage anxiety had been worked through, and my confidence as a live
performer had finally overcome it. However, as nerves started to kick
in on a level I'd never known before, and with the predisposition to
stage fright that stemmed from my childhood performing in adult environments that made me uncomfortable, I finally reached the limit
of pressure I could take. I was in a spotlight that was bigger than
I'd ever imagined would flood me, and I was scared. I found it extremely difficult to find enough confidence to sing properly under
the pressure. My throat tightened, and I felt as though I was choking. The sound just didn't come out the way it was supposed to.
Squeezed, shaky notes were all I could muster, and each time I failed
to control what sounded from my voice, the more insecure I became,
and it slowly began to compound.

Now all of a sudden I was thrilled about the ability technology
had to "fix" a live vocal I was disappointed with. Studio recording
felt safe enough, and live stage performances had come a long way
since my childhood of hiding behind my guitar. I began to sympathize
with other singers who I admired on studio recordings but was disappointed with in live performances. Were they experiencing stage
fright, doubting their own ability under the pressure? I understood
and related to their experience. I was now more sympathetic to the
singer who was more than capable of singing live perfectly well in the
studio, but not able to project that ability as well on a stage. What

During the video shoot of "Dance with the One That Brought You," with actors Charles Durning (left) and Sean Penn (right). *(Courtesy of Mercury Records, a Division of UMG Recordings, Inc.)*

Sean Penn directing me in the video of "Dance with the One That Brought You." *(Courtesy of Mercury Records, a Division of UMG Recordings, Inc.)*

Photo shoot with Tim.

BELOW: In Cairo filming "The Woman in Me" video, July 1995. (*Courtesy of Mercury Records, a Division of UMG Recordings, Inc.*)

A John Derek picture of me wearing Bo Derek's pink hat, California, 1995.
(*Courtesy of Mercury Records, a Division of UMG Recordings, Inc.*)

Before a tour break, I played a prank on my band and had them wear spandex outfits.

With my band during the Come On Over tour.

Dancer in Central Park, after special permission was granted for me to bring him there to ride for the day during the Come On Over tour.

The first time I met Elton John, in 1998.

With Tim on the video shoot of "That Don't Impress Me Much," El Mirage Dry Lake, November 1998. (*Courtesy of Mercury Records, a Division of UMG Recordings, Inc.*)

Video director Paul Boyd, costume designer Marc Bouwer, and hairstylist Cyril Lanoir on the video shoot of "That Don't Impress Me Much," November 1998. (*Courtesy of Mercury Records, a Division of UMG Recordings, Inc.*)

With Marc Bouwer on the video shoot of "Man! I Feel Like a Woman!," New York, January 1999. (*Courtesy of Mercury Records, a Division of UMG Recordings, Inc.*)

ABOVE: With Eja in Milan, fall 2001.

LEFT: Eja's first snow, Switzerland, winter 2001.

Eja and Tim at the chateau, Switzerland, winter 2001.

Taking a break with Eja from a photo shoot, spring 2002.

At the CMA Awards in 2003 with Jason Owen, my publicist at the time and my manager today. *(Credit: Ed Rode/ EdRode.com)*

BELOW: Performing in front of 50,000 great fans at a concert in Chicago's Grant Park, July 27th 2003. *(Credit: NBCU Photo Bank/Paul Drinkwater)*

A cozy evening with Fred
at the Canadian cottage,
Lake of Bays, 2010.

Las Vegas, October 2010.

Me and Eja feeding a young moose, Christmas 2009 in Canada.

Pages spread out at the Blackstone House, Mustique, while writing my book,
March 2010.

At home in Switzerland, happily back to songwriting, 2010.

Eja and I on a mountain hike, overlooking our hometown on Lake Geneva, 2010.

Eja and I, Lake Geneva, summer 2010.

was the difference? Live is live, whether in the studio or on a stage. But psychologically, trying to be perfect when you are aware that there are potentially millions of viewers watching can really put you on edge. I care about doing my best, and when I think there is any chance my best might not be good enough, I get nervous, and anxiety takes over.

For some reason, the studio and my own live concert stage remained a comfortable zone throughout the Come On Over tour, and I was able to enjoy the experience vocally. But live TV was where my nerves first started to rear up again, like a ghost from my childhood performing past. I really felt on the spot, and it affected my self-esteem to the point that my voice began to close from the tension in the muscles around my neck and larynx, which were slowly becoming chronically tight and beginning to constrict my vocal freedom. At the time, this would only interfere with my singing voice when I was under great stress or pressure, which was pretty much limited to television performances.

I decided it was time to start touring six months after the *Come On Over* CD was released. Putting the tour together required a lot of advance time, so the preproduction stage began while the album was still being recorded. The process began with the search for the band musicians. After I went through the hours of audition cassette demos, I was ready to call musicians in for live auditions. Regarding musicianship, Mutt was the main critic, as he knew what it was going to take from the musicians technically to pull the album off live. I was looking more at personality, stage presence, and the ability to multitask as a good musician and a stage performer. I wanted the musicians to be musically accurate on their instruments, while being able to sing backing vocals and have the physical stamina to keep the energy onstage up and pumping for an hour and a half to two hours, nonstop. Attitude was also key. I had to like them as people and sense a genuine good character in their personalities. "No troublemakers or egomaniacs allowed, no matter how good they are," was a big part of the criteria. I wanted to work with nice people who had humility, honesty, and professionalism, and that is what I got, after a time-consuming screening process, of course.

Here's the rundown of those who shared the stage with me on both the Come On Over and Up! tours and countless television performances and specials. With me the longest from the *Shania* CD promotional touring period, Allison Cornell was on keys, violin, mandolin, and backing vocals. Marc Muller, recommended by Allison, was on electric, acoustic, and slide and steel guitars. Likewise, bassist-vocalist Andy Cichon turned me on to Randall Waller, one of the lead electric guitarists and backing vocalist. Roddy Chiong played violin and sang backing vocals, and J. D. Blair was on drums. Hardy Hemphill played piano and percussion and sang backing vocals, and Cory Churko was on acoustic and electric guitars, violin, and backing vocals. Brent Barcus was on lead guitar and backing vocals.

I really can't single out any one member of the band as more special than the others, as they all contributed uniquely to the success of every show over the years. They were a supportive, positive-thinking, energetic, low-drama group of individuals, and I salute them with the deepest respect possible. They were also a culturally mixed group: Roddy, a classically trained Chinese American musician; J.D., an African American with a funk music background; Andy and Randall, from Australia; Cory, from Canada; Brent and Hardy, from a Christian music background; Marc, a Californian surfer and musician; and Allison with Juilliard training. Most of the musicians played more than one instrument and were truly multitalented.

Rehearsals for the Come On Over tour were like boot camp. I wanted each concert to be a *show*, brimming with energy. And I didn't want the spotlight to shine only on me. As I explained to the musicians the first day of rehearsal, they were an integral part of the performance, not just a backup band. "I want you guys to run around, connect with the audience, so that the whole stage comes alive," I told them.

Well, in order to do that without the playing and singing suffering, you have to know your parts so well that the music becomes an extension of yourself—but without sounding as though you're on automatic pilot. One aspect of playing live that people don't always appreciate is the physicality it demands. Ever try scooting around a stage while wielding an electric guitar or bass? By the time you're midway through a set, it can feel as if someone strapped an anchor around your shoulders using battleship chains. Musicians need to be up to the task physically as well as mentally. And the only way to do that is to rehearse repeatedly until you build up those calluses on your fingers and commit every movement to muscle memory, just like an athlete. Also, if you're going to develop the onstage telepathy that characterizes any great performing unit, there is no substitute for practice, practice, practice. How else do you think musicians learn to play together with genuine precision? Jamming is great, and there is a lot to be said about feeling your way through a song, but lots of times this can be sloppy as well. Although it may be amusing to them, musicians who just make it up as they go along can make for painful listening. Jamming can be like a private joke: the only ones enjoying it are the ones who can make sense of what's being said/played. My personal feeling is that if you have your chops up to scratch and know exactly where you are going with your part, then you have true liberty to ad lib without crashing into anyone else.

We drilled the approximately twenty-song set for weeks on end in the gym at Loon Echo, until we were all exhausted and about as perfect as you could get. Marc Muller, our extraordinary pedal steel guitarist, worried aloud that all this rehearsing might dull everyone's spontaneity. "I honestly think we're ready," he said.

"Not yet," I replied. Everyone looked up. "When you can do cartwheels while singing and playing at the same time, *then* we're ready." I might have said this with a half smile, as I never did ask any of my band members to cartwheel while performing, but I was serious. By the time we wrapped up dress rehearsals, with lighting, full sound— the whole shebang—here's how tight we were: the versatile Hardy Hemphill could play guitar or piano and sing while knocking off one of his beloved crossword puzzles *in ink*. One time during a run-through, violinist Allison Cornell wandered over to Hardy's side of the stage, looked over his shoulder, and yelled over the gale of sound, "Six down: *deceased!*" without missing a note. They both doubled over with laughter at the realization of how far we had come as a band.

Was it overkill? Maybe. I know that most of the musicians thought so. But I'd always been big on aiming for excellence and shooting for the best performance possible, and I couldn't hold a candle to Mutt in the department of getting things spot on. Anyone working with the two of us was going to be involved in the quest for perfection. I believe it all paid off. Our very first show was on May 29, 1998, at the 4,600-seat Sudbury Community Arena in my old hometown. It was surreal being back in Sudbury, where I spent some of my childhood career in clubs and talent shows, to now be preparing for my international concert tour as a bona fide recording artist. My parents were missing the before and after of Eilleen Twain, but they were there with me in spirit on that rehearsal stage, as if I were in a time warp. So much had changed, yet I still felt so close to the small-town Northern girl I had always been.

Jon Landau came backstage and remarked, "Wow! You guys sounded like you've already been on tour for three months, not just one day." That was high praise coming from someone who had stood in the wings for probably hundreds of shows by Bruce Springsteen and the E Street Band, widely regarded as one of the greatest live outfits ever to grace a stage.

Even with all that rehearsing, I had to get used to singing while being in perpetual motion from trying to command such a vast stage. In most of the little clubs I used to play, there was no need to move about, seeing as how there wasn't any room. Truthfully, I was never entirely satisfied with my vocals, but I came to realize that unless I stood still, I just wasn't going to give a studio-level performance. On-stage, it was more important to me to touch as many members of the audience as possible, whether shaking hands, signing autographs, or simply making eye contact while singing. My only goal was to leave the fans who came to my show satisfied that their hard-earned money had been well spent.

The set list was rapidly filling up with hits. *Come On Over*'s first two singles, "Love Gets Me Every Time" and "Don't Be Stupid (You Know I Love You)," reached number one and number six, respectively, on the Hot Country Songs chart. Oddly enough, the tenderhearted love song "You're Still the One," a personal favorite of mine, started slowly upon its release at the beginning of 1998. The first week in May, shortly before the tour kicked off, the single finally nicked the number one spot, then fell back. But "You're Still the One" would spend the next two months at number two on the Hot 100, giving me my first Top 10 pop hit. It also was my first record to receive airplay on adult contemporary radio, staying at number one for most of the summer. Although the song has country elements of warm, acoustic strumming, the verses are dominated by piano, while a smoldering organ, my least favorite instrument, stands out as the most prominent sound on the choruses. The music, I believe, transcended genres, and the universal message of the lyrics gave it broad crossover appeal. For sure, "You're Still the One" stood as a career landmark for me.

My two years of promoting *The Woman in Me* taught me what I did and did not like about being on the road. Above all else, I craved personal space and control; a measure of consistency, too, would help to preserve my sanity. So this time around, I traveled mostly by bus, with as little flying as possible. To me, living out of the bus was preferable to staying in hotels, because it allowed me to keep my clothes folded in drawers and not in a suitcase. It was my home on wheels. It cost me $1 million to buy my road home. It was worth it.

Two familiar faces from Timmins accompanied me: Larry and Helene Bolduc, my ex-boyfriend Paul's father and mother. They'd always been like adoptive parents to me, and even though Paul and I had broken up five years before, we'd remained close. Larry, who'd driven transport truck for more than twenty years for Sears, was my bus driver, and Helene filled in as my personal assistant, as Kim had two young children and needed to be home working in the upstate New York office.

One other benefit of traveling by bus was that we could hit the road immediately after the show, giving us an hour's head start on the trip to the next destination. As soon as the encore ended and the houselights came up, I was hustled offstage and ushered into a waiting car for a police escort to the bus, which was parked just off the nearest highway—usually a few minutes outside of town. The bus was too big to maneuver easily through traffic, so taking the car instead enabled us to get out of there just ahead of the concertgoers.

Nevertheless, the driver had to move quickly before we got caught up in the congestion like a fly in honey, or we'd be marooned for an hour, along with everyone else. Larry would swerve around other cars, braking suddenly, turning sharply, while I bounced around in the backseat. It reminded me of a car chase scene from *The Dukes of Hazzard*.

The whole time, Helene or my sister Carrie would be trying to help me wriggle out of my shirt. For this tour, we'd arranged for me to end each show wearing a local sports jersey, which I'd then autograph and give to the promoter to auction off for charity. However, I couldn't take the shirt off without first removing the battery pack to the inner-ear monitors that I wore in order to hear myself onstage. We'd duct tape the battery pack to the back of my bra, so that it stayed hidden under my long hair; a wire then ran up between my shoulder blades and connected to a pair of budlike earpieces. After a show, my hair was usually damp with sweat, and the wire would often get all tangled up in it. So as we're sliding around the backseat, Helene or Carrie is trying to carefully take off this gear without yanking out my hair or tearing off some skin—sometimes succeeding, sometimes not. I'd be cursing and ouching until I was finally freed. I must have looked like Houdini trying to escape from a straitjacket.

As soon as I climbed on the bus, I headed for my bedroom compartment, where Tim waited for me on my bed. I'd brought him along in order to help stave off the loneliness of the road and also to provide security.

Tim was a proud, classically handsome German shepherd with the typical golden tan coloring with black markings, large, imposing head, and long, pointy ears. He'd received two years of intensive Schutzhund training in Austria, personal protection schooling. *Schutzhund* simply means "protection dog" in German, and German shepherds are but one of a number of breeds to compete for and win a Schutzhund title. Tim stuck with me everywhere I went. He slept beside my bed, followed me to the bathroom door, and, in short, never let me out of his sight, no matter what.

In fact, when I first got Tim, I didn't realize how seriously he took his "job" until we were on a video shoot together and he was so insistent on staying near me that he kept barging his way into the frame. Finally, I took a heavy leather lead and tied him outside my wardrobe trailer in the shade, gave him some water, and returned to the set. Maybe ten minutes later, a panicked Tim came darting onto the set, ruining a scene. He'd chewed completely through the leash. I learned my lesson, and from then on made sure to tie him up close by so that he could at least see me and hear my voice at all times. That kept him calm. Still, taking no chances, I replaced the leather lead with a metal chain. He came close to gnawing his way through that on several occasions.

I loved Tim, and we shared the tour bus for the entire eighteen-month tour. The crowd noise and pyrotechnics of the show would have been too much for him, so while I performed, he waited patiently on the bus, lying on my bed. I tried taking him to sound checks at the beginning of the tour, but the pyro tests with the rifle-like concussive sound made him wild in defense mode. He would start barking, with the hair on his back standing on end, searching incessantly for where the sound was coming from. The fire of a gun was especially alarming to Tim, as it was part of his training to become alert and try to protect against a perpetrator when he heard the shot of a firearm. He was taught to find and retrieve firearms, in fact, so he was going nuts, desperate to do his job and protect me

Tim and I had a little routine: I used my bedroom as my dressing room. After I finished getting dressed, I'd call him up on my bed, kiss him on the head, and tell him to stay there until I got back. And he did. The moment I returned, he'd practically bowl me over. He was so overwhelmed with excitement and relief that he had me in his sights once again, and that he was now able to do his job. He was obviously panicked from the separation anxiety he'd endured in my absence. We were only apart for the one-hour sound check on show days and the approximately two-hour shows, but it didn't take much for Tim to get worked up, as his training was to never leave the side of the person he was meant to be protecting. I'd take him outside for his last bathroom break, when what I really wanted to do was get out of my sweaty stage clothes, hit the shower, slip into some PJ's, and relax for the ride ahead. Naturally, Tim made it his business to take his sweet time before doing his business, especially if it happened to be raining out.

As soon as I'd finished showering, I'd signal Larry, and off we'd roll into the night. (Trying to shower on a moving bus is like taking a shower during a major earthquake while standing on a bar of soap. I tried this once and realized that unless I wanted to break my neck, showering on the bus while it was stationary was necessary.) I probably should have gone right to sleep, but I never slept well in a moving vehicle, making mobile living not the most practical choice while touring, but the pros outweighed the cons. I'd usually stay up and talk to Helene or chat on the phone or watch a movie during the first hours of making our way to the next city, while rewarding myself with my naughty late-night snack of orange soda and yellow cheddar cheese popcorn.

It's amazing how much living space can be squeezed into a bus. My personal space was in the center area, closed off from the driver and from Helene's sitting and sleeping area in back. Helene and I shared a side door, but the layout afforded me a surprising amount of privacy.

The trip from city to city could range from six to ten hours, and I'd typically be awake for much of it before finally drifting off—only to be jolted awake a few hours later when we'd arrived at our parking spot either at the venue or nearby. As the bus was maneuvered into its space, it shimmied and jerked till it finally stilled in parked position. It was impossible to sleep through the parking of the bus. Larry, having driven all night, would then head off with Helene to a hotel, where they could get a more comfortable sleep, leaving me and Tim to ourselves.

My dog was impatient to go right outside. I didn't share Tim's excitement, as you might imagine, but I didn't have to. Check this out: I'd had the bus customized with a special floor hatch that opened to a ramp leading down to a luggage bay below. Without having to leave my compartment, I could hook Tim to a lead attached to a run line outside and let him out through the hatch in the floor. He could then take care of business and run around to his heart's content, and if he wanted shade, he could always lie down in the bay. A security camera kept him in my view at all times until he was ready to come back in. It really worked beautifully.

Sometimes we were able to park on neighboring farms, which gave me an opportunity to ride Dancer. That's right: he came along, too, for much of the tour, riding in a mobile stall. Being able to ride him while enjoying nature definitely helped to clear my head, but I really made the most of my limited free time. By late afternoon—and remember, since I'd be up half the night, I generally didn't get out of bed until around ten or eleven—I'd either ride Dancer when he was there or take long walks with Tim, and before I knew it, it was approaching three in the afternoon, time to head to the venue for the pre-performance sound check. All in all, I had a pretty good setup and lifestyle on the road. Having it so personalized helped make the eighteen months manageable.

The first U.S. leg of the tour took us to approximately eighty cities, ending with two shows at the Miami Bayfront Park Amphitheater in mid-January 1999. By then the *Come On Over* album had been out for more than a year and had delivered two more number one country hits, the rock-heavy "Honey, I'm Home" and the dramatic love song "From This Moment On."

"Honey, I'm Home," which draws you in with an infectious, danceable groove before changing tempo on the choruses, is sort of my playful take on the Johnny Paycheck classic "Take This Job and Shove It," but from the female perspective. While I can't vouch for this 100 percent, I think it's safe to assume that it's the only chart topper in country music history to contain a reference to premenstrual syndrome. "From This Moment On," practically a wedding vow set to music, was my first record to feature another recording artist, Bryan White, and for the international version, the lead singer from the group Boyzone, Ronan Keating. A few times during both tours, men were proposing to their girlfriends during the performance of this song. I was told by countless fans that it was a popular wedding song. This was an unexpected fact about the song that pleased me. The song was living a life of its own, independent of me. It now belonged to the public, and a large number of them decided it was going to be their wedding song. Some couples even came to my concerts in full wedding apparel. I just loved this.

Music moves people, and I was touched by how much my music did this for the fans. This was what I was doing it for; this was what made all the hard work so worth it. I took pleasure in the pleasure the music brought to them and their lives. "You're Still the One" and "From This Moment On" went to number one on the Adult Contemporary chart and reached the top five on the Hot 100.

When we flew off to Australia for seven dates in February, "That Don't Impress Me Much" was on its way into the Top 10 on both the country and pop charts. A tongue-in-cheek put-down song about men who think they're hot stuff but, in reality, leave the woman singing the song ice cold, it could be a cousin of Carly Simon's biting 1973 number one hit "You're So Vain." Except that in her song, the guy in question is so besotted with himself that it's inconceivable to him that she might be referring to someone else. My man, on the other hand, is so conceited and condescending, but, above all, clueless, that it would never dawn on him that he was the star of "That Don't Impress Me Much." In fact, he'd probably listen to the lyrics, grunt, and say, "Man, what a jerk *that* guy must be!" This character was fictitious, but it spanned a stereotype that most women, by their thirties, have met at least once in their travels, so in that sense, I was confident I was writing about a sort that really did exist.

The cowbell-propelled song had an unhurried rhythm and marked a bit of a return to more traditional country rock. It was the sixth release from *Come On Over,* and we still had five more singles to go, plus four solid months of shows in North America without a breather.

# 24

## Come On Overseas

Until I was almost twenty-seven, I was about as provincial as they came, having never even been outside of Canada. Being married for the past five years to Mutt, who'd lived and worked on several continents, had expanded my world considerably, and in 1995 I got to go to Egypt to shoot the video for "The Woman in Me (Needs the Man in You)." Now, in 1999, the ongoing—make that never-ending—Come On Over tour would be taking me to Australia and Europe, after which my husband and I were set to move to Switzerland.

We'd bought a French château–style estate in an area referred to as the Swiss Riviera. "The world is our oyster" type thinking made us consider many different places to settle. Any corner of the world was a possibility. We were open to trying something new, but our goal was to choose somewhere we could enjoy some anonymity, an attractive landscape, and convenient access to North America. We figured that if the local language was not English, which language could we live with and actually enjoy learning? Croatian might not have been our number one choice of second languages to learn, for example, but we were attracted to the Latin-based languages such as Italian, Spanish, and French.

Since I'd had a base in French from my bilingual exposure growing up in Northern Ontario, I had an ear for the language. We scanned the French-speaking countries, and when we toured Switzerland as one of those on the list, we were captivated by the dramatic views of the Alps and Lake Geneva's stunning shade of emerald. The food was exquisite, with everything from rustic to gastronomic. The people came across stern and distant, at first, but we figured we were looking for somewhere to keep to ourselves anyway, as a portion of our year would always be spent traveling internationally for work.

The château we found had world-class views from every window and was a historic landmark, with impressive architecture and design. This was the place we wanted to be. Our plan was to finish renovating by the end of the year, just as the tour was wrapping up. Mutt flew back and forth to oversee the work on the house; although I couldn't be there, I'd direct the renovation and decorating from a seat on the tour bus, a set of blueprints spread out before me. Living in Saint Regis Falls permanently was not our plan; after four years of near constant travel—and my largely nomadic life prior to that—I was *so* looking forward to putting down roots. But until then, I had another nine months ahead of me, playing sixty-four dates in sixty-one cities.

From March through June, following our return from Down Under, our convoy of buses and equipment trucks crisscrossed North America, from as far east as Moncton, New Brunswick, our first show; to Vancouver, British Columbia, on Canada's West Coast; and all the way down to Jacksonville, Florida. The trip to Australia was particularly rewarding for me, knowing that my music had reached the other end of the planet, literally. I took advantage of the outback experience and made a horse trek through the bush with some local ranchers one afternoon on a down day from the tour. We were lucky to come across a herd of kangaroo, which was such a rush, and I felt as if I were seeing storybook creatures right before my eyes. *Come On Over* brought me to this exotic, faraway land, giving me one of the highest-selling albums ever, reaching fifteen times platinum and spending nineteen weeks at number one and 165 weeks in the Top 100. In Australia, it is the bestselling album of the 1990s.

A music tour very much resembles a traveling circus. The Come

On Over tour employed more than one hundred people: besides me and the nine-member band, there were drivers, roadies, soundmen, riggers, caterers, carpenters—you name it. I take off my hat to these skilled folks for the dedication they exhibited every day. Their job was harder than mine: the road crew essentially constructs the equivalent of a good-sized house, then tears it down and packs it up, four or five times a week for months at a clip. As Jackson Browne sang in his affectionate tribute to his roadies, "The Load Out," "They're the first to come and the last to leave," and although they traveled the same number of miles that I did, they probably got half the sleep.

The monotony and pressure of road life get to everyone, not just the star, and under those conditions, you bond together like family, especially since you are far away from home and loved ones. We all had jobs to do, but we did have ourselves some fun. To break up the daily grind, I initiated a "crew lottery": at every sound check, I would pull a name out of a hat or a bowl, and the winner would receive $500. On weekends, we had two draws. A small thing, perhaps, but it helped to keep up morale. Plus, I got a real kick out of watching the smiles and hearing the cheers each time a crew member's name was announced.

One time I just wanted to give the bus and truck drivers a break. I forget where we were and where we were going (after a while, the cities seem to blend in to each other), but as a surprise/prank, I hired substitute drivers to drive the tour buses, and one separate party bus for our drivers to ride on as passengers instead of drivers, so for a change they could sit back, relax, and enjoy the ride. But they didn't know this yet. I stocked the party bus with food and refreshments and arranged for a meeting to be called on this bus for all the drivers. Once the last driver was on board, thinking they were about to have a meeting, the hired driver closed the door and drove away, abducting our driver/passengers for the overnight journey to the next city. The initial reaction of many of the drivers was panic. They were anxious and uncomfortable with the fact that someone else would be sitting in their driver's seat, operating their bus, and don't forget, as it was a surprise, they hadn't grabbed personal effects like cell phones or toothbrushes. They just weren't prepared for this surprise kidnapping. In the end, they had a good time and were grateful for the break and thoughtfulness.

Practical jokes are a time-honored tradition of the road, and if I say so myself, mine were pretty creative, especially two that I played on my band. We had a rare break coming up, and I wanted to throw a surprise appreciation lunch for everyone, with the help of a handful of crew members who were sworn to secrecy. So that no one would suspect anything, we planned to hold it in the afternoon at the arena I was playing, since that's when most of the crew would be there anyway, loading in the equipment.

The band members were informed that I wished to meet with them privately before sound check to discuss an upcoming concert that would be filmed for a TV special. In general, musicians, like most onstage performers, pay attention to their appearance. Sometimes to an obsessive degree. With that in mind, I had ordered them the skimpiest, tightest spandex outfits you had ever seen, like something a wrestler would squeeze into. Everything bared and nothing spared. To top it off, they came in garish blue, pink, yellow, and purple. At the meeting, I excitedly called up the band members one by one and handed them their outfits.

You should have seen the horrified expressions on their faces, and you could all but read their minds: *I'm expected to walk out onstage in this? And for a performance that's going to be filmed, for posterity?!?* Even Andy Cichon, our hunky bassist, who has a buff bodybuilder's bod, was visibly uncomfortable with the painted-on look of his stage wear. They were all holding them out at arm's length, as if a skunk had sprayed them.

"Okay, well, go try 'em on!" I said brightly. They eyed one another as if they were thinking, *She can't be serious.* "I can't wait to see you in them!" *Oh. My. God. She's serious.* A few minutes later, they emerged stiffly from the dressing room wearing the outfits, not to mention pained expressions, in front of the whole crew. On cue, a marching band came trumpeting in, the caterers rolled in a banquet table full of fabulous fare, a mass of balloons soared over our heads after being released, and the ribbon scoreboard, a band-type screen that wrapped around the venue, flashed the names of everybody on the tour. The cat was out of the bag.

The band members were good sports about it, considering the laugh that everyone had enjoyed at their expense.

If they handed out a prize for Best Gag Played on a Bunch of Musicians, this next one would have brought home the trophy. And it was a high-tech prank to boot. Guitar techs are the people responsible for making sure the guitarists' instruments are all polished and restrung, tuned, and ready to go. Before one show I conspired with them to detune all the stringed instruments that would be used for "No One Needs to Know," an all-acoustic number. The techs twisted the tuning pegs this way and that, making for one wince-inducing sound.

Okay, here's the genius part: of course, I didn't want to inflict any of this on the audience, so in preparation for this practical joke, I got the crew to secretly record us performing the song the night before. When you're playing a big stage, where the musicians stand far apart from one another, you don't hear what the audience hears, only what the soundman sends you through your earpiece.

As we counted in the song, the sound engineer rolled the tape of all the guitars from the night before. The only live sounds actually emanating from the stage were my voice and J. D. Blair's drums. The audience heard a wonderfully played "No One Needs to Know," not realizing that the instruments were on tape. And each musician heard only the wretched sound coming out of his sabotaged instrument. Every string, totally out of tune. Best of all, he had no idea that the others were trapped in the exact same nightmare. As far as he knew, he and he alone was massacring the song. *What the hell is going on?! Oh, man, Shania is gonna be pissed!* Their panicked expressions had the guitar techs laughing so hard that they nearly passed out.

J.D. kept playing, as of course there was no way of messing up his drums, and he had to be live, so if the band decided to stop in the middle of the song out of confusion, J.D. would be the only one that to the audience would have been noticeably *not* playing. The other musicians could stop and start off and on in their confusion, but it's hard to decipher who's playing what in that song, as it's a wall of acoustic instruments.

But we were not finished with them yet. Nope. One by one, Brent, Randy, and Andy snuck off to the side of the stage to have one of the guitar techs take the unplayable instruments off their hands and replace them with ones that worked. The techs just ignored them. In that moment, I am sure that three guitar techs could easily have been sent to the hospital with injuries sustained from an out-of-tune guitar employed as a deadly weapon. But all Brent, Randy, and Andy could do was glare at them.

Each of the guys eventually caught on and played air guitar for the rest of the song. The audience never suspected a thing, but only because I managed to keep myself from cracking up in the middle of singing. You have no idea how hard that was.

When you're on tour, the music usually continues after the show, on the bus. "But that's your day job. Don't you get tired of it?" Singing with other people? Never. I passed a number of late nights jamming with the opening act, Leahy. I had seen this eclectic Canadian group consisting of four multitalented brothers and seven sisters, ranging in age from about their early twenties to their midthirties, on the 1998 Juno Awards and thought they would make for a terrific show opener. Not only did they play and sing, but they were also first-rate Irish step dancers. Very impressive.

Whenever we could coordinate our two buses in the convoy to the next town, I would hop on theirs until bedtime. It was crowded, but it seemed the more the merrier. I'd snack on Froot Loops out of the box and join in the laughter and dancing. The girls taught me how to swing dance, and we'd all dance in twos, sister-to-sister, sister-to-brother, and as the girls knew the guy moves, they made great partners for me as well, and I never ran out of partners. The Leahy bus would rock down that highway until the last man was standing. That was usually me.

During the course of the two-year tour, some of the smaller Leahy children sometimes tagged along on the bus as well. I was thankful to be around this close-knit family; it lent me a badly needed sense of reality and kept me from drowning in isolation—an unfortunate consequence of both fame and being on an endless road.

Finding freedom and solitude during touring was not easy for me, so the people who surrounded me were important for keeping my own morale up. I was also feeling the wear from the lack of freedom I had to do simple things like go to a park for a walk by myself or pop out for a pizza without planning it. Doing anything outside the venue walls without planning was almost impossible. I loved being around my road family, but I also liked being out in the world, alone. Sitting on a bench along a river with the world happening around me, lost in my own solitude, anonymous and free to be there undisturbed in my thoughts without having to isolate myself to do it . . . this I missed.

There were periods I felt like a babysat child while out on tour, someone knowing where I was at all times. Frustrated by the lack of independence, one day I just decided to break away. Completely and irresponsibly ignore security concerns and without a plan, without telling anyone . . . just walk out. Stomp out like a little kid fed up with being told what to do all the time. At the time what was really going through my head was that I was damned if I was going to live in Michael Jackson–type isolation and seclusion. I imagined how lonely it must've been for him; hibernating and hiding from the outside world was something I could not live with. I needed out of the prison bubble and didn't want to take a simple stroll with a whole production of elaborate disguise and undercover security. I accepted that as my professional life, not my real one!

Wearing some sweats and a cap, I walked out of the venue onto the street and just like that, I was free. It was a show day after sound check, so it was about four in the afternoon. I still had a few hours before showtime, so I picked a direction and just started walking. I felt so free and light. Giddy and chirpy, I skipped along so pleased with myself that I'd made the decision to just take the plunge and head out somewhere on my own. No security, not telling anyone that I was going or where I was going, just like any other normal citizen in the civilized world, I'd simply gone out for a walk. No big deal. I kept my head down for the most part, avoiding eye contact, and for a time I got away with my escape really well. It was a temperate, sunny afternoon, perfect for a stroll, and I was enjoying my freedom adventure thoroughly. Too soon, however, the time came when I had to start heading back to the surreal, real world of my bubble cage.

I got about ten minutes out from the venue and I noticed the streets were getting pretty thick with other walkers. With every block there were more and more strolling bodies that soon became a crowd, and before I knew it, I was locked in the mob of people inching their way to the various entrances of the venue. My venue. Shoulder to shoulder with people wearing my face across their chests and backs, I was right among the audience. So freaky to be walking behind some-one, looking eye level at myself on the back of her T-shirt. I thought, *Oh no, how am I going to get through this without anyone noticing me? I really got myself into it this time.* I actually felt like a naughty child preparing for my scolding once I got in the door. I imagined hearing things like: *Where have you been, young lady? We were worried sick about you. You could have gotten yourself into trouble out there. You have a responsibility and you better start taking it more seriously and stop running off like that whenever you feel like it.* It was true, I hadn't thought it through very well with the timing; it hadn't dawned on me that I was going to be trying to get back into the venue at the same time as twenty thousand other people, all there to see . . . me, and I'd be standing right among them.

I did not have a cell phone with me, so I had no choice but to blend in with the crowd of twenty thousand or so fans until I made it inside. The thought that I could very easily be late to my own show made me giggle. I resigned myself to the fact that I was in for a scolding and decided to just enjoy the moment. Everyone was all pumped and chattering away. I tuned in to the conversations around me:

"What song do you think she'll open with?"

"Wonder what Shania will be wearing tonight?"

"I hope she sings 'You're Still the One.' That's my absolute favorite."

"I'm gonna try to make it to the stage and get an autograph."

I allowed myself to become temporarily lost in the audience's vibe and fantasized that I was there for one of my own favorite artists. I understood how the fans felt as I imagined that every inch toward the entrance was one inch closer to seeing Prince or Michael Jackson, for example, both of whom I adored and had never seen live in concert.

I can't imagine many performers get the chance to stand anonymously among their fans and experience firsthand the run-up to the show, feel that excitement build. I have to tell you, it was a rush, and something that I will cherish forever. Especially since I probably will have the good sense never to do it again, at least if I don't want to risk being late for my own show!

Finally, I made it to the entrance. "Where's your ticket?" demanded the local security guy. Obviously, I didn't have one.

"It's me," I whispered. Not that I expected him to believe me. Before I could find out, a crew member walking by spotted me and whisked me inside. "What were you doing outside?!" were his first words. "Outside." That word strikes me even now as I reflect. When I was in the sheltered environment of touring, there was a threshold to cross and I went "outside" of it, like passing from one reality into another. Anyway, I made a long story short and told him that I'd gone for a walk and just timed my return badly. He looked at me quizzically, like, "*That* was a weird thing to do," and escorted me backstage to prepare for the show.

The North American leg ended on July 1 with a concert in Hollinger Park before twenty-two thousand people, making it the largest event in the history of Timmins. This park is the same park me and my two sisters, Carrie and Jill, walked to in our little threesome, growing up. The pool was just up the road, and the McDonald's where I worked in high school was directly across the street. In summer the park holds local concert events, one of which I participated in one year with the band Longshot. We entered a talent contest in a "battle of the bands" type category, and we won first place. (In the photo I included of that performance, I'm wearing the mukluks my grandmother gave me.) The park built stages for these events, the same way they built one for me eighteen years later during my Come On Over tour.

I was giddy throughout that entire show, spotting so many familiar faces in the audience. It was nonstop identifying people I knew or recognized, as my eyes shifted and scanned the audience: family, friends, schoolmates I hadn't seen since high school, neighbors, merchants. I felt like I knew everyone personally, and a sort of hometown pride came over me, knowing they'd all come to celebrate with me. It's maybe like the way you might feel if you organized a birthday party and a lot of people showed up. It makes you feel cared about, thought of, like your existence has some importance and meaning to them. This is probably ego coming forth, giving a false sense of worth, but after you toil for years to accomplish something, it's rewarding to know that you are appreciated. I'm not always sure where to draw the line between self-worth and actual worth, I guess. All I know is, that day, I felt as though I'd earned that support. It hadn't come free, and I was relishing that satisfaction.

I wondered what my hometown people must think of this event, of me. Were they there as genuine fans, did they even listen to my music, or were they there because they were curious to see me again in person after all this time, like you might feel at a reunion? Did they find it novel that one of their own actually made it to the big time, or were they just taking advantage of a day at the park because something was going on? I didn't really know what to expect from my hometown, and I supposed what they were thinking and their reasons for being there that day were probably a bit of all of the above. My own friends and family were proud of my success and were there to enjoy the moment along with me. Overall, the feeling from the crowd was one of support and enthusiasm. For me it was a walk down memory lane and a way I could get some perspective on where I'd come to in my life, by connecting to where I'd come *from*.

From Timmins, we flew to Glasgow, Scotland, for the first of four shows in the United Kingdom. Nineteen ninety-nine was to mark *Come On Over*'s breakthrough in Europe.

But before heading to Europe, I'd sent Dancer to Switzerland, where our château was now complete, and we'd moved in and settled once and for all in our Swiss home. The night before I had to leave, Dancer was frolicking out in the paddock with the other horses and got kicked in the knee. It was hard to tell the extent of the damage that night, as he had to be brought to a clinic for X-rays. I didn't feel good about leaving Dancer but had to fly out for the next show.

A couple of days later, I got a call from Mutt that would break my heart in two. It was late morning, not long before sound check. "Dancer is gone," my husband told me. Nothing could be done to save the knee, which had shattered completely, and given that Dancer was pushing fifteen years old, the vet felt that there was no other choice but to put him down. I was out of my mind with anguish. How could the vet kill Dancer? Why didn't he speak to me first to at least explain before he took the liberty of killing my prince, my beloved friend? A rush of anger and grief overtook me. I'd lost my beautiful boy.

I felt empty and lonely after the news about Dancer. I already had such a small circle of comfort in my bubble as it was, and losing him at that moment was like losing a limb. I'd lost a part of me like someone had just hacked off my arm. Just a brutal attack on my being, and it left me feeling like there was less of me, less of everything at that point. I was now even more lonely, more insecure, more unhappy. I was numb for days after the news of Dancer's death and went through my shows on automatic pilot in my sadness. I would never get over the loss of Dancer and still miss him so much.

We were now in our last three weeks of the Come On Over (and Over and Over) tour, which ended just before Christmas in West Palm Beach, Florida. I learned everything I needed to know about being an international artist on tour at this point, and I learned more about being lonely, tired, isolated, and creatively uninspired than anything. I didn't do any songwriting, and as my closest friend was my horse, it speaks volumes of where my personal life was at. And now even he was gone. Despite all this, it was one of the biggest concert tours of 1998 and 1999. Meanwhile, the album showed no signs of slowing down. In fact, during Christmas week, *Come On Over* sold 355,000 copies, more than in any week since its release two-plus years before. The CD would hit worldwide sales of thirty-nine million.

While I acknowledge this is all something to be proud of, breaking records is not why I got into music. This is an art form, not a sport like hockey, where someone's always gunning, say, for Wayne Gretzky's record for most goals in a single season. As much as I love performing and singing to large audiences, the biggest thrill for me is as a songwriter. Those outrageous numbers containing all those zeros sprang from a simple song composed on an acoustic guitar. It didn't even have words or a title at first.

To this day, how a song is written remains a mysterious, elusive process, which is part of what makes it so rewarding. Every writer has individual approaches, reasons, inspirations behind each one. Songs are like fingerprints, they are one-of-a-kind creations. What the songs mean to the listener is also extremely unique to each one. One mother told me that her favorite song was "From This Moment On" because it was the song she played while giving birth to her son. Another mother wrote to tell me that my music will live forever for her, as it was the music requested by her child to play during his funeral, so it would bring cheer to those around him rather than sorrow. Although not my thinking when I wrote the song, I believe like any song, it belongs to whoever claims it, and its purpose becomes whatever it means to that individual.

Okay. Now you finish the song, polish it, and record it to the best of your ability. Eventually you have a whole litter of songs, and you send them out into the world, never really knowing what effect they will have. They excite *you* and are fraught with meaning for *you*, but will anybody else hear it? When you receive validation that the feelings you put into words connected in some way with other human beings around the world . . . whoa! It doesn't always have to be that profound, either. For every couple who has adopted "From This Moment On" as "their" song, there's someone who likes "Rock This Country" just because it's fun and catchy. Other listeners couldn't even tell you why they like a particular song. They just know it moves them when it comes on the radio. That's enough.

At the end of the Come On Over tour, Bo Derek invited me to go along on a weeklong horse trip to Spain and Portugal with her and a few of her girlfriends: actresses Daryl Hannah and Tatjana Patitz; Diandra Douglas, Michael Douglas's wife at the time; and Shekar, a Turkish princess. It was quite a crowd, and although I didn't feel I fit in with the likes of all these regal beauties, I went along to admire my favorites of all God's creatures as a present to myself after a good three years of dedicated work on *Come On Over*. All the radio and television promotions of every single; video productions; endless hours of editing; photo shoots; interviews; songwriting; recording; and right to the end of the tour, I felt I deserved it. Spain and Portugal pride themselves on their magnificent horses, and we'd be visiting the most noted breeders in the region. Maybe, I thought, I would find a new Andalusian.

Despite all the stunning horses I saw and rode on the trip, my heart wasn't in it. To me, no other horse could live up to my Dancer. I just wasn't ready for a new one yet.

While in Portugal, we watched a game of horseball, which is like a cross between polo, rugby, and basketball. It's played on horseback, naturally, by two teams of four. The object is to score a goal by hurling a ball into the opposing team's hoop-shaped net. Sounds tame enough, except that we have not gotten to the rugby element yet.

As a team gallops across the field toward the goal, its players must pass the ball back and forth. The ball, about the size of a soccer ball, has a leather, ropelike netting around it for handling easily with the fingers. It was explained to me that originally, this game was played with a human head, and the hair was what one grabbed on to with the fingers. The defending team tries to prevent their opponents from scoring, either by blocking the shot, or wresting the ball out of another player's hands, or using their horses to push rival players' horses off course. There is more to it than that, but you get the basic idea. It's fast, furious, and physical. The sport is said to have originated in Argentina during the eighteenth century and at one point had to be outlawed because too many participants died playing it.

Maybe it's the hockey fan in me, but I found horseball thrilling to watch. At the end of the trip, when Bo and the other girls went back to their lives, I had an open week for a change and decided to stay on to learn how to play. It was the first time in a year and a half that I didn't have a manager, an assistant, or security with me. To be in a foreign country, not speaking any Spanish, with total strangers, was really stepping out for me. And it turned out to be exactly what I needed in order to get back in touch with myself: do something spontaneous and completely unrelated to my professional life. I always enjoyed athletic challenges, and horseball was physically demanding enough to qualify for that.

Let me tell you, I had the time of my life. My body ached from the physical strain inflicted upon it; every morning, I woke up so stiff that I was ready to limp to the telephone and cancel going to practice. But once I coaxed my legs into the shower, my determination flickered to life, and I was ready to rumble. By the end of the week, I was hooked. My fingers were taped for support, as they were strained and bruised, and my thumb was actually sprained, but once I was warmed up the excitement and adrenaline of the game masked the pains. After the hardest working period of my career, beyond a success I could ever have imagined, and the loss of my beloved Dancer, I was going to enjoy spoiling myself by basking in the pleasure of doing something self-indulgent and rejuvenating. Even if it hurt a little.

# 25

## Home at Last

We welcomed the new millennium from our new home in our new country. And, unlike at our previous place in upstate New York, I would actually get to feel as if I belonged here, because after five years of almost incessant traveling, my calendar was clear. It took until I was almost thirty-five, but finally I could feel settled in one place.

And what a place. I'll start with the house, the elegant Swiss, French-style château I started telling you about earlier. It was perched atop an imposing hill overlooking Lake Geneva and the French and Swiss Alps. A designated historical landmark, it had been an art school in recent years, and although the mansion and grounds were in decent shape, they required extensive work to convert this magnificent building back into a home. Practically every room had something that needed fixing, such as repairs to walls, doors, rewiring, and plumbing. All the sinks, showers, and toilets had to be replaced, too.

Plus, it needed a new kitchen. Make that *a* kitchen, period. It didn't have one; it must have been removed instead of refurbished, as art schools needed classes, not kitchens, after all. I never knew where the original kitchen would have been, but I believe it was probably in the basement, as most noble families did not cook for themselves but rather had staff cook, who worked in a discreet area in the building. I decided that the kitchen needed to be at the heart of the house, a central location where everyone could congregate together easily from anywhere in the home.

Having never had a permanent home of my own before, I enjoyed the novelty of building the nest where Mutt and I would live and love happily ever after. It was like a fairy tale. During the last several months of the tour, you would find me studying blueprints and floor plans, surrounded by decorating books and piles of fabric swatches. Thankfully, much of the structure's original materials had been preserved, such as the detailed parquet flooring throughout, and the various stone and marble staircases, pillars, and fireplaces. Handsome French oak panels made from trees no longer in existence lined the high-ceilinged living room, and the whole house still had its original door and window frames, also made of oak with the original brass handles.

After visiting Versailles and learning to appreciate the different periods of architecture and design during my international travel, just out of interest's sake I started to take more detailed note of the materials, lighting fixtures, fabrics, colors, and shapes. I was especially drawn to the Renaissance period when Versailles was built. I wanted to put our own imprint on the centuries-old château—make it cozy and homey—yet keep the decor in its original period style. My feeling was, you just don't tamper with an architectural jewel such as this. We chose mostly classic French fabrics in the style of the 1700s and 1800s, which went back to the days when Marie Antoinette still had her head. The carved wood frames evoked a palace tearoom setting, only with furniture in larger scale and more comfortable and lofty than the originals. I'd ordered brass fireplace screens custom designed from the original molds of Versailles, while the floors were graced with Renaissance-style Savonnerie and Aubusson rugs, some of which were antiques in their own right but from the period. Crystal chandeliers, antique alabaster and ceramic lamps, and several antique bronze sculptures completed the look. It was all very palatial, lush, and fit for a princess. I learned as I went, leafing through

Renaissance and Baroque design books and browsing European antiques markets to try to do justice to the already beautiful palate of
the naked house. Given my humble beginnings, at times I did feel a
bit like Cinderella at the ball. Am I really going to live here?

My favorite rooms were the kitchen and the bedroom that would
become my son's room. The stove, a radiant-heat Aga made of cast
iron, was a stunning piece of art in itself, finished in French vanilla
enamel, with brass and black fittings. Without my having to go on
tour anytime soon, it would receive quite a workout.

Mutt, meanwhile, being the passionate landscape designer that
he was, completely transformed the garden. We had several hundred
different varieties of roses everywhere; they poured out of the flower
beds to cling to the trellised walls and the balconies that offered a
panoramic view over the lake and mountains. You've never seen a
more dramatic landscape: steep, snowcapped mountains plunging
down to meet the lake, which is fed by the alpine glaciers, making it
crystal clear.

Throughout the plateaus and valleys in the region lay farm country. Swiss farms are like no other farms. They are neat and tidy, like
the farms depicted in children's books: wood chalet-style barns and
houses with roofs made from cedar shake or stone-tiled roofs. The
windows have colorful, blooming window boxes, bursting with buds
that cascade over the edges like floral fountains. Every windowpane
has delicate and intricate hand-crocheted curtains gracing it and
water troughs overflowing with gushing glacier-fed streams. All buildings are perfect, compact, and so well maintained. Smurfville comes
to mind for me. It's like a million Smurfs must live in these handsome
hamlets to keep everything so perfect and pristine. It's as though your
eyes are looking through high-definition lenses exaggerating this already splendid view. Or like someone pushed the "enhance" option
key on the Photoshop program of the computer. I want to eat these
sweet little farm clusters up every time I see one, each of them posing like a model for its postcard opportunity.

The first time I took in this pastoral view, I thought happily, *I'm in love with this. I want to live here, love here, snuggle sheep here, and eat chocolate.* (And I don't even *love* chocolate, but Swiss chocolate is exceptionally good.) Tim, Mutt, and I took to hiking the hills. One time, as Tim bent down to drink from one of the mountain water troughs that zigzag the terrain, his tail grazed an electric fence belonging to a livestock farm. *Zap!* Suddenly I heard my poor dog yelping in pain. Those fences are pumped with enough voltage to discourage thousand-pound cattle from escaping, so Tim was pretty lucky that he didn't get seriously hurt.

Other than that, the lake region was the perfect place to be after leaving the road and the craziness of the entertainment world. For one thing, almost no one even knew who I was. I mean, they may have been familiar with the music of *Come On Over*—as it sold something like seven million copies in Europe—but I, the artist, wasn't considered a big deal in Switzerland. That by itself brought a kind of freedom I hadn't experienced in years. It's not that I mind being recognized in public; I mean, if you've sold millions and millions of records and suddenly nobody stops you on the street, you might want to call your manager to inquire about the health of your career, but it's heartening to be reminded that sometimes when strangers approach you, it's not because you're famous, but rather that they just want to be friendly. (In some cases, they just wanted directions and figured that I must be a local!) Let's face it, celebrity or not, sincerity can be frustratingly hard to find and is something to be valued.

Living away from the magnifying glass of fame had a healthy effect on me. I slowly began to shed the protective shell that I'd built up over the last few years and even began making eye contact with strangers again. To be able to wander the streets just like everybody else was a revelation to me. Every once in a while someone, usually a tourist, would recognize me and ask for an autograph or a picture. It had become so unexpected that it actually caught me off guard. And you know what? Now it came as a pleasant surprise, like a child finding a piece of candy that she'd left in her pocket and forgot about.

• • •

The only downside to living in a place where no one knew me was that I didn't know anyone. I missed Kim, and Stacy, and Helene, and my family back home in Canada. Bear in mind that I'd just come off the road, where you're surrounded by a surrogate family of musicians and crew. For all my damned griping about the exhaustion of touring, that's the part I treasure most: the relationships you establish.

At first, I felt very much out of my element in my new country, where I didn't yet speak the language. The only friend I had at first was an Italian-French woman, five years younger than me, named Marie-Anne, who'd been serving as Mutt's secretary and interpreter while we were renovating, because none of the workers spoke English. She'd spent most of her life in the area, and so I had to rely on her to an uncomfortable degree, including when it came to learning how to operate the parking meters.

At first Marie-Anne acted a bit chilly toward me, which I attributed to shyness. Or perhaps it was a language barrier between us that prevented deeper communication. We started to bond when the two of us became pregnant within four months of each other.

Mutt and I had not made a firm decision to start a family early on in our marriage, but I left myself open to the possibility of someday having a child. Still, I had no specific time period in mind. I also respected Mutt's preference to not have children at all, although he wasn't against it. So we both just left the decision loose. Once the Come On Over tour ended and I began settling into being off the road, we made the decision to have a child after all. I learned I was pregnant in November 2000, with a due date of August 22, 2001.

I missed having family around during my pregnancy, as it was something I wanted to share not only with my husband but also with the women in my life. Female companionship helps you feel like you have a sisterhood of other mothers' support. My own mother was gone; my sisters were on another continent, along with Mary, Helene, Kim, and Stacy. I felt quite alone during this time.

As Marie-Anne and I were both pregnant, we began sharing

a more personal friendship. We went to Lamaze classes together, shared the same obstetrician, had the same delivery room, and basically walked each other through the incredible experience of becoming mothers for the first time. I respected Mutt's wishes to keep our lives very private even during my pregnancy, so I saw my family very rarely during that time and into the first weeks after my delivery. I regret that neither of my sisters was there for Eja's birth. Marie-Anne was my only companion through this very special period of my life.

Right after midnight on Sunday, August 12, 2001, almost two weeks before my actual due date, my water broke. Mutt and I were at home in the château.

"What happens now?" he asked nervously. Eja was his first child, so he was as new at this as I was.

I assured him there was no need to rush to the hospital, which was just three minutes away; I told him we had about twenty-four hours before the baby would arrive, or that's at least what I understood from the Lamaze instructor. "Let's shower and take our time getting there," I said. "No problem." I was genuinely not panicked or concerned.

Not even fifteen minutes later, my contractions were only two minutes apart, then one minute apart and so intense that I was doubled over in pain within the first hour after my water broke. We called my obstetrician, Dr. Stoll, and I could barely get out the words as I tried to explain what was happening. He instructed us to meet him at the hospital right away.

When he got our call, Dr. Stoll had been stargazing at the Perseid meteor shower lighting up the sky. As he would tell me afterward, he didn't mind being interrupted. "I was delighted," he explained, "because I felt that it was a special sign to have a birth occurring as the universe displayed its magic."

My husband and I could have used some supernatural intervention right about then, because halfway to the hospital, we came upon flashing yellow lights and orange detour signs. Construction? At this hour? You've got to be joking.

"Is there a way to go through here?" asked Mutt. "My wife is having a baby, and we need to get to the hospital straightaway." The fellow manning the intersection site either couldn't understand Mutt's broken French or just didn't care what was coming—baby, bomb, or the end of the world. He just pointed in the direction of the longer route. By this point, I felt like a medieval torture victim on the rack, my pelvic joints being pulled apart.

We met Dr. Stoll in the parking lot of the hospital and I couldn't stand up straight. I was embarrassed to be so crippled by this common pain, but it was clutching me and forcing me into this involuntary bent shape. As much as I wanted to control my body and maintain some dignity, I had to walk into the hospital hunched over. Where was my strength, my ability to tolerate pain and suck up my desire to break under the pressure? I learned an important lesson: a body about to give birth *doesn't care*. With body buckled in half, strained smile, and clenched fists, I managed to make my way to the maternity floor in this half-squat position but nevertheless on my own two feet after stubbornly declining the wheelchair offered by the doctor.

We entered a pitch-black, extremely quiet hallway of the maternity wing. All lights off, we couldn't see in front of us as the elevator door opened. Dr. Stoll jumped ahead to the light switch and literally flicked on the lights as we made our way down the corridor. I was the only one delivering that night and there was no one else on the floor, it seemed. It was surreal to be opening up the floor especially for me to have my baby. I doubted momentarily that I was somewhere capable of delivering my firstborn, but the immediacy and sharpness of my pelvic pain took over and reeled me into accepting where I was and what was happening. No questions asked, I was having this baby here and now, no matter what! Of course, I was in good hands being in a Swiss hospital with a doctor who'd been delivering babies for as many years as I was old.

Sure enough, after a quick inspection of my baby's position, the doctor announced that I was already eight centimeters dilated. Intravenous went in abruptly, and I was prepped for the delivery table. I felt a bit like a turkey being prodded, poked all round, and exposed, ready for the pan. Everything was new and mysterious; even though I'd taken the tour and done the Lamaze classes, I still didn't really know what was happening and what would happen next. Everything explained in French or broken English made it that much more mysterious and scary. I trusted my doctor, though, and felt confident that he knew what he was doing.

Before being transferred, however, I argued with the nurse that surely there must be time for me to try delivering in the large, round bathtub I intended trying as my first option, but no one was taking me seriously and I was ushered along. There was no time to experiment with less conventional delivery methods other than lying flat on my back. My pain increased while my ability to talk diminished, so off to the delivery table it was. I wanted to flash my hands up in the air in a "stop" position to say, "Can we just hold on a minute here and slow down? This is going way too fast and I feel like I'm missing this amazing experience." But there was no time for any of the fancy stuff like putting my favorite atmospheric music on the stereo system.

Nothing else mattered once my little son was born and all was good in the world. I had a healthy baby boy, and who cared on what table or by which method I had delivered him? He was here, finally. His dad cut the umbilical cord and bathed him in a basin beside me, then the doctor put my baby to my breast to nurse. Eja, our little angel. The Hebrew meaning is "the Lord is my God," and to me it was the saying of an angel. We also just liked the ring to "Eja," pronounced *Asia*. It was original, and we'd chosen it even before knowing if we were having a boy or a girl.

Over my five days in the hospital, I had Marie-Anne drop by periodically to help translate with the hospital staff—none of whom spoke English—but otherwise, there was no female companionship. But I was thrilled when my sister Carrie came to visit me shortly after I came home. My nephew Dylan was also with her, and it was beautiful for me to see the kids together. It made me sad knowing it would only be brief, that this was only a visit and that I would soon be without family again. Making the most of their time with us, we took long strolls along the lake and enjoyed the summer weather. One afternoon while wheeling Eja in his stroller along the lake walk, I had to stop to nurse, and Carrie said, "I'll watch out for photographers." She was used to the way I had to be cautious in public back in America and Canada and figured (correctly) that the last thing I wanted was for my exposed boob to turn up in some tabloid.

"No need to be so paranoid," I insisted. "They barely pay any attention to me here."

My anonymity went only so far, apparently, because a week later a picture of me burping Eja pressed up against my shoulder—immediately after having finished nursing him—appeared in the gossip rags. I'll never know if the person who snapped the photo had also taken shots of me actually nursing and had the decency not to sell them, or if he just happened to miss the moment. It was a disturbing reminder that you never know when you're being watched through a camera lens and photographed, even in private, intimate moments.

# 26

## Up! Up! and Away

Eja was still nursing the whole time we were recording *Up!*, as he was only a few months old when we started in the studio. I would take him into the vocal room with me at night, and he'd sleep peacefully in his carriage next to me while I sang. Occasionally he'd chirp or squeak or sigh in his sleep, and it would leak into the mic, so I'd have to do another take. But how cool it was to be a new mom and recording artist at the same time. I felt like a modern-day version of a woman from a time in the distant past, who gives birth and then goes right back to work in the fields, with the baby strapped to her back, working away like nothing ever happened. I'd stop and feed when necessary, then get right back to it. Bouncing back and doing it all made me feel strong and capable.

We traveled a lot during the whole writing and recording of *Up!*, keeping the three of us hopping between various places in Europe and the Caribbean. We enjoyed the travel, soaking in the creative inspiration it gave and the variety of musicians Mutt tapped into along the way.

I had been frustrated by being boxed into the country genre with *The Woman in Me* CD, as I felt the title track and "If You're Not in It for Love" were both pop-sounding records. I'd hoped they would have had more international and crossover success and believed I was held back from that by being labeled "country," and therefore relegated to the one genre, no matter what the music actually sounded like. I did not want to be limited by this music prejudice, the same way Dolly had not been when she crossed over from country to pop, Elvis from rock to country then gospel, Olivia Newton-John from pop to country, George Michael from pop to R&B, Elton John from pop rock to soft rock, R&B, and even to country, and more.

Most well-written songs are genreless, I believe, and are instead appealing works of music and lyrics combined to tell a short story. Anyone who wants to hear them is interested in their appeal, not in what genre they're in. What is done with a song once it's written isn't always obvious. The production and arrangement of any given song can take it in a multitude of directions, and it's usually the style of the performer's influence that determines the direction. A good example of this is the song "I Will Always Love You," written by Dolly Parton. Dolly's original recording hit number one on the *Billboard* Hot Country Songs chart in 1974 but was limited there. Its more epic, commercial success came with Whitney Houston's version released in 1992, which topped the pop, R&B, and soul charts all over the world.

For the *Up!* CD, Mutt and I were motivated to create three different musical arrangement styles for all the songs, to avoid getting boxed in to one genre. I'd thought often about how most artists, including myself, had remixes of the singles off our original CDs. For example, it was common to do dance remixes for clubs and shortened versions with solos removed, reworked intros and endings for some radio programming, or bonus tracks for promotional releases, which circulated internally for promotional use. Then there were mixes specifically for movie soundtracks or television campaigns. I thought, why not just create the whole album in three distinct versions to begin with and let the public and industry decide which version of what song they preferred? So Mutt produced and arranged a more traditionally country-feeling version with the classic fiddles and steel guitar sounds; a more progressively pop-rocky version with more electric guitar, bigger-sounding drums, and no country instruments; and a dance version that had an East Indian flavor with authentic, traditional instruments, in place of what he had recorded from the American musicians for the other two pop and country versions. In the discussions with the label on how to market this unusual package of three CDs and how to identify the difference between them, I thought it was appropriate to code them according to colors that represented the feel of each style best. Green, I figured, for "country" (thinking of pasture, the green, green grass of home). Red felt sexier and progressive for the pop version, and blue suited the international version, as I saw blue representing open sky, a space without boundaries.

Released in November 2002, *Up!* became my first number one on both the country chart and the *Billboard* Top 200. (In fact, it debuted at number one on both charts.) It yielded five Top 20 country hits and sold twenty million copies around the world, going to number one in Canada, Australia, New Zealand, and Germany, and number two in my new homeland of Switzerland! This was the red version, well at work in pop and in the international markets.

The green version was doing its job in the country arena, and in the end, the album as a whole made me the only woman performer (also, the only Canadian performer) to ever have three consecutive CDs exceed ten million in sales. In 2003, *Up!* was named the Country Album of the Year by *Billboard,* and won me the Billboard Music Award for Country Artist of the Year.

The blue version was more of an artistic interpretation, and as with dance mixes, it wasn't made for radio airplay and circulated on a smaller scale. My favorite version of any of the songs from all three CDs is the blue version of "When You Kiss Me." The video for this song was one of my favorites as well. I was on a beach in New Zealand, wearing men's jeans and an oversized wool sweater, which was *soooooo* me.

The fact that the album was categorized in pop, pop rock, and country pop was my dream: to be an international recording artist, recognized as an artist not of any specific genre, but just appreciated as an artist by *all* lovers of music. To not be confined meant more to me than the chart numbers, sales figures, and awards. To me success was achieving what you set out to do. I never had numbers in my head, but I had a vision of being heard by people of all walks of life, from all over the world.

Just as the Come On Over tour marked an improvement over my first time out on the road, my 2003–04 jaunt around the world for *Up!* was even more enjoyable for me, mainly because this time Eja, Mutt, and Tim came along. Carrie accompanied us as well off and on, bringing her son, Dylan, and husband, Jeff.

Once again, we had a great band, all the same members as from the Come On Over tour. The crew was a mix from the last tour and some new members, and the stage was completely different, being positioned in the center of the venues. The Up! shows were "in the round," as we called it, on a 360-degree revolving stage. There were ramps, stairs, and platforms suspended through the stage surface so I could get from one side to the other by either crossing over the middle or by going around the perimeter. The technical crew, sound, lights, instrument technicians, quick changes, were all in the bottom center of the stage, where normally they would be in side wings, not visible. I wanted them right among us, like the pilots of a space shuttle, part of the experience for the audience. Once we all got on board and took off, we were there to stay until the show was over. Fans were eye level with the crew, and I walked between, in, up, and around them throughout the entire show. It was a great design, and I enjoyed the all-directions access to the fans instead of the usual side-to-side, band-in-back, audience-in-front setup. The audience was within arm's reach, and I could actually *touch* them. This made for a lot of interaction, both between myself and the crew and the fans and the crew. The stage design concept resembled some contemporary restaurant setups you see fairly often now, with kitchens completely open to the tables, where the patrons can see everything going on behind the scenes. My stage was planned with much the same purpose.

The schedule during this tour wasn't quite so rigorous as the tour before because I insisted on time with my son: three legs consisting of a few months each and several weeks in between to recharge. September through Christmas was spent in the United States and Canada. February and March took us on my first extended excursion through Europe—which was now much closer to home than North America. We played thirty shows in twenty-five cities, including Paris, Berlin, Oslo, and Glasgow. I was received by pumped-up crowds and felt welcome and at home, even though I was far from home itself. I did my best to learn a few words in the various languages of each country, but got by best in France, where at the time I at least knew a few basics.

We played more international-sounding versions with fewer fiddles, and more electric guitars and synthesized loops and effects to the arrangements of the crossover hits that had gone international, including "Man," "I'm Gonna Getcha Good!," and "Ka-Ching!" Ireland had by far the loudest and most enthusiastic audiences during the European leg.

Then we returned to North America in April for another three months. Although the tour was shorter, I was a mom now, and—typical me—trying to do everything perfectly. Having to juggle too many balls at once caught up with me: I was constantly run down and sick with colds and the flu. Being a singer, you do everything in your power to protect your instrument, because there is nothing more frustrating than losing your voice. If you're a guitar player and you pop a string onstage, you just turn around, a member of the road crew straps on a replacement, and you carry on as if nothing happened. Vocalists, of course, don't have that luxury. Some mornings during the North American swing, I would wake up and try to talk, never mind sing, but could produce nothing more than a wheeze.

I probably should have taken time off to get well and let my throat recover, but I was adamant about not canceling any shows, and the schedule was tight, with one date right on top of the next. I opted for steroid injections to reduce the swelling in my throat. Within a couple of hours, my voice would be better than ever: all the high notes present and accounted for, and I had energy to spare. However, you eventually max out on steroids, which was the point I had reached. I was told by doctors that repeated injections can cause muscle atrophy around the larynx. At any rate, my voice just wasn't working properly.

This became a chronic problem in the last few months of the tour, and I managed to get through, but it was stressful, and I felt I was walking a high wire every show day. The band had to start lowering keys for me, and I adjusted melodies and used tracked vocals in some places on really bad nights. My voice was unpredictable, so I had to wing it before every show, making last-minute decisions on song lists, the order of songs, keys, and the use of any tracked vocals. It kept everyone on edge, and I wasn't enjoying the strain and pressure.

Fortunately, the dedicated people around me kept up my morale. Although I stood alone in the spotlight, I always felt the support from everyone else onstage and backstage. The fans were forgiving, which also gave me strength. Ultimately I felt that despite my vocal challenges, we were still entertaining the audiences every night. And if they were happy, I was happy. Not much else you can do when you have twenty thousand or so people waiting to see you. But at this point I was no longer feeling like I was the woman who could "do it all."

I was still blessed with the realization of what an awesome spectacle it was for me to watch the enthusiastic crowds streaming into the arena from every direction, every night. Unbeknown to them, I'd be sitting behind the dark tinted glass windows of the tour bus parked just outside the loading dock, taking in the celebratory scene: the "Shania We Love You" banners, the faces painted with my name, the T-shirts emblazoned with the tour logo and itinerary. The fans were beautiful, and it moved me to hear them chanting my songs as they skipped excitedly toward the entrances. I hoped that I would be able to please them and make it worth their while. I wanted to open the window and call out to them—wish them a fun time and apologize in advance for not feeling up to par. Sometimes fans would make eye contact with me through the pane without their realizing it, which was . . . surreal. It was like they were looking right through me, as if I were a ghost.

I remember standing backstage with Eja one night, watching the arena fill up. Usually by showtime, I'd be on the bus giving him his bath and getting him ready for bed. Then I'd get myself ready and head back just in time to hit the stage. My two-and-a-half-year-old had been reading a book about ants earlier in the day, and I guess they were still fresh in his mind, because Eja turned to me and observed, "Mommy, they look like ants. You're the queen, and they're all here for you." It's amazing how children can be perceptive beyond their years. That he understood my role as the one they were all coming to see. The people all the way across the venue *did* resemble ants from that distance, and they *were* all there to see me. So I could understand his child logic and how he made the connection.

However, I've never wanted Eja to get confused by the image of celebrity and develop a false impression that I was in any way superior to anyone, so I reminded him that I wasn't a queen. "In fact," I said, "I work for those people. They don't work for me, the way that army ants do for their queen. They're here to be entertained by me, and I have to get out there and make them happy."

It was showtime. I left him with his little thoughts of his queen mommy and walked toward the stage.

# 27

## Give Me a Break

Our final show in Fort Lauderdale, on July 10, 2004, closed the curtain not only on the Up! tour but on nearly twelve years of relentlessly striving for success and then sustaining it.

I felt as if something immense had been accomplished, but I was exhausted, too—physically, mentally, emotionally. For all the record sales, awards, and accolades of the past decade, my confidence was rattled and my self-esteem low. I realized that the things that brought me the deepest satisfaction were not necessarily related to my professional accomplishments at all. The timing was good in regard to devoting myself to being a mom and housewife for a while. I was enjoying the change of pace at the château in Switzerland.

As it would turn out, my timing could not have been better career-wise, as well, because the record industry was, to be blunt, undergoing a seismic shift. There are a number of reasons for this, including the lost revenue from fans downloading songs for free on the Internet, an array of entertainment choices besides music, and a lack of foresight on the part of record companies to have adjusted to the new landscape.

Nothing more beautiful has come out of any effort I've ever made than my baby boy. It was time for me to enjoy this reward in my life, take a break from my career, and allow my personal life to dominate my time and energy. It was time to take pride in things like keeping a clean house, parenting a happy child, and being a wife and homemaker.

Reflecting on my past, I can see now that having grown up amid some harsh circumstances caused me to develop a hard shell, something I've had to work at overcoming ever since. Not much came easy when I was a kid, and so I felt that I had to fight my way up throughout my youth. The struggle continued into adulthood, perhaps because of the highly competitive profession I chose, except that as a grown-up, you're expected to be more diplomatic and patient, less openly opinionated and controlling. It took me a while to realize that even though I still had to battle to get where I wanted to go, all in all, life was gentler, less complicated emotionally, and more civilized than when I was a child. I was surrounded by a lot of wonderful people who rewarded me with loyalty, appreciation, and kindness, and I had more opportunities to stop, think, and communicate. Most things that I do in my life I do because I enjoy the process, not because I think there is going to be a payoff at the end. The reward is in the experience itself.

Cooking is a good example of this for me because I love to create in the kitchen. Anyone who enjoys cooking knows that the ultimate reward is the pleasure your food brings to those eating it. What I like most about cooking is that, as with music, you can improvise. Sometimes, in fact, that's how you develop your best recipes. Sure, I could follow a cookbook recipe to the letter, but then I'm just reproducing *someone else's* creation. I've found that it's usually more fulfilling—in all aspects of life, not just in the kitchen—to take whatever I've learned and adapt it to my own personality, experience, and skills. Of course, in doing so, you risk failing and winding up with a dish that sends everyone running from the table. However, life has taught me that it's worth taking the chance.

When not bent over my Aga range, I spent my time with Eja. He was starting preschool, and I enjoyed pushing him to and from school in his stroller every day. It was forty minutes each way, which helped keep me in shape. You'd be amazed at how many calories you burn onstage, and without that physical outlet, I missed the exercise. I was sad when my little boy outgrew the stroller, for both sentimental and practical reasons.

As much as Mutt and I both loved the château and its gardens, I missed Canada. I don't mean the cold, but sitting around a campfire on a lakefront somewhere where I could reach out and touch the water, not just look over it from a mansion on a hill. I wanted to be right amid the nature on the shore. In 2007, we decided to move into a small bungalow right on the edge of magnificent Lake Geneva. Given the benefit of hindsight, I think that the move was somewhat symbolic of other changes to come soon in my personal life. I felt torn about leaving the château, as I'd gone through my pregnancy there and had fond memories of helping Mutt plant the garden during my last trimester. Eja spent his early years eating rose petals and munching happily on freshly grown basil and sage there.

Tim was buried in the garden, too, which made leaving even harder. He had died at the age of ten, which is about the average for a German shepherd. Entering the last weeks of the Up! tour, we sent him home to Switzerland because the cities we were playing were too spread out, and he was too old to be put through such long flights. Just a week after I got back, Eja had to go into the hospital to have his tonsils removed. When I put the overnight bag in the back of the car, Tim started to panic, thinking, of course, that I was going away again. As I pulled out, he trotted alongside the car, frantic that he wasn't coming. It broke my heart, but I knew we'd be away only overnight.

No sooner had my son been administered anesthesia than our caretaker called to say that Tim had suffered a heart attack and was at the vet. He'd call me back with an update. I held Eja's hand, knowing in my heart that the news about Tim wouldn't be good, and it wasn't: my beloved Schutzhund had died. I felt so sad and so guilty, too, as I really believe that Tim died of a broken heart, thinking that I was leaving him behind.

• • •

Just as we were about to refurbish the bungalow, the villa that I currently live in popped up. It was the better property, with a boathouse and much more room, so we abandoned the bungalow. I turned my attention to the much larger renovation that our new home would require. At the same time, I was not only planning to overhaul a Swiss farm that we'd purchased but also in the final stages of constructing a huge complex on a farm in New Zealand that we bought in 2004.

The New Zealand property was on the Motutapu, a high-country sheep-farming station on the south island. I started designing a homestead for us shortly after we bought it and began putting my heart, soul, and dreams into the plans. I dreamed of riding horses across the vast plains, along winding riverbanks and through golden tussocks in the sharp, beaming sunshine of the land of the Kiwi. Every year Mutt, Eja, and I would go there for several months, living in a small caravan (at least, that's what it's called there; another word would be *trailer*) parked in one of the sheep paddocks. It was pretty cramped for the three of us, but we enjoyed camping out while our home was being built.

Essentially, renovating properties became my full-time job, and I relished the challenge. Piles of architectural and engineering plans, interior design catalogs, and magazines cluttered the kitchen table in the bungalow in Switzerland, as we were living in the basement while the house itself was under renovations, so there was no office or desk space. There were stacks of email correspondence from architects, engineers, contractors, and decorators. My time, energy, and love went into building these nests for my family.

During the several months we lived in the bungalow, Marie-Anne and I took up tennis lessons, as Eja and her daughter, Johanna, had been taking them together for a couple of years already. We figured we'd give it a try to get more exercise in, since the kids were now both six years old and well out of their strollers, and we were walking less. Between regular long walks and tennis, Marie-Anne and I were doing pretty well with our attempts to stay fit, and the long walking allowed us to talk and share as friends without men or kids around. It was good girl bonding time.

Marie-Anne could be hot and cold at times, but after nine years of friendship, I shrugged it off as just the way she was. In the months leading up to our annual trip to New Zealand, however, our conversations became more personal than ever, like we'd suddenly broken through some barrier. I confided to her that Mutt had grown distant, to the point where I felt our marriage was in trouble. Marie-Anne always listened attentively and offered sensible, objective advice. After all, although she was my friend, she'd known my husband longer than she'd known me. For the first year that we had the château, I was still on the Come On Over tour while she was already working for Mutt in Switzerland.

Sharing my secret concerns with her made me feel better. It was highly unusual for me to talk with anyone about my personal life, especially my marriage. I was incredibly tight lipped in that regard with everyone in my life. But I was making a real exception opening up the way I did with Marie-Anne, and for some reason, she went so out of her way like she never had before to make me comfortable with that. Interestingly enough, Marie-Anne let on that she and her husband, Fred, were trying to work through marital problems of their own; maybe I took comfort in knowing that I wasn't alone, and the fact that she was the only longtime friend I had who was close enough to talk with in person.

In the fall of 2007, however, Marie-Anne started canceling tennis and turning down walks. I was getting quite enthusiastic about tennis and wanted to play more, not less, so I started playing and taking lessons with another mother of one of the kids in Johanna and Eja's tennis class. Sandra and I enjoyed our tennis together, and I was appreciative of her company. I was developing a new friendship locally, and it felt good, as my social life had always been so closed. Sandra and I shared similar views on life and had many stimulating conversations about much more than men and kids, having more intellectual things to talk about, and I was motivated by this companionship. I didn't understand Marie-Anne's sudden distance, but we would leave Switzerland very soon for the Christmas holidays and then head on to New Zealand to finally see the building project through to the finish, so I figured we'd just pick up where we left off and things would be back to normal when we got back four months later. The Motutapu farm in New Zealand was my dream house; my wish list of every possible detail had been fulfilled in the design and architecture. This had been an enormous project spanning four years of work. I was beyond excited to see 2008 approaching and this dream finally becoming a reality.

Our plan was to spend Christmas in Canada with my family, hit Utah for ten days of skiing, then begin the New Year in our new, second home just outside of Wanaka, New Zealand. Nevertheless, I was unusually sad to leave Switzerland and our friends there, especially Marie-Anne, Fred, and Johanna. We missed them whenever we traveled, and our New Zealand trips were usually spent in three- to four-month stretches. Something else was tugging at me this particular time, though, but I couldn't explain it then.

During this stretch in New Zealand, Mutt returned to Switzerland twice, while Eja and I stayed behind. He was going to prepare for some upcoming music projects, and I needed to oversee the finishing touches on the house. It was a lot of work to bear alone, and I was overwhelmed and not happy that he had to go.

Tension between us had started building slowly in the previous couple of years, but it was quite noticeable in the recent weeks since we left Switzerland before Christmas. Communication was just breaking down more and more, to the point where I felt he was avoiding me altogether. I've practiced meditation regularly for the past seventeen years as a method of reconnecting with myself in a peaceful place, a place within, where I practice the discipline of not thinking, let alone overthinking. For me, meditation is an exercise in stilling the mind, but at that time I was constantly thinking about the strain in my marriage, and it was consuming an overwhelming amount of my thoughts, sending my mind spinning during meditation instead of quieting it. At that time I needed meditation for more than just disciplinary reasons; I needed it to escape my anguish over the deteriorating state of my relationship with the man I loved and didn't want to lose, yet felt slipping away. Now I was depending on meditation for answers on how to keep him. I consider it fruitful meditation when I achieve thoughtless concentration, but now my meditation had become a place I went to loaded with questions and expectations.

In order to preserve it as the spiritual retreat it was meant to be, it was time to turn to a more intellectual therapy as another method of guidance for the worldly, marital problems I was having. I'd ordered a tall stack of books on how to save a marriage and how to be a better spouse, friend, and person overall. In order to tackle the discontent in my life, it was my responsibility to learn how in the hell I could get to a place where I might find some sort of peace that would allow me to accept my unhappy marriage for what it was and not be one of those people always thinking the grass is greener on the other side. I wanted to learn to appreciate what I had and make the most of it, to take a realistic and practical approach. This was my intent, and my books were going to educate me on how to do this.

Among my pile of self-help books were:

*The Secret* by Rhonda Byrne
*The Artist's Way* by Julia Cameron and Mark Bryan
*The Book of Secrets* by Deepak Chopra
*The Seven Principles for Making Marriage Work*
    by John M. Gottman
*The Power of Now* by Eckhart Tolle
*Buddha: A Story of Enlightenment* by Deepak Chopra
*The Rules of Life* by Richard Templar
*Too Soon Old, Too Late Smart* by Gordon Livingston, MD
*Eat, Pray, Love* by Elizabeth Gilbert

I wanted to save my marriage and work on it, but I could sense that something was almost too seriously wrong between us now, as our communication had dwindled to strained conversation and little to no eye contact. A panic began to well up inside me, and I became anxious and afraid. I sensed there was something he wasn't telling me.

At least if we were in Switzerland, I could have called Marie-Anne to go for one of our lengthy walks-slash-marital-therapy-sessions. Instead, I was way up in New Zealand's high country, while my friend was at the base of the Swiss Alps.

One night, a few days after he left for Switzerland, I was in such despair that I just *had* to talk to someone, so I called Marie-Anne at home while Eja was asleep. My husband's silence was causing me to imagine all sorts of terrible things, I told her.

"Maybe he's ill and doesn't want to upset me," I worried aloud. "If you see Mutt while he's in Switzerland, could you just see if you notice anything . . . *strange* about him? Like, if you think he looks sick in any way or is acting out of character." As she was our local assistant in Switzerland, it was logical to assume Mutt would contact her while he was there to help with any administrative tasks or run errands. She assured me that she would keep an eye out and for me not to worry, commenting on how I had enough to worry about with the workload of tying up all the loose ends with the building, alone. She was very sympathetic and comforting.

Then I blurted out my other fear.

"Do you think he's having an affair?" I asked.

Marie-Anne's reply didn't surprise me because I sheepishly agreed with her response—that it was absurd to even think my husband could possibly be having an affair.

The almost scolding tone of her voice in response made me feel foolish for even having entertained such a notion. After all, how *could* he possibly carry on an affair without my noticing, since we lived such an isolated life, especially in the last few years living in Switzerland?

Caution: when someone within your circle is having an affair, it can be very hard for anyone to see, and easily masked by excuses that are easy to legitimize, especially if it's a neighbor, mutual friend, or the notoriously obvious and predictable secretary.

I believed it was foolish of me to entertain such a paranoid assumption and that my husband's peculiar behavior might even have been in my own imagination. Marie-Anne calmed me down and convincingly reassured me that everything was fine, that she hadn't personally seen anything unusual in his behavior. She told me she would observe him and let me know if she noticed anything odd. I thanked her as she verbally wrapped her arm around my shoulder and comforted me. I was relieved when I got off the phone with her. I believed her completely. I believed my friend was looking out for me and that everything was going to be okay.

# 28

## Never in Ten Million Years

Upon our return to Switzerland at the end of March 2008, I would face the most painful shock of my life since the death of my parents twenty years earlier.

My husband was having an affair with Marie-Anne.

Marie-Anne my confidante, the same friend who'd comforted me over the phone only weeks before, expressing how absurd it was of me to have any such suspicions of my husband. The idea that she was the mistress, after all the confiding I'd done in her, had not even entered my mind.

Denial can have multiple layers, and rationalizing is common when you're trying to absorb something you just don't want to believe. I thought: *Okay, so maybe they made a mistake. My husband and my friend will come to their senses and realize that.* I was ready to forgive, forget, make things right, move on, and get on with our lives. Not like nothing had happened, but like something had happened that I thought was fixable. But this was not to be.

Despite everything, I still loved my husband. And I still loved my friend. I put myself in their shoes with the understanding that accidents happen, we're all human, and we all make mistakes. It was love that allowed me to take that perspective at that moment, but considering my desperation to keep everything from falling apart, it was probably also in my naïve (and shell-shocked) state of mind that I wrote the following letter to Marie-Anne, treating her as a decent friend who'd temporarily lost her way and behaved in a manner that wasn't really her. I just wanted everyone to get on with healing, including her:

*Regardless of what has and hasn't been said and done up to now, and that things have been changed forever for all of us, I do hope we all go into the future never having secrets from each other ever, ever again of any kind. That we take responsibility to make sure the ones we love can know they can trust us and never do things they cannot know about.*

This is all extremely personal stuff, and I've questioned myself often about whether or not to include it in the book, as it's against my nature to open up like this. But since having a traitor in your midst is such a difficult thing to recognize—especially when he or she is so good at it, it makes you wonder if that person has somehow been professionally trained—it's helpful and almost a responsibility for someone with experience to warn others. There are affairs that fall out of the sky, like the typical unhappy husband who bumps into a woman in the grocery store aisle and realizes that his life has just begun at that moment, is lovestruck, and leaves his wife and kids as a result of his undeniable urge to fulfill his wants and desires. Although these affairs are unsavory and still morally unacceptable, they happen. But a friend who is already in the life of a couple who are struggling and vulnerable, who has a bird's-eye view with a great advantage to observe, and who is able to circle and wait until the opportunity to strike arises—this is not something that "just happens." This is more like the behavior of a vulture, slowly scoping, patiently waiting and hovering. Beware of these sneaky creatures.

I mistakenly thought I was so aware of the people around me, and I'm sharing this because I know it is not my shame alone to hide; it's a reality that happens to many people, no matter who you are. This is campfire talk, where you can sit around and share things with mutual friends and neighbors. Information you want to communicate with a community spirit, an exchange of knowledge and experience shared out of generosity, not malice. Give me a handful of women to sit around a fire with on this subject, and there would be plenty to talk about, no matter what age, class, or education. This topic is a true equalizer.

Eventually, I even came to the point of accepting the end of my marriage. It's not as though I was oblivious to the fact that our communication had frayed in recent years. At times, I thought that perhaps the universe was telling me that I'd been stuck in a rut, and it was dragging me kicking and screaming to my own freedom.

I believe that relationships are a give-and-take, an exchange of good and bad that travels in both directions. Over fourteen years together, Mutt and I both had our share of give-and-take. There was an equal exchange between us, and when the energy of that exchange died, so did the relationship. We weren't victims of each other, only victims of the one taking advantage of our vulnerable state as a couple and as a family. No one is to blame for the end of our marriage, only responsible for the manner in which it ended. *That* was unforgivable, if there is any such thing.

For the first week after finding out about the affair, I was ready to die—to go to bed forever and never wake up. Or to hurt someone. I was ready to do *something* desperate, but in reality, there was nothing to do but to suffer through it. Fortunately, when you're a mom, the responsibility of caring for your child can keep you going. You have the routine of preparing your child for school in the morning, dragging yourself out of bed on autopilot, and cheerfully keeping a brave face. And as soon as he's off, at least in my case, I'd slip back into my pajamas and spend the day in bed, crying and sleeping fitfully. I wasn't eating at all; in fact, I went a whole week without any solid food and just drank orange juice. This can be considered healthy during a cleansing fast, for example, but I wouldn't recommend it while trying to cope with the grief of a deep emotional crisis.

I was freezing cold all the time, and my only relief came when I'd strip off my clothes and climb into a steaming-hot bath. Five times a day. Yet I'd be shivering most of the time, shaking uncontrollably, my teeth chattering violently. Out of the bath, I'd wear a winter coat over my pajamas, plus wool socks and a scarf. It made no difference. I couldn't get rid of the chills and at the same time, I was sweating profusely. It was as if my body were trying to purge itself of the emotional agony inside by forcing the pain out of my pores so that I didn't drown in it. I hurt physically, too, aching as though someone had sandpapered all my nerve endings.

But when four o'clock arrived, and it was time to kick back into Mommy the Brave for the evening, I was there for my son with a hug and a smile. Believe me, it took all the courage I could muster to get through our morning and afternoon routines like everything was "okay." However, the way I looked at it, this sudden, major change in our lives was going to be hard enough on him; I was not about to subject him to the pain that I was feeling on top of his own. All things considered, I think I did a pretty good job of managing this "double life," as my son didn't seem unusually stressed.

I resented Marie-Anne a great deal, knowing which end of the stick she was on. We were both new, single moms, going through our daily routines with our children, only I was drained of all my energy, as the façade I tried to keep up for my child's sake took everything I had. She was going through her daily routine, however, while in a new and exciting romance with a man who decided to put her first, above his wife and his family. Love is energizing, and new love is especially blissful and makes you feel invincible. Boy, were she and I at opposite ends of the stick, all right. It must have felt so empowering to know that he risked it all for her. Is this the way a mistress feels? That she is more valuable and important to the man than his wife and family? Perhaps it's the unfaithful husband convincing her that she's important enough to stake such a claim. Or is it her own sense of self-entitlement? In any case, at the time my perception was that my husband's mistress was the winner, the one defended by my own husband. And when he wasn't looking, she had the confidence to parade her cockiness and fearlessness with snarly looks and hisses when by chance our paths crossed in person, as they inevitably did, since we lived in the same small village. This was extremely painful for me and left me feeling weak and defeated. She had nothing left to fear, and I'd lost. Every time she kicked me when I was down, she made sure my husband wasn't looking, and when I tried to explain to him what he couldn't see, he refused to listen and didn't want to know. I felt as if I were trapped in some kind of childish game with my sadistic opponent standing just far enough away that I couldn't reach her, all the while sticking out her tongue at me. It was degrading. I hated her because I felt she was making a fool of my husband, someone I considered to be intelligent, mature, and anything but vulnerable to the cliché of the temptress secretary, as she shamelessly "displayed" an attitude that seemed to say, "Your husband will never see my other face, and I will never show it to him, because I have his compassion, his sympathy, and his credit card, and there is nothing you can do about it." She was right, and I felt helpless for myself and for Mutt. I was disgusted that another woman's lust for a lifestyle upgrade was worth the devastation of my family. She was pitiless, and I was a pitiful mess of "woe is me."

There was one occasion in the initial days when I was too wrung out to keep up the masquerade in front of my son. I felt a big sob coming on, so I ducked into another room and tried to pull myself together. Nothing doing. I sat down at the computer and began tapping out my angst while listening to some music. That didn't help either. I was crying all over my keyboard and going through tissues like crazy.

My son walked into the room. "Mom, you're crying," he said. "Why are you crying? I've never seen you cry before." He was surprised more than anything else, because he really had never seen me cry in his life. (I told you, I'm working on it.) I'm sure it was awkward for him. I'd had sad moments, of course, but, as is my nature, I always felt strongly about never burdening my child with my own personal pain in life.

But I had no family around, my husband was gone, and I was simply alone. Alone with my grief, trying to be strong and hide it from my son. For that moment, I just couldn't do it. I was quick on my feet, though. "It's okay," I told him. "It's important to know that mommies cry, too, sometimes." I went on to explain that music is very powerful and can move us emotionally. It can make us happy, angry, or sad, and the song that was playing on my iTunes happened to make me feel sad, that's all. "It is good to cry when something makes us sad." He accepted this explanation, hugged me, and went back to playing. And I went back to sobbing.

I was gutted that I'd been such a fool, to have been tricked by a traitor, but as shocked as I was at the news of the affair, I was equally surprised that I didn't suspect more earlier, that I had been such a blind idiot. But such is the talent of a crafty con. Although my husband's distance—and what I realize now was the transparency of his conscience—created suspicion in me, Marie-Anne's award-winning acting was what really threw me off. She kept reassuring me that everything was okay, that I was jumping to conclusions, and then distracting me with comfort, suggesting I should question my thinking, diverting me calmly and coolly from my concerns. Absolutely an Oscar performance that I could not see through. It gives me chills just thinking about how she was able to do this. I read something that struck a chord recently on the Internet from Roderick Anscombe's "When the art of the question meets the art of the Lie": I can't say I find it healthy to live life being suspicious all the time, but you do need to pay attention and keep a reasonable sense of awareness to protect yourself against anyone trying to take advantage of you. In day-to-day life, it's over-the-top to be distrustful of your spouse every time he or she comes home late from work or doesn't seem comfortable with questioning. But I do think it's wise to remain in close communication with your partner in every way your relationship has meaning to you: parenting, romance, friendship. Gaps allow devious outsiders to come in and take advantage of space between you, and they see it as an opportunity to fill in the missing parts. Address gaps with your partner and talk about them, acknowledge them. Don't ignore areas you are having trouble connecting on, and talk about the fact that you are aware the gap is there and that you are interested in finding a solution to fill it, even if you don't have that solution. Show your interest in finding out what you can do and suggest that it be a mutual effort. Share the responsibility. If you blindly expect your partner to see all this on his or her own, then I believe you are taking the risk your partner won't live up to your expectations. Be more proactive with weaknesses in any relationship you value, recognize your responsibility in keeping gaps and empty, vulnerable areas filled with communication, understanding, and awareness, and you will improve your chances of surviving unnecessary breaks. Stay in touch and you stay connected. Once you let go of communication, some bloodsucking standby will almost surely step in and grab your end. Good luck trying to get it back once you've lost hold.

They say that the lying and sneaking around—the "intrigue"—add to the excitement of an illicit affair. Even after the cat was out of the bag, the deceit continued. In the first days after my return from New Zealand, while I was still in the dark that my friend Marie-Anne was a traitor, she came to the hotel where I was staying while waiting to move into our renovated lakeside villa, to comfort me over my concerns about my marriage. I sensed a defensive attitude in her tone when I asked her some direct questions about my husband, and that set off an alert in me. Over dinner and drinks, with our kids playing next to us on the carpet, I eventually got up the nerve to ask her what was going on between her and my husband. I assumed that she knew something I didn't and that she was helping him keep it from me as his loyal secretary, but I still wasn't suspicious that she was actually a part of the secret.

Her response was unbelievably convincing. "I'm heartbroken that you would even think that I was hiding something from you," she said innocently, her eyes tearing up. Although I was suspicious of something, I didn't know what to think, as she successfully managed to confuse me with her act. "We've been friends for all these years," she reminded me. "I can't believe you are questioning my loyalty and honesty." I wound up apologizing for having doubted her.

The morning after this dinner in my hotel room with Marie-Anne, Fred took on the painful chore of telling me about the affair, as he could no longer bear her lying to me so cruelly, even across from me at my own table. Although I do not want to minimize the pain Fred endured through the process of discovering the affair, as he had parallel suffering on the flip side of things, I have simplified this part of the story to broad strokes, to avoid getting bogged down in details. I considered chopping this section out of the book altogether, as it's so uncomfortable to review, let alone write. But someone scammed her way into my trust, so completely under the radar, that my astonishment compelled me to share how these events unraveled, in case they help readers recognize this happening in their own lives, before it's too late. Whether it be in business, family, friendship, or marriage, it's so important to keep your eyes open for cons, liars, and cheats who will comfort you with one hand on your shoulder and rob you with the other. Marie-Anne made the old saw "With friends like that, who needs enemies?" a reality for me.

Fred explained that his wife had spent some time with my husband in luxury spas in the area over the last months. Of course, I demanded proof, and outside of what he'd witnessed personally, he had the classic evidence in the form of phone bills, hotel information, and receipts, and the memory of a garter belt and lingerie he saw packed in her luggage. She was meant to be going away for time "alone," the same story she gave me through our email exchanges.

Bonjour,

I got all your emails for Mutt. I will print them and give them to Mutt tomorrow.

I am actually at the spa now and will go back tomorrow to Vevey [a district in Switzerland] and do my last night in Montreux Palace. I really enjoy it!

I will write you more when I will be back home.

Lot of love,

Marie-Anne

Bonjour,

I hope you are doing well and not too tired with all the works. Next week, I am leaving for a few days by myself, alone, in a spa without husband and daughter! I am really happy to do it! It will be so relaxing!

Marie-Anne

And me, not catching on at all, wrote back:

Bonjour,

It's after midnight, and I am going to bed now. I'm sorry for not writing sooner. There is really no excuse to not stay in better touch, but I feel like my days just go by so fast here. Too much to do and so little time.

We miss you all, and it's nice to hear from you. Even if I don't write back regularly, it doesn't mean we don't talk and think about you. We always do.

Have fun on your alone spa time. Very nice, and I'm happy for you. I am not resting much at all right now, so I am jealous. Ha! Enjoy!

Love, E

That one just kills me. "I really enjoy it!" she says. Oh, I'll bet she did. How could any friend write something like that while in the company of the other's husband? This was all happening with Fred's awareness, and even though he tried to intervene, short of chaining his own wife to the house, how could he keep them apart when they were so intent on being together? He had a demanding, full-time job and a daughter to look after, and I was no help being on the other side of the globe and, worse, still oblivious to the situation.

Fred apologized profusely to me—both for not having told me as soon as he discovered the affair, weeks earlier, as well as for my pain at hearing what he had to say. He felt so guilty having to be the one to break my heart. Of course, there was no reason for him to feel sorry; it wasn't his fault this was all happening. People who are not concerned with trying to protect the ones they've hurt often protect themselves by avoiding unpleasant confrontations. I said, "Fred, we aren't exactly at the top of our spouses' lists of people they're concerned about." I had to reassure him that he did the right thing answering my questions honestly and not remaining a part of their lie.

I thanked Fred for coming clean and sparing me further humiliation by turning on the light. That's one of the most painful aspects of being the spouse who remains in the dark. Not only do you hurt and grieve, but you feel like a fool, insulted that those you love don't feel you're worthy of the truth, that you have no right to know their truth, as if it has nothing to do with you. The chorus from a 1970s hit song, "How long has this been going on?" kept playing in my head, and my mind was racing with a zillion questions. But I wasn't going to get any answers on that one. Once the door was closed, there were no more answers coming, no explanations, no consideration or compassion for my need to know, and that was how it remained.

Recently I was reading Jane Fonda's autobiography, and I had to laugh when I got to the part where she wrote about her painful divorce from media mogul Ted Turner. She confessed to having written several angry letters expressing things that, had she mailed them, she would have regretted later. But she knew not to send them, that merely writing down her feelings brought some measure of healing. Her advice: "Best not leave *everlasting* proof of your *temporary* insanity."

She is so right, and I wish I'd read that bit of wisdom before I'd sent my venting letters. I suppose I did go through a temporary period of insanity, and my language reflected this. I used every hurtful word I could find to express my desperation and helplessness. After it dawned on me that this was permanent, and that neither my husband nor Marie-Anne had any intention of putting their families back together, my letters went from angry to pleading:

*Please leave us in peace! Please! I'm begging you. I am so low, so brokenhearted I can't take it anymore. I wish you love and happiness, but I am dying, and I can't take it anymore. This is killing me. Have mercy. I loved him so much, and I can't cope anymore. I don't want life or love anymore. I just want peace. Why are you torturing me? Let it go. Pleeeeeaaaaaassssseeee!!!!!!! If you could see me crying and suffering, maybe you would have pity. Find love somewhere else from someone else that isn't hurting two families so much. All of us have to suffer for the two of you. It just isn't right!*

Okay: I wish I could have taken *that* one back. My pathetic pleading made no difference at all to Marie-Anne, but I had to try. Besides, the way I look at it, the letters that I did send were meant to be sent, and those that I stashed in a drawer weren't. Under the circumstances, I'm not about to beat myself up for expressing my genuine anguish.

I admit I'm embarrassed about being so vulnerable, but I'm sharing it with you as a way of letting it go. If there is anyone who is going through or has gone through something similar, I want you to know that there is no shame in expressing your pain or even things that embarrass you. There is a time to force yourself to let go of your inhibitions in order to embrace new thinking, to share your feelings even if you have to force yourself a little. In fact, it's harmful not to. So at the risk of making a fool of myself or being judged for indulging such vulnerable thoughts and emotions, I feel liberated in being able to laugh at myself, to laugh even at what once made me cry, to be able to say that I've grown and progressed toward a new way of looking at things. It's like being able to admit that you were the one who farted.

# 29

## Digging My Own Hole

Freeing myself from the rubble of anger, confusion, frustration, and the sheer emotional agony of the double betrayal took longer than I expected. It was like a bad flu, something that needed to run its course, no matter how badly I wanted it to go away and stop incapacitating me. Some days the despair was so all-consuming, I'd feel like it was coursing through my veins. I felt sick with grief and wished, like in the case of a grave illness, there was a blood transfusion for the suffering of loss. Maybe then I'd be all better, able to start fresh, with new, untainted, "happy" blood. I was becoming impatient with myself, in a hurry to somehow snap myself out of this awful state.

I never considered harming myself, but I *was* harming myself—torturing myself, really, by trying to make sense of it all. What happened to me, and why? How could he? How could she? I'd been robbed of trust, love, hope, things that belonged to me, I believed. These thoughts held my mind captive day and night. In hindsight, I realize that I was trying to apply logic to love and desire—and what could be more illogical than that? I wanted desperately to turn my brain off, but I just could not find the switch. Jim Morrison once said about pain, "You should stand up for your right to feel your pain." My emotions would not quiet; they were hurting me, and I wanted them to quit. I was desperate to shut them off, and I reached out many times searching for something in the dark to flick or push, anything, but there is no such thing. You can pretend your pain is not there, but it is. It's real, and neither you nor anyone else around you should try to convince you that it isn't. Work through your pain, and you will get to the other side of it. There is no other way; shutting it off is not an option. The situation you are in may not be in your control, but your right to feel the pain from the affliction is. As humans, we cannot order emotion away like a naughty child. It's necessary to allow ourselves time to feel our doom, that all is lost, if that is genuinely what we are feeling. We grow and learn from our suffering, so why let anyone take that away from you?

From the time I was a little girl, I would write my feelings out of me. Unbeknown to me at the time, this was a very healthy thing to do. Expressing my emotions in a song or poem really helped me to see things more clearly and come to terms with them. It was my way of working through and addressing them. But not this time. In fact, writing them out became a self-destructive exercise. I typed obsessively in endless circles about Mutt and Marie-Anne and me, each keystroke digging me deeper and deeper into the emotional hole I'd created for myself, so that now I was mentally drained in addition to being just plain sad, except when I put it all on hold when I was around my son.

However, as so often happens in life, something positive emerged from a terrible time: namely, this book.

I was writing in a frenzy every day for hours and hours, piling up tens of thousands of words, and yet the relief and answers I sought were as elusive as ever. I figured all I'd done was waste a whole lot of time.

Or maybe not. It occurred to me that I felt satisfied and rewarded reflecting on my life *as a whole* and had found the importance of thoughtfully writing it down. So why not keep writing? But instead write about the forty-two years that preceded having my heart broken and not just in an effort to empty myself of my current suffering. Writing about my entire life meant I could feel the creative fulfillment that comes from expressing myself, and it would interrupt my preoccupation with the heartbreak I was trapped in. I didn't want that one crisis to be what defined my life, as it was really only a *moment* in my life within a larger story. A story that deserved that I start . . . at the beginning!

The act of writing helped me regain some badly needed perspective. When you're in the depths of despair—over anything; it doesn't have to be a romantic breakup—it's easy to lose sight of the fact that you weren't always in this much pain, and the time will come again when that crushing sensation in your chest finally lifts and the weight of feeling that maybe you're going crazy will dissolve. Grief is not a mental illness, even though while you're in the midst of it, it may very well feel that way. I also understand that if I were feeling such despair not having had an *experience* of loss associated with it, then perhaps I should be more concerned about my psychological health. Fourteen years of marriage to someone you deeply love, and with whom you have a child, ended by an affair with a close friend? That's something to be devastated by. But thanks to a great deal of reading about grief, personal struggle, and loss in my effort to climb out of my deep hole, I began to learn to be less hard on myself and to ease up on putting a time frame on my grief, while still keeping a healthy eye on it or allowing those who cared about me to do so.

In her book *Living Through Personal Crisis*, Dr. Anne Kaiser Stearns talks about the need to keep good friends and family around you in times of crisis. I chose a few descriptions from her list of what makes an "empathetic person" that I particularly related to. An empathetic person is someone who "does not shock easily, but accepts your human feelings as human feelings," "reminds you of your strengths when you forget that you have these strengths within yourself," and "recognizes that you are growing." For those who do not have the rare empathetic person in their lives, this is a good reason to seek out a professional. Dr. Stearns's advice is, "A well-trained professional is someone who listens well, with acceptance and without judgment. If more people had accepting friends capable of good listening, there would be less need for professional helpers."

So I've learned that I need people who are good for me as I go through this healing process, as there are those who are bad for me. I realize it's wise to remember that people who bestow suffering on you are usually in a rush for you to "get over it" so they can feel less guilty about the grief they've caused you. I paid too much attention to this in the first year of my marital and friendship betrayal crisis, allowing that pressure to make me question myself and my own state of mental health.

Here, another quote from Dr. Stearns on "Destructive People": "The destructive person may harm you and complicate your mourning in a wide variety of ways. He or she . . . labels your feelings or behavior as 'silly,' 'sick,' 'weird,' 'selfish,' or 'feeling sorry for yourself.'" She gives good advice to avoid placing ourselves in settings that are alien to healing.

Learning to avoid the judgment of my healing process by my husband and Marie-Anne was one thing, but part of that process was revisiting it through writing it down, so it became a bit of a vicious circle for a while. I thought that if I just kept writing it out, it would eventually be gone. The idea was to put it down on paper and forget about it. But it wasn't as easy as that, although what I did find great about putting my story in words was that as the pages mounted, I could actually "see" the different stages of my life in a physical pile. I was able to measure the stacked pages I'd written about this awful year or so, and they were far outweighed (literally) by all the good stuff.

I wrote and climbed my way back up, one chapter at a time. Of course, autobiographies are not written overnight, so this would be a lengthy process, like long-term therapy, I guess. To get through those first months, I relied on a small group of family and friends who rallied around me and stayed by my side. These were my beloved, empathetic care providers.

Frederic was there for me despite his own emotional turmoil. A true, empathetic person through it all, he emailed me regularly once everything was out in the open. He sent a quote to remind me I was not *really* alone, when I felt I was, as none of my friends or family could get to me in the first days after I found out the bad news that my marriage was over. This quote could not have come at a better time: "A friend is someone who knows the song in your heart and can sing it back to you when you have forgotten the words."

Still, I thought, *Finally, Easter is over, I'm facing the new reality that my marriage is over, my friend is my husband's new love interest, and I'm struggling to cope alone.* Stacy was finally able to come to Switzerland, but only several days after I got the bad news, which felt like an eternity. Those days alone with Eja were terrifying and desperate, and Fred's calls and emails comforted me and kept me going. Mary then came to take over from Stacy as soon as she could get to Switzerland from Canada, so I wouldn't be alone.

With the affair right under my nose, I needed time to catch my breath before I could cope with the reality that it was real. I refused to accept it overnight. I resisted it and demanded that it stop, explaining to both of them that it was cruel, ruthless, and unfair, but my pleas fell on deaf ears. I begged for compassion, but it didn't come. I felt as if my marriage was dead but still warm, yet there was already dirt being thrown over the grave. I couldn't take both those hits at the same time. Reality does not wait for you to catch your breath, and when you are reminded of what your new reality is, what your loss is, and your lack of control over it, it's natural to panic, over and over again, with each reminder, in the initial weeks of mourning. I'd have periods of the day when I was calm and able to function, going in and out of episodes of shock, numbness, and weeping. The song that came to mind regularly during that initial period of battling with acceptance was Bonnie Raitt's "I Can't Make You Love Me."

It's a couple of weeks after the bad news, and I have an emotional breakdown while having tea with Mary at a nearby café one afternoon. This was my true breaking point, which sent me back to family and friends in Canada. As we were talking about the painful scenario, everything just hit me harder than I could stand, and an intense flood of emotion came over me, till I was hardly able to walk the short distance back to our hotel without Mary supporting me. My knees kept giving out from under me. Mary reminded me that no one understood the situation as deeply as Fred, the other victim in all of this, and she urged me to go to him to talk. But we had no real contact or relationship at this point, and besides, he worked long days as international operations manager for the worldwide coffee company Nespresso and rarely got home before eight in the evening. If only my family were here and not halfway across the world. I called him anyway, and in short, panicked breaths, hyperventilating, I tried to explain that I could not take it anymore. From his cell phone Fred told me, "Meet me at my place. I'm coming right away."

Fred's office was a good thirty minutes away. I walked about halfway to his apartment, where he, Marie-Anne, and Johanna had lived together for the last year, and just—froze. My purse slipped from my fingers and fell at my feet. I stood there, hanging my head; there was no more life force left in me to move another inch. I'm guessing that I remained there, statue-like, for at least a half hour. I was conscious of everything around me: the warmth of the sun, the birds chirping and swooping and circling above, the joggers breezing by me, the spring poppies and tulips on my left, the rowers gliding silently by on my right, the dramatic snowcapped mountains shining like beacons. Baby strollers, walkers, talkers, bikes, dogs—all going by in both directions, blurry, as if seen in my peripheral vision. The only thing in focus were my own two feet. I could not lift my head. My heart holding my thoughts and my thoughts holding my heart, neither of them strong enough to snap me out of it.

It was like the rest of the world existed around me, but I no longer existed within it. Living was over for me. *This is where I get off, off this living place. Do with me what you will, life,* I thought. *I have nothing left, and I give up.* Ashamed and humiliated, I really had given up. I was at my lowest, and I was shutting down—physically, mentally, emotionally.

Eventually, I became aware of a sharp *clip-clop* sound coming toward me. A jangle of keys and spare change in a jacket pocket. Then Fred's arms wrapped around me and his wordless sigh of sympathy against my cheek. When he arrived at his apartment house and did not see me waiting there, he went running around the block, frantically trying to find me.

We headed toward his place, with Fred holding me up. I remember feeling his heart still pounding from his running and panic to find me, as his ribs pressed up against me to support my weight. I could feel how alive and real he was, and his energy gave me a sense of comfort that perhaps some of that life might transfer to me and resuscitate me. Some human warmth and sincerity I could physically feel, a real, beating heart, capable of genuine compassion.

When Fred talks about it now, he simply says, "When I found you along the lake that day, you were totally broken." He wrapped me in a blanket, since I was shivering, sat me on the office sofa in his apartment, and gave me a half glass of vodka. According to Fred, I didn't speak for several hours. I just sat there, numb. He was extremely sensitive and understanding, waiting patiently for me to communicate when I was ready. We just sat there together in silence.

Now when I hear stories of spouses losing their partners to another love, to sickness, or just because they are no longer in love, I feel their pain, I understand them, especially when it's someone who's had a long-term marriage. I'm sensitive to the shock and fear of having to start over alone. When you've been married for so long, you don't know how to be alone in life anymore. It can be nothing short of terrifying and depressing. Outside support is crucial to anyone going through this. I have to say that before this happened to me personally, I took it too lightly, thinking, *It's only a divorce; it happens every day.* But the individual circumstances of divorce have huge effects on those involved, and they should not be minimized or generalized, nor should their potential complexity be underestimated.

In mid-April 2008, after the breakdown by the lake, I took Eja with me to our Ontario cottage. I said good-bye to Fred and wished him luck with the nasty divorce and custody battle he'd already been dragged into by his wife. I did not know when Eja and I would see him again, and it felt like a final farewell.

I needed to be closer to those who would nurture me through the next several months. Thank God for them. They held me compassionately when I was shaking and felt like a baby bird that had fallen from its nest, lost, broken, and scared. I was pretty helpless at times. My family and friends also shouted at me when I needed to hear painful truths—particularly at the beginning, when I was still deluding myself that maybe this was all a big mix-up and somehow still fixable. I remember my sisters expressing great impatience with me, demanding I stop referring to Marie-Anne as "my friend" and calling my ex-husband "Love."

"We've had enough of this! They are selfish, heartless people, that's what they are, and that's what you should be referring to them as." I really was in a pathetic state, still seeing my husband and Marie-Anne as people who'd just made a mistake and would eventually see that they were wrong, then come to me apologizing with humility and compassion in their hearts. I was dreaming! My whole world had just come crashing down around me, and I could not face it all at once. I hadn't made their identity switch in my mind yet. It wasn't sinking in that what they used to be to me, they no longer were. In reality, my "friend" was now my backstabber, and my husband was now my backstabber's new love interest. They were open about their intolerance of my grief and impatient for me to "get over it" already. I was mourning the loss of these relationships and the potential they held in my dreams for the future. But change wasn't instant or final, like any death. It would take time.

Weeks later while at the cottage, a friend called to help cheer me up. I was still in a fragile state and started going on and on about how "maybe this isn't what we all think it is. Maybe one of the reasons that Mutt constantly defends Marie-Anne is because she really is innocent. Maybe she didn't see this coming." My friend wasn't having any of it, and he cut me right off.

"Eilleen!" he barked. "*Come on!* She is having an affair with your husband of fourteen years. Your own friend! Someone who knew your marriage was going through a vulnerable time. She is a bitch! In fact, she's a *cunt*! Say it, Eilleen: 'She's a cunt.' That's the word for her. Come on, say it out loud! I want to hear you say it!" he demanded.

It was hard saying it, even as angry as I was, but he really did help draw me out of my dark, insecure place. I still hadn't crossed the threshold of identifying her as my deceiver, and I found it hard to bring myself to say such a thing out loud about her; it seemed childish and vulgar. But her behavior was vulgar, and my friend was helping me face that by pulling the realization out of me with this free-spirited conversation. I engaged in repeating after him. It *was* kind of cathartic. (Harsh, I know, but after all, it *is* only a word.) My emotions were so balled up inside me that it felt good to release some pressure.

# 30

## Love Story

Double betrayal is a doozy. My mother died when she was forty-two years old, and it strikes me that a part of me died at the same age. With one knife in my heart and another in my back, my ability to trust died along with my will to live, love, and grow, but it was temporary, as if it were a near-death experience. God said, "Nope, not ready for you yet. You have to keep on going. These wounds may hurt, but they won't kill you. You're gonna live."

I reflected on my mother a lot during this time. In the past, I'd often think about her during happy events, like when I wished she were in the audience when I received my first Grammy Award or here to greet my baby boy when he came into the world. It didn't have to be something momentous, though; anything meaningful made me miss her, such as the time I first made molasses cookies using an old recipe she'd handwritten on the inside cover of one of my grandmother Eileen's cookbooks. Now, hurting as much as I did, I felt very lonely without my mom and wished we could be sitting around the kitchen table talking the way we used to.

When my mother died, I didn't have anyone close to me in the same way, to really share my music with, and I was feeling similarly stranded again. Any time a marriage splinters, it's painful and tragic. It's even more complicated when the two people involved are not just romantic partners but also business partners and collaborators. I didn't lose just my husband, I lost my songwriting partner and record producer. I was at loose ends professionally. I've always had a sound sense of myself artistically but had relied on Mutt for commercial direction on the musical front. Once a song is written, it can go off in an infinite number of directions in the way of arrangement, style, feel, and overall sound. It takes a producer with a vision to home in on the direction that best serves the song and then shape the record accordingly. Mutt is a master at this. I enjoyed the involvement of my artistic direction in the process, but Mutt's domain was clearly the production side of the music, and I hadn't developed any confidence in being more involved once I'd written and recorded my vocals. He was the captain of the space shuttle, which is kind of what his studio looks like with its vast collection of gear: sound effects units, instruments, knobs, buttons, switches, riders, and screens, a wall-to-wall flashing, blinking music cockpit. It's a fantastic, creative atmosphere, as any legendary producer's workplace should be, the perfect pad for a music genius. This is where Mutt thrives. My place was more in the background when it came to making the record, the quieter voice that piped up to give my two cents and make final touches. I had definite opinions, and they were respected, but there wasn't time or room for me to experiment and develop any producer skills once we were in the middle of a record. Mutt certainly didn't need my help, or anyone's for that matter, when it came to music production. It's a learning experience just watching him work, and I think I probably learned more by doing that than by actually being involved.

In the wake of this major upheaval, I began to seriously reevaluate everything in my life. My confusion was so great, I didn't know where to begin, as you can see from this letter I wrote to myself in an effort to get focused:

*Do I work again? Sing again? Run away and hide? Hibernate in motherhood and lock the rest of the world out, how do I share my son with his father now, do I split myself in every direction in the hope to find balance, try harder to forgive and forget, or just forget and move on? What? "What the fuck do I do now?" I cried out loud. Sometimes I think it's best just to sit and let life come to me, for that bus to speed by and run me over. Why be proactive at all? Why bother trying to see it coming and jump out of the way? Why bother planning, thinking, helping, hurting, loving? Just be and let life behold me instead of beholding life. I'd say I'm a little disorientated . . . wouldn't you? Major understatement!*

About the only thing I was sure of was that I could never trust other people again outside of a close-knit circle of family and friends. Honestly, my faith in human nature had really been damaged—permanently, I thought. I had always been emotionally self-protective anyway, wondering what was next, expecting life would have more shit to throw at me when I least expected it. I figured it was best to accept it was coming at all times. That way I could forget about it. But after this happened, my guard was up, and I was really ready to protect myself. Nobody was going to get too close; that way, I would never hurt this badly again.

I am grateful to Dr. Deepak Chopra for enlightening me, showing me that to disengage emotionally was no way to live. I first met Deepak in Zurich at a convention where he was to give a lecture at the end of 2007. I asked if it was possible for us to meet in private during his stay, as it was just over a two-hour drive from where I lived on Lake Geneva. My request to meet with him was primarily to discuss the distance forming between my husband and me, in my effort to try to understand what I could do. His advice and recommended reading material, although right on target in regard to saving a marriage, came too late to save mine. But I left Deepak with a few books filled with advice and guidance under my arm and a heart full of hope.

The next time I would see Deepak was about two years later, one afternoon in Geneva, prior to a Red Cross charity ball we were both attending that evening. This time we were meeting so I could get his thoughts on what to do about the knives in my heart and back, explaining that I was exhausted from anger, sleeplessness, confusion, disappointment, and sadness, and that I would settle for a feeling of indifference, as I figured that at least this would give me some peace. He explained, "You might deflect some of the inevitable pain of life, but you will also miss out on its abundant pleasures."

"I know, you're right. I don't want to go through life disconnected; I just want relief." He assured me that I would reach that point, comparing my pain to a fruit that's about to ripen and fall to the ground, freeing me. He said that the fruit had to become full and heavy before it could be released from the tree, before it could be enjoyed and appreciated. I admit I was impatient, as his advice seemed so vague, with no deadline to look forward to. *Like, when can I expect this fruit to fall, for crying out loud?* was my thinking. "Can't you be more specific?" I wanted to ask, but I was too ashamed to reveal my lack of composure and what I knew was spiritual immaturity talking. I was so tired of waiting around for answers. So many questions were still out there, and I just wanted someone to explain something definitive for a change, to look into my future and let me see clearly that everything was going to be okay.

But there was no crystal ball, and Deepak was not a fortune-teller, but he was right. I'm glad I took his advice and didn't harden my heart. Because of Deepak's very wise words, I left myself open to the inevitability of logic, that eventually the fruit would ripen and when it did, I would have my juicy taste of what possible good might come out of all my pain. If I had not had faith in the wise keepsake shared with me that day, I might have shut myself off from the love of my life.

Although I had known Frederic for about nine years, I had never really *known* him; I mean, he was my close friend's husband. I thought he was a wonderful, considerate person, and anyone could see that he was an attentive husband and father, but we were friends by association only. It was he and Mutt who were friends, the two of them often meeting alone over dinners to discuss politics, sports, current events, and life in general. I always believed it's one thing to be close to your friend, but another to be closer to your friend's husband. The men had their bond, and Marie-Anne and I had ours. That is at least what I believed, of course. Fred was always the one to take the kids on Saturday mornings for bike rides or to the carnival passing through town. He loved being with the kids, and I admired his energy and dedication to his daughter. He would take Johanna on father-daughter vacations to give Marie-Anne time to herself, and his bond with my own son from the very beginning was also very touching. The two of them were always the best of friends, and both Mutt and I were happy that Eja had another male figure in his life, as the Thiébauds were the only friends we had in the country. We all spent time together, but the kids gravitated toward Fred. He and I shared much of our family lives together, but in our appropriate places as the spouses of our friends.

It stands to reason that we supported each other during this time of our mutual betrayal, staying in touch, mostly by phone and email every couple of days, as I'd left for Canada at this point. After all, who else could understand better what the other was going through? However, since our previous interactions had always been in the context of our two families, we almost didn't know how to act with each other directly. We were polite, almost formal. Fred is especially traditional when it comes to social boundaries, always very friendly but appropriate. For both Mutt and me, teaching our son good manners has always been very important. Mutt reminds Eja often that "manners maketh man," and I believe this is true. I also believe there is another layer to this philosophy that is equally important, if not more so: honesty maketh humanity.

Fred is someone who possesses both manners and honesty with a natural ease. Raised in a family of doctors and lawyers on both his mother's and his father's sides, Fred grew up in a formal, refined social environment—a privileged upbringing. Considering the comfort and stability of growing up almost sheltered from social and economic struggle, Fred is still a real salt-of-the-earth kind of person. An open book, and deep in his natural being, he is a genuine and sincere human being. It is one thing to be mindful of your manners, to be polite and respectful, but if you don't mean it, what does it stand for? Sincerity holds incredible value to me personally, and as much as I think it's important to have good manners, if you question something or someone but you hide behind your manners because they're easier and less messy to manage, you are being deceitful and compromising your integrity. I would rather teach a child to speak his mind or live out actions that are true to what he thinks and believes, while at the same time expressing himself with grace, humility, and consideration. I feel strongly that you can be honest and achieve all this at the same time. This is a worthy intention, to remain truthful but considerate. This is how I would describe Fred: a true gentleman.

Together Fred and I tried to hash out what had happened to each of us. Sometimes we argued over who was to blame for this disaster. "He" must have done this. No, "she" must have done that. We didn't want any of it to be true and simply didn't know who was responsible. I didn't want it to be my husband any more than he didn't want it to be his wife, and neither of us wanted to believe our friend would do such a thing. There were so many angles and tangles to the long web of lies and deception, it was enough to make you dizzy.

Nearly six months later, in September 2009, I returned to Switzerland from the cottage in Canada so that Eja could go back to school. Fred and I continued bonding over our lives, our children, our woes, our dreams, our recovery. It was fall and getting cooler, and we would often have evening campfires outside the front door of the annex, as the main house was still under renovations. Roasting marshmallows, playing music, dancing, and singing—we had so much fun, and Fred and I were getting very good at swing dancing. The kids would join in and sometimes stand on the side to cheer us on. One night in December they were both up on the second-floor bedroom balcony watching us with a bird's-eye view, while Fred and I danced below beside the campfire, unaware of their gazing down on us. Fred and I must have appeared to be pretty lost in each other because at one point the kids piped up and said, "Why don't you guys kiss?"

Fred and I stopped dead, stunned, and said in unison, "What?"

"Why don't you guys just kiss?" they repeated, rolling their eyes while smiling from ear to ear. We looked at each other, quite surprised that the kids had recognized a connection between us that we'd been feeling for some time but felt uncomfortable revealing openly. We responded to the kids with an "okay," and we kissed on the cheek. The kids said, "No, on the lips." Fred and I couldn't believe our own children were cheering us on to kiss, for real, so we did. Fred and I perked our kissers, pecked on the lips, and the kids smiled and giggled. We were happy. Relief came rushing through us, as the ice had been broken. Fred and I were surprised and relieved by our children's encouragement to be ourselves in love, and from that moment on, the four of us began to form a reassembled family, building a nest, a new foundation, reconstructing our lives as a unit after the fall of the ones we'd lost.

Fred and I proceeded with caution, because we were both keenly aware that our mutual grief might be the main thing binding us together. We also considered the dangers of confusing the children with a rebound romance. But it wasn't.

What attracted me to Fred was his selflessness. He was going through the same agony as I was—maybe even worse, because as a father, he would have to battle his soon-to-be ex for the right to see his own daughter. At least that was something I never had to face. Yet he was never too busy to nurse me through my emotional lows. I think it's fair to say that he was more of a support to me than I was to him at first. While I was a self-pitying spigot of never-ending sadness in the initial period of my grief, he showed strength, kept a healthily clear, pragmatic perspective, and was infinitely patient and understanding. I admired him.

He was also there for Eja, who had known Fred his whole life. In fact, not long ago, Fred showed me a picture taken of my son only hours after he was born. "I don't recall ever seeing this photo before," I said to Fred. "I don't remember who took this photo."

"Me," he responded.

That warmed my heart. He really was always there, like a gift under the Christmas tree, pushed to the back where I couldn't see it. A gift with my name on it, only hiding, as I wasn't meant to open it till much later when it was time to take the tree down, then all of a sudden there it was, this present, for me! As if labeled, "From heaven—to Eilleen," Fred was for me; it was just a matter of time.

I describe what happened to Fred and me this way: we were two people who had been jettisoned from our lives as if we'd been shoved off the edge of a high cliff. Thankfully, we managed to grab on to each other on the way down in midair and break each other's fall.

It would be easy to say that we eventually fell in love because we were a couple of castaways in the same lifeboat, adrift at sea with no one else to turn to for comfort. Believe me, when we first realized that we had feelings for each other, it scared me. I was in denial, in fact. I didn't want to love again; I wanted Fred to know up front that love was the last thing I needed. Although I was going to work hard to avoid my true feelings for Fred, his only request was to leave him the right to love, care, and worry for me, even if I didn't want to love in return. The fact that I was honest about my new pessimistic point of view on love and men in general did not deter Fred.

I spent months shutting myself off from any thoughts of a relationship, but Fred loved me and was brave enough to come out and say it, even though I had made it clear that the thought of ever being in love again scared me out of my wits. I made it very clear that I was not ready.

Fred would email me quotes like this one from an anonymous author: "Love comes to those who still hope even though they've been disappointed, to those who still believe even though they've been betrayed, to those who still love even though they've been hurt before." Whoever wrote these words must have had a Frederic Nicolas

Thiébaud in his or her life, too. Or this one, from fiction writer Maria Robinson: "Nobody can go back and start a new beginning, but anyone can start today and make a new ending." He was right, I knew it, and I also recognized how irresistible this beautiful person was becoming to me. It turned out that my heart was still connected after all, and I finally stopped fighting my true emotions. I was falling in love with him.

The realization that our marriages were over was already nine months behind us. Nine months of emptiness, loneliness, fear of what was next, confusion over what had happened and why. There were still no answers, no closure or healing of the open wounds. Although I didn't feel ready to open the door, kindness, understanding, and love were tapping. I just had to accept that it wasn't my offenders tapping, the ones I expected to be offering these things I needed so badly. I had been so preoccupied with waiting for them to come knocking with compassion, explanation, and remorse that at first I couldn't hear Fred, the one who really cared.

The more time we spent together, however, the more I/we discovered how much we shared in common and that there was an undeniably natural bond forming between us. We had a surprisingly long list of things in common: sports, music, parenting, and our overall philosophies on life, and these launched us into hours of conversation, where time just disappeared. Soon it felt as though we were constantly running out of time, with never enough of it to be together. That December, I accompanied Fred on a business trip to Miami. While in Florida, we went skydiving. It was Fred's idea, and when he asked me, my response was, "Why not?" I was ready to throw caution to the wind, to let go completely, to experience losing control by choice, unlike the loss of control I had over my marriage ending, who loved me, or who I loved. I wasn't afraid, only ready to follow through with accepting that whether I lived through this experience or not was out of my hands, and that was part of the liberation for me: making a choice to do something potentially fatal, not needing to know what was going to happen next. That is truly letting go.

We also took in a Michael Bublé concert at Madison Square Garden in New York before heading home to Switzerland in time for Christmas. We'd been listening to a lot of Bublé's music, as Fred is a real fan of crooners, and we both love to dance to big-band swing, so it was a treat to see Michael in person. Two of our favorite tunes he recorded are "I'm Your Man" and "Everything." It's very romantic music, perfect for falling in love.

Fred got his first taste of what it's like to travel with a celebrity in our star-crazed culture. I had been living a hermetic existence in Switzerland for several years, so I was completely unprepared for the onslaught of paparazzi waiting for us the moment we landed in the United States. That was naïve of me, and I really should have known better. The flashing cameras caught us together but apart, so nobody knew what to make of this athletic-looking, handsome man who *appeared* to be with me. Fred wasn't used to this, naturally, and found the intrusion very annoying—as anybody in his right mind would. We both realized quickly that from that point on, the only place for us to find privacy would be behind closed doors.

Fred and I decided to spend our first Christmas as rejected spouses together in Verbier, a charming ski resort not far from our home. Even though we were finding solace through each other's company and support, special occasions—especially Christmas and New Year's—are tough when you've experienced deep loss. There are so many memories from the past that come flooding back to haunt you, reminders of how much has changed, that things will never be the same, and the finality and permanency hits you all over again. Fred and I were determined to face the future with bold hearts, however, and bring in the New Year with a positive attitude. We stayed busy with friends and family, and we would all have a splendid holiday and New Year's together. I cooked my heart out; we laughed our heads off, filled up with food and fun, played seasonal music ad nauseam, and bathed in the atmosphere of Noel in the winter-land beauty of the Swiss Alps, with its snow, evergreens, and smoking chimneys. There were occasional lows—but we held each other up. And the seasonal cheer kept our hearts warm and cozy.

December 28 would mark my fifteenth wedding anniversary. I was facing my first wedding anniversary separated from Mutt. It was Eja's first Christmas without his father and overall, a struggle for me emotionally.

Fred planned a surprise for me earlier in the week as my Christmas gift, but it didn't pan out due to the weather, so the first opportunity for it to happen, ironically, fell on the twenty-eighth. My heart was broken. It was so hard not to think that, that very day a year ago, Marie-Anne was wishing us a happy anniversary, and all the while she was seducing my husband. It was going to take something powerful to change my focus that day, and little did I know that it could happen because of an incredibly special person.

Fred's amazing surprise was to ski with me to two airplanes, so Fred could get there first, that would take us to a Swiss glacier, where we would toast to new beginnings with a glass of champagne. This amazing day helped me forget my sorrow, created new memories for me at that time of year, and made me fall further in love with Fred. It was fifteen below zero with no wind, sunny, and we were alone. The pilots agreed to leave us for forty-five minutes on our glacier plateau so we could celebrate our excitement for life and love in complete peace. Fred presented me with a gorgeous watch engraved with a "love" dedication, and the date, and he presented it down on one knee. He had been to the site before me, as he'd gone ahead with his own pilot to carve out a bench in the snow, spray paint a huge, red heart over the white surface, and place roses along the perimeter. He even had a bottle of pink champagne and glasses chilling in the snow. It was magic, and Fred created this magic. He wanted to set a romantic atmosphere to declare his love for me. It was like a marriage proposal, only he wasn't asking for a commitment of marriage. He was asking me to allow him to love me. "Sunshine," he said, "just let me love you." Even if I wasn't ready for commitment, he wanted me to know how he felt, expecting nothing in return. He was merely asking me to accept the engraved watch as a token of his love. He wanted us to move into 2009 with him having declared his love for me.

Fred had more romantic plans to come and loved to catch me off guard with the most beautiful ideas I could ever dream of. Fred is a romance god, and I lap it up. I'm spoiled rotten, and I admit it. Another one of his best was the time he rented his friend's movie theater for the night to surprise me with the most elaborate, romantic experience. He walked me into the empty foyer of the movie house with my eyes closed and led me up to a table decorated with glowing tea candles, a bouquet of roses in the center, and champagne on ice. Fred had gone to the theater during lunch that day to set up everything, and he'd instructed his friend to light the candles just before we entered and then disappear so there was no one in sight. It was magical.

Fred put on some of my favorite tunes while we danced and sipped champagne. I was so taken by this romantic surprise and never would have imagined there was more to come. Fred left me for about three minutes, and I assumed he'd gone off to the bathroom. Upon his return he said, "Now for the next part." I was breathless, not believing there was a "next part." How could there be more to this beautiful, thoughtful surprise? He walked me to the theater door with my eyes closed, and when he asked me to open them, I immediately began to tear up as he guided me to view the platform below. My eyes fell on a table for two draped in white linen with another vase of roses set beautifully for a romantic dinner. Fred had made the lighting very theatrical, with blue and red color gels on the spotlights, aimed to highlight our private table. Candles were lit all around the edge of the platform, and the rest of the room was black. It was incredibly dramatic and looked like a set for a play.

I couldn't believe this was happening, and just as I was trying to get my head around how on earth he put all this together, Fred began to escort me down to the table, and a side door swung open. A formally dressed waiter came in with our first course as if he'd walked on the set from backstage, his timing perfectly cued. Fred chose the menu himself right down to the dessert, and the restaurant was conveniently next door to the theater. It was so gorgeous and touching. I was in awe. The waiter was caught up in the whole romantic spirit of it and had a smile from ear to ear as he swept in and out from the theater with our delights. Fred had thought of everything. This was not only the most romantic thing I had ever experienced, it was the most romantic thing I'd ever heard of. Fred is full of these ideas, and from small to elaborate, he fills my life with surprise and wonder every day.

It's true I swore I would never allow myself to love again, but Fred is impossible not to love. This man goes the extra mile and loves in a truly unconditional way. Pure, honest, selfless love. Sweet, humble, compassionate. Little by little, he would win my heart.

# 31

## Rearview Mirror

Three years after our hearts were broken, together, I feel more love now than any other emotion I've felt since that time. I consider myself the luckiest woman on the planet that I have Fred to share the rest of my life with. Our wedding day was January 1, 2011, 1/1/11. It was a big decision to take the plunge of tying the knot, not because we had any doubts regarding our love for each other, but for me personally, I was torn by my knowledge that a wedding and marriage contract weren't going to make me any less or more committed to the relationship. One of the things that did it for me was that I was uncomfortable calling Fred my boyfriend. It just seemed like such a juvenile term at forty-five years old. Call me old-fashioned, but Fred prefers the word *traditional*. In any case, we both agreed that we were in love, wanted to spend our lives together, and knew more than ever before what it meant to make a lifelong commitment. That was what we wanted, together.

We've grown together through a very unusual set of circumstances, and we both agree that we've developed a unique love as a result. We're so grateful for having discovered each other in this new light. If our lover can also be our best friend, we've found the ultimate partner. I've never experienced this as completely as I do with Fred. I trust his observations of me and am not ashamed to say that I rely on him to hold up the mirror for me.

Fred makes me feel good about myself and helps me focus more on my positive attributes rather than my faults. He helps me see that although I may never be completely satisfied with myself, *he* is, and there is no pressure from him to be anything other than who I already am. This is precious, and I value this love, acceptance, and appreciation. I am loved, and I know it; what more could I ask for?

Passion for romance is something that I have rediscovered since allowing myself to love and be loved by Fred. I'll be honest: when your husband leaves you, and falls into the arms of your close friend, the other woman, your self-esteem can really suffer. I was sure that there must be something wrong with me. The rejection made me feel self-conscious, and I was sure that no man would desire me. I'd always been rather conservative when it came to romantic intimacy, not being terribly open or comfortable expressing myself with a new lover. Just feeling shy about it, basically. I had to know my partner well before feeling safe and confident in the bedroom. It was going to take strong communication with a very sensitive partner for me to feel appreciated again romantically. When it came to romance, Fred was able to give me back the confidence I needed to relax about loving again.

Physical attraction is essential to a healthy romantic relationship, and, thankfully, there is no shortage of that between the two of us. Fred makes me feel as if I'm the most gorgeous woman on the planet. Of course, I know I'm not, but he means it and shows it. When I tell Fred that I'm feeling fat and ugly or have general complaints about my appearance, he says, "Well, Sunshine, I'm just going to have to try harder. I guess I'm not doing my job, and no matter how many times a day I have to tell you how beautiful and sexy you are, I'm going to say it until you believe me." He seems so genuinely perplexed when my self-image is low. What a gift! I wish I could love myself as much as he loves me. I think this is a worthy goal to work toward, and so I put it on my list of priorities.

The irony is that I have a man who is highly attracted to me, and yet I'm more dissatisfied with my body lately than I've ever been in my life. The best years of my fitness and body shape were during my first marriage, as I was so physically active and just younger. I had very little extra body fat, an hourglass silhouette, and a taut tummy, even after the birth of my son. But lately my body has gone through a change that I'm not liking. I was reading that emotional stress can cause weight gain, especially in the abdomen area, and I believe it. For the first time in my life, I have cellulite on my stomach. In fact, I have a flabby layer of fat over my entire body. I'm not complaining about size here, I'm talking about texture and shape. These unwanted changes came on over the course of just a few months following the discovery of the betrayal, and I've had a very hard time getting rid of it. In comparison to the high percentage of surgically perked and plumped breasts today, mine seem droopier than usual, and probably really are. I'm letting "the girls" hang loose under my sweat clothes around the house and when someone comes to the door, I cross my arms under them for support to avoid making it obvious that I'm not wearing a bra but should be. Fred thinks I have a warped sense of my body image and am too critical. Maybe he's right.

I'm pretty insecure about my changing body, as it came about so suddenly that I haven't had time to get my head around it yet. I asked Fred recently, "What if I can't get rid of my flab? Will you be okay with that?" He said exactly the right thing and reassured me that with or without my squishy layer, he's still totally attracted to me. I lecture myself regularly to just be happy with what I have and even happier that I have a man who is, too. When I express this nagging insecurity about my self-image to Fred, he pulls out his research ammunition, and as I roll my eyes he reminds me that in 2009 *Hello!* magazine voted me "Most Beautiful Canadian," and a study by researchers at the University of Toronto cited me, actress Jessica Alba, and model Elizabeth Hurley as having perfectly proportioned faces. Fred found that one in an actual scientific journal, *Vision Research*; he loves researching this stuff, taking pleasure in using it as a means of turning my self-confidence around. Now, that's what I call "a good man," and every woman deserves one! I prefer to remain realistic about what I really look like when I'm not glammed up. The only other option is to remove all mirrors from the house, which sometimes Fred threatens to do when he feels I'm being too hard on myself.

I've decided to be proactive about my changing body and my attitude toward my new self-image. I've started by being realistic. I had the body of a twenty-five-year-old until I was forty-two, and seemingly overnight, I now have the body of a forty-five-year-old. So, part of my daily practice is to stop and reflect when I find I'm beating myself up over it, and to take action rather than moan. I've hiked up my level of physical activity and clamped down on my eating habits, but without my whole quality of life going to pot (as my new potbelly is enough pot for me to deal with as it is), and I remember to balance pleasure with discipline. I'll let you know how it goes, but for now, I'm still on the road to finding the solution to all this change. If I don't see any results within a reasonable amount of time, then I will resign myself to learning to live with it and concentrate on changing my attitude and not being so hard on myself.

There has to be a point in our lives where we simply accept that time catches up with us eventually. As much as medical advancements have made it possible to forestall aging, I'm not sure I'm someone who is willing to invest excessive time and effort in the quest to preserve beauty. The healthier thing to do, it seems to me, is to learn to be comfortable in your own skin and love yourself as you are. Besides, the character lines on my face have branded me with a number somewhere in the range of my real age.

At the moment I'm clearly at a crossroads with my self-image. Maybe I'm entering a phase of my life where this will become a never-ending battle from here on out. Maybe my hormones have taken my body in a new direction, and there is nothing I can do about it. Maybe at forty-five, this is my new body, like it or lump it, lumps and all.

The first time I think I even gave any thought to the appearance of my body was in the seventh grade. I was athletic and still tomboyish; skinny and scrawny, but strong, with muscular legs. Then I sprouted, or at least part of me did. At twelve, I was already a C cup, busting out of last year's shirts and developing an hourglass shape. One day while I was walking down the hallway at Pinecrest Junior High, a boy reached out and ripped open my snap-up, red-and-white-checkered shirt. I was embarrassed, of course, but mostly pissed at the nervy kid who did it. I never let boys intimidate me and had their number at an early age; most were quite sexist in an instinctive way, almost as though they couldn't help it or something.

I wasn't overweight, but I started noticing what fat was. I saw a classmate wearing very short shorts walking toward me. She was tanned and pretty, but I noticed her thighs jiggling as she walked. My thighs were hard, carved, and masculine. I was proud of my boyish athleticism and found her jiggly thighs unattractive. The tomboy in me saw this as a sign of someone lazy and soft. A girly girl was behind those thighs; someone weak, fragile, and not equal to boys. A girl with thighs like that couldn't possibly run as fast, or kick as hard, or jump as far, or stand as firm.

As my jiggly-thighed classmate came closer, I noticed that not only was she jiggly, she was bumpy, too. Each time she took a step, I could see a blanket of lumpy, bumpy skin. *Gross!* I thought. *What is that?* A boy with me said, "Eilleen, you'll never look like that." *Man,* I thought, *I hope not.*

The next summer, I started wearing short shorts, too. I was becoming more aware of the fact that I was a girl, with bulges and curves that boys admired. I was still very athletic and masculine in attitude, to the point of strapping down my breasts, as they painfully and annoyingly bounced out of control if I moved any faster than walking. I had to control these balloons that had grown without my consent.

I managed to maintain my boyish thighs until I was probably in my early twenties. It's hard to say because, to be honest, I avoided wearing bathing suits altogether in my teens after coming out of the lake one time with one breast completely hanging out, for what felt like the whole world to see. There were no full-length mirrors around our house, and no one would have seen my thighs to notice them transforming.

By the time I became a photographed celebrity in my thirties, I not only had a floppy, soft, orange-peel texture to my thighs, I had *cellulite*. I was horrified. I wasn't fat—in fact, I was quite thin—but still had this horrible texture to my legs when I squeezed down on them. It wasn't obvious when I was standing still and in flattering light, but squeeze them down with my fingers or put me in the wrong light, and it was obvious that I had this dreaded female nightmare.

In my daily life, I see girls and women all over the planet walking around with tummies bulging out of their shirts and thighs flapping around, as if they are proud of their earned chub. After all, we have babies, cravings, menstrual cycles that keep us famished no matter how much we cram into ourselves, and moods that demand immediate and desperate relief that only something fattening and indulgent will satisfy. Hello, chocolate, potato chips, alcohol, ice cream, and so on.

I envy girls who wear their extra weight like a badge of honor; clearly, they are comfortable in their own skin. They are not worried about what I or anyone else thinks of them. These girls are not miserably avoiding the foods they love and forcing themselves to be more active than they want to be. They are eating what they want, when they want, and not apologizing for it. How their bodies end up after that is not their concern. I admire the sense of freedom they possess. But at the same time, I also hear so many of them eventually moan about how they wish they could lose weight. I think that describes most women, and at least every woman I know personally.

My conclusion is that it's more important to be comfortable with your weight, no matter what it is, as long as you are healthy and energetic enough to meet the personal goals and demands you have set in your life. Those might be the ability to kick a soccer ball around with your child, host a Sunday gathering with your family, manage your job and domestic life without it completely exhausting you, not avoiding sexy lingerie if you secretly wish to wear it, feeling sexy and attractive to your lover, and having enough energy at the end of the day to actually engage in intimacy. If you meet your own expectations, what are you questioning? I ask myself this every day. The expectations that the fashion industry puts on us are not realistic.

Throughout the peak of my career, right up to the time I turned forty, my body went through interesting changes. I worked like a dog with little time to pee, let alone eat. I was always a very conscientious eater and made sure that my few bites between interviews or performances were light and healthy. I remained thin because of this but often had serious energy lows. I'm still not sure if some of the extreme exhaustion was due to how little I ate, lack of sleep, or simply being overworked. There were times when those around me would comment that I was too thin and needed to eat more. I wasn't deliberately trying to be skinny; I just couldn't keep the weight on. I even went to the extreme of adding cream and cheese to as many foods as I could. I was never into greasy foods, but I decided to add natural fats to my diet. My personal assistant was adding pure heavy cream to my breakfast and fruit milkshakes, lots of cheese to my lunches and dinners, and I enjoyed pancakes on Sundays made with whole cream and served with melted butter and lots of maple syrup. I can tell you, if I tried that now, I'd be as big as a house.

When I was touring, I was at my slimmest. There were a couple of promotional periods when I'd gained back a bit of weight, and I remember it bothering me. I recall looking in the mirror and gauging my limit thusly: if my thighs touched when I placed my ankles together, I needed to lose weight. Honest! I was constantly in and out of designer clothes and dresses that were almost always uncomfortably tight and unkind in exposing all my body flaws. Each time I had a major event—a national television appearance, for example—I would make sure that the designer was aware of any changes in my measurements so that there wouldn't be any last-minute disasters or humiliation for me. Designers would often comment to me how horrified they were when I added a little weight. It was traumatic to have to announce such a "catastrophe." Imagine, not only did I have to admit my weight gain, but I also had to measure myself in all the key places and give these incriminating details on paper to an assistant, who would hand it to another assistant, who would bring it to the designer—who would then most likely cringe in response.

Most top fashion designers have models displaying their magnificent drapes like human clothes hangers. Honestly, in many cases, the catwalk model is unrealistically thin to the point of literally resembling skin and bones. These skeletal figures make any other body type look fat and unworthy of wearing the fashions, and it's enough to make you never want to shop again. I never understood the logic in showcasing clothing most women would never have the confidence to wear and are actually intimidated by. I've often said out loud while watching certain fashion shows, "As if I could ever wear that!" After all, most women simply aren't walking bone racks in real life unless they are seriously ill with an eating disorder, and neither are the majority of us six feet tall and up. We can't wear this stuff and actually look good, in reality.

I always had full breasts even when I was at my thinnest; my brothers nicknamed me "Leeny, Weeny, Chesty Morgan" after the giant-boobed sex symbol, as I was a size 32D by the time I was thirteen, with a very small frame barely supporting them. Once they reached full inflation, I eventually gave up tying them down to prevent the relentless chin boxing when I ran, and decided to cut back on sports instead. I carried on with basketball, though; I discovered that wearing two underwire granny-style bras kept me secure enough to jump around without getting black eyes. In all seriousness, this worked well until I would eventually discover the luxury of the sports bra.

As for food, it has been a source of guilt for me all my life, but for different reasons. When I was a kid growing up in an impoverished home, I had to make sure that I never took more than my share so everyone got some. Now, in my midforties, I feel guilty for telling my son that he's not allowed to have a cookie while I have one myself but know full well I shouldn't.

Used to be that I could eat a lot and never gain an ounce. In my teens, an age when many girls start putting on the pounds, I could eat three eggs over easy with two slices of buttered toast and a bowl of cereal for breakfast; french fries and a triple-scoop banana split for lunch; and then a meatball sandwich with cheese for dinner. That was often topped off with a late-night pizza during band practice nights.

By the time I was in my midteens, my parents were doing better and better each year, so that even the cupboards at home were rarely bare now. Being a teenager, however, I was more attracted to eating out with my friends. You know what that means: high-calorie fast food with little nutritional value. It didn't show on me, though. I stayed thin, maybe due to how active I was. As I grew older and understood more about nutrition, I not only learned to avoid commercially prepared foods but became a vegetarian. I've been meatless now for eighteen years.

I've worn many different styles of hair in my life, from long and straight to high and curly, long and curly, slicked back, bangs, no bangs, even cropped and reddish for the "That Don't Impress Me Much" video. I was always looking for something new for interest's sake on my own part, and on one occasion, I got it in my head that I wanted braids. Lots of cascading, cornrow braids that fell long down my back. Well, braids I got. An expert on braiding hair came in to create my wish look for the special I was filming the following night in Dallas, Texas, before a live audience.

Daisy, the lovely lady who came to braid my hair, arrived with mounds of brunette extensions to weave into my own locks. My hair was already very long, but I didn't have enough of it to braid and have a full enough look. I'd never had this done before, although on many occasions I'd had extensions of different kinds. Just never a weave and braiding, cornrow style. Of the other extension methods I've had done, the longest was my first and took three hours. It was for the video for "The Woman in Me," which was shot in Egypt at the base of the great pyramids. Those extensions were sewn onto a series of cornrows braided flush to my scalp, each spaced about an inch apart so that my own hair fell free in between to create a natural blend for a natural look. These extensions were put in to give length, as they were longer than my own. Mostly I used extensions for volume or texture rather than for length, as I kept my own hair quite long for many years anyway and I often performed with just my natural hair.

The extensions that Daisy was going to weave in for the Dallas special took much longer than anticipated. We started before dinner, and at *midnight* she was still far from finished. I had ten o'clock rehearsal the next morning and would not get a chance to rest again till showtime. It was a very busy day due to the fact that we would be filming, so extra rehearsal and staging were required throughout the day.

As the hours passed and it became clear how long this cornrowing hair-extension adventure was taking, I didn't know if I should pull the plug on the idea and just call it quits, losing the several hours already invested, or carry on and hope it moved faster now that there was a rhythm going.

It's painful getting cornrows put in, especially when it's a tight weave like what Daisy was doing. She was extending my own hair with longer braids, so the weight of the hair was pulling on the rows braided against my scalp, and the cornrows had to be solid. My head was *throbbing*, I was exhausted, but I didn't have the heart to pressure Daisy to go any quicker, as she was working as fast as she could. I felt so bad for her own fatigue after all the hours of fingering through what seemed to be miles of hair. She was a trouper and said that she could carry on and was determined to finish. So we carried on, but it was five o'clock in the morning before we would finish. I was ready to cry and so upset to think that I'd have to go through such an important show having pulled an all-nighter, all for the sake of beauty. "A look." I felt stupid for making the call in the first place to experiment with my hair just before a crucial event such as filming a live television special. There was enough pressure as it was. But how was I to know it would take so long? Not even Daisy, the expert, had anticipated it taking all night.

Nevertheless, the show went on, the lighting and cameras did their job hiding any fatigue that might have shown around my eyes from the lack of sleep, and I did the special with all the cascading, braided hair I'd wished for. Beauty definitely has its price at times, and this experience was one of the expensive ones for me. Hair is always the most tiring of the beauty needs I have when I'm working, as it requires what seems to be endless pulling, tugging, fingering, scrunching, pinning, slicking, spraying, and fussing. I often find that maintaining beauty is one of my most shackling commitments to the expectations of any onlooker. If I were ever to completely liberate myself from the need to live up to my public image, the first thing I would do is shave my head. Of course, I would look plain ugly if I did this, as I have such a goofy head shape, probably due to my having been born a blue baby. Some people have beautifully shaped heads and would look great bald. Well, I'm not one of those people. Still, I figure that maybe when I'm old, I'll take the plunge and shave it off. Free myself of the constant battle to tame it to a decent shape and flatter my face. I actually have contemplated, at times, shaving it off now and just wearing wigs. That way I would only have to worry about my hair when I go out of the house, and it would take about thirty seconds to decide what hair I wanted. At least I'd have diversity at my fingertips, and changing my mind at the last second could actually be fun instead of stressful.

Shortly after I turned forty-four, I sat for a photo shoot. Now, I am one of these girls who needs to wake up very early in order to look good for the camera. Otherwise I just look . . . ordinary; at best, someone with potential with bags under her eyes. Trust me: without professional hair and makeup, I don't look like Shania the superstar/celebrity/sex symbol. That's true of most people in the entertainment world, if they're being frank. We rely on costly "glam squads" (hair, makeup, and wardrobe professionals) to reach into their bag of tricks and work their magic. They can make anyone look good.

Anyway, the photo session went wonderfully, and I was thrilled with the results. The pictures masked my flaws and made me appear sexy, taller, younger, and fitter. What more could a girl ask for? I left there for the airport feeling good about myself. Of course, the mere act of projecting confidence enhances a person's appearance, and vice versa.

I stroll into the waiting lounge and immediately sense myself being "noticed" by my predominately male fellow travelers. At my age, I savor any flattery directed my way. Why not?

I sit down to wait for the plane to start boarding and get myself situated. Out comes my BlackBerry, a computer, and a book. Suddenly there's a shift in the air. It's a good thing I didn't take my two minutes of male appreciation for granted, because now there's a new girl in town, and she's blonde and beautiful, runway height, fit and thin, seemingly flawless—and, above all, young. I think I'm doing pretty well for my age, but I don't hold a candle to this beauty. Every man's eyes are superglued to her, and I'm thinking, *Well, that glory was short-lived.* I have to admit that even *I* couldn't take my eyes off of her. I did develop a bit of an attitude fart as she flounced up to the food bar and, *of course,* nibbled rabbitlike *at* some grapes and poured herself a bottled water. Ugh! Why not go for the cheese, cake, or crepes? Even a sandwich would have gotten her off the hook with me, but, jeez, she was living out her perfection too much for my comfort. *Eat some potato chips, for crying out loud!* I grumbled to myself.

All right, all right, I wasn't thrilled by the fact that she'd stolen my two minutes of attention on a day when I happened to feel better about myself than I had in a long time. However, the more I studied her, I realized a few things. One, this blonde was beyond bleached, and her lips were so unnaturally puffy, you'd have thought she'd been stung in the kisser by a hive of bees. It's not for me to judge, but why would anyone so young and naturally beautiful opt for such fake augmentation? But the men around me didn't seem to notice any of this, not surprising, or if they did, they didn't particularly care.

# 32

## From This Moment On

Even when life hits you like a Mack truck that's come out of nowhere, there is still a chance that you will survive, and although the road to recovery may be slow, long, and even permanent, this doesn't mean you can't enjoy the rest of your life and be happy again.

Time is a healer, and it has moved me along through many difficult moments in my life because of the way it so ingeniously brings change along with it. If you are walking around with deep, open wounds, however, it can actually make things worse, as emotional wounds are like unsolved mysteries, full of unresolved pain and suffering. The more time passes, the longer a wound stays open and the more likely it will never close. In the event it does eventually close, however, it will leave a bigger, more painful scar than had it had the chance to close much sooner. Time is like sleep: once you lose it, you never make up for it. The lesson for me is: when there is a situation that creates suffering, try to resolve it, don't leave it to fester.

What I have gained from the generosity of time, though, is acceptance that so much was out of my control. I believe deeply that like all the good that has come to me in my life, I'm meant to enjoy it and not feel guilty for my fortunes, as I do have to accept the bad without disappointment or regret. I believe negative feelings are toxic, and I've learned with the grace of time and the butt-kicking teachings of experience that my energy should be spent avoiding negative thoughts and emotions rather than allowing my need for answers to spin me into obsession and suck all my energy dry. It takes energy to enjoy life, and if we spend it all on figuring out the answers to "why me" and "poor me," every time we go through a challenge in life, we will never have the energy to run with our children, play with the dog, go sailing, take dance lessons, climb mountains, get a degree, plant a tree, sing a song, or love and nurture our family and friends. I am learning to leave the "goes around" of "what comes around, goes around" to the universe, destiny, the Creator, and all the elements and forces more powerful than me. This frees me up *soooo* much from a responsibility I thought was mine. I was trapped in the feeling that if someone hurts me, I have to make sure he or she doesn't just walk away like nothing ever happened and get away with it.

At the age of six, I was perplexed by the behavior of a creature I knew nothing about, something entirely different from myself: a bumblebee. Cycling along the sidewalk this one time, I saw a cute, furry little ball that I felt guilty for half squashing with the tire of my bike, and I wanted to make it better by taking it in my hand to comfort it, to make sure it was okay. Because I was so unfamiliar with this unusual little being, I didn't understand it had a stinger. I wasn't aware of its ability to hurt me or that my compassion toward it could turn to hate in a matter of seconds. This injured bee, which had my complete sympathy at the time, stung me. I was shocked and instantly angry with it for turning on me when all I was trying to do was say "sorry" and be its friend.

We all have to grow up, however, and try to see things with more maturity than we did when we saw life through the eyes of a naïve child who has youth as an excuse for her thoughts, actions, and reactions. With Marie-Anne, for example, all I wanted was for us to be friends, not realizing we didn't share the same moral values until I'd already been stung. So what does that make Marie-Anne in the end? If I'm really being fair and objective, all it makes her is someone I did not understand, someone who was so unlike myself that I could not recognize what she was made of or capable of. All it makes her, when all is said and done, is different from me.

Putting effort into recognizing and acknowledging my own flaws, I find I'm learning to better tolerate and understand the shortcomings of others. I know deep down that I'm no better than the next guy. I'm struggling through life trying to keep my head on straight, my thoughts pure, and my actions exemplary at all times, but it's a daily effort, and, if I dare say, impossible. I'm too realistic to imagine I will ever be so perfect as to arrive at such saintly behavior, but I will keep trying and aiming for it anyway because I figure if I keep shooting for the stars, should I miss, at least I'll have a chance at landing on the moon. The moon was hung for a reason, and you couldn't get more excellent real estate for stargazing, after all.

The more straightforward emotions I experience most days of my life, I express pretty freely, except for sadness. I rarely cry. It's not that I don't get sad, because I do, even sometimes daily in small ways, but my sadness is often expressed falsely. I might get edgy or short instead of tearing up. It's like I'm fighting it, and like a fighter, I act more defensive than sad. My heart beats faster, my throat chokes up, squashing my sadness down into my gut, and it stays there, not getting the chance to flow out through tears. I don't believe this is a good thing for my health, and even though I want to cry when I'm sad, knowing it's the best thing to do, the truest reaction and healthiest outlet for my feelings, it's as though I just can't be bothered with the drama it causes. Your face goes red, your nose starts running, and everyone stops to mother you as if you're some wounded puppy. Instead, I like being loved and taken care of when my feet are sore and someone offers to massage them, or when I'm hungry and I'm offered a plate of food. I take well to these acts of kindness and accept help and generosity much better than I used to. I have come to enjoy receiving as well as giving over time, which came slow and hard for me. The vocal problems I developed over the years and that manifested during the Up! tour were related to emotional blockage, which is logical considering I have such a hard time crying. I want to let it out, but I have too many excuses waiting at the floodgates, and they dam up the ducts and block the flow.

A voice specialist I visited in 1999 told me that, in his opinion, my complaints of the strained vocal sound I had gone to see him about were not at all related to the whiplash injury I suffered ten years earlier on a roller-coaster ride. Rather, the problem was an emotional block. I was annoyed with what I considered to be a nonsense theory, but he assured me that the muscles around my larynx, which I explained felt as if they were clutching my voice box, were actually voluntary muscles. In other words, they were controlled by me, not by my injury, the way an involuntary muscle would be. The heart, for example, is involuntary, and no matter how sad or "heartbroken" you feel, your heart keeps beating and won't stop beating until you are physically dying. The doctor explained that this particular group of muscles that were tightening up my throat were the same muscles that choke you up when you are anxious about something or about to cry. Hence the term "choked up." When you're fighting back the tears, these muscles really tighten, and I was going through a chronic period of being "choked up." Even though the doctor's explanation was perfectly logical and acceptable to me intellectually, I didn't accept it as being possible. As if my emotions could be so weak that I would be choked up like that all the time?

Until I was to revisit this issue again, however, the doctor left me with some very good advice: he told me I needed to cry. He believed that from lack of expression, for whatever reason, I was holding in my emotions, and they had to flow and become unblocked. I had to free my pent-up sadness. As he said all this, I thought to myself, *What nerve. He doesn't even know me. How can he assume I've got blocked emotions? He's a voice box specialist, for crying out loud!*

Just as I was leaving, his advice to me was if I found it too hard to cry naturally, I should watch sad and funny movies regularly. Any kind of emotional expression that brought tears would work. In our period of intense emotional healing after our separations, Fred and I decided we'd stick to comedy and laugh our way to tears until I felt ready to do the tearjerker method. I just didn't want to get dragged back down into the depths of sorrow for a while. I know I'll have to go back to it, but one thing at a time. I still feel the need to function and allow life to pull me back down when it wants to, and I roll with it when it does and allow myself to be sad. This is when I find watching sad cinema works. It's often unexpected and feels good.

I also am learning to accept that I won't shine any more or less than I was created to. I just have to follow my heart, never intentionally hurting anyone in the process, and I'll shine as much as I'm meant to. I don't expect any more from others, either. This is all any of us can do. Less expectation means less disappointment. I expected too much from Mutt, for example. I expected him to be my life partner. I expected more from his dedication, compassion, and maturity, and set him too high on my list of people with unshakeable integrity, as if there even is such a list in reality. It was my own expectations of human nature that let me down so hard, and I take full responsibility for that. This has been a valuable lesson.

Since my last record, my attitude has taken a turn regarding professional priorities and goals. I believe that what will come of this period of healing and growing is a different woman from the one the world knows as Shania, in many respects. My views on certain things have changed, which has had a ripple effect. I approach music differently now in the sense that I have a deep desire to reconnect with my noncommercial voice—that is, my singing-around-the-house voice. Likewise, my approach to songwriting has changed, too, as I need more time to play and experiment without being preoccupied with what the finished product will be like. I'm taking the liberty to say and do things I would not have considered before (like writing an autobiography, for one thing).

Whereas I used to see a division between Eilleen the person and Shania the personality, now they have merged into one: I want to be one person who designates a time and a place for all aspects of her personality and character. Just as swimming is done in the water and soup is eaten with a spoon, making love is for behind closed doors; intimate time with my family belongs to us personally; and public appearances and performances are confined to the stage, studio, and cameras. I can be and do all the different things that make me happy and keep me fulfilled without having to compromise who I am supposed to be. I've defined those things for myself now and don't allow them to be dictated by anyone else.

I am more comfortable in my own skin these days musically, and although, overall, this freer approach to going about my life will probably result in my making mistakes here and there, I'm not afraid of that. If there's one thing I've realized over the years, it's that not only do we learn from our mistakes—but when everything goes without a hitch, where's the challenge, the opportunity to find out what you're made of? You can't grow in any aspect of life if you're not willing to take risks. I find that it's more fun, too, than always playing it safe. I love to dream up crazy ideas even though I know that most of them will never come to fruition. That's okay. No dream is a waste of time and energy, just like there's no such thing as a dumb question. What *is* dumb is to *not* ask and, therefore, never know the answer.

In my recent dreamy state, I see my career becoming guided more by exploration than calculation. I want to go off in search of whatever excites me creatively, intentionally leaving my maps and flashlights at home. Getting lost can be a blessing, as you never know what you'll stumble upon. Above all else, I crave freedom. I think I may have achieved that both in my personal life as well as artistically.

In the Swiss Riviera, however, I was still not free of a deep-seated anxiety over possibly running into Marie-Anne after the fallout with the betrayal. It was more than possible, actually; it was inevitable. Understandably, I think, the prospect of coming face-to-face with the "other woman" was something that I really preferred to avoid, but the area around Lake Geneva consists of a mere five-kilometer stretch.

Sure enough, one day I was walking along the lake, and I suddenly spotted her coming in my direction. Big, black high-fashion sunglasses covered half her face. I froze, and my mouth went dry. She confidently marched past me in what felt like slow-motion speed, her body language posturing like a mean, hissing cat, a posse of support pals in tow. Her arrogant air made me feel small and alone. A part of me wanted to confront her, but I was still pretty vulnerable then, and whatever courage I had dissipated quickly. Overwhelmed with intimidation, my heart was racing, and I was pretty much shitting my pants.

Once there was finally a bit of physical distance between us again, the fear loosened its grip on me, and I felt my breathing returning to normal. The thing I'd been dreading had finally occurred on that first encounter; now it was over, and I'd survived. I was okay. And I would get more okay as time went on. It's happened more than once now, crossing paths with her in our neighborhood along the shores of the lake. Even a year ago this type of encounter made my heart race, with me not knowing what to do, and although a part of me still wants to confront her, I feel less and less vulnerable to that urge all the time.

But being anywhere near Marie-Anne still just makes me feel bad, and time may never change that, but distance does help. In the same way you might avoid stinky smells that won't wash away, if you keep your distance and turn your face to the wind, at least the stench will stay behind you. That was cheeky; but when I'm feeling sour about something I figure it's better to have a sense of humor.

At present, I wake up every morning to a dream. I have the perfect partner, lover, and friend who spoils me rotten and is intelligent, gorgeous, athletic, fun, interesting, and interested. He loves my son and is a mature, conscientious, and sensitive parent. When I feel down, all I have to do is look at the incredible son God gave me, the little daughter to love and cherish, the long-standing group of reliable, supportive friends, family, and old friends I'm rediscovering; I enjoy financial independence that I have the satisfaction of having earned through hard work, and life is good. This beautiful life is mine to live. I am free to take my life in any direction I want as long as my little family is happy. I want to now start living each day like it's the vacation of my life because it actually is. I haven't been living it that way, but this is my new goal. I want to wake up each day aware of this amazing journey I'm on and make the most of it, whether I stay in bed and just rest, take a jump in the lake, hop in a kayak for a paddle, get on my bike and ride, go for a walk, write a song or a poem (or a book), read, play tennis, smell my roses, get cooking in the kitchen— the list goes on. No matter what our age or lifestyle, we all have simple things we can take advantage of that we more often than not take for granted.

I've often thought what a good idea it would be to post a passage on the wall at the foot of my bed so when I sit up in the morning, the first thing I see is a posted reminder of how beautiful life is, a reminder of how fortunate I am. To be in love and loved, a beautiful family, a home, trusted friends, music, creativity, and health. I want to embrace this feeling of gratitude by being reminded daily that my life is like the most amazing vacation, no matter where I am. No matter how fantastic life may actually be, however, the key is remaining aware of it. It's easy to forget all the good in your life when something hard and heavy hits you. This is why I think a posted reminder called something like "Good morning, you lucky lady," or "Rise and shine to another perfect day in your beautiful life," or "Your life rocks and here's why," followed by a list of things I love about my life, is a good idea. Out with the bad and in with the good. This has become my new thinking, and I believe reinforcing the good is a great way to leave less room for the bad to take hold of your time and energy.

I recognize through personal experience that money can improve the quality of life in some respects, but by no means is it wise to believe it can actually buy happiness.

I have been on both sides of a few fences in life, and I can tell you with certainty that there is always someone worse off and someone better off no matter what your lot in life. Your fortune or misfortune is relative to whatever surrounds you. Sometimes you are worse off and other times better off, but at every stage along the way—rich, poor, loved, betrayed, hungry, satisfied, lonely, crowded, nobody, or famous—everyone deserves compassion, respect, and consideration. I can speak from experience on both sides. I suffer no less from life's emotional struggles now that I am comfortable monetarily than I did when I was poor, for example. I allow myself as much compassion during any struggle now as I did when I was on the other end of the economic spectrum. I find that in fame and fortune, you are given less compassion and consideration during challenging times because now that you "have it all" you have no right to complain. It's not possible to suffer when you have money and fame, in other words. You're almost not allowed to be unhappy if you are rich and famous, and if you are, you're considered spoiled and selfish by those observing and judging you.

It's usually arrogance, ignorance, or jealousy that suggests the rich and famous have no right to be unhappy or to feel or express their unhappiness. This thinking can only come from those who give too much value to money and fame. These are the people who believe that money and fame are the most important things in life, that once you have them, there is nothing more to need or want. When you believe that someone rich and famous has no rights to public sympathy, it's because you believe the only things that bring happiness are material and superficial. Those who believe that love, sincerity, honesty, and integrity are the more valuable elements in life also realize that fame and fortune can, in many ways, actually add grief and stress to one's life rather than make it easier.

When you come from an underprivileged life, ready to meet the rest of it with a heart full of dreams and ambitions, you had better also be ready to face a world that, at times, will take pleasure in kicking the shit out of you. A world that will try to steal your precious gifts away. Expect life to be cruel and to make it as hard as possible for you to reach your goals, seemingly on purpose. There is little room for big success in life, as it's often granted to an elite group squeezed into a small space. However, I don't believe success belongs only to society's elite of the best educated, most privileged, or lucky. Success *does,* however, belong to anyone willing to earn it, and who has the talent and ability to be there. All capable people have the right to access the opportunity of success.

Regardless of what status you were born into in this world, human nature has equipped you with the skills to survive. I've learned during my own climbs through life so far that it's better to be realistic and prepare for a few falls if you're going to tackle a steep mountain, as mountains get narrower at the top, and there you see everyone fighting for space, footing, and oxygen. The air gets thinner as you get higher, and so does the difference between fair and unfair, and your ability to see clearly while your head is in the clouds. The trick is to hold your head above the clouds to keep a cool mind and clear vision so you don't lose sight of your goals.

My personal feeling is that if you are able to survive the climb of life on whatever mountain it is you've set out to master, and if in the bit between the base and the peak you learn something from both the good and the bad alike, and if you live to tell about it with gratitude, you've succeeded.

# Acknowledgments

T hanks to my parents, Sharon and Jerry Twain, whose lives inspired me to see the importance of writing and sharing this book. May they rest together forever, in peace. Thank you, Fred, my husband, for your endless love, devotion, and tireless encouragement throughout the journey. You were there during those moments when I lost sight of my conviction and needed to be reminded of why I was putting myself through the gigantic feat of documenting my memoirs. For reading my pages from top to bottom, several times over, printing, copying, cutting, pasting, backing up, and mostly for keeping me focused and rational during such an emotional project. Thank you, my Sweet Man, for helping me fulfill my stubborn wish of writing my story myself. Thanks also to my sister Carrie-Ann, who has always been the loyal, selfless wind beneath my wings, my strongest and most dedicated supporter. Thank you to all the family and friends who cheered me on during the times I felt apprehensive and discouraged.

The months of long hours writing these pages took particular patience and understanding from my son, Eja, as the book became somewhat of a permanent guest in our life over the course of a year. He was always gracious and accepting about the moments the book preoccupied my time and attention, and I hope he takes fond memories with him of us writing side by side during many evenings after school: Eja working on his creative writing homework or personal poems and songs while I worked on the pages of this book. One day he will read these pages, and my wish as he makes his way through the chapters of my life is that he comes to appreciate the importance of documenting what's in your heart and recognizes the value in sharing such intimacy with purpose and honesty. To respect and honor the truth, the process of discovering it, and the gift of learning from what it has to teach us along the way—to cherish the written word as a precious expression that is neither spontaneous nor fickle; and unlike the spoken word, writing allows more time for reflection and revision. This places a greater demand on the writer to take responsibility for its meaning and what it represents. Regardless of whether this memoir is praised or criticized, my wish is that my son finds peace in having the opportunity to learn about my life, from the words of his mother.

I started with a story; I ended with a book. This was a team effort and I would like to thank the dedicated group of individuals who contributed to its creation. To my manager Jason Owen, for thinking outside the box, and my business manager Stacy Smith for her wisdom and nurturing. A sincere thanks to the publisher of Atria Books, Judith Curr, who, before even reading a word, believed. Thanks to Atria's director of publicity, Paul Olsewski, and a big thank-you to Bob Barnett for taking me seriously when I said I'd written a book. It's likely he may have thought, *You mean, a song?* But no, I meant a book, and he got it! Thank you, Philip Bashe and Patty Romanowski Bashe, who contributed their time and talent throughout the shaping and editing process. A special thank-you to Jeanne Lee, Sarah Cantin, Jessica Chin, and Chris Lloreda at Atria. I can't thank Sarah Durand enough for being my gentle guide and lifeline through the cover-to-cover experience. I thank you for your patience, sensitivity, and respect for authenticity. Authoring a book is new territory for me, and without the foundation of support from those who contributed, my life story would have remained printed on hundreds of loose pages, stacked at the bottom of a drawer, under jeans that no longer fit but which I can't bring myself to throw away.

A portion of my proceeds from this book will be donated to Shania Kids Can, a foundation dedicated to helping underprivileged children. Thank you to everyone who makes this charity possible and thanks especially to the children whose lives this foundation reaches.

"Mommy, you're so sweet, your face is like a candy."

Mommy replies, "Well, son, your face is as beautiful as a flower."

The five-year-old boy then says without skipping a beat, "And Mommy, you picked me."

I cannot take credit for choosing my incredible son, as Heaven picked him for me. Thank you, Heaven!

# Index

# About the Author

SHANIA TWAIN rose to fame in the early 1990s with her debut album, *Shania Twain* (1993), and achieved worldwide success with her 1997 album, *Come On Over*, which became the bestselling album of all time by a female musician, and the bestselling country album of all time. A five-time Grammy Award winner, Twain has also achieved major success as a songwriter, winning twenty-seven BMI Songwriter awards. She has sold more than 75 million albums worldwide to date, including 48 million in the United States. Her docuseries on Oprah Winfrey's OWN network debuted in spring 2011. This is her first book.